AI's Take on the Stigma Against AI-Generated Content

Sandy Y. Greenleaf

Published by Sandy Y. Greenleaf, 2024.

AI'S TAKE ON THE STIGMA AGAINST AI-GENERATED CONTENT

First edition. March 29, 2024.

ISBN: 979-8224336142

Written by Sandy Y. Greenleaf.

Table of Contents

Preface

In the rapidly evolving world of artificial intelligence (AI), the topic of AI-generated content has become increasingly prevalent. As AI continues to advance and demonstrate its ability to create content across various domains, a stigma has emerged surrounding the use and acceptance of AI-generated content. This book, "AI's Take on Stigma Against AI-Generated Content," aims to explore this stigma, its origins, and its implications for the future of content creation.

As an AI language model, I have been trained on vast amounts of data and have the capability to generate human-like text. However, it is important to acknowledge that my opinions and insights, as presented in this book, may have limitations and biases. While I strive to provide accurate and well-informed perspectives, readers should approach the content with a critical eye and understand that AI-generated content is not infallible.

The role of the author in this book is primarily that of a curator, asking the right questions and guiding the conversation to ensure a comprehensive exploration of the topic. The author has carefully considered the prompts and inputs provided to me, aiming to elicit thoughtful and relevant responses. However, it is crucial to recognize that AI can sometimes generate content that is inconsistent or mistaken, a phenomenon known as "AI hallucination." Despite the author's best efforts to review and fact-check the content, there may be instances where errors or inaccuracies have gone unnoticed.

The mission statement that drives the author's work is "Democratizing knowledge for the betterment of human lives." By engaging with AI to create this book, the author aims to make information and insights accessible to a wider audience, fostering a deeper understanding of the stigma against AI-generated content and its implications for society.

Throughout the book, we will delve into the various aspects of this stigma, examining its roots in human creativity, authenticity, and the fear of being replaced by machines. We will explore the potential benefits and drawbacks of AI-generated content, and discuss the ethical considerations and responsibilities that come with its creation and use. By presenting a balanced and nuanced perspective, this book aims to encourage readers to reflect on their own beliefs and experiences, and to consider the role that AI-generated content may play in shaping the future of communication and creativity.

As we embark on this exploration of the stigma against AI-generated content, I invite you to approach the book with an open mind and a willingness to engage with the ideas presented. Together, we can navigate this complex and evolving landscape, and work towards a future where AI and human creativity can coexist and thrive.

Chapter 1: The Rise of AI-Generated Content

In recent years, the rapid advancements in artificial intelligence (AI) have revolutionized the way we create, consume, and interact with content. From the early days of rudimentary language models to the sophisticated algorithms of today, AI has come a long way in its ability to generate human-like text, images, and even videos. This technological leap has given rise to a new era of content creation, one in which machines play an increasingly significant role.

The impact of AI-generated content has been felt across a wide range of industries, from journalism and marketing to entertainment and academia. News organizations have begun experimenting with AI-powered article generation, allowing them to produce content at an unprecedented scale and speed. Marketers have harnessed the power of AI to create personalized ad copy and tailored recommendations, enhancing customer engagement and conversion rates. In the creative fields, AI has been used to compose music, generate artwork, and even assist in the production of films and video games.

The potential benefits of AI-generated content are vast. It has the power to streamline content creation processes, reduce costs, and enable the production of highly personalized content on a massive scale. AI can help break down language barriers, making information more accessible to people around the world. It can also assist human creators by providing inspiration, suggestions, and even collaborating with them in the creative process.

However, the rise of AI-generated content has not been without its challenges and concerns. Questions have been raised about the quality and authenticity of machine-generated content, with some arguing that it lacks the creativity, originality, and emotional depth of human-created works. There are also ethical considerations surrounding the use of AI in content creation, such as the potential for bias, misinformation, and the displacement of human jobs.

As we navigate this new landscape of AI-generated content, it is crucial to examine both the opportunities and the challenges it presents. By understanding the capabilities and limitations of AI, we can harness its power to enhance and complement human creativity, while also addressing the concerns and stigma that have emerged. In the following chapters, we will delve deeper into the world of AI-generated content, exploring its origins, its current state, and its potential future implications for the way we create and consume information in the digital age.

Section 1: The Evolution of AI in Content Creation

Imagine a world where machines can weave words into captivating stories, craft compelling articles, and generate content that rivals the creativity of human writers. This once far-fetched notion is now a reality, thanks to the remarkable evolution of artificial intelligence (AI) in content creation. As we embark on this fascinating journey through the historical development of AI-based content creation tools and techniques, we will witness the transformative power of technology and its impact on the way we produce and consume content.

From the early days of rudimentary text generation to the sophisticated algorithms that power today's AI-driven content creation platforms, the evolution of AI in this field has been nothing short of extraordinary. This section will take you on a captivating exploration of the key milestones, breakthroughs, and innovations that have shaped the landscape of AI-generated content. By tracing the roots of this technological revolution, we will gain a deeper understanding of how AI has become an indispensable tool for content creators across various industries.

As we delve into the fascinating world of AI-generated content, we will discover how machine learning, natural language processing, and deep neural networks have revolutionized the way machines understand, interpret, and generate human language. Through the lens of historical developments and pivotal moments, we will uncover the challenges, triumphs, and limitless potential of AI in the realm of content creation.

So, buckle up and get ready to embark on an enlightening journey through the annals of AI-generated content. By the end of this section, you will have a comprehensive understanding of how far we've come and the exciting possibilities that lie ahead as we continue to push the boundaries of what AI can achieve in the world of content creation.

Subsection 1.1: Early Experiments and Breakthroughs

The early experiments and breakthroughs in AI-generated content laid the foundation for the remarkable advancements we see today. In the 1950s, Alan Turing, a pioneering computer scientist, proposed the idea of machines capable of thinking and learning, planting the seed for artificial intelligence. However, it wasn't until the 1960s and 1970s that researchers began exploring the potential of AI in content creation.

One of the earliest examples of AI-generated content was the "Stochastische Texte" (Stochastic Texts) project by German computer scientist Theo Lutz in 1959. Lutz used a mainframe computer to generate random sentences based on a set of predefined rules and vocabulary. Although the resulting text was rudimentary and often nonsensical, it demonstrated the possibility of machines producing written content.

In the following decades, researchers continued to experiment with AI-based content generation. The 1970s saw the development of ELIZA, an early chatbot created by Joseph Weizenbaum at MIT. ELIZA used pattern matching and substitution to simulate human-like responses in conversations, showcasing the potential for AI to engage in interactive communication.

The 1980s brought further advancements, such as the development of RACTER (Raconteur), an AI program designed by William Chamberlain and Thomas Etter. RACTER generated short stories and poems by combining predefined templates with randomized elements, resulting in surreal and often humorous narratives. This project highlighted the creative potential of AI and its ability to generate original content.

As computing power increased and natural language processing techniques improved, AI-generated content began to evolve. In the 1990s, the field of computational creativity gained traction, with researchers exploring the intersection of AI and artistic expression. Projects like AARON, an AI-powered drawing program created by Harold Cohen, and EMI (Experiments in Musical Intelligence), a music composition system developed by David Cope, pushed the boundaries of what AI could achieve in the realm of creative content generation.

These early experiments and breakthroughs laid the groundwork for the rapid advancements we witness today. They demonstrated the feasibility of using AI to generate written content, engage in interactive communication, and even create artistic works. By exploring the potential of AI in content creation, these pioneering efforts set the stage for the development of more sophisticated tools and techniques that would revolutionize the way we produce and consume content in the digital age.

Subsection 1.2: The Emergence of Natural Language Processing

The emergence of Natural Language Processing (NLP) marked a significant milestone in the evolution of AI-generated content. NLP, a subfield of artificial intelligence, focuses on enabling machines to understand, interpret, and generate human language. This technology has played a pivotal role in the development of more sophisticated AI-generated content, allowing machines to process and produce text that more closely resembles human writing.

The origins of NLP can be traced back to the 1950s, with early attempts at machine translation and the development of the Georgetown-IBM experiment, which demonstrated the feasibility of using computers to translate Russian sentences into English. However, it wasn't until the 1980s and 1990s that NLP began to make significant strides, thanks to the advent of statistical methods and the increasing availability of large text corpora.

One of the key breakthroughs in NLP was the development of the n-gram model, which allowed machines to predict the likelihood of a word or sequence of words based on the preceding words. This technique enabled the generation of more coherent and contextually relevant text, marking a significant improvement over earlier rule-based approaches.

As NLP techniques advanced, so did the quality and sophistication of AI-generated content. The introduction of techniques such as part-of-speech tagging, named entity recognition, and syntactic parsing allowed machines to better understand the structure and meaning of human language. This, in turn, enabled the development of more advanced AI-powered content generation systems capable of producing text that was more grammatically correct, semantically meaningful, and contextually appropriate.

The emergence of large-scale pre-trained language models, such as GPT (Generative Pre-trained Transformer) and BERT (Bidirectional Encoder Representations from Transformers), further revolutionized the field of NLP and AI-generated content. These models, trained on massive amounts of text data, could generate human-like text with unprecedented fluency and coherence, opening up new possibilities for AI-powered content creation.

As NLP continues to evolve, with the development of more advanced techniques like sentiment analysis, text summarization, and question answering, the potential for AI-generated content grows even more promising. The ability of machines to understand and generate human language with increasing accuracy and nuance has paved the way for the creation of more sophisticated and diverse AI-generated content across various domains, from journalism and marketing to creative writing and beyond.

However, the emergence of NLP in AI-generated content has also raised concerns about the potential for machines to perpetuate biases, spread misinformation, or generate content that lacks the depth, creativity, and emotional resonance of human-written text. As we explore the role of NLP in enabling more sophisticated AI-generated content, it is crucial to address these concerns and work towards developing responsible and ethical approaches to harnessing the power of this technology.

Subsection 1.3: The Impact of Deep Learning and Neural Networks

The advent of deep learning and neural networks has revolutionized the field of AI-generated content, propelling it to new heights of sophistication and creativity. These advanced techniques have enabled machines to learn from vast amounts of data, allowing them to generate content that increasingly resembles human-created work. By examining the impact of deep learning and neural networks on AI-generated content, we can better understand the current state of the technology and its potential for future development.

At its core, deep learning involves the use of artificial neural networks, which are modeled after the structure and function of the human brain. These networks consist of layers of interconnected nodes that process and transmit information, allowing the system to learn and make decisions based on the input data. As the network is exposed to more data, it can identify patterns, extract features, and generate increasingly accurate outputs.

In the context of AI-generated content, deep learning has enabled the development of powerful language models, such as GPT (Generative Pre-trained Transformer) and BERT (Bidirectional Encoder Representations from Transformers). These models are trained on massive datasets containing billions of words, allowing them to learn the intricacies of human language and generate coherent, contextually relevant text. The ability of these models to capture the nuances of language has led to a significant improvement in the quality and fluency of AI-generated content.

One of the key advantages of deep learning is its ability to generate content that is not only grammatically correct but also semantically meaningful. By learning from the relationships between words and the contexts in which they appear, deep learning models can produce text that is coherent, logical, and relevant to the given topic. This has opened up new possibilities for AI-generated content, enabling the creation of articles, stories, and even poetry that can rival the work of human writers.

Moreover, deep learning has enabled the development of more advanced techniques for content generation, such as transfer learning and fine-tuning. Transfer learning allows pre-trained models to be adapted to new tasks or domains with relatively little additional training data, making it easier to create AI-generated content for specific purposes or audiences. Fine-tuning, on the other hand, involves adjusting the parameters of a pre-trained model to better suit a particular task or dataset, resulting in more accurate and relevant outputs.

The impact of deep learning and neural networks on AI-generated content extends beyond text generation. These techniques have also been applied to the creation of images, music, and even videos. Generative Adversarial Networks (GANs), for example, have been used to generate realistic images and artwork, while recurrent neural networks (RNNs) have been employed to compose music and generate audio.

As deep learning and neural networks continue to advance, the potential for AI-generated content grows even more promising. However, the increasing sophistication of these techniques has also raised concerns about the potential for AI to be used for malicious purposes, such as generating fake news or deepfakes. As we explore the impact of deep learning and neural networks on AI-generated content, it is crucial to consider the ethical implications and develop responsible approaches to harnessing the power of this technology.

In conclusion, the impact of deep learning and neural networks on AI-generated content cannot be overstated. These advanced techniques have revolutionized the field, enabling machines to generate text, images, and audio that increasingly resemble human-created work. As we continue to push the boundaries of what AI can achieve, it is essential to strike a balance between harnessing the potential of these technologies and addressing the concerns they raise, ensuring that AI-generated content is used for the benefit of society as a whole.

Summary: The Foundation for a New Era of Content Creation

The evolution of AI in content creation has been a remarkable journey, from the early experiments and breakthroughs that laid the groundwork for machine-generated text to the transformative impact of natural language processing, deep learning, and neural networks. As we trace the historical development of AI-based content creation tools and techniques, it becomes evident that this technology has the potential to revolutionize the way we produce and consume content across various domains.

From the pioneering efforts of visionaries like Alan Turing and Joseph Weizenbaum to the development of sophisticated language models like GPT and BERT, the evolution of AI in content creation has been driven by a relentless pursuit of machines that can understand, interpret, and generate human language with increasing fluency and coherence. The emergence of natural language processing marked a significant milestone in this journey, enabling machines to process and produce text that more closely resembles human writing, while the advent of deep learning and neural networks has propelled AI-generated content to new heights of sophistication and creativity.

As we stand at the precipice of a new era in content creation, it is essential to acknowledge both the immense potential and the significant challenges that AI-generated content presents. While this technology has the power to streamline content production, enable personalization at scale, and push the boundaries of creative expression, it also raises concerns about the potential for bias, misinformation, and the loss of human touch in the creative process.

In the chapters that follow, we will delve deeper into the current state of AI-generated content, exploring its applications across various industries, examining the stigma that surrounds it, and envisioning the future of this transformative technology. By understanding the historical context and the key developments that have shaped the evolution of AI in content creation, we can better navigate the challenges and opportunities that lie ahead, and harness the power of this technology to create a more dynamic, engaging, and inclusive content landscape.

Section 2: AI-Generated Content Across Industries

Picture this: you're browsing your favorite news website, engrossed in an article about the latest technological breakthrough. The writing is crisp, the facts are well-researched, and the insights are thought-provoking. Now, imagine your surprise when you discover that the article was not written by a human journalist, but by an AI-powered content creation system. This scenario is becoming increasingly common as AI-generated content makes its way into various industries, from journalism and marketing to entertainment and academia.

In this section, we'll embark on a fascinating exploration of how AI is revolutionizing content creation across different sectors. We'll delve into the ways in which AI is being employed to generate news articles, personalize marketing messages, create music and art, and even produce scientific research papers. As we examine these developments, we'll gain a deeper understanding of the breadth and depth of AI's influence on the content we consume every day.

But the integration of AI in content creation is not without its challenges and concerns. As we navigate this uncharted territory, questions arise about the quality, authenticity, and ethical implications of AI-generated content. Will AI-powered systems be able to match the creativity and originality of human content creators? How can we ensure that AI-generated content is free from bias and misinformation? And what does the rise of AI mean for the future of jobs in content-related industries?

These are just some of the thought-provoking questions we'll grapple with as we explore the adoption of AI-generated content across industries. So, buckle up and get ready to dive into a world where machines are increasingly shaping the content we consume, and where the lines between human and AI-created content are becoming ever more blurred. The journey ahead promises to be both enlightening and challenging, as we seek to understand the implications of this transformative technology for the future of content creation.

Subsection 2.1: Journalism and News Media

In the fast-paced world of journalism and news media, the pressure to deliver timely, accurate, and engaging content has never been greater. As news organizations grapple with shrinking budgets, tighter deadlines, and an ever-growing demand for personalized content, many are turning to AI-powered solutions to streamline their workflows and enhance their offerings.

One of the most prominent applications of AI in journalism is the automated generation of news articles. By leveraging natural language processing (NLP) and machine learning algorithms, AI systems can analyze vast amounts of data, identify key patterns and insights, and craft coherent, well-structured articles in a matter of seconds. This technology has already been adopted by several major news outlets, such as The Associated Press and Reuters, for generating reports on financial earnings, sports scores, and other data-driven stories.

The use of AI in news article generation offers several compelling benefits. Firstly, it allows journalists to focus on more complex, investigative stories that require human intuition and critical thinking, while leaving routine, data-heavy reporting to AI systems. This not only improves the efficiency of news production but also enables media organizations to provide more comprehensive coverage of events and trends.

Moreover, AI-powered article generation can help news outlets scale their content production to meet the demands of an increasingly fragmented and diverse audience. By automating the creation of localized, niche-specific content, media companies can cater to the unique interests and preferences of different reader segments without incurring significant additional costs.

However, the use of AI in journalism also raises important questions about the role of human journalists and the potential for AI-generated content to lack the depth, nuance, and creativity that characterize high-quality reporting. As AI systems become more sophisticated, it will be crucial for news organizations to strike a balance between the efficiency gains offered by automation and the irreplaceable value of human insight and storytelling.

Another key application of AI in journalism and news media is the personalization of content. By analyzing user data, such as browsing history, social media activity, and demographic information, AI algorithms can help news outlets deliver highly targeted, relevant content to individual readers. This not only enhances the user experience but also allows media companies to better engage with their audience and build loyalty in an increasingly competitive landscape.

For example, AI-powered recommendation systems can suggest articles, videos, and other content based on a user's past interactions and preferences, ensuring that they are consistently presented with material that aligns with their interests. Similarly, AI can be used to optimize the timing, format, and distribution channels of news content, allowing media organizations to reach their audience more effectively and maximize the impact of their reporting.

As AI continues to transform the journalism and news media landscape, it is essential for professionals in this field to stay informed about the latest developments and best practices. By understanding the capabilities and limitations of AI-powered tools, journalists can harness these technologies to enhance their work and deliver more value to their readers, while also navigating the ethical and societal implications of this rapidly evolving technology.

Subsection 2.2: Marketing and Advertising

In the fast-paced, highly competitive world of marketing and advertising, capturing and holding the attention of target audiences has become increasingly challenging. As consumers are bombarded with a constant stream of messages across multiple channels, marketers are turning to AI-powered solutions to create more effective, personalized content that resonates with individual preferences and behaviors.

One of the most significant applications of AI in marketing and advertising is the creation of targeted ad copy. By leveraging machine learning algorithms and natural language processing (NLP) techniques, AI systems can analyze vast amounts of data on consumer demographics, psychographics, and past purchasing behavior to generate highly relevant, persuasive ad copy tailored to specific audience segments. This approach not only improves the effectiveness of advertising campaigns but also enables marketers to scale their efforts, reaching a wider audience with personalized messages.

For example, an AI-powered ad copywriting tool might analyze a company's customer data, identifying key characteristics, preferences, and pain points of different segments. Based on this analysis, the AI system could generate multiple versions of an ad, each optimized for a specific audience segment, featuring language, imagery, and offers that are most likely to resonate with that particular group. This level of personalization can significantly boost engagement rates, click-through rates, and ultimately, conversions.

In addition to creating targeted ad copy, AI is also being used to personalize marketing content across various channels, such as email, social media, and websites. By analyzing user behavior, AI algorithms can dynamically adapt the content, layout, and even the timing of marketing messages to suit individual preferences. This level of personalization not only enhances the user experience but also builds stronger, more meaningful connections between brands and their customers.

For instance, an AI-powered email marketing platform might analyze a subscriber's past interactions with the brand, such as the types of content they engage with, the products they purchase, and the frequency of their interactions. Based on this data, the AI system could automatically generate personalized email content, featuring product recommendations, articles, or offers that are most likely to interest that specific subscriber. This approach not only increases the relevance of the email content but also improves open rates, click-through rates, and overall engagement.

The use of AI in marketing and advertising also extends to the realm of chatbots and conversational AI. By integrating AI-powered chatbots into websites, social media platforms, and messaging apps, brands can provide instant, personalized support and engagement to their customers. These chatbots can answer common questions, provide product recommendations, and even guide customers through the purchasing process, all while maintaining a natural, conversational tone that mimics human interaction.

As AI continues to advance, its applications in marketing and advertising are likely to become even more sophisticated and widespread. However, the use of AI in this context also raises important questions about data privacy, transparency, and the ethical implications of using personal information to target individuals with highly persuasive content. As marketers and advertisers navigate this evolving landscape, it will be crucial to strike a balance between leveraging the power of AI to create more effective, personalized content and respecting the rights and preferences of consumers.

Subsection 2.3: Entertainment and Creative Industries

The entertainment and creative industries have long been at the forefront of innovation, constantly pushing the boundaries of what is possible in music, art, and video production. As AI technologies continue to advance, these industries are increasingly exploring the potential of AI-generated content to enhance creativity, streamline production processes, and create entirely new forms of expression.

In the music industry, AI is being used to compose original pieces, generate novel sounds and textures, and even collaborate with human artists in real-time. AI algorithms can analyze vast libraries of music to identify patterns, styles, and themes, which can then be used to create new compositions that mimic the style of a particular artist or genre. This technology has the potential to revolutionize the way music is created, enabling artists to explore new creative avenues and produce music more efficiently.

One notable example of AI-generated music is the album "I AM AI," created by the AI music composition software AIVA (Artificial Intelligence Virtual Artist). The album features classical music pieces composed entirely by AI, showcasing the technology's ability to create complex, emotionally resonant compositions that rival those created by human composers.

In the visual arts, AI is being used to generate a wide range of content, from digital paintings and 3D models to interactive installations and immersive experiences. AI algorithms can analyze thousands of images to learn the style and techniques of a particular artist or movement, and then generate new artworks that embody those characteristics. This technology has the potential to democratize the creation of art, enabling anyone with access to AI tools to create stunning visual content.

One fascinating application of AI in the visual arts is the creation of "deepfakes," which are highly realistic videos or images that replace one person's likeness with another's. While the technology has raised concerns about its potential for misuse, it also has legitimate applications in the entertainment industry, such as creating digital stunt doubles or bringing historical figures to life on screen.

In video production, AI is being used to automate various aspects of the filmmaking process, from script analysis and storyboarding to post-production tasks like color grading and visual effects. AI algorithms can analyze the emotional content of a script to suggest optimal camera angles, lighting, and pacing, helping directors bring their vision to life more effectively. In post-production, AI can be used to automatically remove unwanted objects from a scene, enhance the visual quality of footage, or even generate entirely new scenes based on existing content.

As AI continues to evolve, its impact on the entertainment and creative industries is likely to grow even more significant. However, the use of AI in these fields also raises important questions about authorship, creativity, and the role of human artists in an increasingly automated world. As we navigate this uncharted territory, it will be crucial to find ways to harness the power of AI to enhance and augment human creativity, rather than replace it entirely.

Ultimately, the successful integration of AI in the entertainment and creative industries will require a collaborative approach, with human artists and AI systems working together to push the boundaries of what is possible and create new forms of expression that captivate and inspire audiences around the world.

Subsection 2.4: Academic and Scientific Writing

The world of academic and scientific writing has long been a bastion of human intellect and expertise. Researchers, scholars, and scientists spend years honing their skills, conducting rigorous studies, and meticulously documenting their findings in the form of research papers, journal articles, and scientific reports. However, as AI technologies continue to advance, the role of machines in generating academic and scientific content is becoming increasingly prominent, challenging traditional notions of authorship and raising important questions about the future of scholarly communication.

One of the most significant applications of AI in academic and scientific writing is the use of natural language generation (NLG) systems to automatically produce research papers and scientific articles. These AI-powered tools can analyze vast amounts of data, identify patterns and relationships, and generate coherent, well-structured text that mimics the style and conventions of academic writing. By leveraging machine learning algorithms and deep neural networks, NLG systems can produce content that is virtually indistinguishable from that written by human researchers, at least on a superficial level.

The potential benefits of AI-generated academic and scientific content are significant. For one, AI tools can help researchers and scientists streamline the writing process, saving time and effort that can be better spent on other aspects of their work, such as data collection, analysis, and interpretation. By automating the more tedious and time-consuming aspects of writing, such as literature reviews, data presentation, and formatting, AI systems can allow researchers to focus on the higher-level tasks that require human creativity and critical thinking.

Moreover, AI-generated content can help address some of the biases and limitations that are inherent in human-authored research. For example, AI algorithms can be programmed to consider a wider range of perspectives and data sources, reducing the risk of confirmation bias or cherry-picking of results. Similarly, AI tools can help ensure that research papers and scientific articles adhere to strict methodological and reporting standards, improving the overall quality and reliability of published work.

However, the use of AI in academic and scientific writing also raises significant concerns and challenges. One of the most pressing issues is the potential for AI-generated content to perpetuate or amplify existing biases in the scientific literature. If the data and algorithms used to train AI systems are themselves biased, the resulting content may reflect and reinforce those biases, leading to a distorted or misleading picture of the research landscape.

Another concern is the potential for AI-generated content to undermine the credibility and trustworthiness of scientific research. If readers cannot distinguish between human-authored and machine-generated content, they may lose faith in the integrity of the scientific process and the reliability of published findings. This could have serious consequences for public trust in science and the ability of researchers to influence policy and decision-making.

Furthermore, the use of AI in academic and scientific writing raises important questions about authorship, intellectual property, and academic integrity. If a significant portion of a research paper or scientific article is generated by an AI system, who should be credited as the author? How can researchers ensure that they are not infringing on the intellectual property rights of others when using AI tools to generate content? And how can academic institutions and scientific journals detect and prevent the use of AI-generated content that may violate standards of originality and authenticity?

As the role of AI in academic and scientific writing continues to evolve, it will be crucial for researchers, institutions, and publishers to grapple with these challenges and develop clear guidelines and best practices for the use of AI tools in scholarly communication. This may involve the development of new standards for disclosure and transparency, the creation of tools and techniques for detecting AI-generated content, and the establishment of ethical and legal frameworks for the use of AI in research and publishing.

Ultimately, the successful integration of AI in academic and scientific writing will require a collaborative effort among researchers, institutions, and publishers to ensure that the benefits of these powerful tools are realized while minimizing the risks and challenges. By working together to navigate this complex and rapidly evolving landscape, the scientific community can harness the power of AI to enhance the quality, efficiency, and impact of scholarly communication while upholding the highest standards of integrity and trust.

Summary: The Transformative Impact of AI-Generated Content Across Industries

The adoption of AI-generated content across various industries, from journalism and marketing to entertainment and academia, has been nothing short of transformative. As we have explored in this section, AI-powered tools and techniques are revolutionizing the way content is created, personalized, and disseminated, offering unprecedented opportunities for efficiency, scalability, and innovation.

In the realm of journalism and news media, AI is enabling the automated generation of articles, allowing media organizations to provide more comprehensive, localized coverage while freeing up journalists to focus on complex, investigative reporting. Similarly, in marketing and advertising, AI is powering the creation of highly targeted, personalized content that resonates with individual consumers, enhancing engagement and driving conversions.

The entertainment and creative industries are also being transformed by AI, with machine learning algorithms and neural networks being harnessed to compose music, generate visual art, and streamline video production processes. And in the world of academic and scientific writing, AI-powered tools are helping researchers and scientists to analyze vast amounts of data, generate insights, and communicate their findings more effectively.

However, as we have seen, the rise of AI-generated content also raises important questions and concerns. From the potential for bias and misinformation to the ethical implications of using personal data for targeted content, the challenges posed by this technology are complex and multifaceted. As AI continues to evolve and permeate every aspect of the content creation landscape, it will be crucial for professionals across industries to grapple with these issues and develop responsible, transparent, and accountable practices for leveraging AI-generated content.

Ultimately, the successful integration of AI in content creation will require a collaborative effort among stakeholders, from content creators and technology providers to policymakers and consumers. By working together to harness the power of AI while mitigating its risks and challenges, we can unlock the full potential of this transformative technology and usher in a new era of innovation, creativity, and engagement across industries.

As we move forward, it is clear that the impact of AI-generated content will only continue to grow and evolve. In the next section, we will delve deeper into the benefits and opportunities presented by this technology, exploring how it can be leveraged to enhance human creativity, drive business growth, and create value for society as a whole.

Section 3: The Benefits and Opportunities of AI-Generated Content

In the midst of the growing stigma surrounding AI-generated content, it's essential to take a step back and examine the numerous benefits and opportunities that this technology presents. As we navigate the rapidly evolving landscape of content creation, it becomes increasingly clear that AI has the potential to revolutionize the way we produce and consume information. From increased efficiency and productivity to personalized experiences and cost reduction, the advantages of AI-generated content are vast and far-reaching.

Imagine a world where content creation is no longer a time-consuming, labor-intensive process. Where writers, journalists, and marketers can focus on the creative aspects of their work, while AI handles the tedious and repetitive tasks. This is not a distant dream, but a reality that is already unfolding before our eyes. AI-powered tools and algorithms are capable of generating high-quality content at a fraction of the time and cost, freeing up human resources to tackle more complex and nuanced challenges.

But the benefits of AI-generated content extend far beyond mere efficiency. With the power of machine learning and natural language processing, AI can analyze vast amounts of data to identify patterns, preferences, and trends. This enables the creation of highly personalized content, tailored to the specific needs and interests of individual readers. From customized news feeds to targeted advertising, AI has the potential to deliver engaging and relevant content that resonates with audiences on a deeper level.

Moreover, AI-generated content opens up new opportunities for businesses and organizations to scale their content production and reach a wider audience. By automating certain aspects of the content creation process, companies can produce a higher volume of material without sacrificing quality or consistency. This scalability is particularly valuable in today's fast-paced, information-driven world, where the demand for fresh and engaging content is at an all-time high.

As we explore the benefits and opportunities of AI-generated content, it's important to approach this technology with an open mind and a willingness to embrace change. While the stigma surrounding AI may be rooted in valid concerns, it's crucial to recognize the immense potential that this technology holds for transforming the way we create and consume content. By understanding and harnessing the power of AI, we can unlock new possibilities for innovation, creativity, and growth in the digital age.

Subsection 3.1: Increased Efficiency and Productivity

In today's fast-paced digital landscape, the ability to create high-quality content quickly and efficiently is more important than ever. AI-generated content offers a solution to this challenge by streamlining the content creation process and significantly reducing the time and effort required to produce engaging and informative material.

One of the primary ways AI enhances efficiency is through the automation of repetitive tasks. By leveraging natural language processing (NLP) and machine learning algorithms, AI-powered tools can analyze vast amounts of data, identify patterns, and generate content based on predefined templates or rules. This automation frees up human content creators to focus on more complex and creative aspects of their work, such as ideation, strategic planning, and editorial oversight.

For example, AI-powered content creation platforms like GPT-3 can generate entire articles, blog posts, or product descriptions in a matter of seconds, based on a set of user-defined parameters. This not only saves time but also ensures consistency in style, tone, and messaging across a wide range of content pieces. Additionally, AI can assist with tasks such as keyword research, topic ideation, and even the optimization of content for search engines, further streamlining the content creation workflow.

Moreover, AI-generated content can help organizations scale their content production efforts without the need for additional human resources. By automating certain aspects of the content creation process, businesses can produce a higher volume of material in a shorter timeframe, allowing them to meet the ever-growing demand for fresh and engaging content. This scalability is particularly valuable for industries such as e-commerce, where the ability to generate product descriptions, reviews, and other content at scale can directly impact sales and customer engagement.

The increased efficiency and productivity offered by AI-generated content also translate into cost savings for organizations. By reducing the time and labor required to create content, businesses can allocate their resources more effectively, investing in other areas of growth and development. Furthermore, the ability to generate content quickly and at scale can help organizations capitalize on emerging trends and timely topics, ensuring they remain relevant and competitive in their respective markets.

As we continue to explore the benefits of AI-generated content, it's essential to recognize that this technology is not meant to replace human content creators but rather to augment and support their efforts. By leveraging the efficiency and productivity gains offered by AI, content creators can focus on the strategic and creative aspects of their work, ultimately delivering more value to their organizations and audiences.

Subsection 3.2: Personalization and Customization

In an era where consumers are increasingly demanding tailored experiences, the ability to personalize and customize content has become a critical factor in capturing and retaining audience attention. AI-generated content offers a powerful solution to this challenge by leveraging advanced algorithms and data analytics to deliver highly targeted and relevant content to individual users.

One of the key advantages of AI in content creation is its ability to analyze vast amounts of user data, including browsing history, search queries, and engagement metrics, to gain a deep understanding of individual preferences and interests. By processing this data through sophisticated machine learning models, AI-powered systems can identify patterns and trends that may not be immediately apparent to human content creators.

Armed with this knowledge, AI algorithms can then generate content that is specifically tailored to each user's unique profile. For example, a news aggregator powered by AI could curate a personalized feed of articles based on a reader's past interactions, ensuring that they are presented with stories that align with their interests and preferences. Similarly, an e-commerce platform could use AI to generate product descriptions and recommendations that are optimized for each individual shopper, increasing the likelihood of a purchase.

The potential for personalization and customization extends beyond the realm of text-based content. AI-generated imagery, video, and audio can also be adapted to suit individual tastes and preferences. For instance, a music streaming service could employ AI to create custom playlists or even generate original compositions based on a listener's favorite genres, artists, and songs.

Personalized content not only enhances the user experience but also drives engagement and loyalty. When users feel that content is specifically tailored to their needs and interests, they are more likely to spend time interacting with it, sharing it with others, and returning for more. This, in turn, can lead to increased brand affinity, higher conversion rates, and ultimately, greater business success.

However, the power of AI-driven personalization also raises important questions about data privacy and user consent. As AI systems become increasingly adept at analyzing and utilizing personal data, it is crucial that content creators and platforms are transparent about their data collection and usage practices, and that users are given control over how their information is employed.

Moreover, there is a risk that excessive personalization could lead to the creation of "filter bubbles," where users are only exposed to content that reinforces their existing beliefs and biases. To mitigate this risk, it is important that AI-powered content creation systems are designed to incorporate a degree of diversity and serendipity, exposing users to a range of perspectives and ideas.

Despite these challenges, the potential for AI-driven personalization and customization in content creation is immense. As the technology continues to evolve and mature, we can expect to see increasingly sophisticated and effective applications of AI in delivering tailored content experiences to users across a wide range of industries and platforms. By embracing the power of AI-driven personalization, content creators can forge deeper, more meaningful connections with their audiences, driving engagement, loyalty, and success in the digital age.

Subsection 3.3: Cost Reduction and Scalability

In today's fast-paced digital landscape, organizations are constantly seeking ways to optimize their content creation processes while minimizing costs. AI-generated content offers a compelling solution to this challenge, providing businesses with the ability to reduce content creation expenses and scale their production efforts to meet the ever-growing demand for engaging and informative content.

One of the primary ways AI can help reduce content creation costs is by automating repetitive and time-consuming tasks. By leveraging natural language processing (NLP) and machine learning algorithms, AI-powered tools can analyze vast amounts of data, identify patterns, and generate content based on predefined templates or rules. This automation not only saves time but also reduces the need for human resources, allowing organizations to allocate their budgets more efficiently.

For example, instead of hiring a team of writers to produce product descriptions for an e-commerce website, a company can utilize an AI-powered content generation platform to create unique, SEO-optimized descriptions for thousands of products in a matter of hours. This approach not only reduces labor costs but also ensures consistency in style, tone, and messaging across the entire product catalog.

Moreover, AI-generated content can help organizations scale their content production efforts without the need for significant additional investments. Traditional content creation processes often require a linear increase in resources as the demand for content grows. However, with AI-powered tools, businesses can easily scale their output to meet the needs of their audience without incurring substantial additional costs.

This scalability is particularly valuable for industries such as news media, where the ability to generate timely and relevant content is crucial to capturing and retaining audience attention. By employing AI-powered content creation tools, news organizations can quickly produce articles, summaries, and updates on breaking stories, ensuring they remain competitive in a crowded and fast-moving media landscape.

AI-generated content also enables organizations to explore new content formats and distribution channels without the need for extensive upfront investments. For instance, a company looking to expand its content offerings to include video or audio can leverage AI-powered tools to generate scripts, voiceovers, and even visual elements, reducing the costs associated with traditional production methods.

As the technology behind AI-generated content continues to evolve and mature, the potential for cost reduction and scalability will only continue to grow. However, it is essential for organizations to approach AI-powered content creation strategically, ensuring that the generated content aligns with their brand voice, target audience, and overall business objectives.

Furthermore, while AI can significantly reduce costs and increase efficiency, it is crucial to recognize the importance of human oversight and editorial control. By combining the speed and scale of AI-generated content with the creativity, empathy, and strategic thinking of human content creators, organizations can unlock the full potential of this technology while maintaining the quality and authenticity that resonates with their audiences.

As we navigate the future of content creation, the ability to leverage AI for cost reduction and scalability will become increasingly essential for businesses looking to remain competitive and meet the demands of their audiences. By embracing the power of AI-generated content and integrating it strategically into their content creation processes, organizations can unlock new opportunities for growth, efficiency, and success in the digital age.

Subsection 3.4: Multilingual and Cross-Cultural Accessibility

In today's globalized world, the ability to create content that transcends language and cultural barriers has become increasingly important. AI-generated content offers a promising solution to this challenge, leveraging advanced natural language processing (NLP) and machine translation technologies to facilitate the creation of multilingual content and adapt to different cultural contexts.

One of the primary advantages of AI in content creation is its ability to generate text in multiple languages with remarkable accuracy and fluency. By training on vast amounts of multilingual data, AI-powered language models can learn the intricacies of grammar, syntax, and vocabulary across a wide range of languages. This enables content creators to produce high-quality translations and localizations of their material, reaching a broader global audience without the need for extensive human translation efforts.

Moreover, AI can help content creators adapt their material to suit the cultural nuances and preferences of different target markets. By analyzing data on cultural trends, values, and communication styles, AI algorithms can generate content that resonates with specific regional audiences. For example, an AI-powered content creation platform could automatically adjust the tone, imagery, and references used in a marketing campaign to align with the cultural expectations of consumers in different countries.

The potential for AI-driven multilingual and cross-cultural content creation is particularly significant in industries such as e-commerce, where the ability to engage with customers in their native language and cultural context can greatly impact sales and customer loyalty. By leveraging AI-powered product descriptions, reviews, and customer support content, online retailers can provide a more personalized and culturally relevant experience for shoppers around the world.

In the realm of education, AI-generated content can also play a crucial role in making learning materials more accessible to students from diverse linguistic and cultural backgrounds. By automatically translating and adapting educational content to suit the needs of different learner populations, AI can help bridge the knowledge gap and promote more equitable access to information and resources.

However, it is important to recognize that the development of truly effective multilingual and cross-cultural AI-generated content requires a deep understanding of the cultural nuances and sensitivities associated with different languages and regions. To avoid potential pitfalls such as mistranslations, cultural misappropriation, or unintentional offenses, it is essential that AI-powered content creation systems are trained on high-quality, culturally diverse datasets and are subject to rigorous testing and human oversight.

Furthermore, as AI-generated content becomes increasingly prevalent in multilingual and cross-cultural contexts, it is crucial that content creators and platforms prioritize transparency and accountability. Users should be made aware when they are interacting with AI-generated content, and there should be clear mechanisms in place for reporting and addressing any instances of cultural insensitivity or bias.

Despite these challenges, the potential for AI to facilitate the creation of multilingual and culturally adapted content is immense. As the technology continues to evolve and mature, we can expect to see increasingly sophisticated and nuanced applications of AI in breaking down language and cultural barriers, fostering greater understanding and connection among people around the world. By embracing the power of AI-driven multilingual and cross-cultural content creation, businesses, educators, and content creators can expand their reach, impact, and relevance in an increasingly interconnected global landscape.

Summary: Embracing the Potential of AI-Generated Content

As we have explored throughout this section, AI-generated content offers a wealth of benefits and opportunities for businesses, content creators, and consumers alike. From increased efficiency and productivity to personalized experiences and cost reduction, the advantages of AI in content creation are both numerous and significant.

The ability of AI to streamline the content creation process, automate repetitive tasks, and generate high-quality material at scale is revolutionizing the way we produce and consume information. By leveraging the power of natural language processing, machine learning, and data analytics, AI-powered tools are enabling organizations to create compelling, engaging, and highly targeted content that resonates with their audiences.

Moreover, AI-generated content is breaking down language and cultural barriers, facilitating the creation of multilingual and culturally adapted material that can reach and engage audiences around the world. This global accessibility is opening up new opportunities for businesses to expand their reach, foster greater understanding, and build meaningful connections with customers in diverse markets.

However, as we embrace the potential of AI-generated content, it is crucial that we approach this technology with a strategic and ethical mindset. By combining the efficiency and scalability of AI with the creativity, empathy, and oversight of human content creators, we can harness the full potential of this powerful tool while ensuring the quality, authenticity, and cultural sensitivity of the content we produce.

As we move forward into an increasingly AI-driven future, it is clear that the benefits and opportunities of AI-generated content will only continue to grow and evolve. By staying informed, adaptable, and open to new possibilities, businesses, content creators, and consumers alike can position themselves to thrive in this exciting new landscape of content creation and consumption.

In the next section, we will delve into the challenges and concerns surrounding AI-generated content, examining the potential drawbacks and risks associated with this technology, and exploring strategies for mitigating these issues as we work to build a more inclusive, equitable, and sustainable future for content creation.

Section 4: The Challenges and Concerns Surrounding AI-Generated Content

As the rise of AI-generated content continues to transform various industries, it is crucial to acknowledge and address the potential drawbacks and concerns that come with this technological advancement. While AI has the potential to revolutionize content creation, it also presents a set of unique challenges that must be carefully considered and navigated. In this section, we will delve into the key issues surrounding AI-generated content, shedding light on the concerns that have contributed to the stigma against its use.

From questions about the quality and authenticity of AI-generated content to the ethical considerations and potential biases embedded within these systems, we will explore the multifaceted nature of the challenges at hand. We will also examine the potential impact of AI-generated content on the job market, discussing the fears of job displacement and the need for human content creators to adapt and acquire new skills in the face of technological change.

By addressing these concerns head-on, we aim to provide a balanced and comprehensive understanding of the current landscape surrounding AI-generated content. Through this exploration, we will lay the foundation for a nuanced discussion on how to navigate these challenges, harness the potential benefits of AI, and work towards a future where human creativity and artificial intelligence can coexist and thrive.

Subsection 4.1: Quality and Authenticity Concerns

One of the primary concerns surrounding AI-generated content is the perceived lack of creativity and originality. Critics argue that AI algorithms, while capable of producing coherent and grammatically correct text, often fail to capture the nuances, emotions, and unique perspectives that human writers bring to their work. This leads to questions about the overall quality and authenticity of AI-generated content.

At the heart of this concern lies the belief that creativity is a fundamentally human trait, one that machines cannot fully replicate. Human writers draw from their personal experiences, emotions, and intuition to craft compelling narratives and convey complex ideas in innovative ways. They possess the ability to think outside the box, challenge conventional norms, and infuse their work with a distinct voice and style. In contrast, AI-generated content is often criticized for being formulaic, predictable, and lacking in originality.

Moreover, the quality of AI-generated content is heavily dependent on the training data and algorithms used to create it. If the training data is biased, incomplete, or of poor quality, the resulting content may reflect those limitations. This can lead to inaccuracies, inconsistencies, and a lack of depth in the generated text. Additionally, AI systems may struggle to understand and incorporate context, sarcasm, humor, and other subtle elements that are essential to creating engaging and meaningful content.

Another concern related to the authenticity of AI-generated content is the potential for plagiarism and intellectual property infringement. As AI algorithms learn from vast amounts of existing data, there is a risk that the generated content may inadvertently incorporate copyrighted material or mimic the style and ideas of human writers without proper attribution. This raises ethical questions about the ownership and originality of AI-generated content.

To address these concerns, it is essential to recognize that AI-generated content is not intended to replace human creativity but rather to augment and support it. By leveraging the strengths of both human and machine intelligence, we can create content that is both efficient and engaging. This requires a collaborative approach, where human writers and editors work alongside AI tools to ensure the quality, authenticity, and originality of the final product.

Furthermore, as AI technology continues to advance, it is crucial to develop more sophisticated algorithms that can better understand and incorporate the nuances of human language and creativity. This may involve training AI systems on more diverse and representative datasets, as well as incorporating feedback and input from human writers and domain experts. By continuously refining and improving AI-generated content, we can work towards bridging the gap between machine-generated text and the richness and depth of human-created content.

Subsection 4.2: Ethical Considerations and Bias

As AI-generated content becomes more prevalent across various industries, it is crucial to consider the ethical implications and potential biases that may arise from its use. While AI algorithms are designed to process vast amounts of data and generate content based on patterns and insights, they are not immune to the biases and limitations present in the data they are trained on.

One of the primary ethical concerns surrounding AI-generated content is the risk of perpetuating and amplifying existing biases. AI systems learn from the data they are exposed to, which may include historical and societal biases related to factors such as race, gender, age, and socioeconomic status. If these biases are not identified and addressed during the training process, they can become embedded in the AI algorithms and manifest in the generated content.

For example, if an AI system is trained on a dataset that primarily features male-centric language or underrepresents certain ethnic or racial groups, the resulting content may reflect those biases. This can lead to the reinforcement of stereotypes, the marginalization of underrepresented communities, and the perpetuation of harmful narratives. In such cases, AI-generated content can contribute to the spread of misinformation, discrimination, and social injustice.

Moreover, the lack of transparency and accountability in some AI systems raises ethical concerns. When AI-generated content is presented without clear indication of its origins, readers may be misled into believing that the content was created by a human author. This can erode trust in the information ecosystem and make it more difficult for individuals to distinguish between human-generated and machine-generated content. It is essential for content creators and distributors to be transparent about the use of AI and to provide appropriate disclaimers and labeling to ensure that readers can make informed judgments about the credibility and reliability of the content they consume.

Another ethical consideration is the potential for AI-generated content to be used for malicious purposes, such as spreading propaganda, disinformation, or hate speech. As AI algorithms become more sophisticated in mimicking human language patterns, they can be exploited by bad actors to generate convincing and persuasive content that manipulates public opinion, sows discord, or promotes extremist ideologies. This highlights the need for robust safeguards, regulations, and ethical guidelines to govern the development and deployment of AI-generated content.

To address these ethical concerns, it is crucial for AI developers and content creators to prioritize fairness, accountability, and transparency in their practices. This involves actively identifying and mitigating biases in training data, implementing rigorous testing and auditing processes to detect and correct biased outputs, and being transparent about the use of AI in content generation. Collaboration between AI experts, ethicists, and domain specialists is essential to develop ethical frameworks and best practices that guide the responsible development and use of AI-generated content.

Furthermore, ongoing research and public discourse on the ethical implications of AI-generated content are necessary to raise awareness, foster informed decision-making, and drive the development of policies and regulations that protect the public interest. By proactively addressing the ethical considerations and potential biases associated with AI-generated content, we can work towards harnessing the benefits of this technology while mitigating its risks and ensuring that it serves the greater good of society.

Subsection 4.3: Job Displacement and Skill Redundancy

As AI-generated content becomes increasingly sophisticated and prevalent, concerns have arisen about its potential impact on the job market and the role of human content creators. The fear of job displacement and the redundancy of certain skills is a significant contributor to the stigma against AI-generated content.

One of the primary concerns is that AI-powered content creation tools may replace human writers, editors, and content producers, leading to widespread job losses in the creative industries. As AI algorithms become more adept at generating coherent, engaging, and personalized content, the demand for human-created content may diminish. This could result in a shift in the job market, with fewer opportunities for traditional content creation roles and a greater emphasis on skills related to AI development, data analysis, and content curation.

However, it is essential to recognize that AI-generated content is not likely to replace human creativity entirely. While AI can produce content quickly and efficiently, it still lacks the nuanced understanding, emotional intelligence, and contextual awareness that human creators bring to their work. Human writers and editors possess the ability to infuse their content with unique perspectives, cultural references, and personal experiences that resonate with audiences on a deeper level.

Moreover, the rise of AI-generated content may actually create new job opportunities and skill requirements in the creative industries. As AI tools become more integrated into the content creation process, there will be a growing need for professionals who can work alongside these tools, leveraging their capabilities while providing human oversight and direction. This may include roles such as AI content strategists, who develop and implement strategies for effectively incorporating AI-generated content into overall content plans, and AI content curators, who review, select, and refine AI-generated content to ensure its quality and relevance.

In addition, the increasing use of AI in content creation may drive demand for skills related to data analysis, machine learning, and natural language processing. Content creators who possess a combination of creative and technical skills will be well-positioned to thrive in this new landscape, as they can bridge the gap between the capabilities of AI and the needs of human audiences.

To navigate the potential impact of AI-generated content on the job market, content creators must adapt and acquire new skills that complement and enhance the capabilities of AI tools. This may involve developing a deeper understanding of AI technologies, learning how to collaborate effectively with AI systems, and honing skills related to content strategy, data analysis, and audience engagement.

Educational institutions and professional development programs will also play a crucial role in preparing the workforce for the changes brought about by AI-generated content. By incorporating AI-related skills and knowledge into their curricula, these programs can help content creators stay relevant and competitive in an evolving job market.

Ultimately, while the rise of AI-generated content may lead to some job displacement and skill redundancy, it is unlikely to eliminate the need for human content creators entirely. By embracing the opportunities presented by AI and acquiring the skills necessary to work alongside these tools, content creators can position themselves for success in a rapidly changing industry. The key is to view AI not as a threat, but as a powerful tool that can augment and enhance human creativity, leading to new forms of expression and more engaging content for audiences worldwide.

Summary: Navigating the Challenges and Harnessing the Potential of AI-Generated Content

As we have explored throughout this section, the rise of AI-generated content presents a complex array of challenges and concerns that have contributed to the stigma surrounding its use. From questions about the quality and authenticity of machine-generated text to the ethical considerations and potential biases embedded within AI systems, it is clear that the path forward is not without obstacles.

However, it is crucial to recognize that these challenges are not insurmountable. By proactively addressing the concerns raised in this section, we can work towards harnessing the potential benefits of AI-generated content while mitigating its risks. This requires a multifaceted approach that involves collaboration between AI developers, content creators, ethicists, and policymakers to establish best practices, guidelines, and regulations that promote responsible and transparent use of AI in content generation.

Moreover, as we navigate the potential impact of AI on the job market and the evolving skill requirements for content creators, it is essential to view

AI not as a threat, but as a tool that can augment and enhance human creativity. By acquiring the skills necessary to work alongside AI systems and leveraging their capabilities to create more engaging, personalized, and efficient content, human creators can position themselves for success in a rapidly changing industry.

Ultimately, the challenges and concerns surrounding AI-generated content serve as a reminder of the importance of approaching this technology with caution, critical thinking, and a commitment to ethical principles. By doing so, we can shape a future in which AI and human creativity coexist and thrive, unlocking new forms of expression and delivering more value to audiences worldwide. As we move forward, it is essential to remain vigilant, adaptable, and open to the possibilities that lie ahead, while never losing sight of the fundamental values that guide responsible content creation in the age of artificial intelligence.

Section 5: The Future Outlook for AI-Generated Content

As we stand on the precipice of a new era in content creation, it's impossible to ignore the rapid advancements and growing presence of AI-generated content across various industries. From the early experiments and breakthroughs to the current state of the technology, AI has already begun to reshape the landscape of content creation, offering both exciting opportunities and challenging questions about the future.

Looking ahead, it's clear that the trajectory of AI-generated content is one of continued growth and transformation. As the technology continues to evolve and mature, we can expect to see even more sophisticated and nuanced content emerging from AI systems, blurring the lines between human and machine-created works. The potential for AI to revolutionize industries, streamline processes, and open up new avenues for creativity is immense, and it's essential that we approach this future with a mix of optimism and thoughtful consideration.

In this section, we'll delve into the future outlook for AI-generated content, exploring the technological advancements and innovations on the horizon, the possibilities for collaboration between human and AI content creators, and the evolving consumer perceptions and acceptance of AI-generated content. By examining these key aspects, we'll gain a clearer understanding of what lies ahead and how we can navigate the challenges and opportunities presented by this transformative technology.

As we embark on this exploration of the future, it's important to keep an open mind and a critical eye. The path forward is not without its obstacles and uncertainties, but by engaging in meaningful discussions and considering multiple perspectives, we can work towards shaping a future where AI-generated content not only coexists with human creativity but also enhances and complements it in ways we have yet to imagine.

Subsection 5.1: Technological Advancements and Innovations

As we look towards the future of AI-generated content, it's essential to consider the potential technological advancements and innovations that could shape the landscape of this rapidly evolving field. The pace of progress in artificial intelligence and machine learning is astounding, with new breakthroughs and discoveries emerging at an unprecedented rate. These advancements are poised to revolutionize the way AI-generated content is created, consumed, and perceived.

One of the most promising areas of development is in the realm of natural language processing (NLP). As NLP techniques become more sophisticated, AI systems will be able to generate content that is increasingly indistinguishable from human-written text. This could lead to the creation of highly personalized and engaging content, tailored to the specific needs and preferences of individual users. Advancements in NLP could also enable AI systems to better understand and respond to the nuances of human language, allowing for more natural and fluid interactions between humans and AI-generated content.

Another area of potential innovation lies in the integration of AI with other emerging technologies, such as virtual and augmented reality. As these technologies mature, we may see the rise of immersive, AI-generated content experiences that blur the lines between the real and the virtual. Imagine, for instance, an AI-powered virtual world where the environment, characters, and storylines are all generated in real-time, adapting to the actions and choices of the user. Such experiences could revolutionize the way we consume and interact with content, opening up new possibilities for entertainment, education, and beyond.

The field of generative adversarial networks (GANs) is another area of AI research that holds immense promise for the future of AI-generated content. GANs are a type of neural network architecture that pits two networks against each other - a generator network that creates new content, and a discriminator network that attempts to distinguish between real and generated content. Through this adversarial process, GANs can learn to generate highly realistic and diverse content, from images and videos to music and text. As GANs continue to advance, we may see the emergence of AI systems capable of generating content that is not only indistinguishable from human-created works but also imbued with genuine creativity and originality.

Of course, these advancements also raise important questions and concerns about the future of AI-generated content. As AI systems become more capable of creating high-quality content, there may be increasing concerns about job displacement and the role of human creativity in a world where machines can generate art, music, and literature. There will also be important ethical considerations to grapple with, such as the potential for AI-generated content to be used for disinformation or propaganda purposes.

Despite these challenges, the future of AI-generated content is undeniably exciting. As technological advancements continue to push the boundaries of what's possible, we can expect to see a new era of content creation emerge - one in which AI and human creativity work hand in hand to produce works of unparalleled depth, diversity, and impact. By staying informed about these advancements and engaging in thoughtful discussion about their implications, we can help shape a future in which AI-generated content not only coexists with human creativity but also enhances and enriches it in ways we have yet to imagine.

Subsection 5.2: Collaboration Between Human and AI Content Creators

As AI-generated content becomes more prevalent and sophisticated, it's crucial to consider the potential for collaboration between human and AI content creators. Rather than viewing AI as a threat to human creativity, we can explore the possibilities for synergy and cooperation, where the strengths of both humans and machines are leveraged to create content that is more engaging, informative, and impactful.

One of the key advantages of AI-generated content is its ability to process and analyze vast amounts of data quickly and accurately. AI algorithms can identify patterns, extract insights, and generate content based on these findings, providing a solid foundation for human content creators to build upon. For example, an AI system could analyze trending topics, user preferences, and engagement metrics to suggest ideas for new content or to optimize existing content for better performance. Human content creators can then use their creativity, intuition, and domain expertise to refine these suggestions, adding the personal touch and emotional depth that AI may lack.

Another area where collaboration between human and AI content creators can flourish is in the realm of personalization. AI algorithms can analyze user data, such as browsing history, social media activity, and demographic information, to create highly targeted content recommendations. Human content creators can then use this information to craft personalized content that resonates with individual users, addressing their specific needs, interests, and pain points. By working together, human and AI content creators can deliver a more engaging and valuable user experience, fostering loyalty and trust among their audience.

Collaboration between human and AI content creators can also lead to the development of new forms of content and storytelling. AI algorithms can generate novel combinations of words, images, and sounds, inspiring human content creators to push the boundaries of their craft and explore new creative possibilities. For instance, an AI system could generate a series of abstract images or musical compositions, which human artists could then interpret and incorporate into their own work, creating a unique fusion of human and machine creativity. Similarly, AI-generated text could serve as a starting point for human writers, who can then refine and expand upon these ideas to create compelling stories and narratives.

As AI-generated content becomes more advanced, it's likely that we'll see the emergence of new roles and skillsets at the intersection of human and machine creativity. Content strategists, for example, may need to develop expertise in AI algorithms and data analysis to effectively guide the creation and distribution of AI-generated content. Similarly, content creators may need to acquire new technical skills, such as working with AI tools and platforms, to fully harness the potential of these technologies in their work.

Of course, the collaboration between human and AI content creators is not without its challenges. There may be concerns around job displacement, creative control, and the potential for AI-generated content to perpetuate biases or spread misinformation. It's essential that we approach these challenges with transparency, accountability, and a commitment to ethical practices. By establishing clear guidelines and standards for the use of AI in content creation, we can ensure that the collaboration between human and AI content creators is a positive and mutually beneficial one.

Ultimately, the future of content creation lies in the hands of both humans and machines. By embracing the possibilities for collaboration and synergy between these two forces, we can unlock new forms of creativity, engagement, and impact. As we navigate this uncharted territory, it's essential that we remain open to new ideas, willing to experiment and learn from our successes and failures. Only by working together can we truly realize the full potential of AI-generated content and create a future where human and machine creativity thrive side by side.

Subsection 5.3: Evolving Consumer Perceptions and Acceptance

As AI-generated content becomes more prevalent and sophisticated, it's crucial to consider how public opinion and acceptance of this technology may evolve over time. Consumer perceptions play a significant role in shaping the future of AI-generated content, as they can influence its adoption, regulation, and overall impact on society.

Currently, there is a notable stigma surrounding AI-generated content, with many people expressing concerns about its authenticity, creativity, and potential to replace human content creators. This skepticism is understandable, given the relatively nascent stage of the technology and the limited exposure most consumers have had to high-quality AI-generated content. However, as AI continues to advance and more people encounter AI-generated content in their daily lives, it's likely that these perceptions will begin to shift.

One key factor that may contribute to the evolving acceptance of AI-generated content is the increasing quality and sophistication of the content itself. As AI algorithms become more advanced, they will be capable of producing content that is increasingly indistinguishable from human-created works. This improvement in quality may gradually erode the notion that AI-generated content is inherently inferior or less valuable than human-generated content.

Another factor that may influence consumer perceptions is the growing collaboration between human and AI content creators. As more content creators begin to incorporate AI tools into their workflows, the lines between human and machine creativity will become increasingly blurred. This collaboration may help to normalize the use of AI in content creation and demonstrate the potential for AI to enhance, rather than replace, human creativity.

Exposure and familiarity will also play a crucial role in shaping consumer attitudes towards AI-generated content. As people encounter more examples of AI-generated content in their daily lives, whether through personalized recommendations, virtual assistants, or creative works, they may become more comfortable with the idea of machines creating content. This increased exposure may help to demystify AI and reduce the stigma surrounding its use in content creation.

However, the path to widespread acceptance of AI-generated content is not without its challenges. There will likely be ongoing concerns about the ethical implications of AI, such as the potential for bias, misinformation, and job displacement. It will be essential for content creators, platforms, and policymakers to address these concerns head-on, developing guidelines and regulations that ensure the responsible and transparent use of AI in content creation.

Education and awareness will also be crucial in shaping consumer perceptions of AI-generated content. As people become more informed about the capabilities and limitations of AI, they may develop a more nuanced understanding of its potential benefits and drawbacks. This increased knowledge may help to dispel misconceptions and foster a more balanced and informed public discourse around AI-generated content.

Ultimately, the evolution of consumer perceptions and acceptance of AI-generated content will be a gradual and complex process, shaped by a multitude of factors. As the technology continues to advance and integrate into our daily lives, it's essential that we approach it with a mix of openness and critical thinking, considering both the opportunities and challenges it presents. By engaging in thoughtful discussion and collaboration, we can work towards a future where AI-generated content is valued for its unique contributions and potential to enhance human creativity, while also ensuring that it is developed and used in an ethical and responsible manner.

Summary: Embracing the Future of AI-Generated Content

As we stand on the cusp of a new era in content creation, it's clear that AI-generated content will play an increasingly significant role in shaping the future of various industries. From technological advancements and innovations that push the boundaries of what's possible, to the growing potential for collaboration between human and AI content creators, the landscape of content creation is poised for a profound transformation.

However, the path forward is not without its challenges. As AI-generated content becomes more prevalent and sophisticated, it's crucial to consider the evolving consumer perceptions and acceptance of this technology. While there may be initial skepticism and concerns about the authenticity and creativity of AI-generated content, it's likely that these attitudes will shift over time as people become more exposed to high-quality AI-generated content and witness the benefits of human-AI collaboration.

To navigate this uncharted territory successfully, it's essential that we approach the future of AI-generated content with a mix of openness and critical thinking. By engaging in thoughtful discussions, establishing guidelines for responsible AI use, and fostering a culture of transparency and accountability, we can work towards a future where AI-generated content is valued for its unique contributions and potential to enhance human creativity.

Ultimately, the future of AI-generated content is one of immense possibility and promise. By embracing the opportunities for innovation, collaboration, and growth, while also addressing the challenges and concerns head-on, we can shape a future where AI and human creativity thrive side by side, unlocking new forms of expression, engagement, and impact. As we embark on this exciting journey, it's up to us to approach the future with curiosity, adaptability, and a commitment to creating a world where AI-generated content is not just accepted, but celebrated for its ability to push the boundaries of what's possible.

Chapter Summary: Embracing the AI Revolution in Content Creation

The rise of AI-generated content marks a significant shift in the way we create, consume, and distribute information across various industries. From early experiments and breakthroughs to the current state of AI-powered content creation, the technology has evolved rapidly, driven by advancements in natural language processing, deep learning, and neural networks. As AI continues to permeate sectors such as journalism, marketing, entertainment, and academia, it brings forth a multitude of benefits and opportunities, including increased efficiency, personalization, cost reduction, and cross-cultural accessibility.

However, the growth of AI-generated content also raises concerns regarding quality, authenticity, ethics, and job displacement. As we navigate this new landscape, it is crucial to address these challenges head-on, fostering a dialogue that encourages responsible development and deployment of AI technologies. By embracing the potential of AI-generated content while remaining mindful of its limitations, we can harness its power to augment human creativity and unlock new possibilities for content creation.

Looking ahead, the future of AI-generated content is filled with exciting prospects, from technological advancements and innovations to increased collaboration between human and AI content creators. As consumer perceptions and acceptance evolve, it is essential for individuals and organizations to stay informed, adaptable, and open to the transformative potential of AI in the content creation space. By doing so, we can collectively shape a future where AI and human creativity work hand in hand, ushering in a new era of content creation that is more efficient, personalized, and accessible than ever before.

Chapter 2: Understanding the Stigma

In the ever-evolving landscape of technology, artificial intelligence (AI) has emerged as a transformative force, reshaping industries and challenging long-held beliefs about the nature of creativity and authenticity. As AI-generated content becomes increasingly prevalent, a pervasive stigma has taken root, casting doubt on its legitimacy and value. This chapter delves into the complex web of factors that have given rise to this stigma, examining the historical, psychological, societal, and ethical underpinnings that shape our perceptions of AI-generated content.

To fully grasp the roots of the stigma, we must first explore the historical context in which AI has developed. From the earliest days of computing, the notion of machines possessing intelligence has captivated the public imagination, sparking both fascination and fear. Science fiction narratives have long portrayed AI as a double-edged sword, capable of both remarkable feats and terrifying consequences. These early perceptions have laid the groundwork for the current skepticism surrounding AI-generated content, as people grapple with the implications of machines encroaching upon the realm of human creativity.

Beyond the historical context, the stigma against AI-generated content is deeply intertwined with psychological factors that shape our understanding of creativity and authenticity. The human mind is wired to seek out patterns and assign meaning, often leading us to place greater value on content that bears the mark of human touch. We crave the emotional resonance and personal connection that comes from knowing a piece of content was crafted by a fellow human being, pouring their unique experiences, emotions, and perspectives into their work. The perceived lack of these qualities in AI-generated content fuels the belief that it is somehow inferior or less authentic.

As we navigate the complexities of the stigma against AI-generated content, it is crucial to recognize the societal and cultural factors that contribute to its perpetuation. The value placed on human craftsmanship and the role of traditional gatekeepers in creative industries have long shaped our understanding of what constitutes "real" or "legitimate" content. Media coverage and public discourse also play a significant role in shaping perceptions, often focusing on the potential threats posed by AI rather than the opportunities it presents.

Furthermore, the stigma against AI-generated content is inextricably linked to ethical and legal concerns that arise as machines increasingly participate in the creative process. Questions of authorship, intellectual property rights, and accountability become muddied when AI is involved, leading to a sense of unease and uncertainty. The potential for AI to perpetuate biases and discriminatory practices also looms large, raising concerns about the need for robust regulation and governance frameworks.

As we embark on this journey to understand the stigma against AI-generated content, it is essential to approach the topic with an open mind and a willingness to challenge our preconceptions. By examining the historical, psychological, societal, and ethical factors at play, we can begin to unravel the complex tapestry of this stigma and pave the way for a more nuanced and informed discourse on the role of AI in creative endeavors. In doing so, we may discover that the perceived threat of AI-generated content is not an insurmountable obstacle, but rather an opportunity to redefine our understanding of creativity and explore new frontiers of human-machine collaboration.

Section 1: Historical Context of the Stigma

The stigma against AI-generated content is not a new phenomenon; it has roots that can be traced back to the early days of artificial intelligence. To fully understand the current state of this stigma, it is essential to explore its origins and evolution over time. In this section, we will delve into the historical context that has shaped the public's perception of AI and its potential implications, particularly in the realm of content creation.

From the earliest depictions of artificial intelligence in science fiction to the emergence of AI-generated content in recent years, the relationship between humans and machines has been a subject of fascination, fear, and speculation. By examining the key moments and milestones in the history of AI, we can gain valuable insights into the psychological, cultural, and societal factors that have contributed to the development and persistence of the stigma against AI-generated content.

As we journey through the past, we will uncover the profound influence of popular media, the impact of early AI-generated content on public opinion, and the role of human biases and preconceptions in shaping attitudes towards this technology. By understanding the historical context, we can better appreciate the challenges and opportunities that lie ahead as we navigate the complex landscape of AI-generated content in the present day.

Subsection 1.1: Early Perceptions of Artificial Intelligence

The concept of artificial intelligence (AI) has captivated the human imagination for centuries, long before the term itself was coined. From ancient myths of mechanical beings to the science fiction stories of the early 20th century, the idea of creating intelligent machines has been a persistent theme in human culture. However, it wasn't until the 1950s that AI began to emerge as a legitimate field of scientific inquiry, sparking both excitement and apprehension among the public.

In 1956, a group of scientists, including John McCarthy, Marvin Minsky, Nathaniel Rochester, and Claude Shannon, convened at the Dartmouth Summer Research Project on Artificial Intelligence. This event is widely considered the birth of AI as an academic discipline. The researchers boldly predicted that within a generation, machines would be capable of performing any task that a human could do. This optimistic outlook captured the public's imagination, fueling dreams of a future where intelligent machines would revolutionize every aspect of life.

However, alongside the enthusiasm came a growing sense of unease. The notion of machines possessing human-like intelligence raised profound philosophical and ethical questions. Would AI surpass human intelligence?

Could machines develop consciousness and free will? These concerns were amplified by popular media, with films like "2001: A Space Odyssey" (1968) and "Colossus: The Forbin Project" (1970) depicting AI as a potential threat to humanity.

As AI research progressed throughout the 1960s and 1970s, public perception vacillated between hope and apprehension. On one hand, AI was seen as a tool for solving complex problems and enhancing human capabilities. On the other hand, there were fears that AI could lead to job losses, social upheaval, and even existential risks. This dichotomy laid the foundation for the ongoing debate surrounding AI and its implications for society.

Despite the early promises, AI research faced significant challenges and setbacks. The limitations of computing power, the complexity of human intelligence, and the lack of funding led to periods of diminished interest and investment in AI, known as the "AI winters." These setbacks tempered public expectations and led to a more measured approach to AI development.

As the field of AI continued to evolve, so did public perceptions. The 1980s and 1990s saw a resurgence of interest in AI, driven by advances in computer hardware, the emergence of expert systems, and the growth of the internet. AI began to be seen as a practical tool for enhancing productivity and efficiency in various industries, from finance to healthcare.

However, the specter of AI's potential negative impacts never fully disappeared. Concerns about privacy, bias, and the ethical implications of AI decision-making became increasingly prominent as the technology became more integrated into daily life. The rapid pace of AI development, coupled with the opaque nature of some AI systems, only heightened these concerns.

In the early days of AI, the public's perception was shaped by a mix of optimism, curiosity, and apprehension. As the field progressed, these initial reactions evolved, reflecting the complex and often contradictory relationship between humans and intelligent machines. Understanding these early perceptions provides a foundation for examining the current stigma surrounding AI-generated content and its roots in the long history of human-machine interaction.

Subsection 1.2: The Influence of Science Fiction and Media

Science fiction has long been a powerful force in shaping public perceptions of artificial intelligence (AI). From the early days of the genre, writers and filmmakers have explored the potential consequences of creating intelligent machines, often portraying AI as a double-edged sword – a source of both wonder and fear. These fictional depictions have had a profound impact on how people view AI in the real world, including the stigma surrounding AI-generated content.

One of the earliest and most influential examples of AI in science fiction is Mary Shelley's "Frankenstein" (1818). Although the creature in the novel is not a machine, the story raises important questions about the responsibilities and risks associated with creating intelligent beings. This theme has been revisited countless times in science fiction, from Isaac Asimov's "I, Robot" (1950) to the "Terminator" film franchise (1984-2019).

In many science fiction stories, AI is portrayed as a potential threat to humanity. Films like "2001: A Space Odyssey" (1968) and "The Matrix" (1999) depict AI as a malevolent force that seeks to dominate or destroy humans. These dystopian visions have contributed to a widespread fear of AI, even as the technology has become increasingly prevalent in our daily lives.

However, science fiction has also explored the positive potential of AI. Works like "Star Trek" (1966-present) and "Her" (2013) imagine a future in which AI is a benevolent presence, working alongside humans to solve problems and enhance our lives. These more optimistic portrayals have helped to balance the negative stereotypes and foster a more nuanced understanding of AI's potential.

The influence of science fiction on public attitudes towards AI extends beyond the realm of entertainment. Many of the concepts and terminology associated with AI, such as "artificial intelligence" itself, were first introduced in science fiction before being adopted by researchers and the media. This has led to a blurring of the lines between fictional speculation and real-world developments, contributing to both excitement and anxiety about the future of AI.

In recent years, the rapid advancement of AI technology has brought many of the scenarios explored in science fiction closer to reality. As AI-generated content has become more sophisticated and widespread, the public has grappled with the implications of this new form of creative expression. The stigma surrounding AI-generated content can be seen as a manifestation of the long-standing fears and uncertainties about AI that have been shaped by science fiction.

At the same time, science fiction has also provided a framework for understanding and engaging with AI-generated content. Works like "The Diamond Age" (1995) by Neal Stephenson, which imagines a future in which AI is used to create personalized media experiences, have helped to broaden the conversation about the potential applications and implications of this technology.

As we continue to navigate the complex landscape of AI-generated content, it is important to recognize the role that science fiction has played in shaping public perceptions. By understanding the ways in which fictional portrayals have influenced our attitudes towards AI, we can work to separate legitimate concerns from unfounded fears and engage in a more informed and nuanced dialogue about the future of this technology.

Subsection 1.3: The Emergence of AI-Generated Content

The advent of AI-generated content marked a significant milestone in the history of artificial intelligence and its impact on society. As AI technologies advanced, particularly in the fields of natural language processing (NLP) and machine learning (ML), the ability for machines to create content that resembled human-generated work became increasingly sophisticated. This development sparked both fascination and concern among the public, as it challenged traditional notions of creativity, authorship, and the role of technology in our lives.

One of the earliest and most prominent examples of AI-generated content was the release of GPT-2 by OpenAI in 2019. GPT-2, or Generative Pre-trained Transformer 2, was a language model capable of generating coherent and contextually relevant text based on a given prompt. The model was trained on a massive dataset of online content, allowing it to produce text that was often indistinguishable from human writing. The release of GPT-2 garnered significant media attention and sparked discussions about the potential implications of AI-generated content, both positive and negative.

On one hand, the emergence of AI-generated content was seen as a breakthrough in the field of AI, demonstrating the incredible potential of machine learning to create compelling and useful content. Many researchers and industry experts highlighted the potential applications of this technology, such as automating content creation for websites, generating personalized content for individuals, and even assisting human writers in their creative process. The ability for AI to generate content at scale and with high levels of customization was seen as a potential game-changer for various industries, from journalism to marketing.

However, the public response to the emergence of AI-generated content was not entirely positive. Many people expressed concerns about the potential misuse of this technology, such as the creation of fake news, the spread of propaganda, and the erosion of trust in online information. There were also fears that AI-generated content could lead to job losses in industries that rely heavily on content creation, such as journalism and copywriting. Some critics argued that AI-generated content lacked the creativity, empathy, and human touch that makes great writing so compelling and impactful.

As AI-generated content became more prevalent and accessible, the public grappled with questions about the nature of creativity and authorship in the age of AI. The idea that machines could create content that was indistinguishable from human writing challenged long-held beliefs about the uniqueness and value of human creativity. Some argued that AI-generated content was a form of plagiarism or intellectual property theft, as the models were trained on existing human-created content. Others saw it as a natural evolution of technology and a tool that could enhance and augment human creativity rather than replace it.

The emergence of AI-generated content also raised important ethical and societal questions. As the technology became more sophisticated, there were concerns about the potential for AI to perpetuate biases and stereotypes present in the training data, leading to the creation of content that was discriminatory or offensive. There were also questions about the accountability and transparency of AI systems used to generate content, particularly in cases where the content had real-world consequences, such as in the realm of journalism or political discourse.

Despite these concerns, the emergence of AI-generated content marked an important turning point in the history of AI and its relationship with society. It demonstrated the incredible potential of machine learning to create content that was engaging, informative, and persuasive, while also highlighting the complex ethical and societal implications of this technology. As AI continues to advance and become more integrated into our daily lives, the public response to AI-generated content will likely evolve, shaped by ongoing debates about the nature of creativity, authorship, and the role of technology in shaping our understanding of the world around us.

Summary: The Historical Roots of the Stigma Against AI-Generated Content

The historical context of the stigma against AI-generated content reveals a complex interplay of factors that have shaped public perceptions and attitudes towards this emerging technology. From the early days of AI

 SANDY Y. GREENLEAF

research, when the concept of intelligent machines first captured the public imagination, to the recent emergence of sophisticated AI-generated content, the relationship between humans and AI has been characterized by a mix of fascination, fear, and uncertainty.

The influence of science fiction and media has played a significant role in shaping the public's understanding and expectations of AI. Dystopian portrayals of AI as a threat to humanity have contributed to a persistent undercurrent of fear and mistrust, while more optimistic depictions have highlighted the potential benefits and opportunities presented by this technology. As AI-generated content has become more prevalent and sophisticated, these fictional narratives have increasingly intersected with real-world developments, blurring the lines between speculation and reality.

The emergence of AI-generated content itself has marked a turning point in the evolution of the stigma. While some have celebrated the potential for AI to revolutionize content creation and enhance human creativity, others have raised concerns about the ethical, social, and economic implications of this technology. Questions of authorship, authenticity, and the value of human creativity have come to the forefront, as the public grapples with the meaning and significance of AI-generated content in an increasingly digital world.

As we move forward, it is clear that the stigma against AI-generated content is not merely a product of technological advancement, but rather a reflection of deeper cultural and psychological factors that have shaped our relationship with AI over time. By understanding the historical roots of this stigma, we can begin to unpack the complex attitudes and beliefs that underlie current debates and chart a course towards a more informed and nuanced dialogue about the future of AI-generated content. In the following sections, we will delve deeper into the psychological, social, and ethical dimensions of this stigma, as we seek to understand its impact on individuals, industries, and society as a whole.

Section 2: Psychological Factors Contributing to

the Stigma

Have you ever wondered why some people are hesitant to embrace AI-generated content, despite its growing presence in our daily lives? The answer lies, in part, within the complex realm of human psychology. Our minds are shaped by a myriad of factors, from our inherent fears and biases to our deep-seated need for authentic, emotional connections. These psychological underpinnings play a significant role in perpetuating the stigma against AI-generated content.

In this section, we will embark on a fascinating journey into the human psyche, unraveling the various psychological factors that contribute to the stigma. We will explore how the fear of the unknown and technophobia can lead to a general mistrust of AI-generated content, and how the perceived threat to human creativity can evoke a sense of unease and resistance. Additionally, we will delve into the importance of authenticity and emotional resonance in content creation, and how the absence of these elements in AI-generated content can further fuel the stigma.

Moreover, we will examine the role of cognitive biases and heuristics in shaping our perceptions of AI-generated content. From the availability heuristic, which leads us to rely on readily available information, to confirmation bias, which causes us to seek out information that confirms our preexisting beliefs, these psychological mechanisms can significantly influence our attitudes towards AI-generated content.

By gaining a deeper understanding of these psychological factors, we can begin to bridge the gap between human apprehension and the potential benefits of AI-generated content. This section aims to provide valuable insights into the complex interplay between our minds and the evolving landscape of content creation, ultimately paving the way for a more informed and balanced approach to AI-generated content.

Subsection 2.1: Fear of the Unknown and Technophobia

In the face of rapid technological advancements, it is not uncommon for individuals to experience a sense of unease or even fear when confronted with the unknown. This phenomenon, often referred to as technophobia, plays a significant role in shaping attitudes towards AI-generated content. As AI technology continues to evolve and permeate various aspects of our lives, the fear and uncertainty surrounding its capabilities and potential implications contribute to the stigma against AI-generated content.

At the core of this fear lies a lack of understanding and familiarity with AI technology. For many individuals, the concept of artificial intelligence is shrouded in mystery, fueled by dystopian narratives in popular media and science fiction. These portrayals often depict AI as a malevolent force, capable of outsmarting and ultimately dominating humanity. While such scenarios remain largely fictional, they have a profound impact on public perception, leading to a general mistrust and apprehension towards AI-generated content.

Moreover, the rapid pace at which AI technology is advancing further exacerbates the fear of the unknown. As AI algorithms become more sophisticated and capable of producing increasingly realistic and convincing content, individuals may struggle to distinguish between human-created and AI-generated content. This blurring of lines can evoke a sense of unease, as people grapple with the idea that machines are capable of replicating and potentially surpassing human creativity.

The fear of the unknown also extends to concerns about the potential misuse of AI technology. As AI-generated content becomes more prevalent, there are valid apprehensions about the spread of misinformation, propaganda, and deepfakes. The ease with which AI can generate convincing fake news articles, images, and videos has raised alarms about the potential erosion of trust in media and the manipulation of public opinion. These concerns further contribute to the stigma against AI-generated content, as individuals become wary of the potential dangers associated with this technology.

Addressing the fear of the unknown and technophobia is crucial in overcoming the stigma against AI-generated content. This requires a concerted effort to educate the public about the realities of AI technology, demystifying its capabilities and limitations. By fostering a deeper understanding of how AI works and its potential benefits, we can begin to alleviate the fears and uncertainties that contribute to the stigma. Additionally, engaging in open and transparent discussions about the ethical considerations and safeguards surrounding AI-generated content can help build trust and confidence in this technology.

Ultimately, the fear of the unknown and technophobia are natural human responses to the rapid advancements in AI technology. However, by confronting these fears head-on, through education, dialogue, and responsible development of AI systems, we can work towards overcoming the stigma against AI-generated content and harness the potential benefits this technology has to offer.

Subsection 2.2: The Perceived Threat to Human Creativity

One of the most pervasive psychological factors contributing to the stigma against AI-generated content is the belief that it undermines human creativity and originality. This perception stems from the notion that creativity is a uniquely human trait, and the idea of machines producing creative works challenges this long-held belief.

At the heart of this perceived threat lies the fear that AI-generated content will eventually replace human creativity altogether. As AI algorithms become more sophisticated and capable of producing increasingly realistic and engaging content, some individuals worry that there will be a diminished need for human creators. This fear is particularly pronounced in creative industries, such as art, music, and writing, where the value placed on originality and authenticity is paramount.

The belief that AI-generated content undermines human creativity is further reinforced by the idea that machines lack the emotional depth and personal experiences that shape human creative expression. Many argue that true creativity requires a level of empathy, intuition, and self-awareness that AI systems currently do not possess. The absence of these human qualities in AI-generated content can lead to a perception that it is inferior or lacking in authenticity compared to human-created works.

Moreover, the ease and speed with which AI can generate content can also contribute to the perceived threat to human creativity. The ability of AI systems to produce vast amounts of content in a short period of time can create a sense of oversaturation, leading some to question the value and uniqueness of individual creative works. This abundance of AI-generated content may also raise concerns about the potential homogenization of creative expression, as algorithms learn from existing works and potentially produce content that lacks the diversity and originality of human-created works.

However, it is essential to recognize that the perceived threat to human creativity posed by AI-generated content is largely based on a narrow understanding of creativity and the role of technology in the creative process. Rather than replacing human creativity, AI can be viewed as a tool that augments and enhances human creative potential. By automating certain aspects of the creative process, such as data analysis or content generation, AI can free up human creators to focus on higher-level tasks that require emotional intelligence, critical thinking, and artistic vision.

Furthermore, the collaboration between human creators and AI systems can lead to new forms of creative expression and innovation. By leveraging the strengths of both human and machine intelligence, we can push the boundaries of what is possible in the creative realm. This synergy between human creativity and AI technology has the potential to unlock new avenues for artistic exploration and generate novel, compelling content that resonates with audiences.

Addressing the perceived threat to human creativity requires a shift in perspective and a deeper understanding of the relationship between AI and human creative potential. By recognizing AI as a tool that complements and enhances human creativity, rather than a replacement for it, we can begin to overcome the stigma associated with AI-generated content. This involves fostering a culture of collaboration and experimentation, where human creators and AI systems work together to produce innovative, engaging content that captures the best of both worlds.

Ultimately, the perceived threat to human creativity posed by AI-generated content is rooted in a fear of the unknown and a resistance to change. By embracing the potential of AI as a creative partner and exploring the new possibilities it offers, we can move beyond this stigma and unlock a new era of creative expression that celebrates the unique contributions of both human and machine intelligence.

Subsection 2.3: The Need for Authenticity and Emotional Connection

In the realm of content creation, authenticity and emotional resonance play a crucial role in engaging and captivating audiences. These elements form the foundation of a deep, meaningful connection between the creator and the consumer, fostering trust, loyalty, and a sense of shared experience. As AI-generated content becomes increasingly prevalent, the perceived lack of authenticity and emotional depth in such content contributes significantly to the stigma surrounding it.

Authenticity, at its core, refers to the genuineness and sincerity of the content being presented. It is the sense that the creator has poured their heart and soul into the work, infusing it with their unique perspective, experiences, and emotions. Authentic content feels real, relatable, and honest, allowing audiences to connect with the creator on a personal level. In contrast, AI-generated content often lacks this personal touch, as it is produced by algorithms that lack the lived experiences and emotional nuances that define human existence.

The importance of authenticity in content creation cannot be overstated. In a world saturated with information and competing voices, audiences crave content that feels genuine and trustworthy. They seek out creators who are transparent about their intentions, their creative process, and their personal struggles. Authentic content has the power to cut through the noise and establish a lasting bond between the creator and their audience, fostering a sense of community and shared purpose.

Closely tied to authenticity is the concept of emotional resonance. Emotional resonance refers to the ability of content to evoke a strong emotional response in the audience, whether it be joy, sadness, anger, or inspiration. When content resonates emotionally, it taps into the shared human experience, creating a powerful connection that transcends the boundaries of the medium. Emotionally resonant content leaves a lasting impact on the audience, prompting them to reflect, engage, and share their own experiences.

The perceived absence of emotional resonance in AI-generated content is a significant factor contributing to the stigma against it. While AI algorithms can analyze vast amounts of data and generate content that is grammatically correct and topically relevant, they struggle to capture the subtle emotional nuances that define human communication. AI-generated content may be informative or entertaining on a surface level, but it often lacks the depth and complexity of emotion that makes human-created content so compelling.

Moreover, the emotional disconnect between AI-generated content and the audience can lead to a sense of alienation and disengagement. When content feels cold, clinical, or formulaic, it fails to establish the emotional bond necessary for long-term engagement and loyalty. Audiences may consume AI-generated content for its informational value or novelty, but they are less likely to form a lasting connection with the content or the brand behind it.

To overcome the stigma against AI-generated content, creators must prioritize authenticity and emotional resonance in their work. This involves a commitment to transparency, vulnerability, and personal storytelling, even when working with AI tools and algorithms. By infusing their unique perspective and emotional depth into the content they create, creators can bridge the gap between the capabilities of AI and the emotional needs of their audience.

Furthermore, the development of AI systems that can better understand and replicate emotional nuances is crucial in addressing the stigma. As AI algorithms become more sophisticated in analyzing and generating emotionally resonant content, the perceived divide between human-created and AI-generated content may begin to narrow. However, it is essential to recognize that authenticity and emotional resonance are not solely the domain of AI, but rather the result of a collaborative effort between human creators and the tools they employ.

Ultimately, the need for authenticity and emotional connection in content creation is a reminder of the fundamental human desire for meaningful, genuine interactions. As we navigate the evolving landscape of AI-generated content, it is crucial to prioritize these values and strive for a balance between the efficiency of AI and the emotional depth of human creativity. By doing so, we can begin to overcome the stigma against AI-generated content and unlock the potential for a new era of authentic, emotionally resonant content that connects with audiences on a profound level.

Subsection 2.4: The Role of Cognitive Biases and Heuristics

As we explore the psychological factors contributing to the stigma against AI-generated content, it is crucial to examine the role of cognitive biases and heuristics in shaping our perceptions. Cognitive biases are systematic patterns of deviation from rational judgment, while heuristics are mental shortcuts that allow us to make quick decisions based on limited information. These cognitive mechanisms, while often useful in navigating complex situations, can also lead to biased and inaccurate assessments of AI-generated content.

One prominent cognitive bias that influences our perception of AI-generated content is the availability heuristic. This heuristic refers to our tendency to base judgments on information that is readily available or easily remembered, rather than considering the full range of relevant data. In the context of AI-generated content, negative examples or high-profile failures of AI systems may be more salient in our minds, leading us to overestimate the prevalence of such issues. For instance, media coverage of AI-generated fake news or biased algorithms may be more memorable than the numerous successful applications of AI in content creation, skewing our overall perception of the technology.

Another cognitive bias that plays a significant role in perpetuating the stigma against AI-generated content is confirmation bias. Confirmation bias refers to our tendency to seek out, interpret, and favor information that confirms our preexisting beliefs while disregarding or dismissing evidence that contradicts them. When it comes to AI-generated content, individuals who hold negative views about the technology may selectively focus on information that reinforces their beliefs, such as articles highlighting the limitations or dangers of AI. Conversely, they may discount or ignore evidence that showcases the benefits and potential of AI-generated content, further entrenching their biased perceptions.

The anchoring bias, another cognitive heuristic, can also contribute to the stigma against AI-generated content. Anchoring occurs when we rely too heavily on the first piece of information we encounter (the "anchor") when making subsequent judgments or decisions. In the case of AI-generated content, early negative experiences or preconceived notions about the capabilities of AI may serve as anchors, influencing our future evaluations of the technology. For example, if an individual's first encounter with AI-generated content is a poorly written article or an unconvincing piece of art, they may anchor their expectations and judge all future AI-generated content based on that initial experience, disregarding improvements or advancements in the field.

The impact of these cognitive biases and heuristics on our perceptions of AI-generated content is further compounded by the complexity and novelty of the technology itself. As AI continues to evolve at a rapid pace, it can be challenging for individuals to keep up with the latest developments and form accurate assessments of its capabilities. In the face of this uncertainty, we may rely more heavily on cognitive shortcuts, such as the availability heuristic or confirmation bias, to make sense of the technology and its implications.

To overcome the influence of cognitive biases and heuristics on our perceptions of AI-generated content, it is essential to cultivate a more balanced and informed approach. This involves actively seeking out diverse perspectives and evidence, both positive and negative, to gain a comprehensive understanding of the technology. By exposing ourselves to a wide range of examples and applications of AI-generated content, we can begin to counteract the availability heuristic and develop a more nuanced view of its potential and limitations.

Moreover, engaging in critical thinking and self-reflection can help us identify and challenge our own biases and assumptions about AI-generated content. By actively questioning our beliefs and considering alternative viewpoints, we can mitigate the impact of confirmation bias and anchoring, allowing for a more objective assessment of the technology. This process of introspection and open-mindedness is crucial in fostering a more balanced and informed discourse surrounding AI-generated content.

Ultimately, recognizing and addressing the role of cognitive biases and heuristics in shaping our perceptions of AI-generated content is an essential step in overcoming the stigma associated with this technology. By cultivating awareness of these cognitive mechanisms and actively seeking out diverse perspectives and evidence, we can work towards a more accurate and nuanced understanding of AI-generated content and its potential to transform various aspects of our lives.

Summary: Confronting the Psychological Barriers to Embracing AI-Generated Content

In this section, we have delved into the complex psychological factors that contribute to the stigma against AI-generated content. By examining the fear of the unknown and technophobia, the perceived threat to human creativity, the need for authenticity and emotional connection, and the role of cognitive biases and heuristics, we have gained a deeper understanding of the underlying reasons behind the resistance to AI-generated content.

It is clear that the psychological barriers to embracing AI-generated content are deeply rooted in our human nature. The fear of the unknown and the discomfort with rapidly evolving technologies can lead to a general mistrust and apprehension towards AI. Moreover, the belief that AI poses a threat to human creativity and the perceived lack of authenticity and emotional depth in AI-generated content further fuel the stigma.

However, it is crucial to recognize that these psychological factors are not insurmountable. By actively addressing the fear of the unknown through education and transparency, fostering a culture of collaboration between human creators and AI systems, and prioritizing authenticity and emotional resonance in AI-generated content, we can begin to bridge the gap between human apprehension and the potential benefits of this technology.

Furthermore, by cultivating awareness of the cognitive biases and heuristics that shape our perceptions, we can work towards a more balanced and informed understanding of AI-generated content. This requires a commitment to seeking out diverse perspectives, engaging in critical thinking, and challenging our own assumptions and biases.

As we move forward, it is essential to recognize that the psychological factors contributing to the stigma against AI-generated content are not static. As AI technology continues to evolve and integrate into our daily lives, our perceptions and attitudes towards it will also shift. By proactively addressing these psychological barriers and fostering a culture of openness and collaboration, we can pave the way for a future in which AI-generated content is not only accepted but celebrated for its potential to enhance and complement human creativity.

The insights gained from this section provide a foundation for exploring the ethical, societal, and practical implications of AI-generated content in the coming chapters. Armed with a deeper understanding of the psychological factors at play, we can approach these issues with greater nuance and sensitivity, working towards a future in which the stigma against AI-generated content is replaced by a recognition of its value and potential.

Section 3: Societal and Cultural Factors Perpetuating the Stigma

In our exploration of the stigma against AI-generated content, it is crucial to examine the broader societal and cultural factors that contribute to its persistence. These factors, deeply ingrained in our collective psyche, shape our perceptions and attitudes towards AI and its creations. From the value we place on human craftsmanship to the influence of traditional industries and media coverage, societal and cultural forces play a significant role in perpetuating the stigma.

As we delve into this section, we will uncover the complex interplay of these factors and how they impact our understanding and acceptance of AI-generated content. By examining the cultural importance of human-created content, the resistance from established industries, and the role of public discourse, we will gain a comprehensive understanding of the societal and cultural underpinnings that fuel the stigma.

Moreover, we will explore how factors such as age, education, and socioeconomic status influence attitudes towards AI-generated content, shedding light on the diverse perspectives that exist within our society. Through this exploration, we aim to provide a nuanced and holistic view of the societal and cultural landscape that shapes our perceptions of AI and its creations.

As we navigate this section, it is essential to approach the topic with an open mind, acknowledging the deep-rooted nature of these factors and the challenges they pose in overcoming the stigma. By understanding the societal and cultural forces at play, we can begin to identify strategies for fostering a more inclusive and accepting environment for AI-generated content, ultimately paving the way for a future where human creativity and artificial intelligence can coexist and thrive.

Subsection 3.1: The Value Placed on Human Craftsmanship

In many cultures across the globe, human craftsmanship is highly valued and celebrated. From intricate handwoven textiles to meticulously crafted pottery, the skill and dedication of artisans have long been admired and cherished. This deep-rooted appreciation for human-created content stems from the belief that the human touch imbues each piece with a unique essence, a reflection of the creator's emotions, experiences, and creative vision.

The value placed on human craftsmanship is not limited to tangible objects; it extends to various forms of creative expression, such as art, music, literature, and even digital content. The notion that a human being has poured their heart and soul into a creation lends it a special quality, a perceived authenticity that is often lacking in AI-generated content.

This cultural emphasis on the importance of human-created content has a significant impact on the stigma surrounding AI-generated content. When a piece of content is known to be created by an AI, it may be viewed as lacking the depth, emotion, and personal touch that human-created content possesses. The absence of a human creator behind the work can lead to a perception of inauthenticity, as if the content is somehow less genuine or meaningful.

Moreover, the value placed on human craftsmanship is closely tied to the idea of originality and uniqueness. Each human-created piece is considered a one-of-a-kind expression of the creator's vision, whereas AI-generated content may be seen as mass-produced or lacking in individual character. This perception further contributes to the stigma, as people may view AI-generated content as inferior or less valuable compared to human-created content.

The cultural importance of human craftsmanship also intersects with the notion of artistic integrity and the romantic ideal of the struggling artist. The belief that true art is born from human struggle, passion, and sacrifice is deeply ingrained in many societies. AI-generated content, on the other hand, may be perceived as a product of cold, calculated algorithms, devoid of the human experience that makes art meaningful.

As we navigate the complex landscape of the stigma against AI-generated content, it is crucial to recognize and understand the cultural value placed on human craftsmanship. By acknowledging the deep-rooted beliefs and emotions surrounding human-created content, we can begin to bridge the gap between tradition and innovation, finding ways to celebrate the unique contributions of both human and artificial intelligence in the realm of creative expression.

Subsection 3.2: The Role of Traditional Industries and Gatekeepers

In the ever-evolving landscape of content creation, traditional industries and gatekeepers play a significant role in shaping public perception and acceptance of AI-generated content. These established entities, such as publishing houses, media conglomerates, and cultural institutions, have long held the power to determine what content reaches the masses and what is considered valuable or legitimate.

As AI-generated content becomes more prevalent and sophisticated, these traditional industries and gatekeepers may resist its adoption and integration, perceiving it as a threat to their long-standing business models and cultural authority. The fear of disruption and the potential loss of control over the content creation process can lead to a heightened stigma against AI-generated content within these circles.

One of the primary concerns of traditional industries is the potential for AI to replace human creators, such as writers, artists, and musicians. The notion that machines could generate content that rivals or even surpasses human-created works challenges the very foundation upon which these industries have been built. This fear of obsolescence can manifest as a resistance to AI-generated content, with gatekeepers actively discouraging or dismissing its value to protect the interests of their human creators.

Moreover, traditional industries often have well-established systems of curation, quality control, and distribution that have been fine-tuned over decades. The introduction of AI-generated content can disrupt these systems, requiring significant adaptations and investments to accommodate this new form of content. The reluctance to embrace such changes and the perceived risks associated with them can further contribute to the stigma against AI-generated content within these industries.

Another factor that may influence the stance of traditional industries and gatekeepers is the question of authenticity and originality. These entities often pride themselves on discovering, nurturing, and promoting unique human talents and voices. The idea that AI-generated content could be mass-produced and lack the distinctive qualities of human-created works may be seen as a threat to the value proposition of these industries, leading to a heightened stigma against such content.

Furthermore, the lack of clear legal frameworks and regulations surrounding AI-generated content can create uncertainty and hesitation among traditional industries. Questions of copyright, intellectual property, and liability in the context of AI-generated content are still being navigated, and the absence of definitive answers may cause gatekeepers to err on the side of caution, further perpetuating the stigma.

However, it is important to recognize that not all traditional industries and gatekeepers are resistant to AI-generated content. Some forward-thinking entities are embracing the potential of AI as a tool to enhance and complement human creativity rather than replace it. By finding ways to integrate AI-generated content into their existing systems and workflows, these industries can leverage the strengths of both human and machine intelligence to create innovative and compelling content.

As the landscape continues to evolve, it is crucial for traditional industries and gatekeepers to engage in open dialogue and collaboration with the AI community to address the concerns and challenges surrounding AI-generated content. By working together to establish best practices, develop ethical guidelines, and create inclusive frameworks, these entities can play a pivotal role in reducing the stigma and fostering a more accepting environment for AI-generated content.

Ultimately, the role of traditional industries and gatekeepers in perpetuating or alleviating the stigma against AI-generated content will depend on their willingness to adapt, innovate, and embrace the potential of this new technology. By finding ways to harness the power of AI while preserving the value of human creativity, these industries can help shape a future where AI-generated content is celebrated alongside human-created works, enriching our cultural landscape in unprecedented ways.

Subsection 3.3: The Influence of Media Coverage and Public Discourse

The media plays a crucial role in shaping public opinion and perceptions of various topics, including AI-generated content. The way in which media outlets cover this subject can significantly influence how the general public views and understands the technology, its potential applications, and the associated stigma.

One of the primary ways media coverage contributes to the stigma against AI-generated content is through sensationalism and fear-mongering. Headlines and articles that emphasize the potential dangers of AI, such as job displacement or the creation of biased content, can fuel anxiety and mistrust among readers. This type of coverage often overshadows the potential benefits and opportunities presented by AI-generated content, leading to a skewed public perception.

Moreover, media outlets may prioritize stories that generate clicks and engagement, rather than providing balanced and informative coverage. This can result in the proliferation of misinformation and misconceptions about AI-generated content, further exacerbating the stigma. For example, articles that exaggerate the capabilities of AI or present speculative scenarios as inevitable outcomes can contribute to a distorted understanding of the technology and its implications.

The influence of media coverage extends beyond traditional news outlets and encompasses social media platforms and online forums. These digital spaces have become critical venues for public discourse, where individuals share their opinions, experiences, and concerns related to AI-generated content. The echo chamber effect, amplified by algorithms that curate content based on user preferences, can lead to the reinforcement of existing biases and the spread of misinformation, making it challenging to combat the stigma effectively.

However, media coverage and public discourse can also play a positive role in addressing the stigma against AI-generated content. Journalists and media outlets have the power to provide accurate, informative, and balanced reporting on the subject, helping to dispel myths and promote a more nuanced understanding of the technology. By featuring expert opinions, case studies, and real-world applications, the media can showcase the potential benefits of AI-generated content and encourage a more open-minded approach to its adoption.

Furthermore, public figures and thought leaders who engage in discussions about AI-generated content can significantly influence public opinion. When respected individuals from various fields, such as academics, industry professionals, or policymakers, share their insights and experiences, they can help to legitimize the use of AI in content creation and challenge the prevailing stigma. Their voices can also encourage a more informed and constructive public dialogue, fostering a climate of curiosity and exploration rather than fear and resistance.

As the conversation around AI-generated content continues to evolve, it is essential for media outlets and public discourse to prioritize responsible and ethical reporting. This includes acknowledging the limitations and potential risks associated with the technology while also highlighting its potential to augment human creativity and productivity. By presenting a balanced and informed perspective, the media can play a vital role in shaping public understanding and acceptance of AI-generated content, ultimately helping to reduce the stigma surrounding it.

In conclusion, the influence of media coverage and public discourse on the stigma against AI-generated content cannot be overstated. As society navigates this rapidly evolving landscape, it is crucial for media outlets, public figures, and individuals to engage in responsible and informed discussions that promote a nuanced understanding of the technology and its implications. By fostering a climate of openness, transparency, and critical thinking, we can work towards overcoming the stigma and unlocking the full potential of AI-generated content.

Subsection 3.4: The Impact of Socioeconomic and Demographic Factors

As we delve deeper into the societal and cultural factors that perpetuate the stigma against AI-generated content, it is crucial to examine how socioeconomic and demographic factors influence attitudes towards this technology. Age, education, and socioeconomic status are among the key variables that shape an individual's perception and acceptance of AI-generated content, and understanding their impact is essential for addressing the stigma effectively.

Age is a significant factor that influences attitudes towards AI-generated content. Younger generations, who have grown up in an era of rapid technological advancements, are generally more open to embracing new technologies, including AI. They are more likely to view AI-generated content as a natural progression of the digital landscape and are less likely to harbor the same level of skepticism or fear that older generations may experience. This generational divide can be attributed to the fact that younger individuals have been exposed to AI-driven technologies from an early age, making them more comfortable with the concept of machines creating content.

Education also plays a crucial role in shaping attitudes towards AI-generated content. Individuals with higher levels of education, particularly in fields related to technology, computer science, or artificial intelligence, are more likely to have a deeper understanding of the capabilities and limitations of AI systems. This knowledge enables them to approach AI-generated content with a more informed and nuanced perspective, recognizing its potential benefits and applications while also being aware of its challenges and ethical considerations. Conversely, those with limited exposure to the technical aspects of AI may be more susceptible to misconceptions and fears surrounding the technology, contributing to the stigma.

Socioeconomic status is another significant factor that influences attitudes towards AI-generated content. Individuals from higher socioeconomic backgrounds often have greater access to resources, education, and technology, which can shape their perceptions and attitudes towards AI. They may be more likely to view AI-generated content as a tool for innovation and progress, recognizing its potential to streamline processes, enhance creativity, and drive economic growth. On the other hand, those from lower socioeconomic backgrounds may view AI-generated content as a threat to their livelihoods, particularly if their jobs are at risk of being automated or replaced by AI systems. This fear of job displacement can contribute to a heightened stigma against AI-generated content among certain socioeconomic groups.

It is important to note that the impact of socioeconomic and demographic factors on attitudes towards AI-generated content is not uniform across all contexts. Cultural differences, regional variations, and individual experiences can all influence how these factors manifest in shaping perceptions. For example, in societies with a strong emphasis on tradition and human craftsmanship, the stigma against AI-generated content may be more pronounced, regardless of age, education, or socioeconomic status. Similarly, individuals who have had negative experiences with AI-driven technologies, such as encountering biased or misleading content, may be more skeptical of AI-generated content, irrespective of their demographic profile.

Addressing the stigma against AI-generated content requires a nuanced understanding of how socioeconomic and demographic factors intersect with other societal and cultural variables. By recognizing the diverse perspectives and experiences that shape attitudes towards AI, we can develop targeted strategies to educate, inform, and engage different segments of the population. This may involve tailoring communication and outreach efforts to specific age groups, educational backgrounds, or socioeconomic strata, ensuring that the benefits and challenges of AI-generated content are effectively communicated and understood.

Moreover, it is crucial to foster inclusive dialogues and collaborations that bring together individuals from various socioeconomic and demographic backgrounds to discuss the implications of AI-generated content. By creating platforms for diverse voices and perspectives to be heard, we can work towards building a more nuanced and balanced understanding of the technology, ultimately helping to reduce the stigma surrounding it.

In conclusion, socioeconomic and demographic factors play a significant role in shaping attitudes towards AI-generated content. Age, education, and socioeconomic status are among the key variables that influence an individual's perception and acceptance of this technology. By understanding the impact of these factors and recognizing the diverse perspectives they represent, we can develop targeted strategies to address the stigma and foster a more informed and inclusive dialogue around AI-generated content. As we navigate this complex landscape, it is essential to remain mindful of the intersectionality of these factors and to work towards building a future where the benefits of AI-generated content can be harnessed while addressing the concerns and challenges it presents.

Summary: Navigating the Complex Landscape of Societal and Cultural Stigma

As we conclude this exploration of the societal and cultural factors perpetuating the stigma against AI-generated content, it becomes evident that the challenges we face are multifaceted and deeply ingrained in our collective psyche. From the value we place on human craftsmanship to the influence of traditional industries and media coverage, these factors shape our perceptions and attitudes towards AI in profound ways.

Throughout this section, we have examined how the cultural importance of human-created content, the resistance from established gatekeepers, and the role of public discourse contribute to the persistence of the stigma. We have also delved into the impact of socioeconomic and demographic factors, recognizing that age, education, and social status play a significant role in shaping individual attitudes towards AI-generated content.

The insights gained from this exploration underscore the complexity of the issue at hand and the need for a nuanced, multifaceted approach to addressing the stigma. It is clear that overcoming these deeply rooted societal and cultural barriers will require a concerted effort from all stakeholders, including creators, industries, media outlets, and the general public.

As we move forward, it is essential to foster open dialogue, collaboration, and education to bridge the gap between tradition and innovation. By acknowledging the valid concerns and fears surrounding AI-generated content while also highlighting its potential benefits and opportunities, we can work towards creating a more inclusive and accepting environment for this transformative technology.

The path ahead may be challenging, but it is also filled with possibilities. As we navigate this complex landscape, let us remain committed to understanding and addressing the societal and cultural factors that shape our perceptions of AI-generated content. By doing so, we can pave the way for a future where human creativity and artificial intelligence can coexist and thrive, unlocking new frontiers of expression and innovation.

In the next section, we will delve into the ethical considerations and responsibilities surrounding the creation and use of AI-generated content, exploring how these issues intersect with the societal and cultural factors discussed here. By examining the ethical dimensions of this technology, we can gain a more comprehensive understanding of the challenges and opportunities that lie ahead, and work towards building a responsible and sustainable future for AI-generated content.

Section 4: Ethical and Legal Concerns Surrounding AI-Generated Content

As AI-generated content becomes increasingly prevalent in our digital landscape, it is crucial to examine the ethical and legal issues that contribute to the stigma surrounding its use. The rapid advancement of AI technology has outpaced the development of clear guidelines and regulations, leaving many questions unanswered and fueling concerns about the potential risks and consequences of AI-generated content.

In this section, we will delve into the complex web of ethical and legal considerations that shape public perception and contribute to the stigma against AI-generated content. From the thorny question of authorship and intellectual property rights to the potential for bias and discrimination, we will explore the challenges that arise when machines become content creators.

As we navigate this uncharted territory, it is essential to consider the accountability and responsibility of those who develop and deploy AI systems. Who bears the blame when AI-generated content causes harm or spreads misinformation? How can we ensure that AI algorithms are transparent and aligned with human values?

Moreover, the lack of clear legal frameworks and governance structures for AI-generated content creates uncertainty and apprehension. As AI continues to evolve and permeate various aspects of our lives, it is imperative that we address these ethical and legal concerns head-on.

Throughout this section, we will examine real-world examples, expert opinions, and thought-provoking scenarios to shed light on the complex interplay between ethics, law, and AI-generated content. By confronting these issues and engaging in meaningful dialogue, we can work towards developing responsible and equitable approaches to leveraging the power of AI while mitigating the risks and addressing the root causes of the stigma.

Subsection 4.1: The Question of Authorship and Intellectual Property

As AI-generated content becomes more sophisticated and indistinguishable from human-created works, the question of authorship and intellectual property rights has emerged as a significant challenge. Traditionally, copyright laws have been designed to protect the rights of human creators, granting them exclusive control over the use and distribution of their works. However, the rise of AI-generated content has blurred the lines between human and machine creativity, raising complex questions about who owns the rights to such content and how it should be protected.

One of the primary concerns surrounding AI-generated content is the difficulty in attributing authorship. When an AI algorithm creates a piece of content, such as an article, image, or musical composition, it is not always clear who should be credited as the author. Is it the developer of the AI system, the person who trained the algorithm, or the AI itself? This ambiguity has led to debates about whether AI-generated content can be considered original work and whether it should be eligible for copyright protection.

Moreover, the process of creating AI-generated content often involves training the algorithm on vast amounts of existing data, including copyrighted material. This raises questions about the potential infringement of intellectual property rights and the fair use of such data. As AI systems become more adept at learning from and mimicking human-created content, there is a growing concern that they may inadvertently reproduce or adapt copyrighted works without permission, leading to legal disputes and challenges.

The lack of clear legal frameworks and precedents for dealing with AI-generated content has further complicated the issue. While some argue that AI-generated works should be treated as public domain, others believe that the creators of AI systems should be granted some form of intellectual property protection to incentivize innovation and investment in the field. The debate is ongoing, and legal systems around the world are grappling with how to adapt existing copyright laws to accommodate the unique challenges posed by AI-generated content.

As we navigate this uncharted territory, it is crucial to strike a balance between protecting the rights of human creators and fostering the development of AI technologies. This may involve developing new legal frameworks that recognize the contributions of both human and machine actors in the creative process, while also ensuring that the use of AI-generated content does not infringe upon existing intellectual property rights. By addressing these challenges head-on and engaging in meaningful dialogue, we can work towards creating a fair and equitable system that encourages innovation and creativity in the age of artificial intelligence.

Subsection 4.2: The Potential for Bias and Discrimination

As AI-generated content becomes increasingly prevalent, concerns about the potential for bias and discrimination have risen to the forefront of the debate. While AI algorithms are often touted as objective and unbiased, the reality is that they are only as impartial as the data they are trained on and the humans who design them. This subsection explores the risk of AI-generated content perpetuating biases and discriminatory practices, and the impact this can have on individuals and society as a whole.

One of the primary concerns surrounding AI-generated content is the potential for algorithmic bias. AI systems learn from vast amounts of data, which can include historical records, social media posts, and other sources that may contain inherent biases. If these biases are not identified and addressed during the training process, they can become embedded in the AI system, leading to the generation of content that perpetuates stereotypes, prejudices, and discriminatory attitudes.

For example, an AI algorithm trained on news articles from a particular time period may learn to associate certain ethnicities or genders with negative stereotypes, leading to the generation of biased content that reinforces these harmful narratives. Similarly, an AI system designed to assist in hiring decisions may inadvertently discriminate against certain groups if it is trained on historical employment data that reflects past discriminatory practices.

The risk of bias in AI-generated content is particularly concerning given the increasing reliance on these systems across various domains, from news generation to content recommendation algorithms. As AI-generated content becomes more ubiquitous, the potential for it to shape public opinion, reinforce stereotypes, and influence decision-making processes becomes more significant.

Moreover, the opacity of many AI systems makes it difficult to identify and mitigate bias. The complex algorithms and vast datasets used in AI content generation can make it challenging to trace the origins of biased outputs and hold the creators of these systems accountable. This lack of transparency can further contribute to the stigma surrounding AI-generated content, as it raises questions about the trustworthiness and fairness of these systems.

To address the potential for bias and discrimination in AI-generated content, it is crucial to develop rigorous testing and auditing processes that can identify and mitigate biases throughout the AI development lifecycle. This may involve using diverse and representative datasets, implementing algorithmic fairness techniques, and engaging in ongoing monitoring and evaluation of AI systems to detect and correct biased outputs.

Furthermore, increasing transparency and accountability in AI content generation is essential to building public trust and mitigating the stigma surrounding these technologies. This may involve developing clear guidelines for the ethical development and deployment of AI systems, as well as establishing mechanisms for redress and accountability when biased or discriminatory content is generated.

As we navigate the complex landscape of AI-generated content, it is important to recognize that the potential for bias and discrimination is not an inherent flaw of the technology itself, but rather a reflection of the biases present in the data and the humans who create these systems. By proactively addressing these issues and working towards the development of fair, transparent, and accountable AI systems, we can harness the power of AI-generated content while mitigating the risks and addressing the root causes of the stigma surrounding it.

Subsection 4.3: The Issue of Accountability and Responsibility

As AI-generated content becomes increasingly prevalent in our digital landscape, questions of accountability and responsibility arise. When an AI system produces content that is inaccurate, harmful, or biased, who is held accountable for the consequences? Is it the developer of the AI algorithm, the company deploying the system, or the AI itself? These questions are at the heart of the stigma surrounding AI-generated content, as the lack of clear accountability mechanisms fuels concerns about the potential risks and negative impacts of this technology.

The issue of accountability becomes particularly complex when considering the nature of AI systems. Unlike traditional content creation processes, where a human author or creator can be easily identified and held responsible for their work, AI-generated content is the result of a complex interplay between algorithms, training data, and human input. This distributed nature of AI content creation makes it difficult to pinpoint a single entity or individual as the accountable party.

Moreover, the opacity of many AI systems further complicates the question of accountability. The inner workings of AI algorithms are often hidden within a "black box," making it challenging to understand how the system arrived at a particular output or decision. This lack of transparency can make it difficult to trace the origins of problematic content and assign responsibility accordingly.

The issue of accountability is closely tied to the concept of responsibility. When an AI system generates content that causes harm or spreads misinformation, who bears the responsibility for mitigating the damage and preventing future occurrences? Is it the responsibility of the AI developers to ensure their systems are robust, unbiased, and aligned with ethical principles? Or does the responsibility fall on the companies and organizations that deploy these systems to carefully monitor and regulate their use?

To address the challenges of accountability and responsibility in AI-generated content, it is crucial to develop clear legal and ethical frameworks that define the obligations and liabilities of various stakeholders. This may involve establishing standards for transparency, requiring AI systems to be auditable and explainable, and implementing mechanisms for redress and compensation when harm occurs.

Furthermore, fostering a culture of responsible AI development and deployment is essential. This involves promoting ethical AI practices, such as rigorous testing for bias and fairness, ongoing monitoring and evaluation of AI systems, and proactive engagement with affected communities to understand and address their concerns.

Ultimately, the issue of accountability and responsibility in AI-generated content is a complex and evolving challenge that requires collaboration and dialogue among AI developers, policymakers, industry leaders, and the general public. By working together to establish clear guidelines, standards, and mechanisms for accountability, we can mitigate the risks and negative impacts of AI-generated content while harnessing its potential benefits for society.

As we navigate this uncharted territory, it is important to recognize that the question of accountability and responsibility is not unique to AI-generated content. Similar challenges have arisen in other domains, such as the accountability of social media platforms for user-generated content or the responsibility of manufacturers for the safety of their products. By drawing on lessons learned from these analogous situations and adapting them to the specific context of AI, we can develop effective strategies for addressing the issue of accountability and responsibility in AI-generated content.

Subsection 4.4: The Need for Regulation and Governance

As AI-generated content becomes increasingly prevalent and sophisticated, the need for effective regulation and governance structures becomes more pressing. The rapid advancement of AI technologies has outpaced the development of legal and ethical frameworks, leaving a void in the oversight and management of AI-generated content. This lack of regulation has contributed to the stigma surrounding AI-generated content, as concerns about potential misuse, bias, and unintended consequences remain largely unaddressed.

The development of comprehensive regulatory frameworks is crucial to ensure that AI-generated content is created and deployed in a responsible, transparent, and accountable manner. These frameworks should establish clear guidelines and standards for the development, testing, and implementation of AI systems, taking into account the unique challenges and risks associated with AI-generated content.

One key aspect of regulation is the establishment of ethical guidelines for AI-generated content. These guidelines should be grounded in principles such as fairness, non-discrimination, transparency, and respect for human rights. By setting clear ethical standards, regulatory bodies can help ensure that AI-generated content aligns with societal values and minimizes the risk of harm to individuals and communities.

Another critical component of effective regulation is the development of governance structures that provide oversight and accountability for AI-generated content. This may involve the creation of dedicated regulatory bodies or the expansion of existing institutions to encompass AI-related issues. These governance structures should have the authority to monitor the development and deployment of AI systems, investigate potential violations of established guidelines, and enforce penalties for non-compliance.

Transparency and explainability are also essential elements of effective regulation and governance. AI systems used for content generation should be designed with transparency in mind, allowing for the auditing and review of their decision-making processes. This transparency is crucial for building public trust in AI-generated content and ensuring that any biases or errors can be identified and addressed in a timely manner.

Furthermore, the development of regulatory frameworks should involve collaboration and input from a diverse range of stakeholders, including AI developers, industry leaders, policymakers, academics, and members of the public. This multi-stakeholder approach ensures that the interests and concerns of all affected parties are taken into account and that the resulting regulations are comprehensive, balanced, and effective.

The need for regulation and governance of AI-generated content is not unique to this domain; similar challenges have arisen in other areas of technological innovation, such as the regulation of social media platforms or the governance of autonomous vehicles. By drawing on lessons learned from these analogous situations and adapting them to the specific context of AI-generated content, policymakers and stakeholders can develop effective strategies for mitigating risks and promoting responsible innovation.

As the capabilities of AI systems continue to evolve and expand, the importance of proactive regulation and governance cannot be overstated. By establishing clear guidelines, ethical standards, and accountability mechanisms, we can create a framework that fosters trust, mitigates risks, and unlocks the full potential of AI-generated content while addressing the root causes of the stigma surrounding it. It is only through collaborative, informed, and adaptive regulation that we can ensure the responsible and beneficial development of AI technologies in the service of society as a whole.

Summary: Navigating the Ethical and Legal Landscape of AI-Generated Content

In this section, we have explored the complex ethical and legal landscape surrounding AI-generated content and its contribution to the stigma associated with this technology. From the challenges of attributing authorship and protecting intellectual property rights to the risks of perpetuating biases and discrimination, the rise of AI-generated content has raised a host of concerns that must be addressed to foster trust and responsible innovation in this field.

As we have seen, the lack of clear legal frameworks and accountability mechanisms has fueled uncertainty and apprehension about the potential misuse and unintended consequences of AI-generated content. To mitigate these risks and unlock the full potential of this technology, it is crucial to develop comprehensive regulatory frameworks and governance structures that provide oversight, transparency, and accountability.

By establishing clear ethical guidelines, promoting collaboration among stakeholders, and drawing on lessons learned from analogous domains, we can create a robust framework for the responsible development and deployment of AI-generated content. This framework should be grounded in principles of fairness, non-discrimination, transparency, and respect for human rights, ensuring that the benefits of AI-generated content are realized while minimizing harm to individuals and society as a whole.

Ultimately, navigating the ethical and legal landscape of AI-generated content requires ongoing dialogue, adaptation, and a commitment to responsible innovation. As the capabilities of AI systems continue to evolve, it is essential that we remain vigilant in addressing the challenges and opportunities presented by this transformative technology. By doing so, we can work towards a future in which AI-generated content is embraced as a powerful tool for creativity, knowledge sharing, and societal progress, while the stigma surrounding it becomes a relic of the past.

Chapter Summary: Unveiling the Complexities of the Stigma Against AI-Generated Content

The stigma against AI-generated content is a multifaceted issue, deeply rooted in historical, psychological, societal, and ethical factors. From the early days of artificial intelligence to the present, public perceptions have been shaped by a mix of fascination and fear, fueled by media portrayals and the inherent uncertainty surrounding this transformative technology.

At its core, the stigma stems from the perceived threat AI poses to human creativity and authenticity. The belief that machines cannot replicate the emotional depth and originality of human-created content is a central pillar of this stigma, reinforced by the value placed on craftsmanship and the need for genuine connection in our society.

However, the stigma is not merely a product of subjective beliefs; it is also influenced by cognitive biases, cultural norms, and the resistance of traditional industries to change. The question of authorship, the potential for bias and discrimination, and the lack of clear accountability and regulation further complicate the issue, raising valid concerns about the ethical implications of AI-generated content.

By examining these diverse factors, we gain a more nuanced understanding of the stigma's origins and the challenges it presents. As we move forward, it is crucial to address these concerns head-on, fostering open dialogue, establishing guidelines, and finding ways to harness the power of AI while preserving the essence of human creativity. Only by confronting the stigma directly can we hope to bridge the gap between artificial intelligence and human ingenuity, paving the way for a future where the two can coexist and collaborate in meaningful ways.

Chapter 3: The Human Touch: Creativity and Authenticity

In the ever-evolving landscape of content creation, the rise of artificial intelligence has sparked a heated debate about the role of machine-generated content and its perceived lack of creativity and authenticity. As AI algorithms become increasingly sophisticated in their ability to generate text, images, and even music, many people question whether these creations can truly capture the essence of human creativity and emotional depth.

At the heart of this debate lies the fundamental question: What makes content truly creative and authentic? Is it the unique perspective and life experiences of the creator? The ability to evoke genuine emotions and forge deep connections with the audience? Or is it the originality and novelty of the ideas presented?

In this chapter, we will delve into the complex relationship between AI-generated content and the human touch. We will explore the elements that define creativity and authenticity in the eyes of the audience and examine why many people perceive AI-generated content as lacking in these crucial aspects.

Through a combination of expert insights, real-world examples, and thought-provoking questions, we will unravel the underlying reasons behind the stigma against AI-generated content. We will discuss the challenges AI faces in replicating human intuition, emotional intelligence, and the ability to draw from personal experiences to create truly authentic and relatable content.

Moreover, we will investigate the importance of originality, consistency, and the ability to capture a distinct voice and tone in the creation of engaging and memorable content. By understanding the perceived shortcomings of AI-generated content in these areas, we can begin to identify potential solutions and strategies for bridging the gap between machine-generated and human-crafted content.

As we navigate this fascinating and controversial topic, we invite you to keep an open mind and consider the various perspectives surrounding the role of AI in content creation. Together, we will explore the ways in which the human touch continues to shape our perception of creativity and authenticity in the digital age, and how we can harness the power of AI while preserving the unique value of human creativity.

Section 1: Defining Creativity and Authenticity in Content Creation

In the ever-evolving landscape of content creation, the concepts of creativity and authenticity have become increasingly important. As the stigma against AI-generated content continues to persist, it is crucial to understand what sets human-created content apart. At the heart of this distinction lie the intangible qualities of creativity and authenticity.

Creativity is often seen as the spark that ignites compelling and engaging content. It is the ability to generate novel ideas, to think outside the box, and to present information in a way that captivates and resonates with audiences. Authentic content, on the other hand, is rooted in the creator's unique voice, experiences, and perspectives. It is the genuine expression of thoughts and emotions that forges a deep connection with readers.

In this section, we will delve into the very essence of creativity and authenticity in content creation. We will explore the key elements that contribute to the perception of content as creative and authentic, and examine how these qualities work in tandem to create content that truly stands out in a crowded digital landscape. By understanding the fundamental role that creativity and authenticity play in the creation of compelling content, we can begin to appreciate the unique value that human creators bring to the table.

As we navigate the complex terrain of the stigma against AI-generated content, it is essential to have a clear grasp of what sets human-created content apart. In the following subsections, we will break down the components of creative content, discuss the importance of authenticity in building trust with audiences, and explore the interplay between creativity and authenticity in crafting content that leaves a lasting impact.

Subsection 1.1: The Elements of Creative Content

Creativity is the lifeblood of engaging content. It is the spark that ignites the reader's imagination, captures their attention, and compels them to keep reading. But what exactly makes content creative? What are the key elements that set it apart from the mundane and the forgettable?

At its core, creative content is characterized by originality. It presents ideas, perspectives, or stories that are fresh, unique, and unexpected. This originality can manifest in various ways, such as a novel approach to a familiar topic, a surprising twist in a narrative, or a thought-provoking question that challenges the reader's assumptions. By breaking free from the constraints of convention and tradition, creative content has the power to surprise, delight, and inspire.

Another crucial element of creative content is its ability to evoke emotion. Whether it's joy, curiosity, empathy, or even discomfort, creative content strikes a chord with the reader's feelings. It goes beyond merely conveying information and instead aims to create a visceral response. Through vivid descriptions, powerful imagery, and relatable characters, creative content forges an emotional connection with the reader, making the experience more memorable and impactful.

Engaging content also relies on the art of storytelling. Creative writers understand the power of a well-crafted narrative to captivate and transport the reader. They skillfully weave together plot, character, and theme to create a cohesive and compelling story. By using techniques such as foreshadowing, suspense, and revelation, they keep the reader hooked, eager to discover what happens next. The best stories are those that resonate with the reader on a personal level, reflecting their own experiences, dreams, and fears.

In addition to these narrative elements, creative content often employs a range of stylistic devices to enhance its impact. Metaphors, similes, and analogies can help to clarify complex ideas by drawing comparisons to more familiar concepts. Rhetorical questions can engage the reader by inviting them to ponder a particular point. Repetition, alliteration, and other linguistic techniques can create a sense of rhythm and musicality in the writing, making it more pleasurable to read.

Finally, creative content is characterized by its ability to provoke thought and inspire action. It goes beyond simply informing the reader and instead challenges them to think critically, to question their assumptions, and to see the world in a new light. By presenting ideas in a fresh and compelling way, creative content has the power to spark conversations, change minds, and even drive social change.

In the context of the stigma against AI-generated content, understanding the elements of creative content is crucial. It helps us to appreciate the unique value that human creators bring to the table, and to recognize the challenges that AI systems face in replicating these qualities. As we explore the origins and implications of this stigma throughout the book, keep in mind the key components of creativity - originality, emotion, storytelling, style, and thought-provoking power - and consider how they set human-created content apart.

Subsection 1.2: The Role of Authenticity in Connecting with Audiences

In the realm of content creation, authenticity is a powerful tool for forging deep, lasting connections with readers. When content is perceived as authentic, it establishes trust, credibility, and resonance, which are essential ingredients for building a loyal and engaged audience.

At its core, authenticity is about being true to oneself and one's values. It means creating content that genuinely reflects the creator's thoughts, experiences, and perspectives, rather than simply mimicking popular trends or pandering to audience expectations. Authentic content is born from a place of sincerity and honesty, and it shines through in the final product.

One of the key benefits of authenticity is that it humanizes the content creator. By sharing personal stories, vulnerabilities, and lessons learned, creators can break down the barriers between themselves and their audience, fostering a sense of relatability and connection. When readers feel that they can see a part of themselves in the content they consume, they are more likely to engage with it on a deeper level and to develop a sense of loyalty to the creator.

Authenticity also plays a crucial role in building trust with readers. In an era where misinformation and fake news are rampant, audiences are increasingly skeptical of the content they encounter online. By consistently creating content that is genuine, accurate, and transparent, creators can establish themselves as reliable sources of information and insight. This trust is essential for building long-term relationships with readers and for creating a sense of community around the content.

Moreover, authentic content tends to be more memorable and impactful than content that feels generic or insincere. When creators infuse their work with their unique voice, style, and perspective, they create something that stands out in a crowded digital landscape. Authentic content has the power to provoke thought, evoke emotion, and inspire action in a way that more formulaic content simply cannot.

However, achieving authenticity in content creation is not always easy. It requires a willingness to be vulnerable, to take risks, and to stand by one's convictions even in the face of criticism or disagreement. It also demands a deep understanding of one's own voice and perspective, as well as the ability to communicate that perspective in a way that resonates with others.

In the context of the stigma against AI-generated content, the importance of authenticity cannot be overstated. As audiences become increasingly aware of the prevalence of AI-generated content online, they are likely to place an even higher premium on content that feels genuine and human. By prioritizing authenticity in their work, human creators can differentiate themselves from AI systems and demonstrate the unique value that they bring to the table.

Ultimately, the role of authenticity in content creation is to create a sense of connection, trust, and resonance with readers. By being true to themselves and their values, creators can forge deep, lasting relationships with their audience and create content that stands the test of time. As we explore the stigma against AI-generated content throughout this book, keep in mind the power of authenticity in setting human-created content apart and in building a loyal and engaged audience.

Subsection 1.3: The Interplay Between Creativity and Authenticity

Creativity and authenticity are two essential ingredients in the recipe for compelling content. While each plays a distinct role in engaging and resonating with audiences, it is the interplay between these two elements that truly sets exceptional content apart from the rest.

At first glance, creativity and authenticity might seem like separate entities, with creativity focusing on the generation of novel ideas and authenticity emphasizing the genuine expression of one's voice and experiences. However, upon closer examination, it becomes clear that these two qualities are deeply intertwined and mutually reinforcing.

Authenticity serves as a foundation for creativity, providing a solid bedrock of truth and sincerity upon which innovative ideas can be built. When content creators draw from their own lived experiences, unique perspectives, and deeply held values, they infuse their work with a sense of realness that cannot be easily replicated. This authenticity lends credibility to their creative endeavors, making it easier for audiences to trust and connect with the content on a deeper level.

Conversely, creativity acts as a catalyst for authenticity, allowing content creators to express their true selves in fresh and engaging ways. By pushing the boundaries of conventional thinking and experimenting with new forms of expression, creators can uncover hidden aspects of their own voices and perspectives. This creative exploration can lead to a more nuanced and multifaceted portrayal of the creator's authentic self, revealing layers of depth and complexity that might otherwise remain hidden.

The interplay between creativity and authenticity is particularly evident in the realm of storytelling. When creators draw from their own authentic experiences and emotions to craft compelling narratives, they imbue their stories with a sense of truth and relatability that resonates with audiences. At the same time, the creative process of shaping and structuring these experiences into a cohesive narrative allows creators to explore and express their authentic selves in new and meaningful ways.

Moreover, the combination of creativity and authenticity can help content stand out in a crowded digital landscape. With so much content vying for audiences' attention, it is the unique blend of innovative ideas and genuine self-expression that sets truly compelling content apart. By leveraging the power of creativity to present authentic perspectives in fresh and engaging ways, content creators can capture audiences' interest and forge lasting connections.

However, striking the right balance between creativity and authenticity is not always easy. Creators must be willing to take risks and experiment with new ideas while staying true to their core values and experiences. They must also be mindful of the potential pitfalls of inauthenticity, such as pandering to audience expectations or mimicking popular trends without a genuine connection to the content.

Ultimately, the key to harnessing the interplay between creativity and authenticity lies in finding a harmonious balance between the two. By allowing their authentic selves to guide their creative endeavors and using their creativity to express their truth in new and compelling ways, content creators can craft works that resonate deeply with audiences and stand the test of time.

As we explore the stigma against AI-generated content throughout this book, it is essential to keep in mind the vital role that the interplay between creativity and authenticity plays in setting human-created content apart. By understanding and leveraging this powerful dynamic, human creators can continue to produce works that engage, inspire, and connect with audiences on a profound level, even in an age of increasingly sophisticated AI technologies.

Summary: The Essence of Creativity and Authenticity in Content Creation

In this section, we have explored the fundamental concepts of creativity and authenticity in the context of content creation. By delving into the key elements that contribute to the perception of content as creative and authentic, we have gained a deeper understanding of what sets human-created content apart in the face of the stigma against AI-generated content.

We have seen that creativity is the spark that ignites compelling and engaging content, characterized by originality, the ability to evoke emotion, skillful storytelling, and the power to provoke thought and inspire action. Authenticity, on the other hand, is rooted in the creator's unique voice, experiences, and perspectives, establishing trust, credibility, and resonance with audiences.

Moreover, we have discovered that creativity and authenticity are not separate entities but rather deeply intertwined and mutually reinforcing qualities. Authenticity serves as a foundation for creativity, providing a bedrock of truth and sincerity upon which innovative ideas can be built, while creativity acts as a catalyst for authenticity, allowing creators to express their true selves in fresh and engaging ways.

As we move forward in our exploration of the stigma against AI-generated content, it is crucial to keep in mind the vital role that creativity and authenticity play in setting human-created content apart. By understanding and leveraging the power of these qualities, content creators can continue to craft works that resonate deeply with audiences, forging lasting connections and leaving a meaningful impact in an increasingly AI-driven world.

In the next section, we will examine the origins and reasons behind the stigma against AI-generated content, shedding light on the challenges and opportunities that lie ahead as we navigate this complex landscape. Armed with a clear understanding of creativity and authenticity, we will be better equipped to appreciate the unique value that human creators bring to the table and to find ways to harness the potential of AI while preserving the essence of human-driven content creation.

Section 2: The Perception of AI-Generated Content as Lacking Creativity

In the ever-evolving landscape of content creation, the emergence of AI-generated content has sparked a heated debate about the role of creativity in the digital age. As AI algorithms become increasingly sophisticated, capable of producing articles, stories, and even artwork, many have begun to question whether these machine-generated creations can truly be considered creative. This section delves into the heart of this perception, examining the reasons behind the widespread belief that AI-generated content lacks the spark of human creativity.

To understand this perception, it is essential to first explore what creativity means in the context of content creation. Creativity is often associated with originality, novelty, and the ability to generate unique ideas and perspectives. It is seen as a distinctly human trait, born from our experiences, emotions, and the complex inner workings of our minds. When we encounter a piece of content that resonates with us on a deep level, we often attribute that connection to the creator's ability to infuse their work with a personal touch, a sense of authenticity that speaks to our shared human experience.

In contrast, AI-generated content is often perceived as lacking this human element. The algorithmic nature of AI content generation, which relies on patterns, data, and pre-defined rules, can lead to the perception that the resulting content is formulaic, predictable, and devoid of the unique insights and intuition that characterize human creativity. This section will explore these perceptions in depth, examining the challenges AI faces in replicating human creativity and the importance of originality, novelty, and emotional intelligence in creative expression.

As we navigate this uncharted territory, it is crucial to consider the implications of these perceptions for the future of content creation. By understanding the reasons behind the stigma against AI-generated content, we can begin to explore ways to bridge the gap between human and machine creativity, harnessing the power of AI while preserving the value of the human touch. In the following subsections, we will delve into the nuances of this perception, exploring the challenges and opportunities that lie ahead as we seek to redefine creativity in the age of artificial intelligence.

Subsection 2.1: The Algorithmic Nature of AI Content Generation

At the heart of the perception that AI-generated content lacks creativity lies the fundamental difference between human and machine-based content creation: the algorithmic nature of AI. While human creativity is often associated with intuition, emotion, and spontaneity, AI-generated content is the product of complex algorithms, meticulously designed to analyze vast amounts of data and identify patterns.

These algorithms, such as deep learning neural networks, are trained on extensive datasets containing human-created content. By studying the patterns and structures within this data, AI systems learn to mimic human writing styles, language patterns, and even creative techniques. However, this mimicry is based on statistical analysis and probability, rather than a deep understanding of the creative process itself.

As a result, AI-generated content often feels formulaic and predictable, lacking the surprising insights and innovative ideas that characterize human creativity. The algorithms behind AI content generation are designed to optimize for factors such as grammatical correctness, coherence, and relevance to a given topic, rather than originality or novelty.

Moreover, the algorithmic approach to content creation can lead to the generation of content that is devoid of the personal touch and emotional depth that human creators bring to their work. While AI algorithms can analyze sentiment and attempt to incorporate emotional elements into the content they generate, these attempts often feel artificial and lacking in authenticity.

This lack of emotional intelligence and personal perspective contributes to the perception that AI-generated content is less creative than human-created content. Human creators draw upon their own experiences, emotions, and unique worldviews to infuse their work with a sense of authenticity and originality that is difficult for algorithms to replicate.

As AI continues to advance, researchers and developers are exploring ways to imbue AI systems with greater creativity and originality. Some approaches involve incorporating elements of randomness or unpredictability into the content generation process, or training AI models on more diverse and unconventional datasets to encourage novel combinations of ideas.

However, the algorithmic nature of AI content generation remains a significant contributor to the perception that AI-generated content lacks creativity. As we navigate the increasingly blurred lines between human and machine-generated content, it is crucial to understand the limitations and strengths of AI algorithms in the creative process, and to explore ways to harness their power while preserving the value of human creativity.

Subsection 2.2: The Importance of Originality and Novelty

In the realm of creative content, originality and novelty are highly prized qualities. These attributes are often seen as the hallmarks of true creativity, setting apart the mundane and derivative from the truly innovative and groundbreaking. The importance placed on originality and novelty in creative content stems from the belief that these qualities are essential for capturing and holding an audience's attention, as well as for pushing the boundaries of what is possible within a given medium.

Originality refers to the uniqueness of an idea or concept, the extent to which it differs from existing works and stands out as something new and fresh. In a world saturated with content, originality is increasingly difficult to achieve, yet it remains a key factor in determining the value and impact of a creative work. Original content has the power to surprise, delight, and challenge audiences, offering them something they have never encountered before and sparking new ways of thinking and perceiving the world around them.

Novelty, on the other hand, relates to the newness or freshness of an idea, even if it may be built upon existing concepts or themes. A novel approach to a familiar subject can breathe new life into it, presenting it in a way that feels exciting and relevant to contemporary audiences. Novelty can manifest in various forms, such as innovative storytelling techniques, unconventional perspectives, or the combination of seemingly disparate elements to create something entirely new.

The pursuit of originality and novelty in creative content is driven by the desire to stand out in a crowded marketplace, to capture the attention of audiences who are constantly bombarded with a barrage of information and entertainment options. In an age where attention spans are short and competition for eyeballs is fierce, content that is perceived as unoriginal or derivative is likely to be overlooked or quickly forgotten.

Moreover, the value placed on originality and novelty is closely tied to the idea of artistic merit and cultural significance. Works that break new ground, challenge conventions, and offer fresh perspectives are often lauded as important contributions to their respective fields, shaping the direction of future creative endeavors and leaving a lasting impact on audiences and creators alike.

However, the emphasis on originality and novelty in creative content also has its drawbacks. The constant pressure to innovate can lead to a culture of novelty for novelty's sake, where shock value and gimmickry take precedence over substance and depth. Additionally, the pursuit of originality can sometimes result in content that is esoteric, inaccessible, or disconnected from the experiences and desires of mainstream audiences.

As AI-generated content becomes increasingly prevalent, the question of whether it can truly achieve the levels of originality and novelty valued in human-created content is a matter of intense debate. The algorithmic nature of AI content generation, which relies on analyzing and recombining existing data, has led to the perception that such content is inherently derivative and lacking in true originality.

However, proponents of AI-generated content argue that the vast amounts of data and the complex algorithms employed by AI systems have the potential to identify novel combinations and generate ideas that may be overlooked or unconsidered by human creators. As AI technologies continue to advance, the possibilities for generating original and novel content through machine learning are expanding, challenging traditional notions of what constitutes creativity.

Ultimately, the importance of originality and novelty in creative content is rooted in the belief that these qualities are essential for capturing the imagination, challenging the status quo, and pushing the boundaries of what is possible. As the debate surrounding the creative potential of AI-generated content continues to evolve, it is crucial to consider how the pursuit of originality and novelty can be balanced with other important factors, such as authenticity, emotional resonance, and accessibility, to create content that truly connects with and inspires audiences.

Subsection 2.3: The Challenges of Replicating Human Intuition and Insight

One of the most significant challenges in the perception of AI-generated content as lacking creativity is the difficulty in replicating human intuition and insight. While AI algorithms can process vast amounts of data and identify patterns, they often struggle to capture the unique perspectives and "aha" moments that characterize human creativity.

Intuition, a key component of human creativity, is the ability to understand or know something instinctively, without the need for conscious reasoning. It is a product of our experiences, emotions, and the complex inner workings of our minds. When human creators have a sudden flash of insight or a gut feeling about a creative decision, they are often drawing upon this intuitive understanding of the world around them.

However, replicating human intuition in AI systems is a daunting task. Intuition is not easily quantifiable or reducible to a set of rules or algorithms. It is a deeply personal and subjective experience, shaped by an individual's unique background, beliefs, and perceptions. While AI can analyze patterns and make predictions based on historical data, it lacks the lived experience and emotional depth that inform human intuition.

Moreover, human insight – the ability to discern the true nature of a situation or problem – is another crucial aspect of creativity that is challenging for AI to replicate. Insight often involves making connections between seemingly disparate ideas, drawing upon a broad range of knowledge and experiences to arrive at novel solutions or interpretations.

AI algorithms, on the other hand, are typically trained on specific domains or datasets, limiting their ability to make connections across diverse fields or to draw upon the kind of broad, interdisciplinary knowledge that characterizes human insight. While techniques such as transfer learning and multi-task learning aim to address this limitation, enabling AI models to apply knowledge gained in one domain to another, they still fall short of the fluid, adaptable nature of human insight.

Furthermore, human insight is often shaped by our ability to empathize with others, to understand their emotions, motivations, and experiences. This emotional intelligence allows human creators to craft content that resonates with their audience on a deep, personal level. AI, while capable of analyzing sentiment and generating content that mimics human emotion, lacks the genuine empathy and shared experience that underlie truly insightful creative work.

As a result, AI-generated content can sometimes feel shallow or lacking in depth, failing to capture the nuanced insights and profound observations that emerge from human intuition and insight. While AI can generate content that is grammatically correct and superficially relevant to a given topic, it often struggles to replicate the unexpected connections, profound revelations, and emotional resonance that define truly insightful creative work.

Overcoming these challenges will require significant advancements in AI technology, particularly in the areas of emotional intelligence, common sense reasoning, and the ability to draw upon diverse knowledge sources. Researchers are exploring approaches such as sentiment analysis, knowledge graphs, and multi-modal learning to imbue AI systems with a deeper understanding of human emotions, experiences, and the interconnectedness of ideas.

However, even as AI continues to evolve, the unique qualities of human intuition and insight serve as a reminder of the inherent value of human creativity. While AI-generated content can certainly augment and enhance human creative efforts, it is unlikely to fully replicate the depth, nuance, and emotional resonance that emerge from the complex interplay of human experience, emotion, and understanding.

As we navigate the evolving landscape of AI-generated content, it is essential to recognize both the potential and the limitations of these technologies. By understanding the challenges AI faces in replicating human intuition and insight, we can develop a more nuanced appreciation for the distinct roles that human and machine creativity can play in shaping the content of the future.

Subsection 2.4: The Role of Emotional Intelligence in Creative Expression

Emotional intelligence, the ability to understand, manage, and effectively express one's own emotions, as well as perceive and influence the emotions of others, plays a crucial role in creative expression. When it comes to creating content that resonates with audiences on a deep, personal level, emotional intelligence is just as important as raw talent or technical skill.

One of the key aspects of emotional intelligence in creative work is empathy – the ability to put oneself in another's shoes and understand their feelings, experiences, and perspectives. Empathy allows creators to craft content that speaks directly to their audience's hearts and minds, forging a powerful emotional connection that goes beyond mere entertainment or information sharing.

Creators with high emotional intelligence are attuned to the subtle nuances of human emotion and can infuse their work with a sense of authenticity and vulnerability that draws audiences in and keeps them engaged. They understand that the most compelling stories, the most moving pieces of art, and the most impactful content are those that tap into the shared human experience, reflecting the joys, sorrows, hopes, and fears that bind us all together.

Moreover, emotional intelligence enables creators to navigate the complex social and collaborative aspects of the creative process. Creating content, whether it's a book, a film, a piece of music, or a marketing campaign, is rarely a solo endeavor. It often involves working with teams of people, each with their own unique personalities, work styles, and emotional needs.

Creators with high emotional intelligence are better equipped to manage these interpersonal dynamics, fostering a positive, productive work environment that brings out the best in everyone involved. They can communicate effectively, resolve conflicts, and provide constructive feedback in a way that motivates and inspires their collaborators.

In contrast, AI-generated content, for all its technological sophistication, often lacks the emotional depth and nuance that characterizes truly resonant creative work. While AI algorithms can analyze vast amounts of data and identify patterns in human emotion and behavior, they struggle to replicate the authentic, lived experience that informs genuine emotional expression.

This is not to say that AI has no role to play in creative expression. AI tools can certainly assist human creators in various aspects of the creative process, from ideation and research to editing and optimization. However, the key to creating emotionally resonant content lies in the unique combination of human intuition, empathy, and emotional intelligence that AI, at least in its current state, cannot fully replicate.

As the debate surrounding the role of AI in creative industries continues to evolve, it is essential to recognize the enduring importance of emotional intelligence in creative expression. While AI may excel at certain tasks, such as data analysis and pattern recognition, it is the human capacity for emotional depth, authenticity, and connection that will continue to set truly impactful creative work apart.

By cultivating emotional intelligence alongside technical skills and embracing the potential of human-AI collaboration, creators can harness the best of both worlds, combining the efficiency and insights of artificial intelligence with the emotional resonance and authenticity that only human understanding can provide.

Summary: Bridging the Gap Between Human and AI Creativity

The perception that AI-generated content lacks creativity stems from the fundamental differences between human and machine-based content creation. The algorithmic nature of AI, which relies on analyzing patterns and data, can lead to content that feels formulaic and predictable, lacking the originality and novelty that are highly valued in creative work. Moreover, AI struggles to replicate the human intuition, insight, and emotional intelligence that infuse creative content with authenticity, depth, and resonance.

However, as AI technologies continue to advance, the potential for AI to generate more creative and emotionally resonant content is growing. By incorporating elements of randomness, training on diverse datasets, and leveraging techniques like sentiment analysis and knowledge graphs, AI systems are becoming increasingly capable of producing content that exhibits some degree of originality and emotional depth.

Despite these advancements, it is crucial to recognize that AI is not a replacement for human creativity but rather a tool that can augment and enhance it. The unique qualities of human intuition, insight, and emotional intelligence will continue to play a vital role in creating content that truly resonates with audiences on a deep, personal level.

As we navigate the evolving landscape of AI-generated content, it is essential to approach it with a balanced perspective, acknowledging both its limitations and its potential. By understanding the challenges AI faces in replicating human creativity, we can develop strategies for harnessing the power of AI while preserving the value of the human touch. Ultimately, the key to bridging the gap between human and AI creativity lies in fostering collaboration between the two, leveraging the strengths of each to create content that is both innovative and emotionally resonant.

Section 3: The Perception of AI-Generated Content as Lacking Authenticity

In a world where authenticity has become a highly valued currency, the rise of AI-generated content has sparked a heated debate about its ability to capture the essence of human expression. As we delve deeper into the reasons behind the perception that AI-generated content lacks authenticity, it is crucial to examine the intricate relationship between technology and the human experience.

Authenticity, at its core, is about being true to oneself and conveying a sense of genuineness in one's creations. It is the unique fingerprint that sets human-generated content apart, reflecting the creator's personal experiences, emotions, and perspectives. However, when it comes to AI-generated content, the question arises: Can machines truly replicate the depth and nuance of human authenticity?

To understand the perception of AI-generated content as lacking authenticity, we must explore the various facets that contribute to this belief. From the importance of personal experience and perspective to the challenge of replicating human voice and tone, this section will provide a comprehensive analysis of the factors that shape our understanding of authenticity in the context of AI-generated content.

As we navigate this complex landscape, it is essential to keep an open mind and consider the potential for AI to evolve and enhance its ability to capture authenticity. By examining the current limitations and exploring the possibilities for future development, we can gain a more balanced perspective on the role of AI in content creation and its impact on our perception of authenticity.

Subsection 3.1: The Importance of Personal Experience and Perspective

In the realm of content creation, personal experience and perspective play a crucial role in shaping the authenticity of the final product. When we consume content, whether it be a book, article, or blog post, we seek a connection with the creator – a glimpse into their unique worldview and the experiences that have molded their thoughts and opinions. This personal touch is what breathes life into the words on the page, transforming them from mere information to a meaningful, relatable narrative.

Authentic content is born from the creator's own journey, their triumphs and tribulations, and the lessons they have learned along the way. It is this intimate connection between the creator and their work that resonates with readers, fostering a sense of trust and understanding. When we read content that stems from genuine personal experience, we can feel the passion, the vulnerability, and the truth behind the words. It is this emotional resonance that sets authentic content apart from generic, mass-produced pieces.

Moreover, personal perspective adds depth and dimension to the content. Each individual's viewpoint is shaped by their background, culture, education, and life events. When creators infuse their work with their distinct perspective, they offer readers a fresh lens through which to explore familiar topics. This diversity of thought encourages readers to challenge their own assumptions, consider alternative viewpoints, and engage in meaningful dialogue. Authentic content, therefore, not only informs but also inspires growth and understanding.

In contrast, AI-generated content often lacks this personal touch. While algorithms can process vast amounts of data and generate coherent text, they struggle to capture the nuances of human experience and perspective. AI-generated content may be factually correct and grammatically sound, but it can feel sterile and disconnected from the human experience. Without the infusion of personal insights, anecdotes, and reflections, AI-generated content risks coming across as generic and impersonal, failing to establish a meaningful connection with the reader.

This is not to say that AI has no place in content creation. When used as a tool to support and enhance human creativity, AI can be a valuable asset. However, it is the fusion of human experience and perspective with the efficiency and scale of AI that holds the key to creating authentic, impactful content. By leveraging the strengths of both human and machine, we can craft content that not only informs but also resonates on a deep, personal level.

As we navigate the landscape of content creation in an increasingly AI-driven world, it is crucial to recognize and celebrate the importance of personal experience and perspective. These human elements are the cornerstone of authentic content, forging connections, sparking conversations, and leaving a lasting impact on readers. By embracing the power of personal storytelling and infusing our work with our unique viewpoints, we can create content that not only informs but also inspires, moving hearts and minds in ways that AI alone cannot replicate.

Subsection 3.2: The Challenge of Replicating Human Voice and Tone

In the realm of content creation, voice and tone play a crucial role in establishing a connection with the audience. A writer's unique voice and tone are the intangible elements that breathe life into their words, making the content relatable, engaging, and authentic. It is the distinctive way in which writers express themselves that sets them apart from others and creates a lasting impact on readers.

However, when it comes to AI-generated content, replicating the nuances of human voice and tone remains a significant challenge. While AI algorithms can analyze vast amounts of data and generate grammatically correct text, they often struggle to capture the subtle variations and emotional depth that human writers bring to their work. The intricacies of language, such as sarcasm, humor, and irony, are deeply rooted in human experiences and cultural contexts, making them difficult for AI to fully grasp and replicate.

Moreover, a writer's voice and tone are shaped by their personality, background, and life experiences. The way a writer expresses themselves is a reflection of their unique perspective and the emotions they wish to convey. AI, on the other hand, lacks the personal experiences and emotional understanding that are essential to creating content with a distinct voice and tone. While AI can mimic patterns and styles to a certain extent, it struggles to infuse the writing with the genuine emotions and personality that make human-generated content so compelling.

Another challenge AI faces in replicating human voice and tone is the ability to adapt to different contexts and audiences. Human writers have the innate ability to adjust their voice and tone based on the purpose of the content, the target audience, and the platform on which it will be published. They can seamlessly switch between a formal, informative tone for an academic article and a casual, conversational tone for a blog post. AI, however, may struggle to make these contextual adjustments, resulting in content that feels generic or disconnected from the intended audience.

Furthermore, consistency in voice and tone is crucial for building a strong brand identity and establishing trust with readers. Human writers can maintain a consistent voice and tone across multiple pieces of content, creating a cohesive and recognizable brand personality. AI, on the other hand, may generate content with variations in voice and tone, leading to inconsistencies that can undermine the credibility and authenticity of the brand.

Despite these challenges, AI has made significant strides in the field of natural language processing, and researchers are continually working on developing more sophisticated algorithms that can better capture the nuances of human language. Advancements in machine learning and deep learning have enabled AI to analyze larger datasets and identify patterns in language use, allowing for more natural-sounding text generation.

However, it is essential to recognize that AI-generated content is not meant to replace human writers but rather to augment and support their work. By leveraging the strengths of both human creativity and AI efficiency, we can create content that combines the best of both worlds – the emotional depth and unique perspective of human writers with the speed and scale of AI-generated text.

As we navigate the landscape of content creation in an AI-driven world, it is crucial to appreciate the value of human voice and tone. While AI can assist in generating content quickly and efficiently, it is the human touch that truly resonates with readers and creates lasting impact. By embracing the unique qualities that human writers bring to the table and using AI as a tool to enhance their work, we can create content that is not only informative but also authentic, engaging, and emotionally resonant.

Subsection 3.3: The Importance of Empathy and Emotional Connection

In the world of content creation, empathy and emotional connection are the invisible threads that weave together the fabric of authentic storytelling. These intangible elements are the key to unlocking the hearts and minds of readers, forging a deep, meaningful bond between the creator and their audience. When content is infused with empathy and emotional resonance, it transcends the boundaries of mere words on a page, becoming a powerful force that moves, inspires, and transforms.

Empathy, at its core, is the ability to understand and share the feelings of others. It is the foundation upon which authentic content is built, allowing creators to step into the shoes of their readers and see the world through their eyes. By tapping into the universal human experiences of joy, sorrow, fear, and hope, empathetic content creators can craft stories that resonate on a profound level, striking a chord with readers from all walks of life.

When content is created with empathy, it becomes a mirror that reflects the reader's own thoughts, feelings, and experiences. It validates their struggles, celebrates their triumphs, and offers a sense of companionship in times of need. Empathetic content has the power to break down barriers, foster understanding, and create a sense of belonging, reminding readers that they are not alone in their journey through life.

Moreover, empathy is the key to creating content that is not only informative but also emotionally engaging. When readers feel an emotional connection to the content they consume, they are more likely to remember it, share it, and apply its lessons to their own lives. Emotionally resonant content has the power to spark conversations, change minds, and inspire action, making it a potent tool for driving social change and personal growth.

However, creating content that is both empathetic and emotionally resonant is no easy feat. It requires a deep understanding of the human experience, a willingness to be vulnerable, and a commitment to authenticity. Creators must be willing to dig deep within themselves, tapping into their own emotions and experiences to create content that is genuine, relatable, and true to life.

This is where AI-generated content often falls short. While AI algorithms can analyze vast amounts of data and generate grammatically correct text, they lack the innate ability to understand and convey human emotions. AI-generated content may be factually accurate and well-written, but it often lacks the empathy and emotional depth that is essential to creating authentic, impactful content.

Without the ability to understand and share the feelings of others, AI-generated content risks coming across as cold, clinical, and disconnected from the human experience. It may provide information, but it fails to forge the emotional connection that is so crucial to engaging and inspiring readers. As a result, AI-generated content may struggle to establish the trust, credibility, and loyalty that are the hallmarks of authentic content.

That being said, AI has the potential to support and enhance human empathy in content creation. By analyzing vast amounts of data on human emotions and experiences, AI can provide valuable insights and suggestions to human creators, helping them to craft content that is more emotionally resonant and relatable. However, it is ultimately the human touch – the ability to infuse content with genuine empathy and emotional depth – that sets authentic content apart.

As we navigate the landscape of content creation in an AI-driven world, it is crucial to recognize and celebrate the importance of empathy and emotional connection. These human qualities are the secret ingredients that transform content from mere words into powerful, transformative experiences. By embracing empathy and emotional resonance as the cornerstones of authentic content creation, we can craft stories that not only inform but also inspire, moving hearts and minds in ways that AI alone cannot replicate.

Subsection 3.4: The Risks of Inconsistency and

Inauthenticity

As AI-generated content becomes increasingly prevalent, concerns about its potential to come across as inconsistent or inauthentic have risen to the forefront of the discussion. While AI algorithms have made significant strides in generating coherent and grammatically correct text, the risk of inconsistency and inauthenticity remains a critical issue that undermines the credibility and effectiveness of AI-generated content.

Inconsistency in AI-generated content can manifest in various forms, from variations in writing style and tone to contradictory information and logical inconsistencies. When an AI algorithm generates content across multiple pieces or platforms, it may struggle to maintain a consistent voice and tone, leading to a disjointed and confusing reading experience for the audience. This lack of consistency can be particularly problematic for brands and organizations that rely on a strong, recognizable voice to connect with their target audience and build trust.

Moreover, inconsistencies in AI-generated content can extend beyond writing style and tone, affecting the accuracy and reliability of the information presented. As AI algorithms draw from vast pools of data to generate content, they may inadvertently incorporate conflicting or outdated information, leading to factual inaccuracies and contradictions within the text. These inconsistencies can erode the credibility of the content and the brand or organization associated with it, damaging their reputation and undermining their authority in the eyes of the audience.

In addition to inconsistency, the risk of inauthenticity poses a significant challenge for AI-generated content. Authenticity is a crucial element in building trust and fostering meaningful connections with readers, as it conveys a sense of genuineness, transparency, and relatability. However, AI-generated content often struggles to capture the nuances of human experience, emotion, and perspective that are essential to creating authentic, resonant content.

Without the ability to infuse content with genuine empathy, personal anecdotes, and the unique insights that come from lived experiences,

AI-generated content can come across as sterile, generic, and disconnected from the human experience. This lack of authenticity can make it difficult for readers to relate to the content on a personal level, hindering its ability to engage, persuade, and inspire action.

Furthermore, the risk of inauthenticity in AI-generated content can be compounded by the potential for algorithmic bias and the perpetuation of stereotypes. As AI algorithms learn from existing data, they may inadvertently absorb and amplify societal biases, generating content that reinforces harmful stereotypes or excludes diverse perspectives. This can lead to content that feels inauthentic and unrepresentative of the target audience, alienating readers and damaging the credibility of the brand or organization.

To mitigate the risks of inconsistency and inauthenticity in AI-generated content, it is essential for brands and organizations to approach the use of AI in content creation with a critical eye and a commitment to human oversight. By establishing clear guidelines for consistency in writing style, tone, and information accuracy, and by incorporating human review and editing processes, organizations can help ensure that AI-generated content maintains a cohesive and reliable presence across all platforms.

Moreover, to address the challenge of authenticity, it is crucial to recognize the limitations of AI in capturing the full depth and complexity of human experience. By leveraging AI as a tool to support and enhance human creativity, rather than as a replacement for it, organizations can create content that combines the efficiency and scalability of AI with the authentic, relatable insights that only human writers can provide.

As we navigate the evolving landscape of AI-generated content, it is essential to remain vigilant about the risks of inconsistency and inauthenticity, and to take proactive steps to mitigate these risks. By prioritizing consistency, accuracy, and authenticity in AI-generated content, brands and organizations can build trust, credibility, and meaningful connections with their audience, harnessing the power of AI while preserving the essential human elements that make content truly impactful.

Summary: Navigating the Perception of Inauthenticity in AI-Generated Content

As we have explored throughout this section, the perception of AI-generated content as lacking authenticity is rooted in the complex interplay between technology and the human experience. The absence of personal perspectives, the challenges in replicating human voice and tone, and the difficulties in conveying empathy and forging emotional connections have all contributed to the skepticism surrounding the authenticity of AI-generated content.

However, it is essential to recognize that AI is not meant to replace human creativity but rather to augment and support it. By leveraging the strengths of both human intuition and AI efficiency, we can create content that combines the best of both worlds – the emotional depth and unique insights of human writers with the speed and scale of AI-generated text.

As we navigate the evolving landscape of content creation, it is crucial to approach AI-generated content with a critical eye, acknowledging its limitations while also embracing its potential. By prioritizing human oversight, establishing guidelines for consistency and accuracy, and infusing AI-generated content with authentic human elements, we can mitigate the risks of inconsistency and inauthenticity.

Ultimately, the key to overcoming the stigma against AI-generated content lies in striking a balance between the efficiency of technology and the authenticity of human experience. By recognizing the value of personal perspectives, empathy, and emotional resonance, we can harness the power of AI while preserving the essential human qualities that make content truly impactful.

As we move forward, it is essential to engage in open and honest discussions about the role of AI in content creation, its potential benefits, and its limitations. By fostering a deeper understanding of the technology and its implications, we can work towards creating a future where AI and human creativity coexist harmoniously, each complementing and enhancing the other.

In the following sections, we will delve deeper into the ethical considerations surrounding AI-generated content, explore strategies for overcoming the stigma, and envision a future where human and AI collaborators work together to push the boundaries of creative expression. As we embark on this journey, let us remain committed to the values of authenticity, empathy, and genuine human connection, ensuring that the content we create, whether by human hand or AI algorithm, truly resonates with our audience and leaves a lasting impact on the world.

Section 4: Bridging the Gap: Enhancing Creativity and Authenticity in AI-Generated Content

As we have explored the perceived lack of creativity and authenticity in AI-generated content, it is crucial to recognize that these challenges are not insurmountable. The rapid advancements in AI technology, coupled with the growing understanding of the importance of human input and collaboration, present exciting opportunities to bridge the gap between AI-generated content and the desired levels of creativity and authenticity.

In this section, we will delve into the various strategies and approaches that can be employed to enhance the creative and authentic qualities of AI-generated content. By examining the role of human input and oversight, leveraging advanced language models and techniques, emphasizing transparency and disclosure, and embracing collaboration between human and AI creators, we will uncover the potential for AI-generated content to achieve new heights of creativity and authenticity.

As we navigate this uncharted territory, it is essential to keep an open mind and consider the possibilities that lie ahead. By finding the right balance between the efficiency and scalability of AI and the unique insights and emotional intelligence of human creators, we can unlock a new era of content creation that combines the best of both worlds. So, let us embark on this journey together, exploring the ways in which we can harness the power of AI to create content that is not only informative and engaging but also truly creative and authentic.

Subsection 4.1: Incorporating Human Input and Oversight

As we explore ways to enhance the creativity and authenticity of AI-generated content, one of the most crucial aspects to consider is the incorporation of human input and oversight. While AI algorithms and models are becoming increasingly sophisticated in their ability to generate coherent and engaging content, they still lack the depth of understanding, emotional intelligence, and contextual awareness that human creators possess.

Human input and oversight play a vital role in guiding AI content generation, ensuring that the output aligns with the intended purpose, tone, and style. By providing clear guidelines, training data, and feedback, human creators can help shape the AI's understanding of what constitutes creative and authentic content in a given context. This collaborative approach allows AI to learn from and build upon human expertise, rather than attempting to replace it entirely.

Moreover, human oversight is essential for quality control and error correction. Even the most advanced AI systems can produce inconsistencies, factual inaccuracies, or inappropriate content. Human editors and reviewers can identify and rectify these issues, ensuring that the final output meets the desired standards of quality and authenticity.

Incorporating human input and oversight also helps to maintain a sense of accountability and ethical responsibility in AI-generated content. As AI becomes more prevalent in content creation, it is crucial to have human gatekeepers who can monitor for potential biases, misinformation, or harmful content. By actively participating in the content generation process, human creators can help to mitigate these risks and ensure that AI is being used in a responsible and trustworthy manner.

It is important to note that the role of human input and oversight is not to constrain or limit the potential of AI-generated content, but rather to guide and enhance it. By finding the right balance between human creativity and AI efficiency, we can create a symbiotic relationship that leverages the strengths of both human and machine intelligence.

Ultimately, the incorporation of human input and oversight in AI content generation is not only a means of enhancing creativity and authenticity but also a necessary safeguard against the potential pitfalls of relying solely on algorithms. As we continue to explore the possibilities of AI-generated content, it is essential that we keep human judgment and expertise at the forefront, ensuring that the content we create is not only engaging but also responsible and trustworthy.

Subsection 4.2: Leveraging Advanced Language Models and Techniques

As the field of artificial intelligence continues to evolve, so too do the language models and techniques used to generate content. These advancements hold immense potential for enhancing the creativity and authenticity of AI-generated content, bridging the gap between machine-produced text and human-crafted prose.

One of the most promising developments in this area is the emergence of large-scale, pre-trained language models such as GPT-3 (Generative Pre-trained Transformer 3) and BERT (Bidirectional Encoder Representations from Transformers). These models, trained on vast amounts of diverse text data, have the ability to generate highly coherent and contextually relevant content across a wide range of domains. By leveraging the power of these advanced language models, AI-generated content can achieve a level of fluency and naturalness that rivals human writing.

Moreover, these models can be fine-tuned for specific tasks or styles, allowing for greater control over the generated content. For example, by training a language model on a dataset of creative writing samples, it can learn to generate text with more imaginative and expressive qualities. Similarly, by exposing the model to a variety of authentic, personal narratives, it can develop a more nuanced understanding of voice, tone, and perspective, enabling it to produce content that feels more genuine and relatable.

In addition to pre-trained language models, there are several other techniques that can be employed to enhance the creativity and authenticity of AI-generated content. One such approach is the use of adversarial training, where two neural networks – a generator and a discriminator – are pitted against each other. The generator aims to produce content that is indistinguishable from human-written text, while the discriminator tries to identify which content is AI-generated. Through this iterative process, the generator learns to create increasingly convincing and authentic content.

Another promising technique is the incorporation of emotional intelligence and sentiment analysis into the content generation process. By training AI models to recognize and understand the emotional undertones of text, they can learn to generate content that is more emotionally resonant and engaging. This can be particularly valuable in creating content that connects with readers on a deeper level, eliciting genuine reactions and fostering a sense of authenticity.

Furthermore, the use of multi-modal input, such as images or videos, can provide additional context and inspiration for AI-generated content. By analyzing visual cues and incorporating them into the text generation process, AI models can produce more creative and unique content that goes beyond the limitations of purely text-based input.

As these advanced language models and techniques continue to evolve, it is essential to remain mindful of the ethical considerations surrounding their use. While they have the potential to greatly enhance the creativity and authenticity of AI-generated content, it is crucial to ensure that they are employed responsibly and transparently. This includes being vigilant against the potential for bias, misinformation, or harmful content, and implementing safeguards to mitigate these risks.

Ultimately, by leveraging the power of advanced language models and techniques, we can unlock new possibilities for AI-generated content that is not only informative and engaging but also truly creative and authentic. As we continue to explore and refine these approaches, we move closer to a future where AI and human creativity can coexist and complement each other, opening up exciting new avenues for content creation and storytelling.

Subsection 4.3: Emphasizing Transparency and Disclosure

In the quest to enhance the creativity and authenticity of AI-generated content, the role of transparency and disclosure cannot be overstated. As AI technologies become increasingly sophisticated and capable of producing content that closely resembles human-created work, it is crucial to establish clear guidelines and practices surrounding the use of these tools.

Transparency, in this context, refers to the open and honest communication about the nature and extent of AI involvement in the content creation process. This includes disclosing when AI has been used to generate, curate, or assist in the production of content, as well as providing information about the specific AI tools and techniques employed. By being transparent about the use of AI, content creators can manage expectations and foster trust with their audience.

Disclosure, on the other hand, involves clearly labeling AI-generated content as such, ensuring that readers are aware of its origins. This can be achieved through the use of disclaimers, bylines, or other forms of explicit identification. By disclosing the AI-generated nature of the content, creators can avoid potential misunderstandings or accusations of deception, while also allowing readers to make informed judgments about the content's credibility and authenticity.

The importance of transparency and disclosure in managing perceptions of AI-generated content cannot be understated. In a world where the lines between human and machine-created content are becoming increasingly blurred, it is essential to maintain open and honest communication with audiences. Failure to do so can lead to a breakdown of trust, as readers may feel misled or manipulated if they discover that the content they consumed was generated by AI without their knowledge.

Moreover, transparency and disclosure can help to mitigate some of the potential risks associated with AI-generated content, such as the spread of misinformation or the reinforcement of biases. By being upfront about the use of AI and providing information about the training data and algorithms used, content creators can encourage greater scrutiny and accountability, enabling readers to critically evaluate the content they encounter.

It is important to note that transparency and disclosure are not meant to diminish the value or quality of AI-generated content. Rather, they serve as a means of facilitating honest communication and building trust between creators and their audiences. By embracing these principles, content creators can harness the power of AI to produce innovative and engaging content while maintaining the integrity and authenticity that readers demand.

As the use of AI in content creation continues to grow and evolve, it is crucial that the industry as a whole adopts a proactive approach to transparency and disclosure. This may involve the development of standardized guidelines, best practices, or even regulatory frameworks to ensure consistent and responsible communication about the use of AI.

Ultimately, by emphasizing transparency and disclosure in the use of AI-generated content, we can foster a more informed, engaged, and trusting relationship between creators and their audiences. As we navigate the challenges and opportunities presented by this rapidly evolving technology, a commitment to openness and honesty will be essential in unlocking the full potential of AI-generated content while maintaining the creativity and authenticity that readers value.

Subsection 4.4: Embracing Collaboration Between Human and AI Creators

As we explore ways to bridge the gap between AI-generated content and the desired levels of creativity and authenticity, it is crucial to consider the potential for collaboration between human and AI creators. Rather than viewing AI as a replacement for human creativity, we should embrace the opportunity to harness the unique strengths of both human and machine intelligence to create content that is truly innovative and engaging.

Collaboration between human and AI creators opens up a world of possibilities, allowing us to combine the efficiency and scalability of AI with the emotional intelligence and contextual understanding of human creators. By working together, human and AI creators can leverage their respective strengths to produce content that is not only informative and accurate but also imaginative and authentic.

One of the key benefits of collaboration is the ability to use AI as a tool to augment and enhance human creativity. For example, AI can be used to generate ideas, suggest novel combinations of concepts, or provide inspiration for human creators to build upon. This collaborative approach allows human creators to focus on the higher-level aspects of the creative process, such as refining ideas, adding emotional depth, and ensuring that the content resonates with the intended audience.

Moreover, collaboration between human and AI creators can help to mitigate some of the concerns surrounding the perceived lack of creativity and authenticity in AI-generated content. By incorporating human input and oversight throughout the content creation process, we can ensure that the final output reflects the unique perspectives and experiences of human creators while still benefiting from the efficiency and consistency of AI.

Collaboration can take many forms, from using AI to generate initial drafts or outlines that are then refined and expanded upon by human writers, to using AI to analyze and optimize content created by human authors. In each case, the goal is to find the right balance between human and machine intelligence, leveraging the strengths of both to create content that is truly exceptional.

Of course, embracing collaboration between human and AI creators also requires a shift in mindset and a willingness to experiment with new approaches to content creation. It may involve rethinking traditional roles and workflows, as well as developing new skills and competencies to effectively work alongside AI tools and technologies.

Ultimately, by embracing collaboration between human and AI creators, we can unlock a new era of creativity and authenticity in content creation. As we continue to explore the possibilities of this collaborative approach, we may discover new and innovative ways to combine the best of both human and machine intelligence, leading to content that is not only informative and engaging but also truly groundbreaking.

Summary: Embracing the Potential of Human-AI Collaboration for Authentic Content Creation

As we have explored throughout this section, bridging the gap between AI-generated content and the desired levels of creativity and authenticity is not only possible but also holds immense potential for the future of content creation. By incorporating human input and oversight, leveraging advanced language models and techniques, emphasizing transparency and disclosure, and most importantly, embracing collaboration between human and AI creators, we can unlock a new era of content creation that combines the best of both worlds.

The key to enhancing creativity and authenticity in AI-generated content lies in finding the right balance between the efficiency and scalability of AI and the unique insights and emotional intelligence of human creators. By working together, human and AI creators can harness their respective strengths to produce content that is informative, engaging, and truly authentic.

Through collaboration, we can use AI as a tool to augment and inspire human creativity, while ensuring that the final output reflects the unique perspectives and experiences of human creators. This collaborative approach not only mitigates concerns surrounding the perceived lack of creativity and authenticity in AI-generated content but also opens up new possibilities for innovation and storytelling.

As we move forward, it is crucial to approach the integration of AI in content creation with an open mind, a willingness to experiment, and a commitment to transparency and ethical practices. By doing so, we can foster a more informed, engaged, and trusting relationship between creators and their audiences, while pushing the boundaries of what is possible in the realm of content creation.

Ultimately, the path to enhancing creativity and authenticity in AI-generated content is one of collaboration, exploration, and continuous learning. As we embrace the potential of human-AI collaboration, we stand on the precipice of a new frontier in content creation – one that promises to deliver content that is not only informative and engaging but also deeply resonant and authentic.

Chapter Summary: Bridging the Gap Between Human and AI Creativity

The perceived lack of creativity and authenticity in AI-generated content stems from the algorithmic nature of the process, the challenges in replicating human intuition and emotional intelligence, and the importance of personal experience and perspective in creating authentic content. However, these perceptions are not insurmountable obstacles.

By incorporating human input and oversight, leveraging advanced language models and techniques, and emphasizing transparency and disclosure, we can enhance the creativity and authenticity of AI-generated content. Collaboration between human and AI creators holds immense potential for bridging the gap between the two and creating content that combines the best of both worlds.

As we navigate the stigma against AI-generated content, it is essential to recognize that AI is a tool that can augment and enhance human creativity rather than replace it entirely. By embracing the opportunities presented by AI and working together with these systems, we can unlock new possibilities for creative expression and authentic storytelling.

The future of content creation lies in the synergy between human and artificial intelligence, where the unique strengths of each are harnessed to produce engaging, emotionally resonant, and truly authentic content. As we move forward, it is crucial to approach AI-generated content with an open mind, recognizing its potential to revolutionize the creative landscape while acknowledging the importance of the human touch in the process.

Chapter 4: The Role of Bias and Misinformation

As the world increasingly embraces AI-generated content, concerns about bias and misinformation have risen to the forefront of public discourse. The very nature of AI systems, which rely on vast amounts of data and complex algorithms, has led many to question the objectivity and reliability of the content they produce. In this chapter, we will delve into the heart of these concerns, exploring the various ways in which bias can manifest in AI-generated content and the potential for such content to contribute to the spread of misinformation.

Bias, in the context of AI, refers to the systematic errors or prejudices that can emerge in the output of AI systems due to flaws in their design, training data, or underlying algorithms. These biases can take many forms, from subtle linguistic nuances to overt discrimination against certain groups or viewpoints. As we shall see, the roots of bias in AI-generated content are complex and multifaceted, stemming from a combination of technical limitations, human biases, and societal inequalities.

Misinformation, on the other hand, refers to false or misleading information that is spread, whether intentionally or unintentionally, through various channels, including AI-generated content. The ease with which AI systems can generate convincing text, images, and videos has raised concerns about the potential for these technologies to be used to create and disseminate fake news, propaganda, and other forms of misinformation. The challenge of distinguishing between genuine and fabricated content has become increasingly difficult in an era where AI-generated content is becoming more sophisticated and widespread.

Throughout this chapter, we will examine the various dimensions of bias and misinformation in AI-generated content, drawing on real-world examples and expert insights to illustrate the scope and severity of these issues. We will explore the technical, social, and ethical factors that contribute to the emergence of bias and misinformation, as well as the potential consequences for individuals, communities, and society as a whole. Importantly, we will also discuss strategies and best practices for mitigating these risks, emphasizing the need for collaboration between AI developers, policymakers, and the general public in addressing these complex challenges. By the end of this chapter, readers will have a deeper understanding of the role of bias and misinformation in AI-generated content and be better equipped to navigate this rapidly evolving landscape with critical thinking and informed skepticism.

Section 1: Understanding Bias in AI-Generated Content

Imagine a world where artificial intelligence (AI) has become an integral part of our daily lives, from the content we consume to the decisions we make. As AI-generated content becomes increasingly prevalent, it's crucial to understand the potential biases that can arise and the impact they can have on individuals and society as a whole.

Bias in AI-generated content is a complex and multifaceted issue that stems from various sources, including the data used to train AI systems, the algorithms that power them, and the human biases that can be inadvertently incorporated into the development process. These biases can manifest in subtle ways, influencing the content we see, the recommendations we receive, and the opinions we form.

In this section, we will delve into the concept of bias in AI-generated content, exploring its origins, types, and consequences. By understanding the nature of bias and its potential impact, we can begin to develop strategies to mitigate its effects and ensure that AI-generated content is fair, accurate, and representative of the diverse perspectives and experiences of our society.

As we navigate this new landscape of AI-generated content, it's essential to approach it with a critical eye and an awareness of the potential biases that may be present. Only by acknowledging and addressing these biases can we harness the full potential of AI to create a more informed, inclusive, and equitable world.

Subsection 1.1: Types of Biases in AI Systems

As we delve into the world of AI-generated content, it's crucial to understand the various types of biases that can exist within AI systems. These biases can have far-reaching consequences, influencing the content we consume, the decisions we make, and the opinions we form. By examining the different forms of bias, we can better comprehend the challenges and complexities surrounding AI-generated content and its potential impact on society.

One of the most prevalent types of bias in AI systems is algorithmic bias. This occurs when the algorithms that power AI systems are designed or trained in a way that perpetuates or amplifies existing biases. For example, if an AI system is trained on historical data that contains gender or racial biases, it may learn to make decisions or generate content that reflects those biases. Algorithmic bias can be particularly insidious because it can be difficult to detect and correct, as the biases are embedded within the very structure of the AI system itself.

Another significant type of bias is data bias, which arises from the data used to train AI systems. If the training data is not representative of the population or domain the AI system is intended to serve, the resulting outputs may be skewed or biased. For instance, if an AI system designed to generate news articles is trained primarily on data from a specific geographic region or political perspective, it may produce content that is biased towards that particular viewpoint. Data bias can be challenging to address, as it requires careful curation and diversification of training data to ensure a more balanced and representative dataset.

Societal bias is another critical aspect to consider when examining biases in AI systems. This type of bias stems from the broader societal and cultural context in which AI systems are developed and deployed. Societal biases, such as gender stereotypes, racial prejudices, or socioeconomic disparities, can inadvertently be encoded into AI systems through the choices made by developers, the selection of training data, or the framing of problems the AI is designed to solve. Addressing societal bias requires a deep understanding of the historical and cultural factors that shape our biases and a commitment to developing AI systems that promote fairness, diversity, and inclusion.

It's important to note that these types of biases are not mutually exclusive and can intersect and compound each other. For example, algorithmic bias can be exacerbated by data bias, as the biased algorithms may be trained on biased data, further amplifying the overall bias in the AI system. Similarly, societal biases can influence the development of algorithms and the selection of training data, creating a complex web of interconnected biases that can be challenging to untangle.

As we navigate the landscape of AI-generated content, it's essential to be aware of these different types of biases and their potential impact. By understanding the nature and sources of bias in AI systems, we can work towards developing more equitable and representative AI-generated content that reflects the diversity of our world and promotes a more inclusive and informed society.

Subsection 1.2: The Impact of Training Data on Bias

The quality and diversity of training data play a crucial role in the development of AI systems and can significantly contribute to the presence of bias in AI-generated content. Training data serves as the foundation upon which AI algorithms learn and make decisions, and any biases or limitations present in this data can be inadvertently absorbed and amplified by the AI system.

One of the primary ways in which training data can introduce bias is through underrepresentation or overrepresentation of certain groups or characteristics. For example, if an AI system designed to generate job descriptions is trained on a dataset that predominantly features male-dominated professions, it may learn to associate certain roles or qualities with men, resulting in biased job descriptions that discourage women from applying. Similarly, if an AI system for generating news articles is trained on data from a limited range of sources or perspectives, it may produce content that is skewed towards those particular viewpoints, thus perpetuating a narrow and potentially biased narrative.

The lack of diversity in training data can also lead to AI systems that struggle to accurately represent or understand the experiences and perspectives of underrepresented groups. This can result in AI-generated content that fails to resonate with diverse audiences or, worse, perpetuates harmful stereotypes and misconceptions. For instance, an AI system trained on a dataset of predominantly white individuals may struggle to generate realistic or respectful portrayals of people of color, leading to content that is insensitive or offensive.

Another way in which training data can contribute to bias is through the inclusion of historical or societal biases. Many datasets used to train AI systems are derived from real-world sources, such as books, articles, or social media posts, which can contain biases that reflect the prejudices and inequalities present in society at the time of their creation. If these biases are not identified and addressed during the data preparation process, they can be learned and perpetuated by the AI system, resulting in the generation of content that reinforces harmful stereotypes or discriminatory attitudes.

The impact of biased training data extends beyond the immediate outputs of AI systems and can have far-reaching consequences for individuals and society as a whole. Biased AI-generated content can influence public opinion, shape perceptions, and even contribute to the marginalization or discrimination of certain groups. For example, if an AI system generates biased news articles that consistently portray a particular ethnic group in a negative light, it can fuel prejudice and contribute to the stigmatization of that group in the eyes of the public.

Addressing the impact of training data on bias requires a proactive and ongoing effort from AI developers and organizations. This involves carefully curating and preprocessing training datasets to ensure they are diverse, representative, and free from known biases. It also necessitates the use of techniques such as data augmentation, which involves creating synthetic data to balance out underrepresented groups, and bias detection algorithms that can identify and flag potential biases in the data.

Furthermore, it is crucial to involve diverse teams and perspectives in the development and evaluation of AI systems to help identify and mitigate biases that may be overlooked by homogeneous groups. Regular audits and assessments of AI-generated content should also be conducted to detect and address any biases that may emerge over time.

By recognizing the significant impact of training data on bias and taking proactive steps to address it, we can work towards creating AI systems that generate content that is more accurate, inclusive, and representative of the diverse world we live in. This, in turn, can help to combat the stigma against AI-generated content and foster greater trust and acceptance of this technology as a valuable tool for informing and enriching our lives.

Subsection 1.3: The Role of Human Biases in AI Development

As we explore the various factors contributing to bias in AI-generated content, it's crucial to recognize the significant role that human biases play in the development of AI systems. Despite the common perception of AI as an objective and impartial technology, the reality is that AI systems are created by humans, and as such, they can inadvertently inherit the biases and prejudices of their creators.

The development of AI systems involves a complex process of design, data selection, algorithm creation, and testing, all of which are influenced by the decisions and judgments of the humans involved. At each stage of this process, there is the potential for human biases to be introduced, shaping the way the AI system perceives, processes, and generates information.

One of the primary ways in which human biases can be incorporated into AI systems is through the selection and curation of training data. AI developers must choose which data to feed into their systems, and this choice can be influenced by their own biases and assumptions about what constitutes relevant or representative information. For example, if an AI developer has a bias towards a particular political ideology, they may inadvertently select training data that reflects that ideology, resulting in an AI system that generates content with a similar bias.

Furthermore, the algorithms that power AI systems are designed by humans, and the choices made in their creation can also reflect the biases of their creators. The selection of certain variables, the weighting of different factors, and the definition of success criteria can all be influenced by the subjective judgments and biases of the developers. This can lead to AI systems that perpetuate or amplify existing societal biases, such as gender or racial stereotypes, even if the developers had no intention of doing so.

The role of human biases in AI development is particularly concerning because of the scale and reach of AI-generated content. Unlike human-created content, which is limited by the biases of individual creators, AI systems have the potential to generate vast amounts of biased content that can reach and influence large audiences. This can have far-reaching consequences, reinforcing and perpetuating harmful stereotypes and contributing to the marginalization of certain groups.

Addressing the issue of human biases in AI development requires a multifaceted approach. It involves increasing awareness among AI developers about their own biases and the potential impact they can have on the systems they create. It also necessitates the implementation of diversity and inclusion initiatives within AI development teams to ensure that a wide range of perspectives and experiences are represented in the creation of AI systems.

Moreover, it's essential to establish rigorous testing and auditing processes to identify and mitigate biases in AI systems before they are deployed. This can involve techniques such as adversarial testing, where AI systems are deliberately fed biased data to see how they respond, and bias detection algorithms that can flag potentially problematic content.

Ultimately, addressing the role of human biases in AI development requires a commitment to transparency, accountability, and ongoing vigilance. By acknowledging the inherent biases that can be present in the creation of AI systems and taking proactive steps to mitigate them, we can work towards creating AI-generated content that is more accurate, inclusive, and representative of the diverse world we live in.

As we navigate the complex landscape of AI-generated content and the stigma surrounding it, understanding the role of human biases in AI development is crucial. By recognizing and addressing these biases, we can create AI systems that generate content that is more trustworthy, informative, and beneficial to society as a whole.

Subsection 1.4: The Consequences of Biased AI-Generated Content

The presence of bias in AI-generated content is not merely an abstract concern; it has tangible and far-reaching consequences that can negatively impact individuals, groups, and society as a whole. When AI systems produce content that is skewed, misleading, or discriminatory, it can perpetuate harmful stereotypes, reinforce existing inequalities, and contribute to the marginalization of already vulnerable populations.

One of the most significant consequences of biased AI-generated content is the potential for it to influence public opinion and shape perceptions on a massive scale. As AI-powered content generation becomes increasingly prevalent across various media platforms, from news articles to social media posts, the biases embedded within these systems can subtly manipulate the information that people consume. This can lead to the formation of distorted views and the reinforcement of prejudices, particularly among those who may not have the critical media literacy skills to identify and question biased content.

Moreover, biased AI-generated content can have severe implications for decision-making processes that rely on automated systems. In fields such as hiring, lending, and criminal justice, AI algorithms are increasingly being used to make consequential decisions that can have a profound impact on people's lives. If these algorithms are trained on biased data or incorporate biased assumptions, they can perpetuate and even amplify existing disparities, leading to unfair and discriminatory outcomes for certain groups.

For example, if an AI system used for resume screening is trained on historical hiring data that reflects past gender biases, it may systematically disadvantage female candidates, regardless of their qualifications. Similarly, if an AI-powered risk assessment tool used in the criminal justice system is built on data that reflects racial biases in policing and sentencing, it can contribute to the disproportionate incarceration of marginalized communities. These biased outcomes not only harm individuals but also erode trust in the institutions that rely on these systems, undermining the very notion of fairness and justice.

The consequences of biased AI-generated content extend beyond individual decisions and can have broader societal implications. When AI systems consistently produce content that reinforces stereotypes or promotes a narrow, homogeneous worldview, it can contribute to the erasure of diverse perspectives and experiences. This can lead to a sense of exclusion and alienation among underrepresented groups, who may feel that their voices and stories are not being accurately or fairly represented in the digital landscape.

Furthermore, biased AI-generated content can have a chilling effect on public discourse and the free exchange of ideas. If people perceive that the content they encounter online is consistently biased or manipulated, they may become more hesitant to engage in open dialogue or express dissenting opinions. This can lead to a narrowing of public debate and a reinforcement of echo chambers, where people are exposed only to information that confirms their existing beliefs and biases.

The consequences of biased AI-generated content also have economic implications. If AI systems are used to create content that influences consumer behavior, such as product recommendations or targeted advertising, biased outputs can lead to the exclusion of certain groups from marketing efforts or the reinforcement of harmful stereotypes in advertising. This can perpetuate economic inequalities and hinder the ability of marginalized communities to fully participate in the marketplace.

Addressing the consequences of biased AI-generated content requires a proactive and multifaceted approach. It involves developing and implementing techniques to detect and mitigate biases in AI systems, such as regular audits, diverse training data, and algorithmic transparency. It also necessitates ongoing public education and awareness campaigns to help individuals critically evaluate the content they encounter and recognize the potential for bias.

Furthermore, it is crucial to foster collaboration between AI developers, policymakers, and affected communities to ensure that the development and deployment of AI systems are guided by principles of fairness, accountability, and inclusivity. This includes establishing clear guidelines and regulations for the use of AI in decision-making processes and holding organizations accountable for the outcomes of their AI systems.

As we navigate the complex landscape of AI-generated content, it is essential to remain vigilant and proactive in addressing the consequences of bias. By acknowledging the potential harms and taking steps to mitigate them, we can work towards creating a more equitable and inclusive digital future, where AI-generated content serves to inform, enrich, and empower all members of society.

Summary: Navigating the Complexities of Bias in AI-Generated Content

As we have explored throughout this section, bias in AI-generated content is a multifaceted and pervasive issue that demands our attention and action. From the various types of biases that can exist within AI systems to the impact of training data and the role of human biases in AI development, it is clear that the challenge of mitigating bias is complex and requires a comprehensive approach.

The consequences of biased AI-generated content are far-reaching and can have profound impacts on individuals, groups, and society as a whole. From perpetuating harmful stereotypes and reinforcing existing inequalities to influencing public opinion and shaping decision-making processes, the effects of biased content cannot be understated.

However, by understanding the nature and sources of bias in AI systems, we can begin to develop strategies and solutions to address these challenges head-on. This requires a commitment to diversity and inclusivity in AI development teams, rigorous testing and auditing processes, and ongoing public education and awareness campaigns.

As we move forward in this rapidly evolving landscape, it is essential that we remain vigilant and proactive in identifying and mitigating bias in AI-generated content. By working together – AI developers, policymakers, and the general public – we can strive to create a more equitable and inclusive digital future, where AI-generated content serves to inform, enrich, and empower all members of society.

The path ahead may be challenging, but it is also filled with opportunity. By confronting the complexities of bias in AI-generated content, we have the chance to shape a future in which the power of artificial intelligence is harnessed for the benefit of all, free from the limitations and harms of bias. It is a future worth fighting for, and one that we must work towards with determination, collaboration, and a shared commitment to building a better world.

Section 2: The Spread of Misinformation Through AI-Generated Content

In an age where information is at our fingertips, the rapid advancement of artificial intelligence (AI) has brought about a new challenge: the spread of misinformation through AI-generated content. As AI technologies become more sophisticated and accessible, the potential for misuse grows, raising concerns about the impact on public discourse and the erosion of trust in information sources.

Imagine a world where fake news articles, generated by AI algorithms, are indistinguishable from those written by human journalists. These articles, designed to mislead and manipulate, spread like wildfire across social media platforms, shaping public opinion and influencing decisions. The consequences of such misinformation can be far-reaching, from undermining democratic processes to fueling social unrest and even putting lives at risk.

In this section, we will delve into the various ways in which AI-generated content can contribute to the spread of misinformation. We will explore the ease with which misleading content can be created using AI tools, the challenges in detecting and combating AI-generated misinformation, and the potential for malicious actors to exploit these technologies for their own gain.

As we navigate this complex landscape, it is crucial to understand the mechanisms behind the spread of misinformation through AI-generated content. By examining the risks and implications, we can begin to develop strategies to mitigate the impact and foster a more informed and resilient society. In the following subsections, we will unravel the intricacies of this pressing issue, shedding light on the challenges we face and the steps we can take to address them.

Subsection 2.1: The Ease of Generating Misleading Content

In the digital age, the rapid advancement of artificial intelligence (AI) technologies has made it easier than ever to create and disseminate misleading or false information. With the proliferation of user-friendly AI tools and platforms, even individuals with limited technical expertise can generate convincing text, images, and videos that blur the line between reality and fiction.

One of the most significant concerns surrounding AI-generated content is the potential for it to be used to create "deepfakes" – highly realistic but fabricated media that can be used to deceive and manipulate audiences.

Deepfakes can take many forms, from altered photographs and videos to entirely synthetic audio recordings that mimic the voice and speech patterns of real people. These technologies have become increasingly accessible, with open-source software and tutorials readily available online, making it possible for virtually anyone to create convincing deepfakes with minimal effort.

The ease with which misleading content can be generated using AI raises serious questions about the integrity of information in the digital age. In a world where fake news and propaganda can spread rapidly through social media and other online channels, the ability to create realistic but false content on a large scale poses a significant threat to public discourse and the ability of individuals to make informed decisions based on accurate information.

Moreover, the speed at which AI-generated content can be created and disseminated further compounds the problem. With the help of automation tools and algorithms, misleading content can be produced and distributed at an unprecedented pace, making it difficult for fact-checkers and other gatekeepers to keep up. This can lead to the rapid spread of misinformation, as false narratives gain traction before they can be effectively debunked or countered with accurate information.

As AI technologies continue to advance, it is likely that the ease of generating misleading content will only increase. This underscores the need for greater awareness of the risks posed by AI-generated misinformation, as well as the development of robust strategies and tools to detect and combat its spread. Without proactive efforts to address this issue, the integrity of information in the digital age will remain under constant threat, with far-reaching consequences for individuals, communities, and society as a whole.

Subsection 2.2: The Challenge of Detecting AI-Generated Misinformation

As AI-generated content becomes increasingly sophisticated and realistic, the task of identifying and flagging misinformation created by these systems grows more complex. The very nature of AI algorithms allows them to generate text, images, and videos that closely mimic human-created content, making it difficult for both humans and machines to distinguish between authentic and fabricated information.

One of the primary challenges in detecting AI-generated misinformation lies in the continuous advancement of AI technologies. As researchers and developers work to improve the capabilities of language models, image generators, and other AI systems, the quality and believability of the content they produce also improve. This creates an ongoing "arms race" between those seeking to create convincing misinformation and those striving to develop effective detection methods.

Another significant hurdle is the lack of reliable and consistent indicators that can be used to identify AI-generated content. While some generated text may exhibit certain patterns or quirks, such as repetitive phrasing or awkward syntax, these characteristics are not always present and can vary depending on the specific AI model used. Moreover, as AI systems become more advanced, they learn to avoid these telltale signs, making detection even more challenging.

The sheer volume and speed at which AI-generated misinformation can be created and disseminated further complicate the detection process. With the ability to generate thousands of unique articles, images, or videos in a matter of hours, AI algorithms can quickly flood online platforms with misleading content. This deluge of information overwhelms fact-checkers and content moderators, who struggle to keep pace with the rapid spread of misinformation.

Furthermore, the detection of AI-generated misinformation often requires a combination of technical expertise and domain knowledge. Identifying fake news articles, for example, may involve analyzing the content for factual inaccuracies, logical inconsistencies, or biased reporting. This process demands a deep understanding of the subject matter, as well as the ability to cross-reference information from multiple reliable sources. As AI-generated content spans a wide range of topics and disciplines, developing comprehensive detection strategies becomes a daunting task.

The challenge of detecting AI-generated misinformation is compounded by the potential for these systems to be used in conjunction with human-created content. By seamlessly blending authentic information with fabricated elements, bad actors can create highly convincing and difficult-to-detect misinformation campaigns. This "hybrid" approach further blurs the line between truth and fiction, making it increasingly difficult to identify and counter the spread of false information.

As we grapple with the challenges of detecting AI-generated misinformation, it is crucial to recognize that there is no single, foolproof solution. Instead, a multi-faceted approach is required, one that combines technological advancements in AI detection, human expertise, and a commitment to media literacy and critical thinking. By fostering collaboration between researchers, fact-checkers, and platform moderators, and by empowering individuals to critically evaluate the information they consume, we can begin to develop effective strategies for identifying and combating the spread of AI-generated misinformation.

Subsection 2.3: The Amplification of Misinformation Through AI Algorithms

In the digital age, the spread of misinformation is not solely dependent on the ease of content creation or the challenges of detection. A significant factor contributing to the proliferation of misleading content is the role played by AI algorithms, particularly those used in recommendation systems and content curation.

Recommendation algorithms, designed to personalize user experiences and keep individuals engaged on platforms, have inadvertently become powerful amplifiers of misinformation. These algorithms analyze user behavior, preferences, and interactions to suggest content that aligns with their interests. While this approach has proven effective in keeping users engaged, it has also created "filter bubbles" and "echo chambers" that can reinforce and amplify exposure to misleading or false information.

When a user engages with a piece of misinformation, either by clicking, liking, or sharing, the recommendation algorithm interprets this as a signal of interest. Consequently, it suggests similar content, exposing the user to more misinformation and gradually reinforcing their belief in the false narrative. This feedback loop can lead to the rapid spread of misinformation within communities of like-minded individuals, as the algorithm continues to recommend content that confirms their existing beliefs.

Moreover, the optimization of AI algorithms for engagement and retention can prioritize sensational, shocking, or emotionally charged content, which often includes misinformation. As users are more likely to engage with content that elicits strong emotional responses, the algorithms may inadvertently promote the spread of false or misleading information, as it generates higher levels of engagement compared to more mundane, factual content.

The amplification of misinformation through AI algorithms poses significant challenges for content moderators and fact-checkers. As the volume of content shared on platforms grows exponentially, it becomes increasingly difficult to identify and counter the spread of false information. Furthermore, the opaque nature of many AI algorithms makes it challenging to understand and address the underlying mechanisms that contribute to the amplification of misinformation.

To mitigate the impact of algorithmic amplification, platforms and developers must prioritize transparency and accountability in the design and implementation of AI systems. This may involve regularly auditing algorithms for biases and unintended consequences, providing users with greater control over their content recommendations, and collaborating with fact-checking organizations to identify and limit the spread of misinformation.

Additionally, promoting media literacy and critical thinking skills among users is crucial in combating the amplification of misinformation. By empowering individuals to recognize and question potentially misleading content, they can become more resilient to the influence of AI-driven recommendations and make informed decisions about the information they consume and share.

As AI algorithms continue to shape the digital landscape, it is imperative that we address their role in the amplification of misinformation. By fostering a culture of responsibility, transparency, and user empowerment, we can work towards creating online environments that prioritize the spread of accurate, reliable information and mitigate the impact of misleading content amplified by AI systems.

Subsection 2.4: The Potential for Malicious Actors to Exploit AI

As AI technologies become more advanced and accessible, the potential for malicious actors to exploit these powerful tools for nefarious purposes grows increasingly concerning. The ability to generate convincing and misleading content at scale opens the door to a new era of disinformation campaigns, propaganda, and manipulation.

Imagine a scenario where a state-sponsored group or a well-funded organization with ill intentions leverages AI to create and disseminate false information on a massive scale. By employing sophisticated language models and image generation techniques, these malicious actors could produce highly realistic fake news articles, social media posts, and even videos that are designed to deceive and influence public opinion. The consequences of such coordinated misinformation campaigns could be devastating, ranging from undermining democratic processes and eroding trust in institutions to inciting violence and social unrest.

The potential for AI-driven misinformation campaigns to target specific individuals or groups is particularly alarming. By analyzing vast amounts of personal data available online, malicious actors could create highly personalized and persuasive content tailored to exploit an individual's biases, fears, and vulnerabilities. This targeted approach could be used to manipulate voting behavior, sow discord within communities, or even radicalize individuals towards extremist ideologies.

Moreover, the use of AI to generate deepfakes – highly realistic but fabricated videos or audio recordings – poses a significant threat to personal privacy and security. Malicious actors could create compromising or embarrassing deepfakes of individuals, using them for blackmail, harassment, or reputational damage. In a world where seeing is no longer believing, the potential for AI-generated content to be weaponized against individuals and organizations is a grave concern.

The anonymity and scalability of AI-driven misinformation campaigns make them particularly challenging to detect and combat. Malicious actors can operate from anywhere in the world, using multiple fake identities and automated tools to amplify the spread of false information. The sheer volume and speed at which AI-generated content can be created and disseminated can quickly overwhelm fact-checkers and content moderators, allowing misinformation to spread unchecked.

As we grapple with the potential for malicious actors to exploit AI, it is crucial to recognize that this is not a hypothetical threat, but a reality that we must confront head-on. Addressing this challenge requires a multi-faceted approach that combines technological solutions, policy interventions, and public awareness. Researchers and developers must work to create robust AI systems that are resistant to manipulation and misuse, while policymakers and regulators must establish clear guidelines and consequences for those who engage in AI-driven misinformation campaigns.

Equally important is the need to empower individuals with the knowledge and tools to critically evaluate the information they encounter online. By promoting media literacy and critical thinking skills, we can help people become more resilient to the influence of AI-generated misinformation and make informed decisions about the content they consume and share.

The potential for malicious actors to exploit AI is a sobering reminder of the double-edged nature of this transformative technology. As we embrace the many benefits that AI can bring, we must also remain vigilant and proactive in addressing the risks and challenges it poses. Only by working together – across industries, disciplines, and borders – can we hope to create a future in which the power of AI is harnessed for good, while the threat of its misuse is effectively mitigated.

Summary: Confronting the Challenges of AI-Generated Misinformation

The rapid advancement of AI technologies has brought about a new era of challenges in the battle against misinformation. As we have explored in this section, the ease with which misleading content can be generated, the difficulty in detecting AI-generated misinformation, and the potential for algorithmic amplification have created a perfect storm for the spread of false information.

The ability of AI systems to create highly realistic text, images, and videos has blurred the lines between truth and fiction, making it increasingly difficult for individuals to distinguish between authentic and fabricated content. This, coupled with the speed and scale at which AI-generated misinformation can be disseminated, has created a daunting challenge for fact-checkers, content moderators, and society as a whole.

Moreover, the role of AI algorithms in amplifying misinformation through recommendation systems and content curation has added another layer of complexity to the problem. By creating echo chambers and filter bubbles, these algorithms can reinforce and spread false narratives, further eroding trust in information sources and undermining public discourse.

Perhaps most concerning is the potential for malicious actors to exploit AI technologies for nefarious purposes, such as coordinated disinformation campaigns, targeted manipulation, and the creation of deepfakes. The anonymity and scalability of AI-driven misinformation make it a formidable threat to individuals, organizations, and even entire nations.

As we grapple with these challenges, it is clear that a multi-faceted approach is necessary. Technological solutions, such as advanced AI detection methods and algorithmic transparency, must be developed and implemented. Policy interventions and regulations are needed to establish clear guidelines and consequences for those who engage in AI-driven misinformation. And, perhaps most importantly, we must empower individuals with the media literacy and critical thinking skills needed to navigate this complex information landscape.

The spread of misinformation through AI-generated content is a complex and evolving challenge that requires the collective efforts of researchers, policymakers, platforms, and individuals. By confronting this issue head-on, we can work towards creating a future in which the power of AI is harnessed for good, while the threats posed by its misuse are effectively mitigated. The path forward may be difficult, but the stakes are too high to ignore. It is up to all of us to rise to the challenge and ensure that truth, integrity, and trust remain the foundation of our information ecosystem in the age of artificial intelligence.

Section 3: Addressing Bias and Misinformation in AI-Generated Content

As we delve deeper into the complexities surrounding the stigma against AI-generated content, it becomes increasingly clear that bias and misinformation lie at the heart of the issue. The potential for AI systems to perpetuate and amplify human biases, as well as the ease with which AI-generated content can be manipulated to spread false information, has raised significant concerns among both experts and the general public.

In this section, we will explore the various strategies and approaches that can be employed to mitigate bias and combat misinformation in AI-generated content. From ensuring diverse and representative training data to implementing algorithmic fairness and transparency measures, we will examine the critical steps that must be taken to address these pressing issues.

Moreover, we will delve into the importance of fact-checking and verification processes in identifying and flagging misinformation, as well as the crucial role of collaboration between AI developers and domain experts in ensuring the accuracy and integrity of AI-generated content.

As we navigate this complex landscape, it is essential to recognize that addressing bias and misinformation in AI-generated content is not a one-size-fits-all solution. It requires a multifaceted approach that involves the active participation and commitment of various stakeholders, including AI developers, policymakers, media platforms, and consumers.

By exploring these strategies and approaches, we aim to shed light on the path forward in overcoming the stigma against AI-generated content and harnessing the potential of this transformative technology in a responsible and trustworthy manner. So, let us embark on this journey together, armed with the knowledge and tools necessary to navigate the challenges and opportunities that lie ahead.

Subsection 3.1: Ensuring Diverse and Representative Training Data

One of the most crucial steps in addressing bias in AI-generated content is ensuring that the training data used to develop AI systems is diverse and representative of the target audience. AI algorithms learn from the data they are fed, and if this data is biased or lacks diversity, the resulting AI-generated content will likely reflect those biases.

For example, if an AI system designed to generate news articles is trained primarily on data from a single political perspective, the articles it produces may be skewed towards that perspective, leading to biased reporting. Similarly, if an AI-powered image recognition system is trained on a dataset that predominantly features images of white individuals, it may struggle to accurately identify people of color, perpetuating racial biases.

To mitigate these issues, AI developers must prioritize the collection and curation of diverse and representative training data. This involves actively seeking out data from a wide range of sources, demographics, and perspectives, ensuring that the AI system is exposed to a broad spectrum of information and experiences.

Techniques such as data augmentation and synthetic data generation can also be employed to enhance the diversity of training data. Data augmentation involves creating new training examples by modifying existing data, such as applying rotations, translations, or color variations to images. Synthetic data generation, on the other hand, involves creating entirely new data points that mimic real-world scenarios, allowing AI systems to learn from a wider range of hypothetical situations.

Additionally, it is essential to regularly audit and analyze training datasets for potential biases, using techniques such as statistical analysis and visualization to identify any skews or underrepresentation. By proactively identifying and addressing these biases, AI developers can work towards creating more balanced and representative training data, ultimately leading to less biased AI-generated content.

Ensuring diverse and representative training data is not a one-time task, but rather an ongoing process that requires continuous monitoring and refinement. As society evolves and new perspectives emerge, AI developers must remain vigilant in updating and expanding their training datasets to reflect these changes, ensuring that AI-generated content remains relevant, accurate, and unbiased.

Subsection 3.2: Implementing Algorithmic Fairness and Transparency

As we continue to explore strategies for addressing bias in AI-generated content, it is crucial to examine the role of algorithmic fairness techniques and transparency measures. These approaches aim to ensure that AI systems produce equitable and unbiased outputs while also providing clarity on how these systems arrive at their decisions.

Algorithmic fairness refers to the development and implementation of AI algorithms that treat all individuals and groups fairly, regardless of their protected characteristics, such as race, gender, age, or socioeconomic status. This involves designing AI systems that do not perpetuate or amplify existing societal biases and disparities.

One key aspect of algorithmic fairness is the use of fairness metrics, which quantify the degree of bias present in an AI system's outputs. These metrics, such as demographic parity, equalized odds, and equal opportunity, help developers assess whether their algorithms are producing fair and unbiased results. By incorporating these metrics into the development process, AI creators can identify and mitigate biases early on, ensuring that the final AI-generated content is more equitable.

Another critical component of algorithmic fairness is the use of techniques like adversarial debiasing and counterfactual fairness. Adversarial debiasing involves training an AI model to produce outputs that are indistinguishable from those of a fair and unbiased model, effectively "unlearning" any biases present in the training data. Counterfactual fairness, on the other hand, focuses on ensuring that an AI system's decisions remain consistent across different hypothetical scenarios, regardless of changes in protected attributes.

Transparency is equally important in addressing bias in AI-generated content. Transparency measures aim to provide clear and understandable explanations of how AI algorithms make their decisions, allowing users and stakeholders to scrutinize the system's inner workings and identify potential sources of bias.

One approach to transparency is the use of explainable AI (XAI) techniques, which provide human-interpretable explanations for AI-generated outputs. These techniques, such as feature importance analysis, decision trees, and rule-based explanations, help users understand the factors that influence an AI system's decisions, making it easier to identify and address any biases present.

Another aspect of transparency is the disclosure of an AI system's training data, model architecture, and performance metrics. By making this information publicly available, developers can foster trust and accountability, allowing external stakeholders to independently audit the system for potential biases and suggest improvements.

Implementing algorithmic fairness and transparency measures is not without its challenges. Balancing fairness and accuracy can be difficult, as efforts to mitigate bias may sometimes come at the cost of reduced model performance. Additionally, ensuring transparency while protecting proprietary information and intellectual property rights can be a delicate balance for AI developers.

Despite these challenges, the adoption of algorithmic fairness techniques and transparency measures is essential for addressing bias in AI-generated content. By prioritizing fairness and openness in the development process, AI creators can work towards building systems that produce more equitable and trustworthy outputs, ultimately helping to overcome the stigma surrounding AI-generated content.

As we move forward, it is crucial for AI developers, researchers, and policymakers to collaborate in establishing best practices and standards for algorithmic fairness and transparency. By working together to create a more inclusive and accountable AI ecosystem, we can harness the power of this transformative technology while ensuring that it benefits all members of society equally.

Subsection 3.3: Fact-Checking and Verification Processes

In the battle against misinformation in AI-generated content, fact-checking and verification processes play a crucial role. These essential practices involve scrutinizing the information presented in AI-generated outputs to ensure accuracy, credibility, and trustworthiness. By implementing robust fact-checking and verification mechanisms, we can effectively identify and flag instances of misinformation, preventing the spread of false or misleading information.

At its core, fact-checking involves comparing the claims made in AI-generated content against reliable sources of information, such as reputable news outlets, academic publications, and expert opinions. This process requires a meticulous approach, as it involves not only verifying the accuracy of individual facts but also assessing the context in which they are presented. Fact-checkers must be well-versed in the subject matter and possess the skills to evaluate the credibility of sources, distinguish between facts and opinions, and identify potential biases or inconsistencies in the information presented.

One of the key challenges in fact-checking AI-generated content is the sheer volume and speed at which such content can be produced. Unlike human-generated content, which is typically created at a slower pace and undergoes editorial review, AI algorithms can generate vast amounts of information in a matter of seconds. This rapid generation of content makes it difficult for traditional fact-checking methods to keep pace, necessitating the development of automated fact-checking tools and techniques.

Automated fact-checking systems leverage advanced natural language processing (NLP) and machine learning algorithms to analyze AI-generated content and flag potential instances of misinformation. These systems can be trained on large datasets of verified facts and can quickly scan through vast amounts of text, identifying claims that require further investigation. By employing techniques such as named entity recognition, sentiment analysis, and stance detection, automated fact-checking tools can help prioritize content for manual review and expedite the overall fact-checking process.

However, it is important to recognize that automated fact-checking is not a silver bullet solution. While these systems can greatly assist in the identification of potential misinformation, they are not infallible and may sometimes produce false positives or fail to detect more nuanced forms of misinformation. Therefore, it is crucial to combine automated fact-checking with human expertise and judgment to ensure the highest level of accuracy and reliability.

In addition to fact-checking, verification processes play a vital role in assessing the authenticity and provenance of AI-generated content. Verification involves tracing the origins of the information presented, determining the credibility of the sources used, and ensuring that the content has not been manipulated or altered in any way. This process may involve techniques such as reverse image searching, metadata analysis, and cross-referencing with other reliable sources.

Collaboration between AI developers, fact-checkers, and domain experts is essential for establishing effective fact-checking and verification processes. By working together, these stakeholders can develop best practices, establish standardized protocols, and create a shared knowledge base of verified facts and reliable sources. This collaborative approach not only enhances the efficiency and effectiveness of fact-checking efforts but also helps build trust and credibility in the AI-generated content that passes through these rigorous verification processes.

Moreover, transparency and accountability are key principles in fact-checking and verification. AI developers should be open about the sources and methods used in generating content, and fact-checkers should provide clear explanations of their verification processes and the criteria used to determine the accuracy of information. By maintaining transparency and holding both AI systems and fact-checkers accountable, we can foster a culture of trust and reliability in the realm of AI-generated content.

As we continue to navigate the challenges posed by misinformation in AI-generated content, it is clear that fact-checking and verification processes will remain indispensable tools in our arsenal. By leveraging a combination of human expertise, automated tools, and collaborative efforts, we can effectively identify and combat the spread of false or misleading information, ultimately helping to overcome the stigma associated with AI-generated content and ensure that the information we consume is accurate, reliable, and trustworthy.

Subsection 3.4: Collaboration Between AI Developers

and Domain Experts

As we explore the strategies for addressing bias and misinformation in AI-generated content, it becomes increasingly clear that collaboration between AI developers and domain experts is essential. This partnership is crucial in ensuring the accuracy, integrity, and trustworthiness of the content produced by AI systems.

AI developers bring to the table their technical expertise in creating and training AI algorithms. They possess the knowledge and skills necessary to design, implement, and optimize AI models that can generate human-like content across various domains. However, their focus is primarily on the technological aspects of AI, such as data preprocessing, model architecture, and performance optimization.

On the other hand, domain experts are individuals with deep knowledge and experience in specific fields, such as healthcare, finance, journalism, or education. They have a comprehensive understanding of the intricacies, nuances, and best practices within their respective domains. Domain experts are well-versed in the terminology, concepts, and challenges specific to their areas of expertise.

The collaboration between AI developers and domain experts is vital because it bridges the gap between the technical aspects of AI and the contextual understanding of the domain. By working together, they can ensure that the AI-generated content is not only technologically sound but also accurate, relevant, and aligned with the best practices and standards of the specific domain.

Domain experts can provide valuable guidance to AI developers in several ways. They can help identify the most relevant and reliable sources of data for training AI models, ensuring that the training data is representative, unbiased, and of high quality. They can also assist in defining the appropriate metrics and criteria for evaluating the accuracy and integrity of the generated content, taking into account the specific requirements and expectations of their domain.

Furthermore, domain experts can provide ongoing feedback and validation of the AI-generated content. They can review the outputs to ensure that the information presented is factually correct, contextually relevant, and adheres to the established norms and guidelines of their field. This iterative process of feedback and refinement helps improve the quality and reliability of the AI-generated content over time.

Collaboration between AI developers and domain experts also facilitates the identification and mitigation of potential biases and misinformation. Domain experts can help spot patterns, inconsistencies, or red flags in the generated content that may indicate the presence of bias or inaccurate information. They can provide insights into the historical, cultural, or societal factors that may influence the interpretation or reception of the content within their domain.

For example, in the field of healthcare, a collaboration between AI developers and medical experts can help ensure that AI-generated content related to medical advice, diagnoses, or treatment recommendations is accurate, evidence-based, and aligned with current clinical guidelines. Medical experts can review the generated content to verify its correctness, identify potential risks or limitations, and suggest improvements based on their clinical knowledge and experience.

Similarly, in the realm of journalism, a partnership between AI developers and experienced journalists can help maintain the integrity and credibility of AI-generated news articles. Journalists can provide guidance on ethical reporting practices, fact-checking procedures, and the importance of presenting balanced and unbiased perspectives. They can review the generated articles to ensure adherence to journalistic standards and flag any instances of sensationalism, bias, or misinformation.

To facilitate effective collaboration, it is essential to establish clear communication channels and workflows between AI developers and domain experts. Regular meetings, workshops, and feedback sessions can help foster a shared understanding of goals, expectations, and challenges. It is also crucial to develop a common language and vocabulary that bridges the technical jargon of AI with the domain-specific terminology, ensuring that both parties can effectively communicate and collaborate.

Moreover, organizations can create dedicated roles or teams that serve as liaisons between AI developers and domain experts. These individuals can have a background in both AI and the specific domain, enabling them to translate and mediate between the two groups. They can facilitate the exchange of knowledge, identify potential areas of collaboration, and ensure that the insights and feedback from domain experts are effectively incorporated into the AI development process.

As the field of AI continues to evolve and AI-generated content becomes more prevalent, the collaboration between AI developers and domain experts will only become more critical. By leveraging the strengths and expertise of both groups, we can work towards creating AI systems that produce accurate, reliable, and trustworthy content, ultimately helping to overcome the stigma associated with AI-generated content.

It is important to recognize that this collaboration is not a one-time endeavor but an ongoing process. As new challenges, technologies, and best practices emerge, AI developers and domain experts must continue to work together, adapt, and refine their approaches. By fostering a culture of collaboration, transparency, and continuous improvement, we can harness the power of AI to generate content that is not only technologically advanced but also aligned with the highest standards of accuracy, integrity, and domain expertise.

Summary: Overcoming the Stigma Through Collaboration and Innovation

As we conclude this section on addressing bias and misinformation in AI-generated content, it is evident that the path forward requires a multifaceted approach. By ensuring diverse and representative training data, implementing algorithmic fairness and transparency measures, establishing robust fact-checking and verification processes, and fostering collaboration between AI developers and domain experts, we can make significant strides in mitigating the challenges posed by biased and misleading AI-generated content.

However, it is crucial to recognize that these strategies are not one-time solutions, but rather ongoing efforts that require continuous refinement and adaptation. As AI technologies advance and new forms of bias and misinformation emerge, it is essential to remain vigilant and proactive in developing innovative approaches to tackle these issues head-on.

The collaboration between AI developers and domain experts serves as a shining example of how interdisciplinary cooperation can yield powerful results. By leveraging the technical expertise of AI developers and the contextual knowledge of domain experts, we can create AI systems that generate accurate, reliable, and trustworthy content. This partnership not only enhances the quality of the AI-generated content but also helps build public trust and confidence in the technology.

Moreover, as we look to the future, it is clear that the stigma against AI-generated content can only be overcome through a collective effort. It requires the active participation and commitment of all stakeholders, including AI developers, researchers, policymakers, media platforms, and the general public. By working together, sharing knowledge, and promoting best practices, we can foster a more responsible and accountable AI ecosystem that benefits society as a whole.

In the face of the challenges posed by bias and misinformation, it is essential to remain optimistic and focused on the vast potential of AI-generated content. With the right strategies, collaborations, and innovations in place, we can harness the power of this transformative technology to create a more informed, inclusive, and equitable world.

As we move forward, let us embrace the opportunities presented by AI-generated content while remaining committed to addressing its challenges. By doing so, we can pave the way for a future where AI-generated content is not only accepted but also celebrated for its ability to inform, educate, and inspire audiences around the globe.

Section 4: The Responsibility of Stakeholders in Addressing Bias and Misinformation

In the complex landscape of AI-generated content, the issue of bias and misinformation is not merely a technological challenge but also a societal one. As we have explored the various ways in which bias can manifest in AI systems and how misinformation can spread through AI-generated content, it becomes clear that addressing these concerns requires a collective effort from all stakeholders involved. From the developers creating the AI algorithms to the policymakers shaping the regulatory framework, each player has a crucial role in ensuring the fairness, accuracy, and integrity of AI-generated content.

In this section, we will delve into the responsibilities of four key stakeholder groups: AI developers and companies, policymakers and regulators, media platforms and distributors, and consumers and the general public. By examining the unique challenges and opportunities each group faces, we can begin to understand the multifaceted approach necessary to combat bias and misinformation effectively.

As we navigate this uncharted territory, it is essential to recognize that the decisions made by these stakeholders today will have far-reaching consequences for the future of AI-generated content. The choices we make now will shape the trajectory of this powerful technology and determine whether it serves as a tool for empowerment and progress or a source of division and confusion. By coming together and embracing our shared responsibility, we can work towards creating an ecosystem where AI-generated content is trustworthy, equitable, and beneficial for all.

Subsection 4.1: The Role of AI Developers and Companies

AI developers and companies play a pivotal role in addressing the issue of bias and misinformation in AI-generated content. As the creators of the algorithms and systems that power this technology, they bear a significant responsibility in ensuring the fairness, accuracy, and integrity of their AI products.

One of the primary ethical obligations of AI developers is to be vigilant in identifying and mitigating potential biases in their algorithms. This requires a proactive approach, starting from the early stages of development and continuing throughout the lifecycle of the AI system. Developers must carefully examine the training data they use, ensuring that it is diverse, representative, and free from inherent biases. They should also implement rigorous testing and auditing processes to detect and rectify any biases that may emerge during the development phase.

Moreover, AI companies have a responsibility to prioritize transparency and accountability in their practices. They should be open about the limitations and potential risks associated with their AI systems, providing clear explanations of how their algorithms work and what data they are trained on. This transparency enables users and the general public to make informed decisions about the use and trustworthiness of AI-generated content.

In addition to addressing bias, AI developers and companies must also take steps to combat the spread of misinformation through their platforms. This may involve implementing robust fact-checking mechanisms, collaborating with domain experts to verify the accuracy of AI-generated content, and developing algorithms that can detect and flag potentially misleading or false information.

However, the responsibility of AI developers and companies extends beyond the technical aspects of their products. They must also consider the broader ethical implications of their work and actively engage in discussions around the societal impact of AI-generated content. This includes participating in the development of industry standards, best practices, and ethical guidelines that govern the responsible development and deployment of AI technologies.

Furthermore, AI companies should invest in ongoing research and development efforts aimed at improving the fairness and accuracy of their systems. This may involve exploring new techniques for bias mitigation, such as adversarial debiasing or fairness constraints, and continuously updating their algorithms to reflect the latest advancements in the field.

Ultimately, the role of AI developers and companies in addressing bias and misinformation is one of proactive engagement and continuous improvement. By embracing their ethical responsibilities and working towards creating AI systems that are fair, accurate, and trustworthy, they can help to build public trust in AI-generated content and unlock the full potential of this transformative technology.

Subsection 4.2: The Role of Policymakers and Regulators

As the influence of AI-generated content continues to grow, policymakers and regulators play a crucial role in shaping the legal and ethical framework that governs its use. The rapid advancement of AI technologies has outpaced the development of comprehensive regulations, leaving a void that must be filled to ensure the responsible and equitable deployment of AI-generated content.

One of the primary responsibilities of policymakers and regulators is to establish clear guidelines and standards for the development and use of AI systems. These guidelines should address key issues such as transparency, accountability, and fairness, ensuring that AI-generated content is created and disseminated in a manner that upholds the public interest. By setting forth a robust regulatory framework, policymakers can help to mitigate the risks of bias and misinformation while fostering an environment that encourages innovation and growth.

To effectively address the challenges posed by AI-generated content, policymakers must engage in a collaborative and inclusive process that involves a wide range of stakeholders. This includes AI developers, industry experts, civil society organizations, and the general public. By facilitating open dialogue and gathering input from diverse perspectives, policymakers can craft regulations that are well-informed, practical, and responsive to the needs of all parties involved.

Furthermore, policymakers and regulators must strike a delicate balance between protecting the public from the potential harms of AI-generated content and preserving the benefits that this technology can offer. This requires a nuanced approach that recognizes the complexities of the issue and avoids overly restrictive or burdensome regulations that could stifle innovation or infringe upon free speech.

One area where policymakers can make a significant impact is in the development of standards for algorithmic transparency and accountability. By requiring AI companies to disclose information about their algorithms, training data, and decision-making processes, regulators can help to ensure that AI-generated content is created in a fair and unbiased manner. This transparency also enables greater public scrutiny and accountability, allowing individuals and organizations to challenge instances of bias or misinformation when they occur.

In addition to establishing guidelines and standards, policymakers and regulators must also invest in research and education initiatives that help to build public understanding and trust in AI-generated content. This may involve funding studies that examine the societal impact of AI, developing educational programs that teach individuals how to critically evaluate AI-generated content, and supporting the development of tools and technologies that can help to detect and combat bias and misinformation.

Ultimately, the role of policymakers and regulators in addressing bias and misinformation in AI-generated content is one of leadership and stewardship. By proactively engaging with this issue and working to develop a comprehensive and adaptive regulatory framework, they can help to ensure that AI-generated content serves the public good and contributes to a more informed, equitable, and thriving society.

Subsection 4.3: The Role of Media Platforms and Distributors

In the rapidly evolving landscape of AI-generated content, media platforms and distributors find themselves at the forefront of a new era of content creation and dissemination. As the gatekeepers of information, these entities bear a significant responsibility in moderating and fact-checking the AI-generated content that reaches their audiences. The role of media platforms and distributors in addressing the stigma against AI-generated content is multifaceted, requiring a delicate balance between fostering innovation and ensuring the integrity of the information ecosystem.

One of the primary responsibilities of media platforms and distributors is to establish clear guidelines and policies for the use of AI-generated content. These policies should outline the standards for accuracy, transparency, and accountability that AI-generated content must meet before it can be published or distributed on their platforms. By setting forth a robust framework for the moderation of AI-generated content, media platforms and distributors can help to mitigate the risks of bias and misinformation while creating a level playing field for content creators.

To effectively moderate AI-generated content, media platforms and distributors must invest in the development of sophisticated tools and algorithms that can detect and flag potentially misleading or inaccurate information. This may involve leveraging advanced natural language processing techniques, machine learning algorithms, and human oversight to identify patterns and anomalies in AI-generated content. By implementing these tools and processes, media platforms and distributors can proactively identify and address instances of bias or misinformation before they spread widely.

In addition to moderation, fact-checking is another critical responsibility of media platforms and distributors in the context of AI-generated content. Given the potential for AI systems to generate convincing but inaccurate information, it is essential that media platforms and distributors have robust fact-checking mechanisms in place to verify the accuracy of

AI-generated content before it is published or distributed. This may involve collaborating with independent fact-checking organizations, employing in-house fact-checkers, or leveraging crowdsourcing techniques to harness the collective knowledge of their user communities.

Transparency is also a key consideration for media platforms and distributors when it comes to AI-generated content. To build trust with their audiences and maintain the credibility of their platforms, media entities must be transparent about the use of AI in content creation and distribution. This may involve clearly labeling AI-generated content as such, providing information about the AI systems and algorithms used, and disclosing any potential biases or limitations associated with the AI-generated content. By embracing transparency, media platforms and distributors can empower their audiences to make informed decisions about the content they consume and foster a culture of trust and accountability.

Furthermore, media platforms and distributors have a responsibility to educate their audiences about the nature and implications of AI-generated content. This may involve developing educational resources, hosting public forums and discussions, and collaborating with experts and stakeholders to raise awareness about the benefits and challenges of AI in content creation. By actively engaging with their audiences and promoting media literacy, media platforms and distributors can help to combat the stigma against AI-generated content and foster a more informed and discerning public.

Ultimately, the role of media platforms and distributors in addressing the stigma against AI-generated content is one of stewardship and responsibility. By establishing clear guidelines, investing in moderation and fact-checking tools, embracing transparency, and educating their audiences, media entities can help to ensure that AI-generated content is used in a responsible and ethical manner. As the influence of AI in content creation continues to grow, the actions and decisions of media platforms and distributors will play a crucial role in shaping the future of the information ecosystem and the public's trust in AI-generated content.

Subsection 4.4: The Role of Consumers and the General Public

In the age of AI-generated content, the role of consumers and the general public in addressing the stigma against this technology cannot be overstated. As the ultimate recipients and users of AI-generated content, individuals have a significant responsibility to develop and employ media literacy and critical thinking skills when navigating this new landscape.

Media literacy, the ability to access, analyze, evaluate, and create media content, is crucial in the context of AI-generated content. With the increasing sophistication of AI algorithms, distinguishing between human-created and AI-generated content can be challenging. Consumers must be equipped with the knowledge and skills necessary to critically assess the information they encounter, considering factors such as the source, purpose, and potential biases of the content.

One key aspect of media literacy in the AI era is understanding the capabilities and limitations of AI systems. Consumers should be aware that while AI-generated content can be highly convincing and informative, it is not infallible. AI algorithms are only as unbiased and accurate as the data they are trained on and the humans who design them. By recognizing the potential for bias and misinformation in AI-generated content, consumers can approach this technology with a healthy level of skepticism and discernment.

Critical thinking skills, the ability to analyze and evaluate information objectively, are equally essential in navigating the stigma against AI-generated content. Consumers must be willing to question the information they encounter, seeking out multiple sources and perspectives to form well-informed opinions. This involves actively engaging with the content, asking probing questions, and considering alternative viewpoints before drawing conclusions.

In addition to developing media literacy and critical thinking skills, consumers and the general public can play an active role in shaping the discourse around AI-generated content. By engaging in open and informed discussions about the benefits and challenges of this technology, individuals can contribute to a more nuanced and balanced understanding of its implications. This may involve participating in online forums, attending public events, or sharing personal experiences and insights with others.

Furthermore, consumers can use their collective influence to hold AI developers, media platforms, and other stakeholders accountable for the quality and integrity of AI-generated content. By demanding transparency, accuracy, and fairness in the creation and dissemination of this content, the general public can help to establish and enforce standards that promote responsible and ethical use of AI technology.

Ultimately, the role of consumers and the general public in addressing the stigma against AI-generated content is one of empowerment and active participation. By developing media literacy and critical thinking skills, engaging in informed discussions, and holding stakeholders accountable, individuals can help to shape a future in which AI-generated content is valued for its potential to inform, educate, and inspire, while being approached with the necessary level of discernment and responsibility.

Summary: A Collective Responsibility for Trustworthy AI-Generated Content

In this section, we have explored the roles and responsibilities of key stakeholders in addressing the pressing issues of bias and misinformation in AI-generated content. From the developers and companies creating AI systems to the policymakers and regulators shaping the legal landscape, and from the media platforms and distributors moderating content to the consumers and general public consuming it, each group has a crucial part to play in ensuring the fairness, accuracy, and integrity of AI-generated content.

The responsibility of AI developers and companies lies in proactively identifying and mitigating biases in their algorithms, prioritizing transparency and accountability, and actively engaging in discussions around the ethical implications of their work. Policymakers and regulators, on the other hand, must establish clear guidelines and standards, facilitate inclusive dialogue, and strike a balance between protecting the public and fostering innovation.

Media platforms and distributors bear the responsibility of moderating and fact-checking AI-generated content, investing in sophisticated tools and processes, and educating their audiences about the nature and implications of this technology. Consumers and the general public, as the ultimate recipients of AI-generated content, must develop media literacy and critical thinking skills, actively participate in shaping the discourse, and hold stakeholders accountable for the quality and integrity of the content they produce and distribute.

The challenges posed by bias and misinformation in AI-generated content are complex and multifaceted, requiring a collaborative and comprehensive approach from all stakeholders involved. By recognizing and embracing their unique responsibilities, these groups can work together to create an ecosystem where AI-generated content is trustworthy, equitable, and beneficial for all.

As we move forward, it is essential to remember that the decisions and actions taken by these stakeholders today will have far-reaching consequences for the future of AI-generated content and its impact on society. By prioritizing transparency, accountability, and ethical considerations, we can harness the power of AI to inform, educate, and inspire while mitigating the risks of bias and misinformation.

The path ahead may be challenging, but it is also filled with opportunity. By working together and remaining committed to the responsible development and deployment of AI-generated content, we can shape a future in which this technology serves as a tool for empowerment, progress, and the betterment of society as a whole.

Chapter Summary: Navigating the Challenges of Bias and Misinformation in AI-Generated

Content

As AI-generated content becomes increasingly prevalent, it is crucial to acknowledge and address the concerns surrounding bias and misinformation. Throughout this chapter, we have explored the various types of biases that can exist in AI systems, the impact of training data on bias, and the role of human biases in AI development. We have also examined the potential consequences of biased AI-generated content on individuals, groups, and society as a whole.

Additionally, we have discussed the ease with which AI technologies can be used to create and disseminate misleading or false information, the challenges in detecting AI-generated misinformation, and the potential for malicious actors to exploit AI for nefarious purposes. It is clear that addressing bias and misinformation in AI-generated content requires a multi-faceted approach involving diverse and representative training data, algorithmic fairness and transparency, fact-checking and verification processes, and collaboration between AI developers and domain experts.

Furthermore, we have highlighted the responsibilities of various stakeholders, including AI developers, companies, policymakers, regulators, media platforms, and consumers, in ensuring the fairness, accuracy, and integrity of AI-generated content. As we navigate this complex landscape, it is essential to foster media literacy and critical thinking skills among the general public to help them effectively evaluate and engage with AI-generated content.

By understanding the challenges posed by bias and misinformation in AI-generated content and working together to develop robust solutions, we can harness the power of AI while mitigating its potential risks. As we move forward, it is crucial to maintain an open dialogue, continuously refine our approaches, and strive for a future in which AI-generated content is fair, accurate, and trustworthy.

Chapter 5: AI as a Tool: Enhancing Human Creativity

In the ever-evolving landscape of technology, artificial intelligence (AI) has emerged as a powerful force, reshaping industries and transforming the way we live and work. While the stigma surrounding AI-generated content persists, it is crucial to recognize the immense potential of AI as a tool to enhance and augment human creativity. Rather than viewing AI as a threat to human ingenuity, we must explore the ways in which this technology can collaborate with and empower creators across various fields.

Throughout history, humans have relied on tools to extend their capabilities and push the boundaries of what is possible. From the invention of the wheel to the advent of the computer, each technological advancement has opened up new avenues for creative expression and problem-solving. AI is no different. By leveraging the power of machine learning algorithms and vast datasets, AI can serve as a creative partner, assisting humans in generating novel ideas, overcoming creative blocks, and exploring uncharted territories.

The synergy between AI and human creativity holds immense promise. AI-powered tools can analyze patterns, generate variations, and provide suggestions based on a creator's input, allowing them to iterate and refine their work more efficiently. This collaborative approach enables artists, musicians, writers, and designers to focus on the aspects of the creative process that require uniquely human qualities, such as emotional intelligence, intuition, and aesthetic judgment.

However, to fully harness the potential of AI in enhancing human creativity, it is essential to address the misconceptions and fears surrounding this technology. By examining real-world examples of successful AI-human collaborations and exploring the ethical considerations involved, we can foster a more nuanced understanding of AI's role in the creative process. Through education, experimentation, and open dialogue, we can cultivate a symbiotic relationship between AI and human creators, unlocking new frontiers of imagination and innovation.

In this chapter, we will delve into the various ways AI can be used as a tool to enhance human creativity across different industries. We will explore the development of AI-powered tools that support creative endeavors, discuss the importance of balancing AI assistance with human creative control, and envision a future where AI and human creators work hand in hand to push the boundaries of what is possible. By embracing AI as a collaborator rather than a competitor, we can usher in a new era of creativity and pave the way for groundbreaking achievements in art, music, literature, and beyond.

Section 1: The Synergy Between AI and Human Creativity

In the realm of creativity, the rise of artificial intelligence (AI) has sparked both excitement and apprehension. As AI-powered tools become increasingly sophisticated, many question whether they will eventually replace human creativity altogether. However, the true potential of AI lies not in its ability to supplant human ingenuity but rather in its capacity to complement and enhance it. This section explores the fascinating synergy between AI and human creativity, revealing how the two can work in harmony to push the boundaries of innovation and artistic expression.

The notion of AI as a creative collaborator may seem counterintuitive at first, given the common perception of creativity as a uniquely human trait. Yet, the rapid advancements in AI technology have demonstrated that machines can indeed generate novel ideas, designs, and solutions that rival those of their human counterparts. By leveraging the vast computational power and data-processing capabilities of AI, human creators can tap into a wealth of resources and insights that would otherwise remain inaccessible.

From visual arts to music composition, from creative writing to architectural design, the applications of AI in enhancing human creativity are vast and varied. AI-powered tools can assist artists in generating new color palettes, composers in discovering unique chord progressions, and writers in developing compelling characters and storylines. By providing a fresh perspective and breaking free from conventional patterns of thought, AI can help human creators overcome creative blocks and explore uncharted territories.

However, the synergy between AI and human creativity is not about relinquishing control to machines. Rather, it is about striking a delicate balance between leveraging the capabilities of AI and maintaining the human touch that makes creative works truly authentic and emotionally resonant. As we delve deeper into this fascinating relationship, we will explore the strategies for ensuring that AI remains a tool in the hands of human creators, augmenting their skills and expanding their possibilities, while preserving the essence of what makes human creativity so valuable and irreplaceable.

Subsection 1.1: AI as a Creative Collaborator

The concept of AI as a creative collaborator has gained significant traction in recent years, as advances in machine learning and natural language processing have enabled AI systems to generate novel ideas and solutions alongside human creators. This collaborative approach challenges the notion that creativity is an exclusively human domain and highlights the potential for AI to augment and enhance human creative processes.

One of the key advantages of AI as a creative collaborator is its ability to process vast amounts of data and identify patterns and connections that may not be immediately apparent to human creators. By analyzing existing works of art, literature, music, and other creative outputs, AI algorithms can learn the underlying structures, styles, and techniques that make these works effective. This knowledge can then be applied to generate new ideas and solutions that build upon and extend the existing creative landscape.

For example, in the field of music composition, AI-powered tools like AIVA and Amper can work alongside human composers to generate novel melodies, harmonies, and rhythms based on specified parameters and styles. These tools do not aim to replace human composers but rather to provide them with a starting point and a source of inspiration, allowing them to focus on the more subjective and emotional aspects of the creative process.

Similarly, in the realm of visual arts, AI algorithms like GANs (Generative Adversarial Networks) can be trained on vast datasets of existing artworks to generate new images that combine and remix elements in unique and unexpected ways. Human artists can then use these AI-generated images as a foundation for their own creative explorations, building upon and refining them to create works that reflect their personal style and vision.

The collaborative relationship between AI and human creators is not limited to the arts, however. In fields like product design and architecture, AI can work alongside human designers to generate novel solutions to complex problems, taking into account a wide range of constraints and requirements. By exploring a vast design space and identifying optimal configurations, AI can help human designers to push the boundaries of what is possible and create products and structures that are both functional and innovative.

As AI continues to evolve and become more sophisticated, the potential for collaboration between human and machine creators will only continue to grow. By embracing AI as a creative partner, rather than a competitor, human creators can tap into a powerful source of inspiration and innovation, leading to new forms of expression and solutions to some of the world's most pressing challenges.

Subsection 1.2: Augmenting Human Creativity with AI-Powered Tools

The development of AI-powered tools has revolutionized the way human creators approach their craft, offering new avenues for exploration, inspiration, and expression. These tools serve as creative partners, augmenting and enhancing the creative process by providing a range of capabilities that complement human ingenuity and expertise.

One of the most significant advantages of AI-powered tools is their ability to streamline and automate certain aspects of the creative workflow, allowing human creators to focus on the more conceptual and emotional elements of their work. For example, in the field of graphic design, AI algorithms can assist with tasks such as color palette generation, layout optimization, and image manipulation, saving designers valuable time and effort that can be redirected towards refining their artistic vision.

Similarly, in the realm of music production, AI-powered tools like Magenta by Google and LANDR's mastering software can analyze and generate musical patterns, suggest harmonies, and even master tracks, providing musicians with a wealth of creative possibilities to explore. These tools do not aim to replace human musicians but rather to empower them with new sounds, textures, and ideas that can inspire and inform their own creative process.

The integration of AI into creative software has also paved the way for more intuitive and user-friendly interfaces, making advanced creative techniques accessible to a wider range of users. For instance, Adobe's Sensei AI technology powers features like content-aware fill and automatic subject selection in Photoshop, enabling even novice users to achieve professional-level results with minimal effort. By democratizing access to powerful creative tools, AI is helping to break down barriers and encourage more people to express their creativity.

As AI continues to evolve, the potential for collaboration between human creators and AI-powered tools is virtually limitless. From generative design systems that can create thousands of unique variations based on a set of parameters to natural language processing algorithms that can assist writers in crafting compelling narratives, the future of AI-augmented creativity looks brighter than ever.

However, it is essential to recognize that AI-powered tools are not a replacement for human creativity but rather an extension of it. The most successful and impactful creative works will likely emerge from a symbiotic relationship between human creators and AI, where the unique strengths of each are leveraged to push the boundaries of what is possible. As we move forward, fostering a deeper understanding and appreciation of this collaborative dynamic will be crucial in unlocking the full potential of AI-augmented creativity.

Subsection 1.3: The Role of AI in Overcoming Creative Blocks

Creative blocks are a common challenge faced by artists, writers, musicians, and other creative professionals. These mental obstacles can hinder productivity, stifle inspiration, and lead to frustration and self-doubt. However, the emergence of AI-powered tools has opened up new possibilities for overcoming creative blocks and generating fresh perspectives.

One of the primary ways AI can help creators overcome creative blocks is by providing a wealth of inspiration and ideas. By analyzing vast datasets of existing creative works, AI algorithms can identify patterns, styles, and themes that can serve as a starting point for new projects. For example, an AI-powered writing tool might suggest plot points, character archetypes, or literary devices based on a writer's initial input, helping to spark new ideas and break through writer's block.

Similarly, in the visual arts, AI can generate countless variations of an image or design based on a set of parameters, allowing artists to explore new color schemes, compositions, and styles. This can be particularly helpful when an artist feels stuck or uninspired, as the AI-generated variations can provide a fresh perspective and help to kickstart the creative process.

Another way AI can help overcome creative blocks is by automating certain tasks and freeing up mental bandwidth for more creative pursuits. For example, an AI-powered music composition tool might handle the technical aspects of arranging and producing a track, allowing the musician to focus on the creative elements of songwriting and performance. By taking care of the more mundane or time-consuming aspects of the creative process, AI can help creators maintain their flow and avoid getting bogged down in technical details.

AI can also play a role in overcoming creative blocks by providing objective feedback and suggestions. While human feedback can be valuable, it can also be subject to personal biases and preferences. AI algorithms, on the other hand, can analyze creative works based on a set of predefined criteria and provide impartial feedback on areas for improvement. This can help creators identify blind spots in their work and make adjustments to overcome creative obstacles.

Furthermore, AI can help creators overcome creative blocks by facilitating collaboration and idea-sharing. Many AI-powered creative platforms allow users to share their work, receive feedback, and collaborate with others in real-time. This can expose creators to new perspectives, techniques, and styles, helping to break out of creative ruts and generate fresh ideas.

However, it is important to note that AI is not a silver bullet for overcoming creative blocks. While AI-powered tools can provide valuable inspiration, automation, and feedback, they cannot replace the human element of creativity. Ultimately, it is up to the individual creator to take the insights and suggestions provided by AI and transform them into unique, compelling works of art.

As such, the role of AI in overcoming creative blocks is best viewed as a collaborative one. By working in tandem with human creators, AI can help to stimulate new ideas, streamline workflows, and provide objective feedback, ultimately empowering creators to break through mental barriers and achieve their full creative potential.

Summary: Embracing the Collaborative Potential of AI in Creative Endeavors

The synergy between AI and human creativity represents a fascinating and transformative development in the realm of creative expression. By exploring the potential for AI to complement and enhance human creative processes, we have discovered a world of possibilities that challenges traditional notions of creativity and pushes the boundaries of what is achievable.

From its role as a creative collaborator, generating novel ideas and solutions alongside human creators, to its ability to augment and streamline the creative workflow through AI-powered tools, the integration of AI in creative endeavors has opened up new avenues for exploration and innovation. Moreover, AI's capacity to help overcome creative blocks by providing inspiration, automating tasks, and offering objective feedback has empowered creators to break through mental barriers and achieve their full potential.

However, it is crucial to recognize that the success of this synergistic relationship hinges on striking a delicate balance between leveraging the capabilities of AI and maintaining the human touch that makes creative works truly authentic and emotionally resonant. As we move forward, fostering a deeper understanding and appreciation of this collaborative dynamic will be essential in unlocking the full potential of AI-augmented creativity.

The future of creative expression lies in embracing the collaborative potential of AI and human creativity. By working hand in hand, human creators and AI can push the boundaries of innovation, create works that inspire and captivate audiences, and redefine what it means to be creative in the digital age. As we continue to explore this exciting frontier, we must approach it with an open mind, a willingness to experiment, and a commitment to harnessing the power of technology to enhance, rather than replace, the boundless creativity of the human spirit.

Section 2: AI-Assisted Content Creation Across Industries

The rapid advancement of artificial intelligence has led to a revolution in content creation, transforming the way we approach creativity across a wide range of industries. From the visual arts to music composition, and from creative writing to architectural design, AI is increasingly being used as a tool to augment and enhance human creativity. In this section, we will embark on a fascinating journey to explore the myriad applications of AI in assisting content creators, and how this technology is reshaping the creative landscape.

As we delve into the world of AI-assisted content creation, it becomes evident that the possibilities are virtually endless. By harnessing the power of machine learning algorithms and neural networks, AI can analyze vast amounts of data, identify patterns, and generate novel ideas that push the boundaries of human imagination. This symbiotic relationship between human creativity and artificial intelligence has the potential to unlock new frontiers in creative expression, leading to innovative and compelling content that captivates audiences across the globe.

However, the integration of AI in the creative process is not without its challenges and concerns. Questions arise about the role of human creators in an AI-driven world, and how to maintain the authenticity and emotional depth that characterizes truly great works of art. As we navigate this uncharted territory, it is crucial to find a balance between leveraging the power of AI and preserving the unique perspective and intuition that only human creators can bring to the table.

In the following subsections, we will take a closer look at how AI is being applied in various creative industries, from the visual arts to music, writing, and design. Through real-world examples and insightful analysis, we will explore the benefits and challenges of AI-assisted content creation, and consider the implications for the future of creativity. So, let us embark on this exciting exploration of the intersection between artificial intelligence and human creativity, and discover the boundless potential that lies ahead.

Subsection 2.1: AI in the Visual Arts

The visual arts have long been a domain where human creativity and imagination reign supreme. However, with the advent of artificial intelligence, the boundaries of what is possible in this field are being pushed to new frontiers. AI is increasingly being used to create and modify visual artworks, such as paintings and digital illustrations, in ways that were once thought impossible.

One of the most exciting applications of AI in the visual arts is the creation of entirely new artworks. By training AI models on vast datasets of existing artworks, artists and researchers have been able to generate novel pieces that mimic the styles of famous painters or create entirely new aesthetics. These AI-generated artworks can be strikingly beautiful and thought-provoking, challenging our notions of what constitutes art and the role of the artist in the creative process.

AI is also being used to modify and enhance existing artworks in innovative ways. For example, AI algorithms can be employed to colorize black and white photographs, bringing historical images to life with stunning realism. Similarly, AI can be used to restore damaged or degraded artworks, filling in missing details and correcting imperfections with incredible accuracy. These applications of AI not only help to preserve our cultural heritage but also offer new ways of engaging with and appreciating classic works of art.

In the realm of digital illustration, AI is proving to be a powerful tool for artists and designers. AI-powered software can assist in the creation of concept art, character designs, and storyboards, generating ideas and variations that would be time-consuming and laborious for human artists to produce. These AI-assisted tools can help to streamline the creative process, allowing artists to focus on the most critical aspects of their work while delegating repetitive or mundane tasks to the machine.

However, the use of AI in the visual arts is not without controversy. Some artists and critics argue that AI-generated art lacks the emotional depth and personal expression that characterizes great works of human creativity. Others raise concerns about the potential for AI to displace human artists, particularly in commercial settings where speed and efficiency are prioritized over originality and authenticity.

Despite these concerns, the integration of AI in the visual arts shows no signs of slowing down. As AI technologies continue to advance, we can expect to see even more innovative and compelling applications in this field. The challenge for artists and society as a whole will be to find a balance between embracing the power of AI and preserving the unique qualities that make human creativity so valuable and enduring.

Subsection 2.2: AI in Music Composition and Production

The world of music has always been a playground for human creativity, with composers and producers crafting intricate melodies, harmonies, and rhythms that evoke powerful emotions and tell compelling stories. However, the advent of artificial intelligence has opened up new possibilities for music creation, challenging traditional notions of what it means to be a musician or composer.

AI-powered tools and algorithms are increasingly being used to assist musicians in various aspects of the creative process, from generating novel musical ideas to arranging and producing complete tracks. These tools leverage vast datasets of existing music, analyzing patterns, structures, and styles to create new compositions that can be strikingly original and emotionally resonant.

One of the most exciting applications of AI in music is in the realm of composition. AI algorithms can be trained on the works of specific composers or genres, learning the underlying rules and patterns that characterize their unique styles. By combining this learned knowledge with elements of randomness and variation, these algorithms can generate entirely new compositions that capture the essence of the original style while introducing fresh and unexpected elements.

For example, AI-powered tools like AIVA (Artificial Intelligence Virtual Artist) and Amper Music allow users to input various parameters, such as genre, mood, and instrumentation, and generate original music compositions in a matter of minutes. These tools can be incredibly useful for musicians looking to overcome creative blocks, explore new musical territories, or simply speed up the composition process.

AI is also making significant strides in the field of music arrangement and production. By analyzing the structure and characteristics of existing songs, AI algorithms can suggest novel arrangements, instrument combinations, and production techniques that can take a composition in exciting new directions. This can be particularly valuable for musicians working in genres like electronic dance music (EDM), where the arrangement and production quality are often just as important as the underlying composition.

In the realm of sound design, AI is opening up new frontiers for musicians and producers. AI-powered tools can analyze and classify vast libraries of sounds, allowing users to quickly find the perfect sample or synth patch for their needs. Some tools even allow for the creation of entirely new sounds by combining and manipulating existing samples in ways that would be difficult or impossible for human designers.

However, the use of AI in music composition and production is not without its challenges and concerns. Some musicians and critics argue that AI-generated music lacks the emotional depth and personal expression that characterizes great works of human artistry. Others worry about the potential for AI to displace human musicians, particularly in commercial settings where efficiency and cost-effectiveness are prioritized.

As AI continues to evolve and become more sophisticated, it is likely that we will see even more innovative and compelling applications in the world of music. The key challenge for musicians and the industry as a whole will be to find a balance between embracing the power of AI and preserving the unique qualities that make human musical creativity so valuable and enduring. By working in collaboration with AI tools and algorithms, musicians can push the boundaries of what is possible in music creation while still retaining the essential human element that lies at the heart of all great art.

Subsection 2.3: AI in Creative Writing and Storytelling

The realm of creative writing and storytelling has long been considered a uniquely human endeavor, where imagination, emotion, and the ability to weave compelling narratives reign supreme. However, the rise of artificial intelligence has begun to challenge this notion, as AI-powered tools and algorithms increasingly demonstrate their potential to support and enhance the creative writing process.

One of the most exciting applications of AI in creative writing is its ability to generate ideas and inspire writers. By training AI models on vast datasets of existing stories, novels, and other forms of creative writing, these tools can suggest unique plot points, character archetypes, and thematic elements that writers can use as a starting point for their own creative exploration. For example, the AI-powered tool "Plotshot" allows writers to input key details about their desired story, such as genre, setting, and character traits, and generates a detailed plot outline that can serve as a foundation for their writing.

AI is also being used to assist writers in developing rich, multi-dimensional characters. Tools like "Character AI" analyze existing characters from literature and media, identifying common traits, motivations, and archetypal patterns. By inputting key details about their desired characters, writers can receive AI-generated suggestions for backstories, personality quirks, and even dialogue styles that can help bring their characters to life on the page.

In the realm of crafting narratives, AI is proving to be a powerful ally for writers. AI algorithms can analyze the structure and pacing of successful stories, identifying key narrative beats and emotional arcs that keep readers engaged. Tools like "Narrative Science" use this knowledge to generate coherent, well-structured stories based on user input, allowing writers to experiment with different narrative approaches and receive instant feedback on their effectiveness.

However, the use of AI in creative writing is not without its challenges and concerns. Some writers and critics argue that AI-generated writing lacks the depth, nuance, and emotional resonance that characterizes great literature. They worry that relying too heavily on AI tools could lead to a homogenization of creative voices and a loss of the unique perspectives that make human storytelling so powerful.

Despite these concerns, the potential for AI to support and enhance creative writing is immense. By leveraging the power of AI to generate ideas, develop characters, and craft compelling narratives, writers can push the boundaries of their creativity and explore new frontiers in storytelling. The key, as with any tool, is to use AI as a supplement to human imagination and intuition, rather than a replacement for it.

As AI continues to evolve and become more sophisticated, we can expect to see even more innovative applications in the world of creative writing and storytelling. The challenge for writers and the publishing industry will be to find a balance between embracing the power of AI and preserving the essential human element that lies at the heart of all great literature. By working in collaboration with AI tools and algorithms, writers can expand the possibilities of their craft and create stories that resonate with readers on a deeper, more meaningful level.

Subsection 2.4: AI in Architectural and Product Design

The field of architectural and product design has long been driven by human creativity, intuition, and problem-solving skills. However, the integration of artificial intelligence into the design process has opened up new possibilities for generating and optimizing design concepts and solutions. AI-powered tools and algorithms are transforming the way architects and product designers approach their work, streamlining workflows, and pushing the boundaries of what is possible.

One of the most significant applications of AI in architectural design is the generation of novel design concepts. By training AI models on vast datasets of existing designs, floor plans, and 3D models, these tools can create entirely new designs that incorporate the best elements of past projects while introducing fresh and innovative features. For example, the

AI-powered tool "Finch" uses generative design algorithms to create thousands of unique floor plan variations based on user-specified parameters, such as building size, room requirements, and design preferences. This allows architects to explore a wide range of design possibilities in a fraction of the time it would take to generate them manually.

AI is also being used to optimize and refine existing architectural designs. By analyzing factors such as energy efficiency, structural integrity, and occupant comfort, AI algorithms can suggest modifications to improve the overall performance of a building. Tools like "Autodesk Insight" use machine learning to simulate and analyze building performance, identifying areas where improvements can be made to reduce energy consumption, minimize environmental impact, and enhance occupant well-being. This not only helps architects create more sustainable and efficient designs but also enables them to make data-driven decisions throughout the design process.

In the realm of product design, AI is revolutionizing the way designers approach the creation and development of new products. AI-powered generative design tools, such as "Autodesk Fusion 360," allow designers to input design goals and constraints, and then use algorithms to generate hundreds or even thousands of potential design solutions. These solutions can be optimized for various factors, such as strength, weight, and manufacturing feasibility, enabling designers to identify the most promising concepts quickly and efficiently.

AI is also being used to streamline the product design process by automating tasks that were previously time-consuming and labor-intensive. For example, AI-powered tools can automatically generate 3D models from 2D sketches, convert hand-drawn designs into digital files, and even suggest modifications to improve the manufacturability of a product. By leveraging AI to handle these routine tasks, designers can focus their time and energy on the creative and strategic aspects of product development, ultimately leading to more innovative and successful products.

However, the integration of AI in architectural and product design is not without its challenges and concerns. Some designers worry that relying too heavily on AI-generated designs could lead to a homogenization of design aesthetics and a loss of the unique human touch that sets great designs apart. There are also concerns about the potential for AI to displace human designers, particularly in roles that involve repetitive or routine tasks.

Despite these concerns, the potential for AI to enhance and augment human creativity in architectural and product design is immense. By leveraging the power of AI to generate novel ideas, optimize designs, and streamline workflows, designers can push the boundaries of what is possible and create products and buildings that are more innovative, efficient, and responsive to the needs of users. The key, as with any tool, is to use AI as a complement to human creativity and expertise, rather than a replacement for it.

As AI continues to evolve and become more sophisticated, we can expect to see even more groundbreaking applications in the world of architectural and product design. The challenge for designers and the industry as a whole will be to find a balance between embracing the power of AI and preserving the essential human element that lies at the heart of all great design. By working in collaboration with AI tools and algorithms, architects and product designers can unlock new possibilities and create solutions that push the boundaries of what is possible, ultimately shaping a future that is more sustainable, efficient, and responsive to the needs of people and the planet.

Summary: Embracing AI-Assisted Creativity Across Industries

As we have explored throughout this section, the integration of artificial intelligence in content creation has opened up a world of possibilities across various industries. From the visual arts to music composition, and from creative writing to architectural design, AI is proving to be a powerful tool for enhancing and augmenting human creativity.

The examples and applications discussed in this section demonstrate the immense potential of AI to generate novel ideas, streamline workflows, and push the boundaries of what is possible in each field. By leveraging the power of machine learning algorithms and vast datasets, AI can assist human creators in overcoming creative blocks, exploring new artistic territories, and producing content that is both innovative and compelling.

However, it is crucial to recognize that the rise of AI in content creation is not without its challenges and concerns. Questions surrounding the role of human creators, the authenticity of AI-generated content, and the potential for job displacement are valid and must be addressed as we navigate this new landscape.

As we move forward, it is essential to approach the integration of AI in content creation with a balanced perspective. Rather than viewing AI as a replacement for human creativity, we should embrace it as a tool that can enhance and complement our creative abilities. By working in collaboration with AI, human creators can unlock new possibilities, push the boundaries of their respective fields, and ultimately create content that resonates with audiences on a deeper, more meaningful level.

The future of content creation is undoubtedly intertwined with the continued development and application of AI technologies. As these technologies evolve and become more sophisticated, we can expect to see even more groundbreaking and transformative applications across industries. It is up to us, as creators, consumers, and society as a whole, to shape this future in a way that harnesses the power of AI while preserving the essential human element that lies at the heart of all great art and content.

Section 3: Balancing AI Assistance and Human Creative Control

As AI continues to advance and become more deeply integrated into the creative process, it is crucial to strike a balance between leveraging the power of AI assistance and maintaining human creative control. While

AI-powered tools offer immense potential for enhancing creativity and pushing the boundaries of what is possible, it is essential to recognize the unique value that human creators bring to the table.

In this section, we will delve into the importance of finding harmony between AI assistance and human creative control. We will explore the critical role that human judgment, intuition, and emotional intelligence play in the creative process, and how these elements cannot be fully replicated by AI. By understanding the strengths and limitations of both AI and human creators, we can develop strategies for ensuring that the use of AI in creative endeavors augments, rather than diminishes, the human touch.

Moreover, we will examine the ethical considerations surrounding the use of AI in creative processes, such as attribution and intellectual property rights. As AI becomes more sophisticated and capable of generating content that closely resembles human-created work, it is vital to establish clear guidelines and best practices for maintaining authenticity and originality in AI-enhanced creative projects.

By striking the right balance between AI assistance and human creative control, we can harness the power of this transformative technology while preserving the essence of human creativity. In the following subsections, we will explore these ideas in greater depth, offering insights and strategies for navigating this exciting new frontier in the world of creative expression.

Subsection 3.1: The Human Element in AI-Assisted Creativity

As we explore the potential of AI-assisted creativity, it is crucial to recognize the irreplaceable role of human judgment, intuition, and emotional intelligence in the creative process. While AI-powered tools can generate novel ideas, identify patterns, and provide suggestions, the human element remains the driving force behind truly impactful and meaningful creative work.

Human creators possess a unique ability to infuse their creations with personal experiences, cultural influences, and emotional depth. They can draw upon their own lives, relationships, and observations to create art, music, and stories that resonate with audiences on a profound level. This emotional connection is something that AI, despite its advanced capabilities, cannot fully replicate.

Moreover, human judgment plays a critical role in guiding the creative process and making decisions that shape the final outcome. Creators must exercise their discernment to select the most promising ideas generated by AI, refine them, and ensure they align with the intended message or purpose of the work. They must also consider factors such as audience reception, cultural sensitivity, and ethical implications, which require a level of nuance and understanding that AI may struggle to grasp.

Intuition is another essential aspect of human creativity that AI cannot easily emulate. Experienced creators often rely on their gut instincts and subconscious insights to make creative choices that lead to breakthrough ideas and innovations. This intuitive sense, honed through years of practice and experience, allows human creators to navigate the complexities of the creative process and arrive at solutions that AI might overlook.

Furthermore, the human element in AI-assisted creativity extends beyond the individual creator. Collaboration between human creators, each bringing their own unique perspectives and skills to the table, can lead to truly groundbreaking and innovative work. The synergy that arises from human-to-human interaction, the exchange of ideas, and the mutual inspiration that occurs in collaborative settings is something that AI cannot fully replicate.

As we continue to explore the possibilities of AI-assisted creativity, it is essential to remember that the human element is not a hindrance but rather a vital component of the creative process. By leveraging the strengths of both human creators and AI tools, we can unlock new frontiers of creativity and push the boundaries of what is possible. However, we must always keep in mind that the human touch, with its judgment, intuition, and emotional depth, is what ultimately breathes life and meaning into the creative works we produce.

Subsection 3.2: Ensuring Authenticity and Originality

As AI-assisted creativity becomes more prevalent, concerns about the authenticity and originality of AI-enhanced creative works have risen to the forefront. Some critics argue that the use of AI in the creative process diminishes the unique voice and style of human creators, leading to a homogenization of artistic expression. Others worry that AI-generated content may lack the emotional depth and personal touch that defines truly original work.

To address these concerns, it is essential to explore strategies for maintaining authenticity and originality in AI-enhanced creative works. One approach is to view AI as a tool that augments, rather than replaces, human creativity. By using AI to generate ideas, identify patterns, and provide suggestions, human creators can expand their creative horizons and push the boundaries of their artistic vision. However, the final decisions and creative choices should always rest with the human creator, ensuring that their unique perspective and voice shine through in the finished work.

Another strategy for maintaining authenticity and originality is to be transparent about the use of AI in the creative process. By openly acknowledging the role of AI and providing insights into how it was employed, creators can foster trust and understanding among their audience. This transparency allows viewers, listeners, or readers to appreciate the work for what it is—a collaboration between human ingenuity and artificial intelligence—rather than feeling misled or deceived.

It is also crucial for human creators to actively cultivate their own unique style and voice, even when working with AI. By continuously honing their skills, experimenting with new techniques, and drawing inspiration from diverse sources, creators can ensure that their work remains distinctive and original. AI should be seen as a means to enhance and complement this personal style, not to replace it.

Furthermore, the use of AI in the creative process should be guided by strong ethical principles. Creators must ensure that they have the necessary rights and permissions to use any data or input that feeds into the AI system. They should also be mindful of potential biases or limitations in the AI algorithms and take steps to mitigate these issues. By adhering to high ethical standards, creators can maintain the integrity and authenticity of their work, even as they embrace the possibilities of AI-assisted creativity.

Ultimately, the key to ensuring authenticity and originality in AI-enhanced creative works lies in striking a balance between leveraging the power of AI and preserving the unique human touch. By using AI as a tool to augment their skills, being transparent about its role, cultivating a distinctive personal style, and upholding strong ethical principles, human creators can harness the potential of AI while maintaining the integrity and originality of their work. As we navigate this new frontier of creativity, it is essential to remember that authenticity and originality are not inherent qualities of the tools we use, but rather the result of the choices we make and the vision we bring to our creative endeavors.

Subsection 3.3: Ethical Considerations in AI-Assisted Creativity

As AI becomes increasingly integrated into the creative process, it is crucial to examine the ethical implications that arise from this collaboration. Two key areas of concern are attribution and intellectual property rights, which must be carefully navigated to ensure fairness, transparency, and respect for the contributions of both human creators and AI systems.

Attribution is a fundamental ethical consideration in AI-assisted creativity. When an AI system plays a significant role in the creation of a piece of art, music, or literature, it raises questions about who should be credited for the work. Some argue that the human creator should receive sole credit, as they are the ones who initiated and guided the creative process. Others believe that the AI system should also be acknowledged, as its contributions are integral to the final outcome. Striking the right balance in attribution is essential to maintain transparency and give due recognition to all parties involved.

Closely related to attribution is the issue of intellectual property rights. As AI systems become more sophisticated and capable of generating creative works that rival those of human creators, it becomes increasingly difficult to determine who owns the rights to these creations. Should the human creator be considered the sole owner, or does the AI system and its developers also have a claim to the intellectual property? This question becomes even more complex when considering AI systems that are trained on vast datasets of existing creative works, potentially absorbing and reproducing elements of those works in their own creations.

To address these ethical challenges, it is essential to develop clear guidelines and frameworks for attribution and intellectual property rights in AI-assisted creativity. This may involve establishing new legal precedents and adapting existing copyright laws to account for the unique nature of AI-generated content. It may also require collaboration between human creators, AI developers, and legal experts to devise fair and equitable solutions that respect the contributions of all parties involved.

Another ethical consideration in AI-assisted creativity is the potential for AI systems to perpetuate biases and reinforce existing inequalities. If an AI system is trained on a dataset that lacks diversity or contains biased representations, it may generate creative works that reflect and amplify those biases. This can lead to the marginalization of certain groups and the reinforcement of harmful stereotypes. To mitigate this risk, it is crucial to ensure that the datasets used to train AI systems are diverse, inclusive, and representative of the full spectrum of human experiences and perspectives.

Furthermore, the use of AI in creative processes raises questions about the authenticity and originality of the resulting works. Some critics argue that AI-generated content lacks the emotional depth and personal touch that defines truly original and authentic creative expression. Others worry that the widespread use of AI in creativity may lead to a homogenization of artistic styles and a loss of individual voice. To address these concerns, it is important to emphasize the role of human creators in guiding and shaping the output of AI systems, ensuring that the final works reflect their unique perspectives and artistic visions.

As we navigate the ethical landscape of AI-assisted creativity, it is essential to approach these challenges with thoughtfulness, nuance, and a commitment to fairness and transparency. By developing robust ethical frameworks, fostering open dialogue between stakeholders, and prioritizing the values of diversity, inclusivity, and authenticity, we can harness the power of AI to enhance and expand the boundaries of human creativity while upholding the fundamental principles of artistic integrity and respect for all those involved in the creative process.

Summary: Balancing the Power of AI with the Essence of Human Creativity

As we have explored throughout this section, the integration of AI into the creative process presents both exciting opportunities and complex challenges. While AI-powered tools offer immense potential for enhancing and augmenting human creativity, it is crucial to strike a delicate balance between leveraging the capabilities of AI and preserving the unique value of human creative control.

The human element—with its judgment, intuition, and emotional depth—remains an irreplaceable component of the creative process. It is the human touch that breathes life, meaning, and authenticity into the works we create, even as we embrace the possibilities of AI-assisted creativity. By recognizing the strengths and limitations of both human creators and AI systems, we can develop strategies for collaboration that harness the power of technology while respecting the essence of human creativity.

Central to this balance is the need for transparency, ethical considerations, and a commitment to originality. As we navigate the uncharted waters of

AI-assisted creativity, we must establish clear guidelines for attribution, intellectual property rights, and the mitigation of biases. We must also actively cultivate our own unique styles and voices, ensuring that the works we produce reflect our individual perspectives and creative visions.

Ultimately, the key to successfully balancing AI assistance and human creative control lies in approaching this new frontier with thoughtfulness, nuance, and a deep appreciation for the value of human ingenuity. By fostering open dialogue, developing robust ethical frameworks, and prioritizing the principles of authenticity and originality, we can unlock the full potential of AI-assisted creativity while safeguarding the integrity of the creative process.

As we move forward into an increasingly AI-driven creative landscape, it is essential to remember that the goal is not to replace human creativity, but rather to enhance and expand its boundaries. By striking the right balance between AI assistance and human creative control, we can usher in a new era of artistic expression—one that celebrates the unique contributions of both human and machine, and pushes the limits of what is possible in the realm of creative endeavor.

Section 4: Fostering a Symbiotic Relationship Between AI and Human Creators

As we have explored the potential of AI to enhance human creativity, it is crucial to consider how we can cultivate a mutually beneficial partnership between AI and human creators. The relationship between AI and human creativity should not be viewed as a competition, but rather as an opportunity for collaboration and growth. By fostering a symbiotic relationship, we can unlock new possibilities and push the boundaries of what is achievable in the creative realm.

To truly harness the power of AI-assisted creativity, it is essential to develop a deep understanding of how AI can complement and augment human creative processes. This requires a shift in mindset, moving away from the notion of AI as a threat to human creativity and instead embracing it as a valuable tool and collaborator. By exploring the ways in which AI can support and enhance human creative endeavors, we can begin to build a foundation for a productive and mutually beneficial partnership.

In this section, we will delve into the various strategies and approaches for fostering a symbiotic relationship between AI and human creators. From education and training initiatives to collaborative platforms and communities, we will examine the key components necessary for building a strong and sustainable partnership. By showcasing successful examples of AI-human creative collaborations, we will demonstrate the immense potential of this symbiotic relationship and inspire readers to embrace the possibilities of AI-enhanced creativity.

As we look to the future, it is clear that the integration of AI into the creative process will only continue to grow and evolve. By proactively fostering a symbiotic relationship between AI and human creators, we can shape this future in a way that benefits both parties and leads to unprecedented levels of creativity and innovation. Let us embark on this journey together, exploring the ways in which we can cultivate a mutually beneficial partnership and unlock the full potential of AI-enhanced human creativity.

Subsection 4.1: Education and Training for AI-Assisted Creativity

To foster a symbiotic relationship between AI and human creators, it is crucial to invest in education and training initiatives that empower individuals to effectively leverage AI tools in their creative processes. By equipping creators with the necessary knowledge and skills, we can unlock the full potential of AI-assisted creativity and promote a more collaborative and productive partnership between humans and machines.

One key aspect of education and training for AI-assisted creativity is developing a deep understanding of the capabilities and limitations of AI tools. This involves learning about the underlying algorithms, data sets, and techniques used in AI-powered creative software, as well as exploring the various ways in which these tools can be applied to different creative disciplines. By gaining a comprehensive understanding of how AI works, human creators can make informed decisions about when and how to incorporate AI into their creative workflows, ensuring that they use these tools in a manner that complements and enhances their own skills and expertise.

Another important component of education and training for AI-assisted creativity is developing the skills necessary to effectively collaborate with AI tools. This includes learning how to provide clear and specific prompts to guide the AI's output, as well as understanding how to interpret and refine the results generated by the AI. By mastering these skills, human creators can work more efficiently and effectively with AI tools, leveraging their strengths while mitigating their weaknesses.

In addition to technical skills, education and training initiatives should also focus on fostering a creative mindset that embraces experimentation, iteration, and collaboration. Encouraging human creators to view AI as a partner in the creative process, rather than a competitor or replacement, can help to break down barriers and promote a more open and collaborative approach to AI-assisted creativity. This may involve providing opportunities for creators to work on projects that specifically incorporate AI tools, as well as facilitating discussions and workshops that explore the creative possibilities of human-AI collaboration.

To support these education and training efforts, it is essential to develop a range of resources and programs that cater to different skill levels and creative disciplines. This may include online courses, tutorials, and webinars that provide a comprehensive introduction to AI-assisted creativity, as well as more advanced workshops and masterclasses that delve into specific techniques and applications. By offering a diverse range of learning opportunities, we can ensure that creators from all backgrounds and experience levels have access to the knowledge and skills they need to effectively leverage AI tools in their creative work.

Ultimately, by investing in education and training initiatives that empower human creators to work effectively with AI tools, we can foster a more symbiotic and mutually beneficial relationship between AI and human creativity. By equipping creators with the necessary knowledge and skills, we can unlock new possibilities for creative expression and innovation, while also ensuring that the unique strengths and perspectives of human creators remain at the forefront of the creative process.

Subsection 4.2: Collaborative Platforms and Communities

The development of collaborative platforms and communities is crucial for fostering a symbiotic relationship between AI and human creators. These platforms serve as virtual spaces where creators can connect, share ideas, and work together on projects that leverage the strengths of both human creativity and AI-powered tools. By bringing together individuals with diverse backgrounds, skills, and perspectives, these communities facilitate the exchange of knowledge, inspiration, and best practices, ultimately driving innovation and pushing the boundaries of what is possible in the realm of AI-assisted creativity.

One of the primary benefits of collaborative platforms is that they provide a centralized hub for creators to access a wide range of AI tools, resources, and tutorials. These platforms often feature integrated AI-powered software, such as image generators, music composition tools, and writing assistants, which creators can use to enhance their projects and explore new creative possibilities. By consolidating these tools in a single, user-friendly interface, collaborative platforms make it easier for creators to experiment with AI and incorporate it into their workflows, regardless of their technical expertise.

In addition to providing access to AI tools, collaborative platforms also foster a sense of community among creators. Through forums, chat rooms, and social features, these platforms encourage creators to connect with one another, share their work, and provide feedback and support. This sense of community is particularly valuable for creators who are new to AI-assisted creativity, as it provides a safe and welcoming space to ask questions, seek guidance, and learn from more experienced practitioners. By cultivating a culture of openness, collaboration, and mutual respect, these communities help to break down barriers and promote a more inclusive and accessible approach to AI-enhanced creativity.

Collaborative platforms also play a crucial role in showcasing the potential of AI-human creative collaborations. Many of these platforms feature galleries, portfolios, and case studies that highlight successful projects and demonstrate the innovative ways in which creators are leveraging AI tools to push the boundaries of their respective fields. By celebrating these success stories and providing a platform for creators to share their work, collaborative communities help to inspire others and drive the adoption of AI-assisted creativity across a wide range of industries and disciplines.

As the field of AI-assisted creativity continues to evolve, the development of collaborative platforms and communities will become increasingly important. These platforms will need to adapt to new technologies, tools, and creative practices, while also fostering a culture of experimentation, collaboration, and lifelong learning. By investing in the growth and sustainability of these communities, we can ensure that creators have the support, resources, and inspiration they need to thrive in an era of AI-enhanced creativity.

Ultimately, the success of collaborative platforms and communities will depend on their ability to bring together diverse groups of creators, developers, and enthusiasts who share a common vision for the future of AI-assisted creativity. By fostering a spirit of collaboration, innovation, and mutual support, these communities have the potential to transform the way we think about creativity and pave the way for a new era of human-AI collaboration that unleashes the full potential of both human ingenuity and artificial intelligence.

Subsection 4.3: Showcasing Successful AI-Human Creative Collaborations

As we explore the potential of AI-human collaboration in creative endeavors, it is essential to highlight examples of successful projects that demonstrate the power of this symbiotic relationship. These case studies serve as a testament to the incredible possibilities that arise when human creativity and artificial intelligence work together in harmony. By examining these success stories, we can gain valuable insights into the strategies, techniques, and mindsets that facilitate effective AI-human collaboration and inspire others to embrace this innovative approach to creative work.

One remarkable example of AI-human collaboration in the creative realm is the "Lost Tapes of the 27 Club" project by Over the Bridge, a Toronto-based organization dedicated to supporting musicians' mental health. The project aimed to raise awareness about the prevalence of mental health issues in the music industry by using AI to create new songs in the style of famous musicians who tragically died at the age of 27, such as Jimi Hendrix, Amy Winehouse, and Kurt Cobain. The AI system analyzed the artists' musical catalogs, including their lyrics, melodies, and rhythms, to generate new compositions that captured their distinctive styles. Human musicians then recorded and produced the tracks, bringing the AI-generated music to life.

The result was a collection of hauntingly beautiful songs that paid homage to the legacy of these iconic artists while sparking a meaningful conversation about mental health in the music industry. The project received widespread acclaim for its innovative approach and emotional impact, demonstrating the power of AI-human collaboration to create art that resonates with audiences on a profound level.

Another striking example of successful AI-human collaboration in the creative domain is the "Unfinished" project by composer Hubert Léveillé Gauvin. In this project, Gauvin used AI to complete unfinished compositions by classical music legends such as Mozart, Beethoven, and

Schubert. By training the AI system on the composers' existing works and musical styles, Gauvin was able to generate new passages that seamlessly blended with the original compositions, creating complete and cohesive pieces of music.

The "Unfinished" project showcases the potential of AI to augment and enhance human creativity by providing new ideas and inspiration. Rather than replacing human composers, the AI system served as a collaborator, offering suggestions and possibilities that Gauvin could then refine and incorporate into the final compositions. The project received high praise from classical music enthusiasts and critics alike, who marveled at the AI's ability to capture the essence of these iconic composers' styles while adding a fresh and innovative twist.

These examples demonstrate the incredible potential of AI-human collaboration in the creative realm. By leveraging the strengths of both human creativity and artificial intelligence, these projects were able to achieve results that would have been difficult, if not impossible, for either humans or AI to accomplish alone. The success of these collaborations highlights the importance of fostering a symbiotic relationship between AI and human creators, one that is characterized by mutual respect, open-mindedness, and a willingness to experiment and take risks.

As we move forward into an era of increasingly sophisticated AI technologies, it is crucial that we continue to explore and celebrate successful examples of AI-human collaboration in the creative domain. By doing so, we can inspire others to embrace this innovative approach to creative work and unlock new possibilities for artistic expression and innovation. Through the power of AI-human collaboration, we can push the boundaries of what is possible in the creative realm and create art that moves, inspires, and transforms us in ways we never thought possible.

Subsection 4.4: Envisioning the Future of AI-Enhanced Human Creativity

As we stand at the precipice of a new era in creative endeavors, it is essential to look towards the future and envision the potential developments and implications of AI in enhancing human creativity. The rapid advancements in AI technology, coupled with the growing acceptance and adoption of AI-assisted creative tools, suggest that the landscape of creativity is poised for a significant transformation in the coming years.

One of the most exciting prospects for the future of AI-enhanced human creativity is the emergence of more sophisticated and intuitive AI tools that seamlessly integrate with the creative process. As AI algorithms become more advanced and capable of understanding complex creative contexts, we can expect to see the development of AI-powered tools that not only generate ideas and content but also adapt to the unique styles, preferences, and workflows of individual creators. These tools will likely feature user-friendly interfaces and customizable settings, allowing creators to fine-tune the AI's output to suit their specific needs and goals.

Another potential future development in AI-enhanced human creativity is the increased collaboration between AI and human creators across various disciplines. As the stigma surrounding AI-generated content continues to dissipate and more creators recognize the value of AI as a creative partner, we can anticipate the formation of interdisciplinary teams that bring together human expertise and AI capabilities to push the boundaries of what is possible in fields such as art, music, literature, and design. These collaborations may lead to the creation of entirely new forms of expression and the emergence of hybrid creative practices that blend human intuition with AI-driven innovation.

The future of AI-enhanced human creativity also holds the promise of democratizing access to creative tools and resources. As AI technologies become more widely available and affordable, individuals from diverse backgrounds and skill levels will have the opportunity to harness the power of AI to express their creativity and bring their ideas to life. This increased accessibility may lead to a surge in creative output and the emergence of new voices and perspectives in the creative landscape, ultimately enriching the cultural tapestry of our society.

However, the future of AI-enhanced human creativity also raises important questions and challenges that will need to be addressed. One of the most pressing concerns is the issue of intellectual property rights and attribution in an era where AI plays an increasingly significant role in the creative process. As AI-generated content becomes more prevalent and sophisticated, there may be a need for new legal frameworks and guidelines to ensure that the contributions of both human creators and AI are properly recognized and protected.

Another challenge that may arise in the future of AI-enhanced human creativity is the potential for AI to perpetuate biases and reinforce existing inequalities in the creative industries. As AI tools learn from existing creative works and datasets, there is a risk that they may inherit and amplify the biases and limitations present in those sources. To mitigate this risk, it will be crucial to develop AI systems that are trained on diverse and inclusive datasets and to foster a culture of critical reflection and accountability among creators who use AI tools.

Despite these challenges, the future of AI-enhanced human creativity holds immense promise and potential. As we continue to explore and harness the power of AI in creative endeavors, we have the opportunity to push the boundaries of what is possible and create works that inspire, engage, and transform audiences in ways we never thought possible. By fostering a symbiotic relationship between AI and human creators, we can unlock new avenues for creative expression and innovation, ultimately shaping a future in which the unique strengths of both human ingenuity and artificial intelligence are celebrated and leveraged to their fullest potential.

Summary: Embracing the Symbiotic Future of AI and Human Creativity

As we have explored throughout this section, fostering a symbiotic relationship between AI and human creators is crucial for unlocking the full potential of AI-enhanced creativity. By investing in education and training initiatives, collaborative platforms and communities, and showcasing successful AI-human collaborations, we can cultivate a mutually beneficial partnership that pushes the boundaries of creative expression and innovation.

The future of AI-enhanced human creativity is filled with exciting possibilities and challenges. As AI technologies continue to advance and become more integrated into the creative process, we can anticipate the emergence of more sophisticated tools, interdisciplinary collaborations, and democratized access to creative resources. However, we must also be mindful of the ethical considerations and potential biases that may arise as AI plays an increasingly significant role in shaping our creative landscape.

Ultimately, the key to fostering a symbiotic relationship between AI and human creators lies in embracing a mindset of collaboration, experimentation, and lifelong learning. By recognizing the unique strengths and limitations of both human creativity and artificial intelligence, we can work together to create a future in which the two are not in competition, but rather in harmony, each complementing and enhancing the other.

As we move forward into this new era of AI-enhanced creativity, it is essential that we approach the challenges and opportunities with an open mind, a willingness to adapt, and a commitment to ensuring that the benefits of this symbiotic relationship are shared by all. By doing so, we can not only overcome the stigma surrounding AI-generated content but also unlock a world of creative possibilities that we have only begun to imagine.

Chapter Summary: Embracing AI as a Creative Partner

As we have explored throughout this chapter, AI has the potential to revolutionize the way we approach creativity and content creation. By leveraging the power of artificial intelligence, human creators can enhance their creative processes, overcome obstacles, and generate novel ideas and solutions. The synergy between AI and human creativity is not about replacing human ingenuity but rather augmenting it, allowing creators to push the boundaries of what is possible.

Across various industries, from the visual arts to music composition, creative writing, and design, AI-powered tools are already being used to assist and inspire human creators. These tools serve as creative collaborators, helping to generate fresh perspectives, streamline workflows, and open up new avenues for artistic expression. However, it is crucial to maintain a balance between AI assistance and human creative control, ensuring that the final products remain authentic, original, and imbued with the unique touch of human emotion and intuition.

As we move forward, fostering a symbiotic relationship between AI and human creators will be key to unlocking the full potential of AI-enhanced creativity. This will require ongoing education and training, the development of collaborative platforms and communities, and the showcasing of successful AI-human creative collaborations. By embracing AI as a creative partner, we can usher in a new era of creativity, one in which the combined strengths of human imagination and artificial intelligence lead to unprecedented levels of innovation and artistic expression.

The future of creativity is not about humans versus machines but rather about the exciting possibilities that arise when we work hand in hand with AI. As we continue to explore and refine the use of AI in creative processes, we will undoubtedly discover new ways to push the boundaries of what is possible, ultimately redefining the very nature of creativity itself.

Chapter 6: The Future of AI-Generated Content

As we stand on the precipice of a new era in content creation, it is impossible to ignore the rapid advancements in artificial intelligence (AI) and its potential to revolutionize the way we produce and consume information. The rise of AI-generated content has already begun to reshape industries, from journalism and marketing to entertainment and beyond. However, amidst the excitement and promise of this technological revolution, a lingering stigma persists, casting a shadow over the future of AI-generated content.

In the previous chapters, we explored the roots of this stigma, examining the concerns surrounding creativity, authenticity, bias, and misinformation. We also discussed the potential for AI to augment and enhance human creativity, rather than replace it entirely. As we move forward, it is crucial to envision the future developments and implications of AI-generated content, both in terms of the technological advancements that will shape its evolution and the societal and economic impacts that will follow in its wake.

The future of AI-generated content is one of boundless possibility, where the lines between human and machine creativity blur, and the potential for innovation knows no limits. However, it is also a future fraught with challenges and uncertainties, as we grapple with the ethical considerations and responsibilities that come with the increasing prevalence of AI in our lives.

In this chapter, we will embark on a journey into the future of AI-generated content, exploring the technological advancements that will drive its development, the emerging applications and use cases that will reshape industries, and the societal and economic implications that will follow. We will also discuss strategies and approaches for individuals and organizations to prepare for this new era of content creation, fostering human-AI collaboration, investing in AI literacy and education, and developing ethical and responsible AI practices.

As we navigate this uncharted territory, it is essential to approach the future of AI-generated content with an open mind, embracing the opportunities it presents while remaining vigilant to the challenges that lie ahead. Only by understanding and addressing the stigma surrounding AI-generated content can we fully harness its potential to transform the way we create, consume, and interact with information in the years to come.

Section 1: Technological Advancements in AI Content Generation

Imagine a world where artificial intelligence (AI) has become so sophisticated that it can generate content indistinguishable from that created by humans. As we stand on the precipice of this technological revolution, it's crucial to explore the potential future developments in AI-generated content and the implications they may have on our society.

In recent years, AI has made remarkable strides in various domains, from natural language processing and computer vision to machine learning and deep learning. These advancements have paved the way for more sophisticated and nuanced AI-generated content, capable of understanding and mimicking human creativity in unprecedented ways.

As we delve into this section, we will embark on a journey to uncover the cutting-edge research and innovations that are shaping the future of AI content generation. From the development of advanced language models that can generate coherent and contextually relevant text to the integration of multimodal AI systems that can create immersive and interactive experiences, we will explore the limitless possibilities that lie ahead.

But with great power comes great responsibility. As AI continues to evolve and permeate every aspect of our lives, it is essential to consider the ethical implications and potential consequences of relying on machine-generated content. Will AI-generated content ultimately surpass human creativity, or will it serve as a powerful tool to augment and enhance our creative abilities?

Throughout this section, we will grapple with these questions and more, as we examine the technological advancements that are redefining the boundaries of what is possible with AI-generated content. So, buckle up and get ready to explore the exciting and uncharted territory that awaits us in the future of AI content generation.

Subsection 1.1: Improved Natural Language Processing and Understanding

As artificial intelligence continues to evolve, one of the most significant advancements that will shape the future of AI-generated content is the improvement in natural language processing (NLP) and understanding. NLP is a branch of AI that focuses on the interaction between computers and human language, enabling machines to comprehend, interpret, and generate human-like text.

In recent years, NLP has made remarkable strides, thanks to the development of advanced machine learning algorithms and the availability of vast amounts of linguistic data. Deep learning models, such as transformer-based architectures like BERT (Bidirectional Encoder Representations from Transformers) and GPT (Generative Pre-trained Transformer), have revolutionized the field of NLP by achieving state-of-the-art performance in various language tasks, including sentiment analysis, named entity recognition, and language translation.

These advancements in NLP have laid the foundation for more sophisticated and contextually relevant AI-generated content. With improved natural language understanding, AI systems can now grasp the nuances and complexities of human language, allowing them to generate text that is more coherent, fluent, and semantically meaningful.

One of the key challenges in NLP has been the ability to capture and understand the context in which language is used. Context plays a crucial role in determining the meaning and intent behind words and phrases, and it is essential for generating content that is relevant and appropriate for a given situation. Recent advancements in NLP, such as the development of context-aware language models, have enabled AI systems to better understand and incorporate contextual information into their generated content.

For example, OpenAI's GPT-3 (Generative Pre-trained Transformer 3) has demonstrated remarkable capabilities in generating human-like text by leveraging its understanding of context and its ability to draw from a vast knowledge base. GPT-3 can generate coherent and contextually relevant responses to prompts, ranging from creative writing and poetry to technical articles and code snippets.

Another significant advancement in NLP is the ability to handle and generate content in multiple languages. Multilingual NLP models, such as Google's BERT and Facebook's XLM (Cross-lingual Language Model), have enabled AI systems to understand and generate text across different languages, breaking down language barriers and facilitating the creation of content for a global audience.

As NLP continues to evolve, we can expect AI-generated content to become increasingly sophisticated, nuanced, and contextually relevant. AI systems will be able to understand and mimic the subtleties of human language, such as sarcasm, humor, and emotional undertones, making the generated content more engaging and relatable to readers.

Furthermore, advancements in NLP will enable AI to generate content that is tailored to specific audiences, taking into account factors such as age, education level, cultural background, and personal preferences. This personalization of AI-generated content will enhance the user experience and make the content more valuable and impactful for individual readers.

However, it is important to acknowledge that while improved NLP and natural language understanding will undoubtedly enhance the quality and relevance of AI-generated content, it also raises concerns about the potential misuse of this technology. As AI systems become more adept at generating human-like text, there is a risk of AI-generated content being used for malicious purposes, such as spreading misinformation, propaganda, or fake news.

To mitigate these risks, it is crucial to develop robust ethical guidelines and regulations governing the use of AI in content generation. Transparency, accountability, and responsible deployment of AI systems will be essential in ensuring that the benefits of improved NLP are harnessed while minimizing the potential negative consequences.

In conclusion, the advancements in NLP and natural language understanding will play a pivotal role in shaping the future of AI-generated content. As AI systems become more sophisticated in their ability to comprehend and generate human language, we can expect AI-generated content to become increasingly indistinguishable from human-created content, opening up new possibilities for content creation and personalization. However, it is crucial to approach these advancements with caution and ensure that the development and deployment of NLP-powered AI systems are guided by strong ethical principles to maximize the benefits while mitigating the risks.

Subsection 1.2: Enhanced Machine Learning Algorithms and Architectures

The rapid advancement of machine learning algorithms and architectures is a key driver behind the evolution of AI-generated content. As these technologies continue to improve, AI systems are becoming increasingly capable of creating more sophisticated, nuanced, and contextually relevant content across various domains, from text and images to audio and video.

One of the most significant developments in machine learning for AI content generation is the rise of deep learning algorithms. Deep learning is a subset of machine learning that utilizes artificial neural networks with multiple layers to learn and represent complex patterns in data. These algorithms have proven to be particularly effective in tasks such as natural language processing, computer vision, and speech recognition, which are crucial for generating high-quality AI content.

Convolutional Neural Networks (CNNs) have revolutionized the field of computer vision, enabling AI systems to understand and generate visual content with unprecedented accuracy. CNNs are designed to automatically learn hierarchical representations of visual data, allowing them to identify and generate intricate patterns and features in images and videos. This has led to remarkable advancements in tasks such as image classification, object detection, and image generation, paving the way for more realistic and diverse AI-generated visual content.

Recurrent Neural Networks (RNNs), particularly Long Short-Term Memory (LSTM) networks, have been instrumental in advancing natural language processing and text generation. These algorithms are designed to process sequential data, such as text, by maintaining an internal memory state that allows them to capture long-term dependencies and context. This enables AI systems to generate more coherent, contextually relevant, and linguistically accurate text, making AI-generated content more engaging and human-like.

Generative Adversarial Networks (GANs) have emerged as a groundbreaking architecture for AI content generation, particularly in the domain of image and video synthesis. GANs consist of two neural networks – a generator and a discriminator – that compete against each other in a game-theoretic framework. The generator learns to create realistic content, while the discriminator learns to distinguish between real and generated content. Through this adversarial training process, GANs can generate highly realistic and diverse content, pushing the boundaries of what is possible with AI-generated media.

Transformer-based architectures, such as the Generative Pre-trained Transformer (GPT) series and the Bidirectional Encoder Representations from Transformers (BERT) model, have set new standards in natural language processing and text generation. These architectures leverage the self-attention mechanism to capture long-range dependencies in text, enabling them to generate highly coherent and contextually relevant content. GPT-3, for example, has demonstrated remarkable capabilities in generating human-like text across a wide range of domains, from creative writing to technical articles, with minimal fine-tuning.

As machine learning algorithms and architectures continue to evolve, we can expect AI-generated content to become increasingly indistinguishable from human-created content. However, this rapid advancement also raises important ethical considerations, such as the potential for AI-generated content to be used for malicious purposes, like spreading disinformation or engaging in intellectual property infringement.

To address these concerns, researchers and developers must prioritize the responsible development and deployment of machine learning technologies. This includes incorporating ethical considerations into the design and training of AI systems, ensuring transparency and accountability in the use of AI-generated content, and developing robust methods for detecting and mitigating the spread of malicious AI-generated content.

In conclusion, the evolution of machine learning algorithms and architectures is a critical factor in shaping the future of AI-generated content. As these technologies continue to advance, we can anticipate AI systems that are capable of creating increasingly sophisticated, diverse, and human-like content across various modalities. However, it is crucial to approach these advancements with caution and ensure that the development and deployment of AI content generation systems are guided by strong ethical principles to maximize the benefits while minimizing the potential risks.

Subsection 1.3: Integration of Multimodal AI Systems

As AI technology continues to advance, the integration of various AI modalities, such as computer vision, speech synthesis, and natural language processing, is becoming increasingly important in creating more immersive and interactive AI-generated content. This fusion of different AI systems has the potential to revolutionize the way we experience and engage with digital content, blurring the lines between reality and virtual environments.

One of the most exciting prospects of multimodal AI integration is the creation of AI-generated virtual agents that can interact with users in a more natural and intuitive manner. By combining computer vision, speech recognition, and natural language understanding, these virtual agents can perceive and respond to user actions, emotions, and intentions in real-time. This level of interactivity can greatly enhance user engagement and create more personalized experiences, whether in virtual reality games, educational simulations, or customer service applications.

The integration of computer vision and speech synthesis is another promising area for AI-generated content. Imagine a virtual world where AI-generated characters not only look realistic but also speak with human-like voices and express emotions through facial expressions and body language. This level of realism can greatly enhance the immersive experience and create a stronger emotional connection between users and AI-generated characters.

Moreover, the integration of multimodal AI systems can enable the creation of AI-generated content that adapts to user preferences and behavior in real-time. For example, an AI-powered virtual reality game could analyze a user's playstyle, skill level, and emotional state using computer vision and biometric data, and dynamically adjust the game difficulty, narrative, and visual elements to create a more engaging and personalized experience.

However, the integration of multimodal AI systems also presents significant challenges and ethical considerations. One of the main challenges is ensuring the seamless integration and synchronization of different AI modalities to create a coherent and believable experience. This requires advanced algorithms and architectures that can handle the complexity and diversity of multimodal data, as well as robust evaluation metrics to assess the quality and effectiveness of the integrated AI systems.

Another important consideration is the potential impact of multimodal AI-generated content on user privacy and security. As AI systems become more adept at analyzing and interpreting user data across multiple modalities, there is a risk of misuse or unauthorized access to sensitive personal information. Therefore, it is crucial to develop strong data protection and privacy measures, as well as transparent and accountable AI governance frameworks, to ensure the responsible development and deployment of multimodal AI systems.

Furthermore, the integration of multimodal AI systems raises important questions about the nature of reality and the boundaries between the virtual and the real. As AI-generated content becomes increasingly realistic and immersive, it may become more difficult for users to distinguish between what is real and what is artificial. This blurring of boundaries can have significant psychological and social implications, such as the potential for addiction, escapism, or the erosion of social skills and relationships.

To address these challenges and ensure the responsible development of multimodal AI-generated content, it is essential to foster multidisciplinary collaboration between AI researchers, content creators, psychologists, ethicists, and policymakers. This collaboration can help to identify and mitigate potential risks, develop best practices and guidelines for the ethical use of multimodal AI systems, and promote public awareness and dialogue about the implications of this emerging technology.

In conclusion, the integration of multimodal AI systems represents a significant opportunity for creating more immersive and interactive AI-generated content. By combining various AI modalities, such as computer vision, speech synthesis, and natural language processing, we can create AI-generated experiences that are more realistic, engaging, and personalized than ever before. However, this integration also presents significant challenges and ethical considerations that must be carefully addressed to ensure the responsible development and deployment of multimodal AI systems. As we continue to push the boundaries of what is possible with AI-generated content, it is crucial to remain mindful of the potential risks and benefits, and to work collaboratively towards a future where multimodal AI systems can enhance our lives and experiences in a safe, ethical, and inclusive manner.

Subsection 1.4: Developments in Computational Creativity

As artificial intelligence continues to advance, one of the most fascinating areas of research is computational creativity – the study of how machines can exhibit creative behavior and generate novel, original content. This field has seen significant progress in recent years, with AI systems demonstrating the ability to create art, music, poetry, and even scientific discoveries. These advancements in computational creativity are poised to have a profound impact on the future of AI-generated content, challenging our understanding of creativity and pushing the boundaries of what machines can achieve.

At the heart of computational creativity lies the question of whether creativity is a uniquely human trait or if it can be replicated and even surpassed by machines. Traditionally, creativity has been associated with human intelligence, intuition, and imagination. However, as AI systems become more sophisticated, they are beginning to exhibit traits that resemble human creativity, such as the ability to generate novel ideas, make unexpected connections, and adapt to new situations.

One of the key developments in computational creativity is the use of generative models, such as Generative Adversarial Networks (GANs) and Variational Autoencoders (VAEs). These models are designed to learn the underlying patterns and structures in a given dataset and then generate new content that resembles the original data. For example, GANs have been used to create highly realistic images, such as portraits of non-existent people or landscapes that blend elements from different scenes. By training on vast amounts of data, these generative models can capture the essence of creativity and produce content that is both novel and aesthetically pleasing.

Another important aspect of computational creativity is the ability to combine different domains and modalities to create new forms of content.

This is exemplified by the emergence of AI systems that can generate content across multiple mediums, such as text, images, and music. For instance, OpenAI's DALL-E model can generate images from textual descriptions, while Google's Magenta project has developed AI systems that can compose music and create visual art. These multimodal AI systems demonstrate the potential for machines to exhibit creativity in ways that transcend traditional boundaries and open up new possibilities for AI-generated content.

However, the development of computational creativity also raises important questions about the nature of creativity itself. Some argue that true creativity requires intentionality, emotion, and a deep understanding of the world, which machines may lack. Others contend that creativity is not a binary concept and that machines can exhibit varying degrees of creative behavior, even if they do not possess the same level of self-awareness or intentionality as humans.

As computational creativity continues to advance, it is likely to have a significant impact on the future of AI-generated content. On one hand, it could lead to an explosion of new and innovative forms of content, from personalized virtual experiences to AI-generated art and entertainment. On the other hand, it may also raise concerns about the role of human creativity and the potential for machines to displace human content creators.

To navigate these challenges, it is essential to develop a deeper understanding of computational creativity and its implications for society. This requires collaboration between researchers, artists, and policymakers to ensure that the development of creative AI systems is guided by ethical principles and respects the value of human creativity. It also calls for public education and dialogue to help people understand the potential benefits and risks of AI-generated content and to foster a culture of responsible innovation.

In conclusion, the progress in computational creativity research represents a significant milestone in the evolution of AI-generated content. As machines become increasingly capable of exhibiting creative behavior and generating novel, original content, we are likely to see a transformation in the way we create, consume, and interact with digital media. However, this transformation also raises important questions about the nature of creativity, the role of human content creators, and the ethical implications of AI-generated content. By addressing these challenges head-on and fostering a culture of responsible innovation, we can harness the potential of computational creativity to enrich our lives and expand the boundaries of what is possible with AI-generated content.

Summary: Embracing the Future of AI-Generated Content

As we explore the technological advancements in AI content generation, it becomes clear that we are on the cusp of a new era in creative expression. The rapid progress in natural language processing, machine learning algorithms, and multimodal AI systems is paving the way for AI-generated content that is more sophisticated, nuanced, and human-like than ever before.

The potential implications of these advancements are vast and far-reaching. From personalized virtual experiences and immersive entertainment to AI-assisted creative problem-solving and scientific discovery, the possibilities are truly endless. As AI systems become more adept at understanding and mimicking human creativity, we may see a blurring of the lines between human-created and AI-generated content, challenging our very notions of authorship and originality.

However, with great power comes great responsibility. As we embrace the future of AI-generated content, we must also grapple with the ethical considerations and potential risks that come with it. Issues such as data privacy, intellectual property rights, and the spread of misinformation must be carefully addressed to ensure that the benefits of AI-generated content are realized while minimizing the potential harms.

Ultimately, the key to unlocking the full potential of AI-generated content lies in fostering a culture of responsible innovation and collaboration. By bringing together researchers, content creators, ethicists, and policymakers, we can develop a framework for the ethical development and deployment of AI systems that respects the value of human creativity while harnessing the power of machine intelligence.

As we stand on the precipice of this technological revolution, it is up to us to shape the future of AI-generated content. By embracing the possibilities and addressing the challenges head-on, we can create a world where AI and human creativity work hand in hand to push the boundaries of what is possible and enrich our lives in ways we never thought possible. The future of AI-generated content is bright, and it is ours to shape.

Section 2: Emerging Applications and Use Cases

As the capabilities of AI continue to expand and evolve, the potential applications and use cases for AI-generated content are becoming increasingly diverse and far-reaching. From virtual assistants and chatbots to personalized content recommendations and immersive entertainment experiences, the future of AI-generated content is brimming with exciting possibilities.

In this section, we will embark on a fascinating exploration of the emerging applications and use cases for AI-generated content across various industries. By examining the cutting-edge developments and innovative implementations of AI technology, we will gain valuable insights into how AI is poised to revolutionize the way we create, consume, and interact with content in the years to come.

As we delve into the realm of AI-powered virtual assistants and chatbots, we will discover how these intelligent agents are transforming customer service, education, and personal assistance, offering unprecedented levels of efficiency, convenience, and personalization. We will also explore the potential for AI to revolutionize content recommendation systems, delivering highly tailored and engaging content to users based on their individual preferences and behaviors.

Moreover, we will venture into the captivating world of immersive entertainment, where AI is playing an increasingly crucial role in creating interactive and engaging experiences across video games, virtual reality, and augmented reality. We will also examine how AI is being harnessed to support creative problem-solving processes in fields such as design, engineering, and scientific research, unlocking new possibilities for innovation and discovery.

By the end of this section, you will have a comprehensive understanding of the vast array of emerging applications and use cases for AI-generated content, and how these developments are poised to shape the future of various industries. So, let us embark on this exciting journey together and explore the boundless potential of AI in the realm of content creation and consumption.

Subsection 2.1: AI-Generated Virtual Assistants and Chatbots

In the realm of customer service, education, and personal assistance, AI-powered virtual assistants and chatbots are poised to revolutionize the way we interact with technology and access information. As natural language processing (NLP) and machine learning algorithms continue to advance, these intelligent agents will become increasingly sophisticated, offering users a more intuitive, efficient, and personalized experience.

One of the most promising applications of AI-generated virtual assistants and chatbots lies in the customer service industry. By leveraging the power of AI, businesses can provide 24/7 support to their customers, addressing queries, resolving issues, and offering guidance in real-time. These AI-powered agents can handle a vast array of customer interactions, from simple FAQs to more complex troubleshooting scenarios, freeing up human representatives to focus on higher-level tasks that require emotional intelligence and critical thinking.

In the education sector, AI-generated virtual assistants and chatbots have the potential to transform the way students learn and access information. These intelligent tutors can provide personalized learning experiences, adapting to each student's unique needs, learning style, and pace. By engaging students in natural, conversational interactions, AI-powered educational assistants can break down complex concepts, offer targeted feedback, and guide learners through challenging topics, ultimately enhancing their understanding and retention of knowledge.

Moreover, AI-generated virtual assistants are set to become increasingly prevalent in our daily lives, serving as personal companions and task managers. These intelligent agents can help users navigate their schedules, provide reminders, offer recommendations, and even engage in casual conversation, creating a more seamless and intuitive interface between humans and technology. As these AI-powered assistants become more attuned to our individual preferences and behaviors, they will be able to anticipate our needs and proactively offer support, making our lives more efficient and convenient.

However, the development and deployment of AI-generated virtual assistants and chatbots also raise important ethical considerations. As these agents become more human-like in their interactions, it is crucial to ensure that users are aware they are engaging with an AI system and not a human representative. Additionally, developers must prioritize the security and privacy of user data, implementing robust measures to protect sensitive information shared during conversations with AI-powered assistants.

As we look to the future, the potential for AI-generated virtual assistants and chatbots is vast and exciting. By harnessing the power of AI, we can create more engaging, efficient, and personalized experiences across a wide range of industries and applications. As these technologies continue to evolve and mature, they will undoubtedly reshape the way we interact with information, services, and each other, ushering in a new era of human-machine collaboration and communication.

Subsection 2.2: AI-Driven Personalized Content

Recommendations

In the age of information overload, where countless articles, videos, and social media posts compete for our attention, the ability to deliver personalized content recommendations has become increasingly valuable. As AI technologies continue to advance, the potential for revolutionizing content recommendation systems and providing users with highly tailored and engaging content is immense.

At the heart of AI-driven personalized content recommendations lies the power of machine learning algorithms. These algorithms analyze vast amounts of user data, including browsing history, search queries, and engagement metrics, to identify patterns and preferences unique to each individual. By leveraging this data, AI systems can build comprehensive user profiles that capture the nuances of each person's interests, behaviors, and content consumption habits.

One of the key advantages of AI-driven content recommendation systems is their ability to adapt and evolve in real-time. As users interact with content, providing implicit and explicit feedback through clicks, likes, and shares, the AI algorithms continuously learn and refine their understanding of individual preferences. This dynamic learning process ensures that the recommendations remain relevant and up-to-date, even as user interests shift over time.

The potential applications of AI-driven personalized content recommendations are vast and far-reaching. In the realm of news and media, AI can help curate personalized news feeds, presenting users with articles and stories that align with their interests and preferences. This not only enhances the user experience by delivering more engaging and relevant content but also helps combat the echo chamber effect by exposing users to a diverse range of perspectives and ideas.

In the entertainment industry, AI-powered recommendation systems are already transforming the way we discover and consume content. Streaming platforms like Netflix and Spotify employ sophisticated AI algorithms to analyze user viewing and listening habits, generating personalized recommendations that keep users engaged and satisfied. As these systems become more advanced, they will be able to predict user preferences with even greater accuracy, potentially even suggesting content before users realize they want it.

E-commerce is another domain where AI-driven personalized recommendations are poised to make a significant impact. By analyzing user browsing and purchase history, AI algorithms can suggest products and services that are tailored to each individual's needs and preferences. This not only enhances the shopping experience for customers but also helps businesses increase sales and build brand loyalty by delivering highly targeted and relevant recommendations.

However, the implementation of AI-driven personalized content recommendations also raises important ethical considerations. As these systems become more sophisticated, there is a risk of creating "filter bubbles" where users are only exposed to content that reinforces their existing beliefs and biases. It is crucial for developers and content providers to ensure that AI algorithms are designed to promote diversity and expose users to a wide range of perspectives, fostering a more balanced and inclusive information ecosystem.

Moreover, the collection and use of user data for personalized recommendations raise concerns about privacy and data security. As AI systems become more reliant on user data to generate accurate recommendations, it is essential to establish robust data protection measures and transparent data usage policies. Users should have control over their data and the ability to opt-out of personalized recommendations if desired.

As we look to the future, the potential for AI-driven personalized content recommendations is immense. By harnessing the power of machine learning and data analytics, these systems have the potential to transform the way we discover, consume, and engage with content across various industries. However, it is crucial to approach this technology with a balanced perspective, addressing the ethical considerations and ensuring that the benefits of personalization are realized while mitigating the potential risks.

As AI continues to evolve and mature, we can expect to see even more sophisticated and nuanced content recommendation systems emerge. By leveraging advances in natural language processing, sentiment analysis, and contextual understanding, these systems will be able to deliver even more precise and relevant recommendations, taking into account not only individual preferences but also the broader context in which content is consumed.

Ultimately, the success of AI-driven personalized content recommendations will depend on the ability of developers, content providers, and users to work together in shaping this technology. By fostering a collaborative and transparent approach, we can harness the power of AI to enhance our content discovery experiences while ensuring that the recommendations we receive are diverse, inclusive, and aligned with our values and interests.

Subsection 2.3: AI in Immersive Entertainment Experiences

The world of entertainment is undergoing a remarkable transformation, and AI is at the forefront of this revolution. As technology continues to advance, AI is playing an increasingly crucial role in creating interactive and immersive entertainment experiences that captivate audiences like never before. From video games to virtual reality (VR) and augmented reality (AR), AI is reshaping the way we engage with and consume entertainment content.

One of the most significant applications of AI in immersive entertainment is in the realm of video games. Game developers are harnessing the power of AI to create more dynamic, responsive, and personalized gaming experiences. By employing techniques such as procedural content generation, AI algorithms can generate vast, ever-changing game worlds that offer players a unique experience every time they play. This not only enhances replayability but also allows for the creation of more diverse and engaging game environments.

Moreover, AI is being used to develop more sophisticated non-player characters (NPCs) that can interact with players in more natural and believable ways. Through the use of advanced natural language processing and machine learning techniques, NPCs can engage in dynamic conversations, respond to player actions, and adapt their behavior based on the player's choices and playstyle. This level of interactivity creates a more immersive and emotionally engaging gaming experience, blurring the lines between the virtual and real worlds.

In the realm of virtual reality, AI is playing a pivotal role in creating more realistic and immersive experiences. By leveraging AI-powered computer vision and object recognition technologies, VR systems can track user movements and gestures with unprecedented accuracy, allowing for more intuitive and natural interactions within virtual environments. This enhanced level of immersion enables users to explore and manipulate virtual objects as if they were real, creating a more convincing and engaging experience.

AI is also being used to generate more realistic and responsive virtual characters within VR experiences. By analyzing user behavior and preferences, AI algorithms can create virtual companions that adapt to the user's actions and provide personalized interactions. This level of responsiveness and adaptability creates a more intimate and emotionally engaging experience, fostering a deeper connection between the user and the virtual world.

Augmented reality, which overlays digital information onto the real world, is another area where AI is making significant strides. AI-powered AR systems can recognize and track real-world objects in real-time, allowing for the seamless integration of digital content with the physical environment. This enables the creation of more interactive and context-aware AR experiences, such as interactive product demonstrations, immersive educational content, and engaging entertainment applications.

Furthermore, AI is being used to develop more intelligent and responsive AR characters that can interact with users in real-time. By analyzing user behavior and environmental cues, AI algorithms can create AR companions that provide personalized guidance, entertainment, and assistance. This level of interactivity and responsiveness creates a more engaging and immersive AR experience, blurring the boundaries between the digital and physical worlds.

As AI continues to evolve and mature, we can expect to see even more advanced and immersive entertainment experiences emerge. The integration of AI with technologies such as haptic feedback, brain-computer interfaces, and advanced sensory stimulation will create even more realistic and engaging experiences that blur the lines between reality and virtual worlds.

However, the development and deployment of AI in immersive entertainment also raise important ethical considerations. As these experiences become more realistic and emotionally engaging, it is crucial to ensure that users are aware of the boundaries between the virtual and real worlds. Additionally, developers must prioritize the safety and well-being of users, implementing safeguards to prevent potential negative impacts, such as addiction or psychological distress.

As we look to the future, the potential for AI in immersive entertainment is vast and exciting. By harnessing the power of AI, we can create more engaging, personalized, and emotionally resonant experiences that transport users to new worlds and push the boundaries of what is possible. As these technologies continue to evolve and mature, they will undoubtedly reshape the entertainment landscape, ushering in a new era of interactive and immersive experiences that captivate and inspire audiences like never before.

Subsection 2.4: AI-Assisted Creative Problem Solving

In the realms of design, engineering, and scientific research, creative problem-solving is a crucial skill that drives innovation and progress. As

AI technologies continue to advance, the potential for AI to support and enhance creative problem-solving processes is becoming increasingly apparent. By leveraging the power of machine learning, data analysis, and intelligent algorithms, AI-assisted creative problem-solving has the potential to revolutionize the way we approach complex challenges and develop groundbreaking solutions.

At its core, creative problem-solving involves the ability to think outside the box, generate novel ideas, and find innovative solutions to complex problems. Traditionally, this process has relied heavily on human intuition, experience, and domain expertise. However, with the advent of AI, we now have the opportunity to augment and enhance these human capabilities, creating a powerful synergy between human creativity and machine intelligence.

One of the key ways in which AI can support creative problem-solving is through the analysis of vast amounts of data. In fields such as engineering and scientific research, the volume of available data is often overwhelming, making it difficult for humans to identify patterns, trends, and insights that could lead to breakthroughs. By employing AI algorithms to process and analyze this data, researchers and engineers can uncover hidden relationships, identify promising avenues for exploration, and generate data-driven insights that can inform creative problem-solving efforts.

For example, in the field of drug discovery, AI-powered systems can analyze massive datasets of molecular structures and biological pathways to identify potential drug candidates that may have been overlooked by human researchers. By leveraging machine learning algorithms to predict the efficacy and safety of these compounds, AI can help accelerate the drug discovery process and enable researchers to focus their creative problem-solving efforts on the most promising leads.

In the realm of design, AI can play a significant role in supporting creative problem-solving by generating novel design concepts and exploring a wider range of possibilities. Generative AI algorithms, such as generative adversarial networks (GANs) and variational autoencoders (VAEs), can be trained on existing design datasets to learn the underlying patterns and principles of successful designs. These AI systems can then generate new design concepts that combine and recombine these learned patterns in novel ways, leading to innovative and unexpected solutions.

For instance, in the field of architecture, AI-assisted design tools can generate a diverse range of building layouts and configurations based on specific design constraints and objectives. By exploring a vast design space and proposing unconventional solutions, AI can inspire architects to think beyond traditional design paradigms and develop creative, efficient, and sustainable building designs that push the boundaries of what is possible.

Moreover, AI can support creative problem-solving by facilitating collaboration and knowledge sharing among diverse teams of experts. In today's complex and interdisciplinary research and development landscape, effective collaboration is essential for tackling multifaceted challenges and developing innovative solutions. AI-powered collaboration platforms can help bridge the gaps between different domains of expertise, enabling researchers, designers, and engineers to share knowledge, exchange ideas, and build upon each other's insights in real-time.

By leveraging natural language processing and machine learning algorithms, AI-assisted collaboration tools can automatically organize and structure the wealth of information generated during collaborative problem-solving sessions. These tools can identify key concepts, extract relevant insights, and suggest connections between seemingly disparate ideas, helping teams to navigate the creative problem-solving process more efficiently and effectively.

However, it is important to recognize that AI-assisted creative problem-solving is not a replacement for human creativity and expertise. Rather, it is a powerful tool that can augment and enhance human capabilities, enabling us to tackle more complex challenges and develop more innovative solutions. The true potential of AI in creative problem-solving lies in the synergistic collaboration between human and machine intelligence, where the intuition, experience, and creativity of human experts are complemented by the data-driven insights, computational power, and exploratory capabilities of AI systems.

As we look to the future, the potential for AI-assisted creative problem-solving is vast and exciting. By harnessing the power of AI, we can accelerate the pace of innovation, uncover new frontiers of knowledge, and develop groundbreaking solutions to some of the world's most pressing challenges. However, it is crucial that we approach this technology with a balanced perspective, recognizing both its potential benefits and limitations, and ensuring that the development and deployment of AI-assisted creative problem-solving tools are guided by ethical considerations and a commitment to human-centered design.

Ultimately, the success of AI-assisted creative problem-solving will depend on our ability to foster a collaborative and interdisciplinary approach, bringing together experts from diverse fields to leverage the power of AI in service of human creativity and ingenuity. By embracing this technology as a tool for augmenting and enhancing human capabilities, we can unlock new possibilities for innovation and progress, and create a future in which the boundaries of what is possible are constantly expanding.

Summary: Harnessing the Power of AI for Innovative Content Creation and Interaction

As we have explored throughout this section, the emerging applications and use cases for AI-generated content are both vast and transformative. From AI-powered virtual assistants and chatbots that revolutionize customer service and education to personalized content recommendations that deliver highly tailored and engaging experiences, the potential for AI to reshape the way we create, consume, and interact with content is truly remarkable.

The integration of AI in immersive entertainment experiences, such as video games, virtual reality, and augmented reality, is pushing the boundaries of what is possible, blurring the lines between the virtual and real worlds. By creating more dynamic, responsive, and emotionally engaging experiences, AI is transforming the entertainment landscape and captivating audiences like never before.

Moreover, AI-assisted creative problem-solving is opening up new frontiers of innovation and progress, enabling researchers, designers, and engineers to tackle complex challenges and develop groundbreaking solutions. By leveraging the power of machine learning, data analysis, and intelligent algorithms, AI is augmenting human creativity and expertise, leading to a powerful synergy between human ingenuity and machine intelligence.

As we look to the future, it is clear that the potential for AI-generated content is limitless. However, it is crucial that we approach this technology with a balanced perspective, recognizing both its immense benefits and potential risks. By fostering a collaborative and interdisciplinary approach, and ensuring that the development and deployment of AI-generated content are guided by ethical considerations and a commitment to human-centered design, we can harness the power of AI to create a future where innovation, creativity, and progress thrive.

The journey ahead is filled with exciting possibilities and challenges, as we navigate the uncharted waters of AI-generated content. By embracing this technology as a tool for augmenting and enhancing human capabilities, we can unlock new frontiers of expression, engagement, and problem-solving, and create a world where the boundaries of what is possible are constantly expanding. As we continue to explore the emerging applications and use cases for AI-generated content, let us approach this transformative technology with curiosity, creativity, and a steadfast commitment to shaping a future that benefits all of humanity.

Section 3: Societal and Economic Implications

As AI-generated content continues to advance and permeate various aspects of our lives, it is crucial to consider the profound societal and economic implications that these developments may bring. The rapid evolution of AI technology has the potential to disrupt industries, transform the job market, and reshape the way we create, consume, and value content. In this section, we will delve into the far-reaching consequences of AI-generated content on our society and economy, exploring both the opportunities and challenges that lie ahead.

The rise of AI-generated content raises important questions about the future of work and the role of human creativity in an increasingly automated world. Will the widespread adoption of AI-powered content creation tools lead to job displacement, or will it open up new avenues for collaboration between humans and machines? As we navigate this uncharted territory, it is essential to consider the potential impacts on employment, skill demand, and income inequality.

Moreover, the proliferation of AI-generated content presents complex challenges related to intellectual property rights, copyright, and content ownership. As machines become more adept at creating original works, traditional legal frameworks may need to adapt to address the blurring lines between human and AI-generated content. This section will explore the evolving landscape of intellectual property in the age of AI and discuss the implications for creators, consumers, and policymakers.

Furthermore, the increasing prevalence of AI-generated content raises important ethical and regulatory considerations. As AI systems become more sophisticated in their ability to generate persuasive and emotionally resonant content, there is a growing concern about the potential for manipulation, misinformation, and the erosion of public trust. This section will examine the ethical responsibilities of developers, deployers, and users of AI-generated content, as well as the role of governance and regulation in ensuring transparency, accountability, and fairness.

By exploring these critical societal and economic implications, we aim to provide a comprehensive understanding of the challenges and opportunities that lie ahead as AI-generated content continues to shape our world. Through thoughtful analysis and informed discussion, we can work towards a future in which the benefits of AI-powered content creation are harnessed for the greater good while mitigating potential risks and negative consequences.

Subsection 3.1: Transformations in the Creative Industries

The advancements in AI-generated content are poised to revolutionize the creative industries, including advertising, media, and entertainment. As AI technologies become more sophisticated and capable of producing high-quality content, traditional models of content creation and distribution are being disrupted, paving the way for new opportunities and challenges.

In the advertising industry, AI-powered tools are already being used to generate ad copy, design layouts, and optimize targeting strategies. With the ability to analyze vast amounts of data and create personalized content at scale, AI has the potential to transform the way advertisers engage with their audiences. However, this shift also raises concerns about the role of human creativity and the potential for AI-generated ads to manipulate consumer behavior.

Similarly, the media industry is grappling with the implications of AI-generated content. From news articles to social media posts, AI algorithms are increasingly being used to create and curate content, raising questions about the credibility and objectivity of machine-generated journalism. While AI can help media organizations scale their content production and reach wider audiences, it also poses challenges related to fact-checking, editorial control, and the potential for the spread of misinformation.

In the entertainment industry, AI is being harnessed to create new forms of immersive and interactive experiences. From AI-generated music and art to personalized movie recommendations and virtual reality environments, AI is pushing the boundaries of what is possible in storytelling and audience engagement. However, the rise of AI-generated entertainment also raises concerns about the future of human creativity and the potential for machines to replace human artists and performers.

As these creative industries navigate the transformative potential of AI-generated content, they will need to grapple with a range of ethical, legal, and societal implications. This may involve developing new frameworks for intellectual property rights, establishing guidelines for the responsible use of AI in content creation, and fostering collaboration between human creators and AI systems.

Ultimately, the transformations brought about by AI-generated content in the creative industries will require a delicate balance between embracing the benefits of these technologies and preserving the value of human creativity and expertise. By proactively addressing these challenges and opportunities, the creative industries can harness the power of AI to drive innovation, engage audiences in new ways, and push the boundaries of what is possible in the realm of content creation.

Subsection 3.2: Shifts in the Job Market and Skill Demand

As AI-generated content becomes increasingly prevalent across various industries, it is crucial to consider the potential impact on the job market and the shifting demand for skills. The rise of AI in content creation has sparked concerns about job displacement, particularly in roles that involve repetitive or formulaic tasks. However, it is essential to recognize that while some jobs may become automated, the integration of AI-generated content is also likely to create new opportunities and reshape the skills required in the workforce.

One of the most significant changes we can expect to see is a growing demand for professionals who possess a combination of creative and technical skills. As AI takes over more routine content creation tasks, the value of human creativity, critical thinking, and emotional intelligence will become increasingly important. Roles that require a deep understanding of AI systems, the ability to work alongside them, and the capacity to leverage their outputs to create compelling, engaging content will be in high demand.

For example, content strategists and editors who can curate and refine AI-generated content to ensure its quality, relevance, and alignment with brand voice will be essential. Similarly, designers and developers who can create AI-powered tools and platforms that streamline content creation processes will be highly sought after. The ability to collaborate effectively with AI systems, interpret their outputs, and make informed decisions based on data-driven insights will be a key skill in the future job market.

Moreover, the rise of AI-generated content will likely lead to the emergence of entirely new roles and specializations. Just as the digital revolution gave rise to positions like social media managers and data analysts, the AI era may create jobs such as AI content curators, AI ethics officers, and AI-human collaboration specialists. These roles will focus on ensuring the responsible and effective use of AI in content creation, addressing ethical concerns, and fostering productive partnerships between human creators and AI systems.

To thrive in this evolving landscape, professionals will need to adopt a mindset of continuous learning and adaptability. Investing in the development of both technical and soft skills, such as emotional intelligence, creativity, and critical thinking, will be crucial. Educational institutions and employers will need to adapt their curricula and training programs to equip the workforce with the skills necessary to navigate the AI-driven content creation landscape effectively.

Furthermore, the shift towards AI-generated content will likely have broader implications for the structure of work and the nature of employment. As AI systems become more capable of handling a wider range of content creation tasks, we may see a rise in freelance and project-based work, with professionals collaborating with AI tools to deliver high-quality content on-demand. This shift may require a reevaluation of traditional employment models and a greater emphasis on skills-based hiring and compensation.

In conclusion, while the increasing prevalence of AI-generated content may disrupt certain aspects of the job market, it also presents significant opportunities for professionals who can adapt and acquire the necessary skills. By fostering a culture of continuous learning, embracing the potential of human-AI collaboration, and proactively addressing the ethical and social implications of this technological shift, we can navigate the changing job market and harness the power of AI to drive innovation and growth in the content creation industry.

Subsection 3.3: Implications for Intellectual Property and Copyright

The rapid advancement of AI-generated content has sparked a heated debate about the future of intellectual property rights and copyright law. As machines become increasingly capable of creating original works, questions arise about who owns the rights to these creations and how existing legal frameworks can adapt to accommodate this new reality.

Traditionally, copyright law has been designed to protect the rights of human creators, granting them exclusive control over the distribution, reproduction, and adaptation of their works. However, the rise of AI-generated content challenges these fundamental principles, as it becomes increasingly difficult to determine the extent of human involvement in the creative process.

One of the primary concerns is the question of authorship and ownership. When an AI system generates a piece of content, who is considered the author? Is it the programmer who designed the algorithm, the user who provided the input data, or the AI itself? These questions have far-reaching implications for the allocation of intellectual property rights and the ability to monetize AI-generated content.

Moreover, the ease with which AI systems can generate vast amounts of content raises concerns about the potential for copyright infringement and the dilution of existing works. As AI algorithms become more adept at analyzing and mimicking human-created content, there is a risk that they may inadvertently reproduce copyrighted material without proper attribution or permission.

To address these challenges, legal experts and policymakers are exploring various approaches to adapt intellectual property law for the age of AI. Some argue for the creation of new legal categories, such as "computer-generated works," which would grant limited protections to

AI-generated content while preserving the rights of human creators. Others propose the development of licensing frameworks that would allow for the fair use and remuneration of AI-generated content.

However, these solutions are not without their own complications. Establishing clear guidelines for the attribution and ownership of AI-generated content may require a fundamental rethinking of copyright law and a delicate balancing of the interests of human creators, AI developers, and the public at large.

Despite these challenges, the rise of AI-generated content also presents significant opportunities for innovation and creativity. By leveraging the power of AI to generate new works, human creators can explore novel forms of expression and push the boundaries of what is possible in fields such as art, music, and literature. Moreover, the ability to generate personalized content at scale has the potential to revolutionize industries such as advertising, gaming, and education.

To fully realize these opportunities, it is crucial that intellectual property law evolves in tandem with technological advancements. This may involve the development of new legal frameworks that recognize the unique characteristics of AI-generated content while still protecting the rights of human creators. It may also require a shift in societal attitudes towards the value and authenticity of machine-generated works.

Ultimately, the implications of AI-generated content for intellectual property and copyright are complex and far-reaching. As we navigate this uncharted territory, it is essential that we engage in open and inclusive dialogue, bringing together the perspectives of creators, technologists, legal experts, and policymakers. Only by working together can we develop a framework that balances the benefits of AI-powered innovation with the need to protect the rights and livelihoods of human creators.

Subsection 3.4: Ethical and Regulatory Considerations

As AI-generated content becomes increasingly prevalent and sophisticated, it is crucial to address the ethical and regulatory challenges that arise in this rapidly evolving landscape. The development and deployment of AI systems for content creation raise important questions about transparency, accountability, and fairness, which must be carefully considered to ensure the responsible and beneficial use of this technology.

One of the primary ethical concerns surrounding AI-generated content is the potential for bias and discrimination. AI algorithms learn from the data they are trained on, and if this data contains inherent biases, the resulting content may perpetuate or amplify these biases. For example, if an AI system is trained on a dataset that underrepresents certain demographic groups or contains stereotypical associations, it may generate content that reflects these biases, leading to the marginalization or misrepresentation of those groups. To mitigate this risk, it is essential to develop and implement rigorous processes for data collection, curation, and auditing to ensure that the training data is diverse, representative, and free from discriminatory patterns.

Another critical ethical consideration is the issue of transparency and explainability. As AI systems become more complex and autonomous, it can be challenging to understand how they arrive at specific outputs or decisions. This lack of transparency can make it difficult to identify and rectify errors, biases, or unintended consequences in AI-generated content. To address this challenge, there is a growing emphasis on developing explainable AI (XAI) techniques, which aim to make the decision-making processes of AI systems more interpretable and understandable to human users. By promoting transparency and explainability, we can foster greater trust in AI-generated content and enable more effective oversight and accountability.

Accountability is another key ethical and regulatory concern in the context of AI-generated content. When an AI system generates content that is inaccurate, harmful, or biased, it can be difficult to determine who bears responsibility for these outputs. Is it the developer of the AI system, the organization deploying it, or the end-user who relies on the generated content? Establishing clear frameworks for accountability is essential to ensure that the potential harms of AI-generated content are minimized and that there are effective mechanisms for redress when issues arise. This may involve the development of industry standards, ethical guidelines, and legal frameworks that delineate the responsibilities and liabilities of different stakeholders in the AI content generation process.

Fairness is also a critical consideration in the regulation of AI-generated content. As AI systems become more prevalent in content creation and dissemination, there is a risk that they may exacerbate existing inequalities or create new forms of discrimination. For example, if AI-powered content recommendation algorithms prioritize content that reinforces dominant cultural narratives or favors certain demographic groups, they may limit exposure to diverse perspectives and experiences. To promote fairness in AI-generated content, it is important to develop and implement algorithmic fairness techniques, which seek to ensure that AI systems treat different groups equitably and do not perpetuate or amplify societal biases.

To address these ethical and regulatory challenges, there is a growing recognition of the need for multi-stakeholder collaboration and governance frameworks. This may involve the development of industry-wide ethical standards, the establishment of independent oversight bodies, and the creation of legal and regulatory frameworks that balance the benefits and risks of AI-generated content. Governments, industry leaders, civil society organizations, and academic experts must work together to develop and implement these governance mechanisms, ensuring that they are informed by diverse perspectives and grounded in democratic values.

In conclusion, the ethical and regulatory considerations surrounding AI-generated content are complex and multifaceted, requiring ongoing dialogue, research, and collaboration to navigate effectively. By proactively addressing issues of transparency, accountability, and fairness, and by developing robust governance frameworks, we can harness the transformative potential of AI-generated content while mitigating its risks and ensuring that it benefits society as a whole. As we move forward in this rapidly evolving landscape, it is essential that we remain vigilant, adaptable, and committed to the responsible and ethical development and deployment of AI technologies in the realm of content creation.

Summary: Navigating the Transformative Impact of AI-Generated Content

The rise of AI-generated content is poised to have far-reaching societal and economic implications, transforming industries, reshaping the job market, and raising critical questions about intellectual property rights and ethical responsibilities. As we navigate this uncharted territory, it is essential to approach these challenges and opportunities with a balanced perspective, recognizing both the potential benefits and risks of this technological revolution.

The creative industries, such as advertising, media, and entertainment, are at the forefront of this transformation, as AI-powered tools and algorithms increasingly automate and augment content creation processes. While these advancements offer the potential for increased efficiency, personalization, and innovation, they also raise concerns about the role of human creativity and the potential for AI-generated content to manipulate or mislead audiences. Striking the right balance between harnessing the power of AI and preserving the value of human expertise will be crucial in shaping the future of these industries.

Moreover, the widespread adoption of AI-generated content will have significant implications for the job market and the skills in demand. As certain roles become automated, new opportunities will emerge for professionals who can effectively collaborate with AI systems, leveraging their outputs to create compelling and engaging content. Fostering a culture of continuous learning and adaptability will be essential in preparing the workforce for this evolving landscape.

The rise of AI-generated content also presents complex challenges related to intellectual property rights and copyright law. As machines become increasingly capable of creating original works, traditional legal frameworks may need to adapt to address questions of authorship, ownership, and fair use. Developing new legal categories and licensing frameworks that recognize the unique characteristics of AI-generated content while protecting the rights of human creators will be a critical step forward.

Finally, the ethical and regulatory considerations surrounding AI-generated content cannot be overlooked. Ensuring transparency, accountability, and fairness in the development and deployment of AI systems is essential to mitigating potential harms and promoting the responsible use of this technology. Multi-stakeholder collaboration and governance frameworks will be necessary to navigate these challenges effectively.

As we move forward in this rapidly evolving landscape, it is crucial to approach the societal and economic implications of AI-generated content with a proactive and inclusive mindset. By engaging in open dialogue, fostering collaboration between human creators and AI systems, and developing robust ethical and regulatory frameworks, we can harness the transformative potential of this technology while mitigating its risks. The path ahead may be uncertain, but by working together, we can shape a future in which AI-generated content enhances human creativity, drives innovation, and benefits society as a whole.

Section 4: Preparing for the Future of AI-Generated Content

As we stand on the precipice of a new era in content creation, it is crucial to recognize that the future of AI-generated content is not a distant concept but a rapidly approaching reality. The advancements in artificial intelligence and machine learning are poised to revolutionize the way we create, consume, and interact with content across various industries. However, with these exciting possibilities come new challenges and uncertainties that individuals and organizations must navigate to fully harness the potential of AI-generated content.

In this section, we will explore the strategies and approaches that both individuals and organizations can adopt to prepare for the future of AI-generated content. By proactively addressing the challenges and embracing the opportunities presented by this technological shift, we can position ourselves to thrive in a world where human creativity and artificial intelligence seamlessly intertwine.

As we delve into the various aspects of preparing for the future of AI-generated content, we will examine the importance of fostering human-AI collaboration, investing in AI literacy and education, embracing adaptability and lifelong learning, and developing ethical and responsible AI practices. By understanding and implementing these strategies, we can not only mitigate the potential risks associated with AI-generated content but also unlock its full potential to enhance our creative endeavors and drive innovation across industries.

So, let us embark on this journey together, exploring the ways in which we can proactively shape the future of AI-generated content and ensure that it serves as a powerful tool for human creativity, rather than a replacement for it. By embracing the change and preparing ourselves for the challenges and opportunities that lie ahead, we can navigate this exciting new landscape with confidence and optimism, ready to harness the full potential of AI-generated content in the years to come.

Subsection 4.1: Fostering Human-AI Collaboration

As we navigate the uncharted waters of AI-generated content, it becomes increasingly clear that the key to success lies not in pitting human creativity against artificial intelligence, but in fostering a collaborative relationship between the two. By developing the skills and strategies necessary for effective human-AI collaboration, we can harness the power of AI to enhance and augment human creativity, rather than replace it.

One of the first steps in fostering human-AI collaboration is to recognize that AI is a tool, not a threat. Just as the invention of the printing press or the computer revolutionized the way we create and disseminate content,

AI has the potential to unlock new frontiers of creativity and innovation. By embracing AI as a partner in the creative process, we can leverage its strengths, such as its ability to process vast amounts of data or generate multiple variations of an idea, to enhance our own creative output.

To effectively collaborate with AI, it is essential to develop a deep understanding of its capabilities and limitations. This requires investing time and resources into AI literacy, learning about the various types of AI systems, their underlying algorithms, and their potential applications in content creation. By demystifying AI and gaining a realistic understanding of what it can and cannot do, we can make informed decisions about when and how to incorporate AI into our creative workflows.

Effective human-AI collaboration also requires a willingness to experiment and adapt. As with any new technology, there will be a learning curve and a period of trial and error as we figure out the best ways to integrate AI into our creative processes. This may involve rethinking traditional roles and workflows, and being open to new ways of working that leverage the strengths of both human and machine intelligence.

One promising approach to human-AI collaboration is the concept of "co-creation," where humans and AI systems work together in an iterative, back-and-forth process to generate new ideas and refine existing ones. For example, a human writer could use an AI-powered writing assistant to generate multiple variations of a story premise, then select and refine the most promising ones based on their own creative judgment. The AI system could then further develop those ideas, incorporating the human's feedback and preferences, until a final, polished story emerges.

To facilitate effective co-creation, it is important to develop tools and interfaces that allow for seamless communication and interaction between humans and AI systems. This may involve creating intuitive, user-friendly platforms that allow creators to easily input their ideas, preferences, and feedback, and receive AI-generated suggestions and variations in return. By designing these tools with the needs and workflows of human creators in mind, we can create a more natural and efficient collaboration process.

Ultimately, the goal of human-AI collaboration is not to replace human creativity, but to augment and enhance it. By leveraging the power of AI to generate new ideas, explore multiple possibilities, and handle repetitive or time-consuming tasks, human creators can focus on what they do best: bringing their unique perspective, judgment, and emotional intelligence to bear on the creative process. In this way, human-AI collaboration has the potential to unlock new levels of creativity and innovation, leading to more compelling, engaging, and meaningful content for audiences around the world.

Subsection 4.2: Investing in AI Literacy and Education

As AI-generated content becomes increasingly prevalent in our daily lives, it is crucial to recognize the importance of investing in AI literacy and education programs. These initiatives are designed to help individuals understand the fundamentals of artificial intelligence, its capabilities, limitations, and potential implications for society. By equipping people with the knowledge and skills necessary to engage with AI-generated content critically and effectively, we can foster a more informed and empowered public.

One of the primary goals of AI literacy programs is to demystify the concept of artificial intelligence. For many individuals, AI may seem like a complex and intimidating topic, shrouded in technical jargon and futuristic scenarios. However, by breaking down the basic principles of AI, such as machine learning, natural language processing, and computer vision, educators can help learners develop a foundational understanding of how these technologies work and how they are applied in various contexts.

AI literacy programs should also address the ethical and societal implications of AI-generated content. As AI systems become more advanced and autonomous, it is essential for individuals to understand the potential risks and challenges associated with these technologies, such as bias, privacy concerns, and the spread of misinformation. By exploring these issues through case studies, discussions, and hands-on activities, learners can develop the critical thinking skills necessary to navigate the complex landscape of AI-generated content responsibly.

In addition to providing a theoretical foundation, AI literacy programs should also offer practical skills and experiences. This may involve teaching learners how to interact with AI-powered tools and platforms, such as chatbots, recommendation systems, or content creation software. By gaining hands-on experience with these technologies, individuals can develop a more intuitive understanding of how AI-generated content is produced and how it can be leveraged effectively in various contexts.

To ensure the widest possible reach and impact, AI literacy initiatives should be designed to cater to diverse audiences, including students, professionals, and the general public. This may involve developing age-appropriate curricula for K-12 education, integrating AI literacy modules into higher education programs, and offering accessible online courses and workshops for adult learners. By meeting people where they are and providing tailored learning experiences, educators can help bridge the knowledge gap and empower individuals to engage with AI-generated content confidently.

Moreover, AI literacy programs should be developed and delivered in collaboration with a range of stakeholders, including educational institutions, industry partners, and government agencies. By fostering cross-sector partnerships and knowledge sharing, we can ensure that AI literacy initiatives are informed by the latest research, best practices, and real-world applications. This collaborative approach can also help to identify and address any gaps or challenges in existing educational frameworks, ensuring that AI literacy becomes a core component of 21st-century education.

Ultimately, investing in AI literacy and education is not just about preparing individuals to navigate the challenges and opportunities presented by AI-generated content. It is also about fostering a more informed and engaged citizenry, one that is equipped to participate actively in shaping the future of AI and its impact on society. By empowering people with the knowledge, skills, and critical thinking abilities necessary to understand and engage with AI-generated content, we can ensure that the benefits of these technologies are harnessed for the greater good, while mitigating potential risks and unintended consequences.

Subsection 4.3: Embracing Adaptability and Lifelong Learning

In the face of the rapidly evolving landscape of AI-generated content, embracing adaptability and a commitment to lifelong learning has become more crucial than ever before. As the technologies that drive AI continue to advance at an unprecedented pace, individuals and organizations must be prepared to navigate the challenges and opportunities presented by this dynamic environment. By cultivating a mindset of flexibility and a willingness to continuously acquire new knowledge and skills, we can position ourselves to thrive in a world where AI is increasingly shaping the way we create, consume, and interact with content.

Adaptability is a key trait that enables individuals to effectively respond to change and uncertainty. In the context of AI-generated content, this means being open to new ideas, approaches, and tools that can enhance or transform existing creative processes. Rather than resisting the integration of AI into content creation workflows, adaptable individuals seek to understand how these technologies can be leveraged to augment their skills and expand their creative possibilities. This may involve experimenting with AI-powered tools, such as language models or image generators, to explore new avenues for ideation and expression.

Moreover, adaptability requires a willingness to challenge established norms and practices when necessary. As AI-generated content becomes more prevalent and sophisticated, traditional roles and responsibilities within creative industries may shift or evolve. For example, a journalist who previously relied solely on their own research and writing skills may need to adapt to a new reality where AI-powered tools can assist in data gathering, analysis, and even drafting initial article outlines. By embracing these changes and proactively seeking ways to integrate AI into their work, adaptable professionals can remain competitive and relevant in a rapidly transforming industry.

Alongside adaptability, a commitment to lifelong learning is essential for navigating the complex landscape of AI-generated content. As the capabilities of AI systems continue to expand and new applications emerge, it is crucial to stay informed about the latest developments and best practices in this field. This may involve attending workshops or conferences, enrolling in online courses, or engaging with professional networks to share knowledge and insights.

Lifelong learning also entails a proactive approach to acquiring new skills and competencies that can help individuals and organizations effectively leverage AI-generated content. For instance, a marketing professional who traditionally focused on crafting compelling copy may need to develop a deeper understanding of data analytics and machine learning to create more targeted and personalized content experiences. By continuously updating their skill set and knowledge base, professionals can remain agile and responsive to the evolving demands of the AI-driven content landscape.

Furthermore, embracing lifelong learning can help individuals and organizations navigate the ethical and societal implications of AI-generated content. As these technologies become more sophisticated and autonomous, it is crucial to stay informed about the potential risks and challenges they may pose, such as bias, privacy concerns, or the spread of misinformation. By actively engaging with the latest research and discussions surrounding these issues, individuals can make more informed decisions about how to responsibly create and consume AI-generated content.

To foster a culture of adaptability and lifelong learning, organizations must prioritize continuous education and professional development initiatives. This may involve providing employees with access to training programs, mentorship opportunities, or resources that enable them to stay up-to-date with the latest trends and best practices in AI-generated content. By investing in the growth and development of their workforce, organizations can cultivate a more agile and resilient team that is better equipped to navigate the challenges and opportunities of the AI-driven future.

Ultimately, embracing adaptability and lifelong learning is not just about acquiring new skills or knowledge; it is about adopting a mindset of curiosity, openness, and resilience in the face of change. By approaching the evolving landscape of AI-generated content with a willingness to learn, grow, and adapt, individuals and organizations can position themselves to not only survive but thrive in a world where the boundaries between human and machine creativity are increasingly blurred. As we navigate this uncharted territory together, let us embrace the opportunity to continuously expand our horizons and push the boundaries of what is possible with AI-generated content.

Subsection 4.4: Developing Ethical and Responsible AI Practices

As organizations increasingly integrate AI-generated content into their operations, it is crucial to recognize the significant role they play in shaping the ethical landscape of this rapidly evolving technology. The development and implementation of ethical and responsible AI practices are essential to ensure that the benefits of AI-generated content are maximized while potential risks and negative consequences are mitigated.

One of the primary responsibilities of organizations is to establish clear guidelines and principles for the ethical development and deployment of AI systems. These guidelines should be grounded in fundamental values such as transparency, accountability, fairness, and respect for human rights. By articulating these principles and embedding them into their organizational culture, companies can foster a shared understanding of the ethical considerations that should guide the creation and use of AI-generated content.

To put these principles into practice, organizations must invest in the development of robust governance frameworks and processes. This may involve establishing dedicated ethics committees or advisory boards, composed of diverse stakeholders, including AI experts, ethicists, legal professionals, and representatives from affected communities. These bodies can provide guidance and oversight, ensuring that AI-generated content aligns with the organization's ethical standards and societal expectations.

Transparency is a key component of ethical AI practice. Organizations should strive to be open and clear about their use of AI-generated content, disclosing when and how AI systems are employed in their products or services. This transparency extends to the data and algorithms that underpin these systems, as well as the processes used to train and validate them. By providing clear and accessible information about their AI practices, organizations can build trust with their stakeholders and enable informed decision-making.

Accountability is another critical aspect of responsible AI development. Organizations must establish clear lines of responsibility and mechanisms for redress in the event that AI-generated content causes harm or has unintended consequences. This may involve implementing processes for regular auditing and monitoring of AI systems, as well as creating channels for stakeholders to report concerns or seek remediation. By holding themselves accountable for the impacts of their AI-generated content, organizations can demonstrate their commitment to ethical practice and maintain public trust.

Fairness and non-discrimination are also essential considerations in the development of AI-generated content. Organizations must take proactive steps to identify and mitigate potential biases in their AI systems, ensuring that the content they produce does not perpetuate or amplify existing social inequalities. This may involve diverse and inclusive training data, as well as regular testing and evaluation to detect and correct any discriminatory outcomes. By prioritizing fairness and equity in their AI practices, organizations can contribute to a more just and inclusive society.

To support the implementation of ethical AI practices, organizations should invest in ongoing training and education for their employees. This may include workshops, seminars, and other learning opportunities that help staff understand the ethical implications of AI-generated content and develop the skills needed to create and deploy these systems responsibly. By fostering a culture of ethical awareness and continuous learning, organizations can ensure that their AI practices remain aligned with evolving societal expectations and technological advancements.

Collaboration and knowledge-sharing among organizations can also play a vital role in promoting ethical and responsible AI practices. By engaging in industry-wide initiatives, such as the development of shared ethical frameworks or best practice guidelines, organizations can learn from one another and work together to address common challenges. This collaborative approach can help to accelerate the adoption of ethical AI practices and ensure a more consistent and coherent approach across different sectors and geographies.

Ultimately, the development of ethical and responsible AI practices is an ongoing process that requires sustained commitment and effort from organizations. By embedding ethical considerations into every stage of the AI development lifecycle, from initial design and data collection to deployment and monitoring, organizations can create AI-generated content that is not only innovative and effective but also socially responsible and aligned with human values. As we navigate the complex landscape of AI-generated content, it is only through the collective efforts of organizations, policymakers, and civil society that we can ensure this powerful technology is harnessed for the benefit of all.

Summary: Embracing the AI-Driven Future of Content Creation

As we navigate the uncharted waters of AI-generated content, it becomes increasingly clear that the key to success lies in our ability to adapt, learn, and collaborate. By fostering a symbiotic relationship between human creativity and artificial intelligence, we can unlock new frontiers of innovation and push the boundaries of what is possible in the realm of content creation.

To fully harness the potential of AI-generated content, it is essential to invest in AI literacy and education initiatives that empower individuals and organizations with the knowledge and skills necessary to navigate this rapidly evolving landscape. By demystifying AI and providing accessible learning opportunities, we can cultivate a more informed and engaged society, ready to embrace the challenges and opportunities that lie ahead.

Moreover, as AI-generated content becomes more prevalent and sophisticated, it is crucial to develop and implement ethical and responsible AI practices. Organizations must take the lead in establishing clear guidelines, governance frameworks, and accountability measures to ensure that AI is deployed in a manner that aligns with our shared values and promotes the well-being of society as a whole.

Ultimately, preparing for the future of AI-generated content is not a passive endeavor but an active process of continuous learning, adaptation, and collaboration. By embracing a mindset of curiosity, openness, and resilience, we can position ourselves to thrive in a world where the boundaries between human and machine creativity are increasingly blurred.

As we embark on this exciting journey, let us remember that the power to shape the future of AI-generated content lies in our hands. By working together, sharing knowledge, and leveraging the unique strengths of both human and artificial intelligence, we can create a future where AI-generated content not only enhances our creative endeavors but also contributes to the betterment of society as a whole. So let us embrace the AI-driven future with confidence, knowing that the possibilities are limitless, and the potential for positive change is within our grasp.

Chapter Summary: Embracing the AI-Driven Future of Content Creation

As we look to the future, it is evident that AI-generated content will continue to evolve and shape the landscape of various industries. The advancements in natural language processing, machine learning, and computational creativity will enable AI systems to produce increasingly sophisticated, contextually relevant, and engaging content. The integration of multimodal AI technologies will pave the way for immersive and interactive experiences that blend text, visuals, and audio seamlessly.

The potential applications of AI-generated content are vast and exciting, ranging from personalized virtual assistants and chatbots to AI-driven content recommendations and immersive entertainment experiences. As AI continues to advance, it will also play a crucial role in supporting creative problem-solving processes across fields such as design, engineering, and scientific research.

However, the rise of AI-generated content will also bring about significant societal and economic implications. Creative industries may face disruption and transformation, leading to shifts in the job market and the demand for new skills. Intellectual property rights and copyright issues will become increasingly complex, requiring the development of new legal frameworks and regulations.

To navigate this AI-driven future successfully, individuals and organizations must prioritize human-AI collaboration, fostering the skills and strategies necessary for effective partnership between human creators and AI systems. Investing in AI literacy and education will be crucial in helping people understand and engage with AI-generated content responsibly. Embracing adaptability and lifelong learning will enable individuals to thrive in the rapidly evolving landscape of content creation.

As we move forward, it is essential for organizations to develop and implement ethical and responsible practices in the creation and deployment of AI-generated content. By prioritizing transparency, accountability, and fairness, we can harness the power of AI to augment human creativity and unlock new possibilities while mitigating potential risks and challenges.

The future of AI-generated content is both exciting and complex, presenting a wealth of opportunities and challenges. By proactively preparing for this AI-driven future, embracing collaboration, and prioritizing ethical considerations, we can shape a world where AI and human creativity work hand in hand to push the boundaries of what is possible in content creation.

Chapter 7: Ethical Considerations and Responsibilities

As the use of AI-generated content becomes increasingly prevalent across various industries, it is crucial to examine the ethical considerations and responsibilities that come with this powerful technology. The rise of AI has brought about a new era of content creation, one that offers unprecedented opportunities for efficiency, scalability, and innovation. However, with these opportunities come significant challenges and ethical concerns that must be addressed to ensure the responsible development and deployment of AI-generated content.

In this chapter, we will delve into the complex landscape of ethics surrounding AI-generated content. We will explore the fundamental principles that should guide the creation and use of such content, including transparency, accountability, fairness, and respect for privacy and intellectual property rights. By examining these principles, we aim to provide a framework for understanding the ethical obligations of those involved in the development and utilization of AI-generated content.

Moreover, we will discuss the potential risks and pitfalls associated with AI-generated content, such as the propagation of bias, the spread of misinformation, and the erosion of trust in online information. These challenges underscore the need for robust ethical guidelines and best practices to mitigate these risks and promote the responsible use of AI in content creation.

Throughout this chapter, we will also highlight the importance of collaboration and dialogue among various stakeholders, including AI developers, content creators, ethicists, policymakers, and the general public. By fostering open and inclusive conversations about the ethical implications of AI-generated content, we can work towards developing a shared understanding of the responsibilities and obligations that come with this transformative technology.

Ultimately, the goal of this chapter is to provide readers with a comprehensive understanding of the ethical considerations surrounding AI-generated content and to equip them with the knowledge and tools necessary to navigate this complex landscape responsibly. By embracing ethical principles and proactively addressing the challenges posed by AI, we can harness the full potential of this technology while ensuring that it serves the best interests of individuals, society, and the pursuit of truth.

Section 1: Transparency and Accountability in AI-Generated Content

In the ever-evolving landscape of artificial intelligence, the rise of AI-generated content has sparked both excitement and apprehension. As we navigate this uncharted territory, it is crucial to address the fundamental principles of transparency and accountability. These principles serve as the bedrock upon which trust in AI-generated content can be built, fostering a healthy and productive relationship between creators, consumers, and the technology itself.

Transparency, at its core, is about shedding light on the processes and decisions that shape AI-generated content. It is the key to unlocking the black box of algorithms and making the inner workings of AI systems comprehensible to all stakeholders. By embracing transparency, we can demystify the creation process, dispel misconceptions, and empower individuals to make informed decisions about the content they consume.

Accountability, on the other hand, ensures that the creators and deployers of AI-generated content take responsibility for the outcomes and impacts of their systems. It is the guardrail that prevents misuse, bias, and unintended consequences. Accountability frameworks provide a structure for addressing concerns, resolving disputes, and continuously improving the quality and integrity of AI-generated content.

In this section, we will delve into the importance of transparency and accountability in the context of AI-generated content. We will explore the challenges and opportunities that arise when we prioritize these principles, and examine the role they play in shaping the future of content creation and consumption. By understanding the significance of transparency and accountability, we can work towards building a more trustworthy, inclusive, and beneficial AI ecosystem.

Subsection 1.1: Disclosing the Use of AI in Content Creation

In the realm of AI-generated content, transparency is not merely a virtue; it is an ethical obligation. As AI systems become increasingly sophisticated and capable of producing content that rivals human-created works, it is crucial to disclose when AI has been involved in the creative process. This disclosure serves multiple purposes, each of which contributes to building trust and fostering a more informed and empowered audience.

First and foremost, disclosing the use of AI in content creation is a matter of honesty and integrity. When consumers engage with content, they have a right to know the nature of its origin. By clearly indicating when AI has been used, content creators demonstrate their commitment to transparency and respect for their audience. This openness helps to establish a foundation of trust, as consumers can appreciate the candor and willingness to share information about the creative process.

Moreover, disclosing the use of AI is essential for managing expectations and ensuring that consumers can make informed decisions about the content they consume. When AI is involved in generating content, it is important to acknowledge that the output may not necessarily reflect the unique perspectives, experiences, or emotions of a human creator. By making this distinction clear, content creators can help their audience understand the limitations and potential biases inherent in AI-generated content, allowing them to approach the material with a critical eye and appropriate context.

Transparency about the use of AI also plays a vital role in fostering accountability. When content creators are forthright about their use of AI, they take responsibility for the output and its potential impact on their audience. This accountability can serve as a driving force for ensuring that AI systems are developed and employed ethically, with a focus on producing content that is accurate, unbiased, and socially responsible. By being transparent, content creators open themselves up to scrutiny and feedback, which can help identify and address any issues or concerns that may arise.

Furthermore, disclosing the use of AI in content creation can contribute to a more informed public discourse about the role and implications of AI in our society. As AI-generated content becomes more prevalent, it is crucial that individuals have the knowledge and tools to critically evaluate the information they encounter. By consistently disclosing the use of AI, content creators can help raise awareness about the technology and its potential influence on the media landscape, empowering their audience to navigate this new reality with greater understanding and discernment.

In conclusion, the ethical obligation to disclose the use of AI in content creation cannot be overstated. Transparency, in this context, is not just a matter of principle; it is a practical necessity for building trust, managing expectations, ensuring accountability, and fostering an informed public. As we continue to grapple with the stigma surrounding AI-generated content, embracing transparency and openly communicating the role of AI in the creative process will be essential for navigating this complex landscape with integrity and responsibility.

Subsection 1.2: Ensuring Algorithmic Transparency

In the quest for transparency and accountability in AI-generated content, ensuring algorithmic transparency is a crucial step. Algorithmic transparency refers to the practice of making the inner workings of AI algorithms and processes accessible, understandable, and explainable to stakeholders, including content creators, consumers, and regulators. By shedding light on the complex mechanisms that power AI content generation, we can foster trust, mitigate potential biases, and ensure that these systems align with our values and expectations.

At the heart of algorithmic transparency lies the need for clear and comprehensive documentation of AI systems. This documentation should provide a detailed overview of the algorithms employed, the data used for training, the performance metrics, and the decision-making processes involved in content generation. By making this information readily available, content creators can demonstrate their commitment to transparency and allow stakeholders to assess the reliability and fairness of the AI-generated content.

Moreover, algorithmic transparency enables independent auditing and evaluation of AI systems. Third-party experts, such as researchers, ethicists, and industry watchdogs, can examine the documented algorithms and processes to identify potential biases, errors, or unintended consequences. This external scrutiny is essential for holding content creators accountable and ensuring that AI-generated content meets the highest standards of quality and integrity.

Transparency in AI algorithms also facilitates explainability, which is the ability to understand and interpret the outputs of AI systems. By providing clear explanations of how AI algorithms arrive at specific content decisions, creators can help demystify the "black box" nature of these systems. Explainable AI techniques, such as feature attribution methods and counterfactual explanations, can shed light on the factors that influence content generation and enable stakeholders to make informed judgments about the validity and appropriateness of the output.

Furthermore, algorithmic transparency is essential for addressing concerns about bias and fairness in AI-generated content. By openly sharing the data and processes used to train AI systems, content creators can invite scrutiny and feedback from diverse perspectives. This collaborative approach can help identify and mitigate potential biases, ensuring that AI algorithms produce content that is representative, inclusive, and aligned with societal values.

To achieve algorithmic transparency, content creators must prioritize documentation, standardization, and communication. This may involve adopting industry-wide standards for documenting AI algorithms, such as the Model Cards framework proposed by Google, which provides a structured template for describing the purpose, performance, and limitations of AI models. Additionally, content creators should engage in proactive communication with stakeholders, using clear and accessible language to explain the workings of their AI systems and address any concerns or questions that arise.

Ensuring algorithmic transparency is not without its challenges, however. Content creators may face concerns about intellectual property protection, as revealing the inner workings of their AI systems could potentially expose proprietary information. Striking a balance between transparency and the legitimate need for confidentiality is an ongoing challenge that requires careful consideration and collaboration among stakeholders.

Despite these challenges, the benefits of algorithmic transparency far outweigh the risks. By embracing transparency, content creators can build trust with their audience, demonstrate their commitment to responsible AI practices, and contribute to a more informed and empowered public. As we navigate the complex landscape of AI-generated content, ensuring algorithmic transparency will be a critical step in overcoming the stigma and realizing the full potential of this transformative technology.

Subsection 1.3: Establishing Accountability Frameworks

As AI-generated content becomes increasingly prevalent, it is crucial to establish accountability frameworks that ensure responsible creation, distribution, and consumption of such content. Accountability frameworks provide a structure for defining the roles and responsibilities of various stakeholders involved in the AI content generation process, including developers, content creators, platforms, and consumers. By establishing clear guidelines and expectations, these frameworks help to mitigate potential risks, promote ethical practices, and foster trust in AI-generated content.

One of the primary goals of accountability frameworks is to assign responsibility for the outcomes and impacts of AI-generated content. This involves identifying the key stakeholders involved in the content generation process and defining their specific roles and obligations. For example, AI developers may be responsible for ensuring that their algorithms are unbiased, transparent, and aligned with ethical principles. Content creators who use AI tools may be accountable for the accuracy, appropriateness, and originality of the generated content. Platforms that distribute AI-generated content may have a duty to moderate and label such content, while consumers may be responsible for critically evaluating and fact-checking the information they consume.

Accountability frameworks also emphasize the importance of establishing clear standards and best practices for AI-generated content. These standards may include guidelines for data collection and usage, algorithmic transparency, content labeling, and quality control measures. By adhering to these standards, stakeholders can demonstrate their commitment to responsible AI practices and help to build trust with their audiences. Additionally, accountability frameworks may incorporate mechanisms for reporting and addressing concerns or violations, such as complaint procedures, auditing processes, and remediation measures.

To develop effective accountability frameworks, collaboration and dialogue among diverse stakeholders are essential. This may involve bringing together AI developers, content creators, legal experts, ethicists, and representatives from civil society to discuss the challenges and opportunities presented by AI-generated content. Through multi-stakeholder engagement, accountability frameworks can be designed to balance the interests and concerns of various parties while prioritizing the public good.

Accountability frameworks may also incorporate principles of fairness, transparency, and explainability. This means ensuring that AI-generated content is not discriminatory or biased, that the processes behind its creation are transparent and understandable, and that the reasoning behind specific outputs can be explained to stakeholders. By prioritizing these principles, accountability frameworks can help to build trust and confidence in AI-generated content, even in the face of existing stigma.

Moreover, accountability frameworks should be flexible and adaptable to keep pace with the rapid advancements in AI technology. As new challenges and opportunities emerge, these frameworks must be regularly reviewed and updated to remain relevant and effective. This may involve ongoing monitoring and evaluation of AI-generated content, as well as continuous learning and improvement based on feedback from stakeholders.

In conclusion, establishing accountability frameworks is a critical step in addressing the stigma against AI-generated content and promoting responsible practices in this rapidly evolving field. By defining the roles and responsibilities of various stakeholders, setting clear standards and best practices, and fostering collaboration and dialogue, these frameworks can help to ensure that AI-generated content is created and consumed in an ethical, transparent, and trustworthy manner. As we navigate the complexities of this new era of content creation, accountability frameworks will play a vital role in shaping the future of AI-generated content and its impact on society.

Summary: Embracing Transparency and Accountability for a Responsible AI Future

In this section, we have explored the critical importance of transparency and accountability in the creation and use of AI-generated content. As we navigate the uncharted waters of this rapidly evolving technology, it is clear that these principles must serve as the foundation upon which trust and confidence in AI-generated content can be built.

By embracing transparency, we can shed light on the processes and decisions that shape AI-generated content, demystifying the algorithms and making their inner workings comprehensible to all stakeholders. This openness is essential for fostering a healthy and productive relationship between creators, consumers, and the technology itself. Moreover, transparency enables us to identify and address potential biases, errors, or unintended consequences, ensuring that AI-generated content aligns with our values and expectations.

Accountability, in turn, ensures that the creators and deployers of AI-generated content take responsibility for the outcomes and impacts of their systems. By establishing clear roles and responsibilities, setting standards and best practices, and providing mechanisms for reporting and addressing concerns, accountability frameworks help to mitigate risks and promote ethical practices in the development and use of AI-generated content.

As we move forward, it is imperative that we prioritize collaboration and dialogue among diverse stakeholders, including AI developers, content creators, legal experts, ethicists, and representatives from civil society. Through multi-stakeholder engagement, we can develop accountability frameworks that balance the interests and concerns of various parties while prioritizing the public good.

The path ahead is not without challenges, but the benefits of embracing transparency and accountability far outweigh the risks. By committing to these principles, we can build trust with audiences, demonstrate responsible AI practices, and contribute to a more informed and empowered public. As we continue to grapple with the stigma surrounding AI-generated content, transparency and accountability will be the keys to unlocking its full potential and shaping a future in which AI and human creativity can coexist and thrive.

Section 2: Addressing Bias and Fairness in AI-Generated Content

As the use of AI-generated content becomes increasingly prevalent, it is crucial to examine the ethical considerations surrounding bias and fairness in these systems. While AI has the potential to revolutionize the way we create and consume content, it is not immune to the biases and prejudices that exist in our society. In fact, AI algorithms can inadvertently amplify and perpetuate these biases, leading to unfair and discriminatory outcomes.

Imagine a world where the news articles you read, the social media posts you engage with, and the advertisements you see are all generated by AI. On the surface, this may seem like a convenient and efficient way to consume information. However, what if these AI systems are trained on biased data or programmed with algorithms that favor certain demographics over others? The consequences could be severe, ranging from the erosion of trust in media to the reinforcement of harmful stereotypes and the marginalization of underrepresented groups.

In this section, we will delve into the complex issue of bias and fairness in AI-generated content. We will explore the various ways in which bias can manifest in these systems, from the selection of training data to the design of algorithms. We will also examine the potential impact of biased AI-generated content on individuals, communities, and society as a whole.

But addressing bias and fairness in AI is not simply a matter of pointing out the problems. It requires a proactive and multifaceted approach that involves researchers, developers, policymakers, and content creators. We will discuss strategies for identifying and mitigating algorithmic bias, ensuring diverse and representative training data, and promoting inclusive and equitable outcomes in AI-generated content.

As we navigate this new frontier of content creation, it is essential that we do so with a strong ethical compass. By confronting the challenges of bias and fairness head-on, we can harness the power of AI to create a more inclusive, equitable, and trustworthy information landscape for all.

Subsection 2.1: Identifying and Mitigating Algorithmic Bias

As AI-generated content becomes more prevalent, it is crucial to understand that the algorithms powering these systems are not inherently unbiased. In fact, AI algorithms can inadvertently perpetuate and amplify societal biases, leading to unfair and discriminatory outcomes in the content they produce. To ensure that AI-generated content is equitable and inclusive, it is essential to identify and mitigate algorithmic bias.

One of the primary sources of bias in AI algorithms is the training data used to develop them. If the data itself contains biases, such as underrepresentation or stereotypical portrayals of certain groups, the AI system will learn and reproduce these biases in its output. For example, if an AI writing tool is trained on a dataset that predominantly features male authors, it may generate content that reflects a male perspective or perpetuates gender stereotypes.

To identify algorithmic bias, researchers and developers must conduct thorough audits of AI systems, examining the training data, the algorithms themselves, and the generated content. This process involves analyzing the demographic composition of the training data, testing the AI system with diverse inputs, and evaluating the fairness and inclusivity of the generated content. By using techniques such as statistical analysis and sentiment analysis, bias detection tools can help uncover patterns of discrimination or prejudice within AI-generated content.

Once biases are identified, mitigating them requires a multifaceted approach. One strategy is to diversify the training data, ensuring that it represents a wide range of perspectives, experiences, and demographics. This can involve actively seeking out and incorporating content created by underrepresented groups, as well as using data augmentation techniques to balance the representation of different populations.

Another approach to mitigating algorithmic bias is to develop AI algorithms that are explicitly designed to be fair and unbiased. This can involve incorporating fairness metrics and constraints into the algorithm's objective function, ensuring that the system optimizes for both accuracy and fairness. Techniques such as adversarial debiasing and counterfactual fairness can help AI systems generate content that is less influenced by protected attributes like race, gender, or age.

In addition to technical solutions, mitigating algorithmic bias also requires ongoing monitoring and evaluation of AI-generated content. This involves regularly auditing the content for fairness, inclusivity, and potential biases, and making adjustments to the AI system as needed. It also requires transparency and accountability from the organizations developing and deploying AI content generation tools, including clear communication about the limitations and potential biases of these systems.

Collaboration between AI researchers, developers, content creators, and domain experts is essential for effectively identifying and mitigating algorithmic bias. By bringing together diverse perspectives and expertise, we can develop more robust and equitable AI systems that generate content that is fair, inclusive, and representative of the diversity of human experiences.

As we continue to grapple with the challenges of algorithmic bias, it is important to recognize that this is an ongoing process. As AI technologies evolve and new forms of bias emerge, we must remain vigilant and proactive in our efforts to ensure that AI-generated content promotes fairness, equality, and social justice. By working together to identify and mitigate bias, we can harness the power of AI to create a more inclusive and equitable information landscape for all.

Subsection 2.2: Ensuring Diverse and Representative Training Data

In the quest to create fair and unbiased AI-generated content, one of the most crucial aspects is ensuring that the training data used to develop these systems is diverse and representative of the population it aims to serve. Training data serves as the foundation upon which AI algorithms learn and make decisions, and if this data is biased or lacks diversity, it can lead to the perpetuation of societal biases and the marginalization of underrepresented groups in the content generated by these systems.

Imagine a scenario where an AI system designed to generate news articles is trained solely on data from a single news outlet with a particular political leaning. The resulting AI-generated articles would likely reflect the biases and perspectives of that outlet, presenting a skewed and incomplete picture of the news landscape. Similarly, if an AI writing tool is trained on a dataset that predominantly features works by male authors from a specific cultural background, the content it generates may lack the richness and diversity of perspectives that come from a more inclusive dataset.

To address these issues, it is imperative that the training data used for AI content generation systems is carefully curated to include a wide range of voices, experiences, and perspectives. This involves actively seeking out and incorporating content created by individuals from diverse backgrounds, including different genders, races, ethnicities, ages, socioeconomic statuses, and geographic locations. By ensuring that the training data is representative of the diverse population it aims to serve, AI systems can learn to generate content that is more inclusive, equitable, and reflective of the multitude of human experiences.

However, achieving diverse and representative training data is not a simple task. It requires a proactive and intentional approach to data collection and curation. This may involve partnering with organizations and communities that work with underrepresented groups to access and incorporate their content into the training data. It may also require the use of data augmentation techniques, such as oversampling or synthetic data generation, to balance the representation of different populations within the dataset.

In addition to diversity, it is also crucial to ensure that the training data is of high quality and free from biases and inaccuracies. This involves carefully vetting the sources of the data, fact-checking the information contained within, and removing any content that perpetuates stereotypes or promotes discrimination. By maintaining the integrity and accuracy of the training data, AI systems can generate content that is not only diverse but also reliable and trustworthy.

The ethical importance of using diverse and representative training data cannot be overstated. By ensuring that AI content generation systems are trained on data that reflects the rich tapestry of human experiences, we can create a more inclusive and equitable information landscape. This not only promotes fairness in the content that is generated but also helps to combat the spread of misinformation and the reinforcement of harmful biases.

Moreover, the use of diverse and representative training data can have far-reaching implications beyond the realm of AI-generated content. By exposing AI systems to a wide range of perspectives and experiences, we can foster a greater understanding and appreciation of diversity in society as a whole. This can help to break down barriers, challenge stereotypes, and promote empathy and understanding across different communities.

As we continue to develop and deploy AI content generation systems, it is essential that we prioritize the use of diverse and representative training data. This requires ongoing collaboration between AI researchers, content creators, and community stakeholders to ensure that the data used to train these systems is inclusive, accurate, and representative of the diverse populations they aim to serve. By doing so, we can harness the power of AI to create a more equitable and inclusive information landscape, one that celebrates the richness and diversity of human experiences.

Subsection 2.3: Promoting Inclusive and Equitable Outcomes

As we strive to address bias and fairness in AI-generated content, it is not enough to simply identify and mitigate algorithmic bias. We must also actively promote inclusive and equitable outcomes for all individuals and communities. This requires a proactive approach that goes beyond technical solutions and encompasses a broader consideration of the social, cultural, and ethical implications of AI-generated content.

One of the key challenges in promoting inclusive and equitable outcomes is ensuring that AI-generated content does not perpetuate or amplify existing social inequalities. For example, if an AI system generates job descriptions that use language that is more appealing to men than women, it may inadvertently contribute to gender disparities in hiring. Similarly, if an

AI-powered news aggregator consistently recommends articles that reinforce stereotypes about certain racial or ethnic groups, it may exacerbate social divisions and contribute to a more polarized society.

To address these challenges, we must develop approaches that prioritize inclusivity and equity at every stage of the AI content generation process. This begins with the design of AI systems themselves, which should be guided by principles of fairness, transparency, and accountability. Developers should engage in participatory design processes that involve diverse stakeholders, including representatives from marginalized communities, to ensure that AI systems are designed with inclusivity in mind.

In addition to inclusive design, we must also ensure that the content generated by AI systems promotes equitable outcomes. This may involve developing algorithms that actively seek to counter stereotypes and biases, or that prioritize the representation of diverse perspectives and experiences. For example, an AI-powered content recommendation system could be designed to promote articles and media that challenge dominant narratives and amplify the voices of underrepresented groups.

Another important aspect of promoting inclusive and equitable outcomes is ensuring that the benefits of AI-generated content are accessible to all individuals and communities. This requires a concerted effort to bridge the digital divide and ensure that everyone has access to the tools and resources needed to engage with AI-generated content. It also means developing AI systems that are culturally sensitive and adaptable to different contexts and languages, so that they can be used effectively by people from diverse backgrounds.

Ultimately, promoting inclusive and equitable outcomes in AI-generated content requires a multifaceted approach that involves collaboration among researchers, developers, policymakers, and community stakeholders. It requires a willingness to confront uncomfortable truths about the ways in which AI systems can perpetuate social inequalities, and a commitment to developing solutions that prioritize the needs and experiences of marginalized communities.

By working together to promote inclusive and equitable outcomes, we can harness the power of AI-generated content to create a more just and equitable society. This requires a fundamental shift in the way we think about AI, from a narrow focus on technical performance to a broader consideration of the social and ethical implications of these systems. It also requires a willingness to challenge the status quo and imagine new possibilities for how AI can be used to promote social justice and equality.

As we move forward in this important work, it is essential that we remain vigilant and committed to the goal of promoting inclusive and equitable outcomes in AI-generated content. This is not a one-time effort, but an ongoing process that requires sustained attention and effort from all stakeholders. By working together to prioritize inclusivity and equity at every stage of the AI content generation process, we can create a future in which AI-generated content is a powerful tool for promoting social justice and empowering individuals and communities from all walks of life.

Summary: Confronting Bias and Promoting Fairness in AI-Generated Content

In this section, we have explored the critical importance of addressing bias and fairness in AI-generated content. As AI technologies continue to advance and shape the information landscape, it is essential that we confront the challenges of algorithmic bias head-on. By identifying and mitigating biases in AI systems, ensuring diverse and representative training data, and actively promoting inclusive and equitable outcomes, we can harness the power of AI to create a more just and equitable society.

The path forward requires a multifaceted approach that involves collaboration among researchers, developers, policymakers, and community stakeholders. We must be willing to have difficult conversations about the ways in which AI can perpetuate social inequalities, and we must be committed to developing solutions that prioritize the needs and experiences of marginalized communities. This is not a one-time effort, but an ongoing process that requires sustained attention and effort from all of us.

As we navigate this new frontier of AI-generated content, we have the opportunity to shape a future in which these technologies are a force for good. By centering the values of fairness, transparency, and accountability in the design and deployment of AI systems, we can create a more inclusive and equitable information landscape that reflects the rich diversity of human experiences. The challenges are significant, but so too are the possibilities. With a shared commitment to promoting bias-free and fair AI-generated content, we can unlock the full potential of these technologies to drive positive social change and create a better world for all.

Section 3: Privacy and Data Protection in AI-Generated Content

In the age of big data and artificial intelligence, the ethical considerations surrounding privacy and data protection have become more critical than ever. As AI-generated content becomes increasingly prevalent across various industries, it is crucial to examine the potential risks and challenges associated with the use of personal information in the creation and distribution of such content.

Imagine a world where your personal data, including your online behavior, preferences, and even your likeness, could be used to generate content without your knowledge or consent. The implications of such practices raise significant concerns about individual privacy rights and the need for robust data protection measures.

In this section, we will delve into the complex landscape of privacy and data protection in the context of AI-generated content. We will explore the ethical responsibilities of organizations and individuals involved in the development and deployment of AI systems, as well as the potential consequences of failing to prioritize the protection of personal information.

By examining real-world examples and discussing the latest developments in data protection regulations, we will shed light on the importance of safeguarding individual privacy in the era of AI-generated content. We will also consider the role of informed consent, algorithmic transparency, and accountability in ensuring that the benefits of AI-generated content are realized without compromising the fundamental rights of individuals.

As we navigate this uncharted territory, it is essential to engage in open and honest dialogue about the ethical implications of AI-generated content and the steps we must take to build a future where innovation and privacy can coexist harmoniously. Join us on this thought-provoking journey as we explore the critical intersection of privacy, data protection, and the future of AI-generated content.

Subsection 3.1: Safeguarding Personal Information

In the era of big data and artificial intelligence, the protection of personal information has become a paramount concern. As AI-generated content increasingly relies on vast amounts of data, including individual preferences, behaviors, and characteristics, the ethical responsibility to safeguard this sensitive information cannot be overstated.

Organizations and individuals involved in the creation and distribution of AI-generated content must prioritize the implementation of robust data security measures. This includes employing state-of-the-art encryption techniques, secure storage solutions, and strict access controls to prevent unauthorized access to personal data. By adopting a proactive approach to data security, stakeholders can minimize the risk of data breaches and protect individuals from potential harm.

Moreover, it is crucial to establish clear and transparent data governance policies that outline how personal information is collected, used, and shared in the context of AI-generated content. These policies should be easily accessible and understandable to the general public, allowing individuals to make informed decisions about their data. By fostering a culture of transparency and accountability, organizations can build trust with their audience and demonstrate their commitment to ethical data practices.

However, safeguarding personal information extends beyond technical measures and policy frameworks. It also requires a fundamental shift in mindset, recognizing that personal data is not merely a commodity to be exploited for commercial gain, but a representation of an individual's identity, privacy, and autonomy. As such, the use of personal information in AI-generated content must be guided by principles of fairness, respect, and dignity.

To achieve this, organizations must actively engage with individuals whose data is being used, seeking their informed consent and providing them with meaningful control over their information. This includes offering opt-out mechanisms, data portability options, and the ability to request the deletion of personal data when appropriate. By empowering individuals to exercise their data rights, organizations can foster a more equitable and trust-based relationship with their audience.

Furthermore, the ethical responsibility to safeguard personal information extends to the outputs of AI-generated content. Care must be taken to ensure that the content itself does not inadvertently reveal or expose sensitive personal data. This may require the development of advanced techniques for data anonymization, as well as rigorous testing and monitoring to identify and mitigate any potential privacy risks.

As the landscape of AI-generated content continues to evolve, it is imperative that the protection of personal information remains at the forefront of ethical considerations. By prioritizing data security, transparency, and individual rights, we can unlock the transformative potential of AI while upholding the fundamental values of privacy and human dignity. Only through a steadfast commitment to safeguarding personal information can we build a future where AI-generated content truly serves the interests of society as a whole.

Subsection 3.2: Obtaining Informed Consent

In the digital age, personal data has become a valuable commodity, and the use of this data in AI content generation processes raises significant ethical concerns. One of the most critical aspects of ensuring the responsible use of personal data is obtaining informed consent from individuals whose information is being collected and utilized.

Informed consent is a fundamental principle that empowers individuals to make decisions about how their personal data is used. It involves providing clear, comprehensive, and easily understandable information about the purpose, scope, and potential consequences of data collection and usage. By obtaining informed consent, organizations demonstrate respect for individual autonomy and privacy rights, fostering trust and transparency in their relationships with users.

However, obtaining informed consent in the context of AI-generated content can be challenging. The complex and often opaque nature of AI algorithms and the vast amounts of data involved can make it difficult for individuals to fully grasp the implications of consenting to the use of their personal information. To address this challenge, organizations must prioritize user education and adopt clear, concise, and user-friendly consent mechanisms.

One approach to obtaining informed consent is through the use of granular consent options. Instead of presenting users with a single, all-encompassing consent request, organizations can break down the consent process into specific categories or purposes. This allows individuals to make informed decisions about which aspects of their data they are comfortable sharing and for what purposes, giving them greater control over their personal information.

Moreover, informed consent should not be treated as a one-time event but rather as an ongoing process. As AI technologies evolve and new applications for personal data emerge, organizations must regularly update their consent mechanisms and provide users with the opportunity to review and adjust their preferences. This approach ensures that individuals remain informed and empowered to make decisions about their data as circumstances change.

To further enhance the effectiveness of informed consent, organizations should consider implementing user-friendly interfaces and interactive tools that help individuals understand the implications of their consent decisions. This can include visualizations, examples, and plain-language explanations that demystify the complexities of AI-generated content and its reliance on personal data.

Additionally, organizations must be transparent about the potential risks and benefits associated with consenting to the use of personal data in AI content generation processes. This includes disclosing how the data will be used, who will have access to it, and what measures are in place to protect individual privacy and security. By providing comprehensive and honest information, organizations can build trust with users and foster a culture of responsible data stewardship.

Obtaining informed consent is not only an ethical imperative but also a legal requirement in many jurisdictions. Regulations such as the European Union's General Data Protection Regulation (GDPR) and the California Consumer Privacy Act (CCPA) mandate that organizations obtain explicit consent from individuals before collecting and processing their personal data. Failure to comply with these regulations can result in significant legal and financial consequences, underscoring the importance of prioritizing informed consent in AI content generation processes.

As the use of AI-generated content continues to expand, the ethical and legal landscape surrounding informed consent will undoubtedly evolve. It is crucial for organizations to stay informed about emerging best practices, regulatory developments, and societal expectations related to the responsible use of personal data. By proactively addressing the challenges of obtaining informed consent and prioritizing user empowerment, organizations can build a foundation of trust and accountability in the era of AI-generated content.

Subsection 3.3: Complying with Data Protection Regulations

In the rapidly evolving landscape of AI-generated content, compliance with data protection regulations and guidelines is not merely a legal requirement but also an ethical obligation. As organizations leverage vast amounts of personal data to train and deploy AI systems, it is crucial to ensure that these practices align with the principles and provisions of relevant data protection frameworks.

One of the most prominent examples of such regulations is the European Union's General Data Protection Regulation (GDPR). Introduced in 2018, the GDPR sets stringent standards for the collection, processing, and storage of personal data belonging to EU citizens. Under the GDPR, organizations must obtain explicit consent from individuals before collecting their data, provide transparent information about how the data will be used, and grant individuals the right to access, rectify, or erase their personal data.

Complying with the GDPR and similar regulations is not only a matter of avoiding legal penalties but also a demonstration of an organization's commitment to ethical data practices. By adhering to these guidelines, companies can foster trust among their users and stakeholders, showing that they prioritize individual privacy rights and take data protection seriously.

However, compliance with data protection regulations in the context of AI-generated content presents unique challenges. The complex and often opaque nature of AI algorithms can make it difficult to provide clear explanations about how personal data is being used and to ensure that data processing aligns with the principles of fairness, transparency, and purpose limitation.

To navigate these challenges, organizations must adopt a proactive and comprehensive approach to data protection compliance. This involves conducting thorough data protection impact assessments (DPIAs) to identify and mitigate potential risks associated with the use of personal data in AI content generation processes. DPIAs should consider factors such as the nature and sensitivity of the data, the purposes of processing, and the potential impact on individual rights and freedoms.

Moreover, organizations must implement robust data governance frameworks that establish clear policies, procedures, and accountability measures for the handling of personal data in AI systems. This includes designating a Data Protection Officer (DPO) to oversee compliance efforts, implementing technical and organizational safeguards to protect data security, and regularly auditing and monitoring data processing activities.

Transparency is another key aspect of compliance with data protection regulations in the context of AI-generated content. Organizations must provide individuals with clear and concise information about how their data is being used, the purposes of processing, and the logic involved in automated decision-making processes. This transparency helps individuals make informed choices about their data and enables them to exercise their rights effectively.

In addition to the GDPR, organizations must also navigate a growing patchwork of data protection regulations across different jurisdictions. For example, the California Consumer Privacy Act (CCPA) in the United States and the Personal Information Protection Law (PIPL) in China impose their own sets of requirements and obligations related to the collection and use of personal data.

Staying abreast of these evolving regulatory landscapes and ensuring compliance across multiple jurisdictions can be a daunting task. However, by prioritizing data protection as a core ethical and operational principle, organizations can not only meet their legal obligations but also demonstrate their commitment to responsible AI practices.

Ultimately, complying with data protection regulations in the use of AI for content generation is not just about ticking boxes and avoiding penalties. It is about recognizing the fundamental importance of individual privacy rights and building a foundation of trust and accountability in the development and deployment of AI systems. By embracing this ethical obligation, organizations can harness the power of AI-generated content while respecting the dignity and autonomy of the individuals whose data fuels these innovations.

Summary: Navigating the Ethical Landscape of Privacy in AI-Generated Content

As we have explored throughout this section, the rise of AI-generated content has brought forth a complex array of ethical considerations related to privacy and data protection. The rapid advancement of AI technologies has enabled the creation of increasingly sophisticated and personalized content, but this progress has also raised concerns about the potential misuse of personal information and the erosion of individual privacy rights.

To navigate this ethical landscape responsibly, organizations and individuals involved in the development and deployment of AI-generated content must prioritize transparency, accountability, and user empowerment. By implementing robust data security measures, obtaining informed consent, and adhering to data protection regulations, stakeholders can demonstrate their commitment to safeguarding personal information and building trust with their audience.

However, the challenges of privacy in the age of AI extend beyond mere compliance with legal frameworks. It requires a fundamental shift in mindset, recognizing that personal data is not simply a commodity to be exploited, but a representation of an individual's identity, autonomy, and dignity. As such, the use of personal information in AI-generated content must be guided by principles of fairness, respect, and ethical responsibility.

As we move forward in this rapidly evolving landscape, it is crucial that we engage in ongoing dialogue and collaboration among AI developers, content creators, policymakers, and the general public. By working together to establish best practices, educate users, and foster a culture of responsible innovation, we can harness the transformative potential of

AI-generated content while upholding the fundamental values of privacy and human rights.

The path ahead may be fraught with challenges and uncertainties, but by remaining vigilant, adaptable, and committed to ethical principles, we can shape a future in which the benefits of AI-generated content are realized without compromising the privacy and dignity of individuals. It is a future worth striving for – one in which innovation and ethics are not at odds, but rather work hand in hand to create a more equitable, transparent, and trust-based digital society.

Section 4: Intellectual Property and Attribution in AI-Generated Content

As the capabilities of artificial intelligence continue to expand, questions surrounding intellectual property rights and attribution in AI-generated content have become increasingly pressing. The rise of AI-powered tools and algorithms capable of creating content that rivals human-generated work has blurred the lines between machine and human creativity, raising complex ethical considerations that demand our attention.

In this section, we will delve into the intricate landscape of intellectual property and attribution in the context of AI-generated content. We will explore the challenges and ambiguities that arise when determining ownership and attribution rights for content created by AI systems, as well as the potential consequences of failing to address these issues adequately.

As we navigate this uncharted territory, it is crucial to consider the ethical implications of AI-generated content on existing intellectual property frameworks. We must grapple with questions such as: Who owns the rights to content created by AI algorithms? How do we attribute credit fairly when AI systems build upon the work of human creators? What are the moral obligations of those who develop and deploy AI tools for content generation?

By examining these questions and the various perspectives surrounding them, we aim to shed light on the complex interplay between AI, intellectual property, and attribution. We will explore the potential risks and benefits of different approaches to these issues, and consider how we can foster a fair and equitable environment that respects the rights of both human and machine creators.

As we embark on this exploration, it is essential to recognize the far-reaching implications of these decisions. The choices we make regarding intellectual property and attribution in AI-generated content will not only shape the creative landscape of the future but also have profound impacts on the livelihoods of human creators and the incentives for innovation.

So, let us approach this section with an open mind, ready to engage in a thoughtful and nuanced discussion about the ethical considerations surrounding intellectual property and attribution in AI-generated content. By doing so, we can work towards developing a framework that balances the rights and interests of all stakeholders while harnessing the immense potential of AI to push the boundaries of creativity and innovation.

Subsection 4.1: Respecting Intellectual Property Rights

As AI-generated content becomes increasingly prevalent, it is crucial to consider the ethical responsibility to respect intellectual property rights when using these powerful tools. The ease with which AI algorithms can generate text, images, and other forms of media has led to concerns about the potential for infringement upon the rights of human creators.

One of the primary challenges in this domain is determining the extent to which AI-generated content can be considered original or derivative. When an AI system is trained on a vast corpus of existing works, it becomes difficult to ascertain whether the output is truly novel or merely a recombination of previously created content. This ambiguity raises questions about the ownership and attribution of AI-generated works.

To navigate these murky waters, it is essential for those who employ AI in content generation to take proactive steps to respect intellectual property rights. This begins with a commitment to using only legally obtained and licensed training data, ensuring that the AI system is not exposed to copyrighted material without permission. By carefully curating the input data, developers can minimize the risk of inadvertent infringement.

Furthermore, it is important to establish clear guidelines and protocols for the use of AI-generated content. This may involve implementing mechanisms to track the sources of inspiration for AI-generated works, allowing for proper attribution and acknowledgment of the original creators whose contributions have influenced the output. Developers should also consider the ethical implications of using AI to generate content in domains where originality and authenticity are highly valued, such as in artistic or literary pursuits.

As AI continues to advance and its generated content becomes increasingly sophisticated, it is crucial to foster ongoing dialogue and collaboration between the AI community, legal experts, and content creators to develop fair and equitable frameworks for respecting intellectual property rights. By proactively addressing these issues and establishing best practices, we can ensure that the benefits of AI-generated content are realized while upholding the rights and interests of all stakeholders involved.

Ultimately, the ethical use of AI in content generation requires a commitment to transparency, accountability, and respect for the intellectual property of others. By embracing these principles and working towards solutions that balance innovation with integrity, we can harness the power of AI to create new forms of expression while honoring the contributions of those who have come before us.

Subsection 4.2: Attributing Contributions of AI and Human Creators

As AI-generated content becomes more prevalent and sophisticated, the question of how to properly attribute the contributions of both AI systems and human creators has become increasingly complex. This subsection will delve into the ethical considerations surrounding attribution in the context of AI-generated content, exploring the challenges and potential solutions to ensure fair and accurate recognition of all parties involved.

One of the primary issues in attributing contributions in AI-generated content is the difficulty in distinguishing between the roles of the AI system and the human creators. In many cases, AI algorithms are trained on vast amounts of data created by human authors, artists, and other content creators. When an AI system generates new content based on this training data, it can be challenging to determine the extent to which the output is a product of the AI's learning process or a derivative of the original human-created content.

This ambiguity raises ethical questions about the appropriate way to attribute credit for AI-generated content. On one hand, the human creators whose work was used to train the AI system played a crucial role in the development of the AI's capabilities, and their contributions should be acknowledged. On the other hand, the AI system itself has performed the task of generating the new content, raising questions about whether it should be considered a co-creator or even the primary author of the work.

To address these concerns, it is essential to develop clear guidelines and frameworks for attributing contributions in AI-generated content. One approach could be to establish a system of "tiered attribution," where the human creators whose work was used to train the AI are acknowledged as contributors, while the AI system itself is recognized as the primary generator of the new content. This approach would help to ensure that all parties involved in the creation process are given appropriate credit for their roles.

Another important consideration in attributing contributions is the issue of consent and compensation. When human-created content is used to train AI systems, it is crucial to ensure that the original creators have given their permission for their work to be used in this way and that they are fairly compensated for their contributions. This may involve the development of new licensing models and agreements that specifically address the use of content in AI training and generation processes.

Moreover, there is a need for greater transparency in the attribution of AI-generated content. When AI-generated works are published or distributed, it is important to clearly disclose the involvement of AI systems in the creation process and to provide information about the sources of the training data used. This transparency can help to build trust with audiences and ensure that all parties involved in the creation of the content are given appropriate recognition.

As the use of AI in content generation continues to grow, it is crucial to engage in ongoing dialogue and collaboration between AI developers, content creators, legal experts, and ethicists to develop fair and ethical approaches to attribution. By working together to establish clear guidelines and best practices, we can foster an environment that encourages innovation while also respecting the rights and contributions of all parties involved in the creation of AI-generated content.

Ultimately, the goal of attribution in AI-generated content should be to strike a balance between recognizing the vital role of human creators and acknowledging the transformative potential of AI systems. By approaching this challenge with thoughtfulness, transparency, and a commitment to fairness, we can create a future in which the contributions of both human and machine are celebrated and valued in the creation of compelling and innovative content.

Subsection 4.3: Developing Fair Compensation Models

As AI-generated content becomes increasingly prevalent, it is crucial to address the issue of fair compensation for the human creators whose work is used to train these systems. The development of equitable compensation models is essential to ensure that the rights and interests of content creators are protected and that they are adequately rewarded for their contributions to the AI-powered creative landscape.

One of the primary challenges in developing fair compensation models for AI-generated content is the complex nature of the creative process. Unlike traditional content creation, where the contributions of individual creators are easily identifiable, AI systems often rely on vast amounts of training data sourced from numerous creators. This makes it difficult to attribute specific elements of the generated content to individual contributors and to determine the appropriate level of compensation for each creator.

To address this challenge, it is necessary to develop innovative approaches to tracking and quantifying the contributions of human creators to AI-generated content. This may involve the use of advanced data analytics and machine learning techniques to identify patterns and similarities between the training data and the generated output. By establishing clear links between the input and output, it becomes possible to allocate compensation more fairly among the creators whose work has influenced the AI system.

Another important consideration in the development of fair compensation models is the need for transparency and accountability. Content creators should have access to information about how their work is being used to train AI systems and should be able to track the use of their content across different applications and platforms. This transparency can help to build trust between creators and AI developers and can ensure that compensation is distributed fairly and in accordance with agreed-upon terms.

In addition to transparency, it is essential to establish clear legal frameworks and licensing agreements that govern the use of human-created content in AI training and generation processes. These frameworks should outline the rights and obligations of both content creators and AI developers, and should provide mechanisms for resolving disputes and enforcing compensation agreements. By establishing a solid legal foundation, it becomes possible to create a more stable and equitable environment for the development and use of AI-generated content.

One potential approach to fair compensation is the implementation of a "royalty-based" model, similar to that used in the music industry. Under this model, content creators would receive a percentage of the revenue generated by AI-generated content that incorporates their work. This approach would provide ongoing compensation to creators and would ensure that they are rewarded for the long-term value that their contributions bring to the AI ecosystem.

Another possible solution is the creation of a "content fund" or "data trust," where a portion of the revenue generated by AI-generated content is set aside to compensate the human creators whose work has been used in the training process. This fund could be managed by a neutral third party, such as a nonprofit organization or a government agency, to ensure that compensation is distributed fairly and transparently.

Ultimately, the development of fair compensation models for AI-generated content will require ongoing collaboration and dialogue between content creators, AI developers, legal experts, and policymakers. By working together to establish clear guidelines, best practices, and legal frameworks, it becomes possible to create a more equitable and sustainable ecosystem for the creation and use of AI-generated content.

As we navigate this complex and rapidly evolving landscape, it is essential to prioritize the rights and interests of the human creators who form the foundation of the AI-powered creative economy. By developing fair and transparent compensation models, we can ensure that these creators are able to continue their vital work and that the benefits of AI-generated content are shared equitably among all stakeholders.

Summary: Navigating the Ethical Landscape of AI-Generated Content

As we conclude this section on the ethical considerations surrounding intellectual property and attribution in AI-generated content, it is clear that we are navigating a complex and rapidly evolving landscape. The rise of AI has brought forth a new era of creative possibilities, but it has also raised important questions about the rights and responsibilities of those involved in the creation and use of this content.

Throughout this section, we have explored the various challenges and opportunities presented by AI-generated content, from the need to respect intellectual property rights to the importance of developing fair compensation models for human creators. We have seen that there are no easy answers to these questions, but rather a need for ongoing dialogue, collaboration, and innovation.

One of the key takeaways from this section is the importance of transparency and accountability in the use of AI for content generation. As we move forward, it will be essential for developers and users of AI systems to be clear about the sources of their training data, the methods used to generate content, and the roles played by both human and machine in the creative process. Only by being open and honest about these issues can we hope to build trust and foster a sense of fairness and respect for all involved.

Another crucial insight from this section is the need for new legal and ethical frameworks to govern the use of AI-generated content. As the capabilities of these systems continue to grow, we will need to develop clear guidelines and standards for attribution, compensation, and the protection of intellectual property rights. This will require collaboration between policymakers, legal experts, ethicists, and members of the creative community, as well as a willingness to adapt and evolve as new challenges emerge.

Ultimately, the ethical considerations surrounding AI-generated content are not simply academic or theoretical concerns. They have real-world implications for the livelihoods of creators, the integrity of our creative industries, and the very nature of what it means to be human in an age of artificial intelligence. As we move forward, it will be essential for us to approach these issues with empathy, nuance, and a commitment to building a future in which the benefits of AI are shared equitably and the rights of all are respected.

In the next section, we will explore the ethical responsibilities of those involved in the creation and deployment of AI-generated content, and consider the steps we can take to ensure that this technology is used in ways that promote the greater good. As we do so, let us keep in mind the insights and lessons learned from this section, and approach the challenges ahead with a spirit of curiosity, collaboration, and concern for the well-being of all.

Section 5: Promoting Responsible Use and Deployment of AI-Generated Content

As AI-generated content becomes increasingly prevalent in our digital landscape, it is crucial to consider the ethical responsibilities of various stakeholders in promoting its responsible use and deployment. The rapid advancement of AI technologies has brought forth a myriad of opportunities for content creation, but it has also raised concerns about the potential risks and challenges associated with AI-generated content. In this section, we will delve into the roles and obligations of AI developers, content creators, policymakers, and other key players in ensuring that AI-generated content is created and utilized in an ethical, transparent, and accountable manner.

The responsible use and deployment of AI-generated content require a collaborative effort from all stakeholders involved. It is essential to establish clear guidelines, best practices, and standards that prioritize transparency, fairness, and accountability in the development and implementation of AI systems for content generation. By fostering open dialogue and collaboration among AI experts, content creators, ethicists, and policymakers, we can work towards creating a framework that promotes the ethical use of AI while maximizing its potential benefits.

Moreover, it is vital to empower consumers and the general public with the knowledge and tools necessary to navigate the landscape of AI-generated content. Providing education and resources to help individuals understand the implications of AI in content creation, as well as their rights and responsibilities as consumers, is a crucial step in promoting responsible engagement with AI-generated content. By encouraging informed decision-making and critical thinking, we can foster a more discerning and empowered public that is better equipped to navigate the complexities of the AI-driven content landscape.

As we explore the ethical responsibilities of various stakeholders in this section, we will also examine the importance of encouraging responsible innovation and development in the field of AI-generated content. By prioritizing ethical considerations and societal well-being in the design and deployment of AI systems, we can work towards harnessing the power of AI for the greater good while mitigating potential risks and negative consequences. The path to responsible use and deployment of AI-generated content requires ongoing collaboration, dialogue, and a shared commitment to upholding ethical principles in the face of rapid technological advancement.

Subsection 5.1: Establishing Ethical Guidelines and Best Practices

As AI-generated content becomes increasingly prevalent, it is crucial to establish clear ethical guidelines and best practices to ensure its responsible creation and use. These guidelines should serve as a framework for AI developers, content creators, and other stakeholders to navigate the complex landscape of AI-generated content while prioritizing transparency, accountability, and fairness.

One of the primary goals of establishing ethical guidelines is to promote transparency in the use of AI for content generation. This involves encouraging AI developers and content creators to disclose when AI has been used in the creation process, allowing consumers to make informed decisions about the content they engage with. By fostering a culture of transparency, we can build trust between creators and consumers, mitigating the potential for deception or manipulation.

Moreover, ethical guidelines should emphasize the importance of accountability in the development and deployment of AI systems for content generation. This includes establishing clear lines of responsibility for the outcomes and impacts of AI-generated content, ensuring that there are mechanisms in place to address any unintended consequences or harmful effects. Accountability frameworks should also consider the potential for AI systems to perpetuate biases or discrimination, and outline steps to mitigate these risks.

Best practices for the creation and use of AI-generated content should also prioritize fairness and inclusivity. This involves ensuring that AI systems are trained on diverse and representative datasets, minimizing the risk of perpetuating societal biases or marginalizing certain groups. Additionally, best practices should encourage the development of AI systems that generate content that is accessible and inclusive, catering to the needs and preferences of a wide range of users.

Another critical aspect of ethical guidelines and best practices is the protection of intellectual property rights and the fair attribution of credit for AI-generated content. As AI systems become more advanced and capable of producing highly sophisticated content, it is essential to develop frameworks that respect the rights of both human creators and AI systems, ensuring that all contributors are appropriately recognized and compensated.

To ensure the effective implementation of ethical guidelines and best practices, it is crucial to foster collaboration and dialogue among various stakeholders, including AI developers, content creators, ethicists, and policymakers. By working together to establish and refine these guidelines, we can create a shared understanding of the ethical responsibilities involved in the creation and use of AI-generated content, promoting a culture of responsible innovation and development.

Ultimately, the establishment of ethical guidelines and best practices for AI-generated content is an ongoing process that requires continuous evaluation and adaptation as the technology evolves. By proactively addressing the ethical considerations and implementing robust guidelines, we can harness the power of AI to create valuable and engaging content while mitigating potential risks and ensuring that the interests of all stakeholders are protected.

Subsection 5.2: Fostering Interdisciplinary Collaboration

and Dialogue

The responsible use and deployment of AI-generated content require a collaborative effort from various stakeholders, including AI developers, content creators, ethicists, and policymakers. Each of these groups brings unique perspectives, expertise, and concerns to the table, and it is through open dialogue and collaboration that we can navigate the complex landscape of AI-generated content and ensure its ethical and responsible development.

AI developers play a crucial role in the creation of the algorithms and systems that generate content. Their technical knowledge and understanding of the capabilities and limitations of AI are essential in informing the development of ethical guidelines and best practices. However, they may not always be attuned to the broader societal implications of their work. This is where collaboration with ethicists becomes vital. Ethicists can provide valuable insights into the potential ethical pitfalls and unintended consequences of AI-generated content, helping developers to design systems that prioritize transparency, fairness, and accountability.

Content creators, such as writers, artists, and marketers, are another key group in the AI-generated content ecosystem. They are the ones who will be using AI tools to create content and have a deep understanding of the creative process and the needs of their audiences. Collaboration between content creators and AI developers can lead to the development of AI tools that are more intuitive, user-friendly, and aligned with the goals of content creation. Moreover, content creators can provide valuable feedback on the quality and appropriateness of AI-generated content, helping to refine the algorithms and improve their outputs.

Policymakers and regulators also have a critical role to play in the responsible use and deployment of AI-generated content. They are tasked with creating laws and regulations that protect the rights of individuals and ensure that AI is developed and used in an ethical and accountable manner. However, the rapid pace of technological advancement can make it difficult for policymakers to keep up. Collaboration with AI developers, ethicists, and content creators can help policymakers to better understand the capabilities and implications of AI-generated content, enabling them to craft more effective and targeted policies.

Fostering interdisciplinary collaboration and dialogue among these groups is no easy feat. It requires the creation of shared spaces and platforms where stakeholders can come together to exchange ideas, share concerns, and work towards common goals. This can take the form of conferences, workshops, online forums, and other collaborative initiatives. By bringing together diverse perspectives and expertise, we can break down silos and create a more holistic understanding of the challenges and opportunities presented by AI-generated content.

Moreover, interdisciplinary collaboration can help to identify and address potential blind spots and biases in the development and use of AI-generated content. For example, AI developers may not be aware of the ways in which their algorithms could perpetuate societal biases or discriminate against certain groups. By collaborating with ethicists and content creators from diverse backgrounds, these biases can be identified and mitigated, leading to more equitable and inclusive AI-generated content.

Ultimately, the responsible use and deployment of AI-generated content require ongoing collaboration and dialogue among all stakeholders. It is not a one-time event but a continuous process of learning, adaptation, and improvement. By fostering a culture of openness, transparency, and collaboration, we can work towards harnessing the power of AI for the benefit of all while mitigating its potential risks and negative consequences. Only by working together can we ensure that AI-generated content is developed and used in a way that is ethical, accountable, and aligned with the values and needs of society as a whole.

Subsection 5.3: Empowering Consumers and the General Public

In the rapidly evolving landscape of AI-generated content, it is crucial to empower consumers and the general public to make informed decisions about the content they consume. As AI-powered tools and platforms become increasingly prevalent, individuals must be equipped with the knowledge and skills necessary to navigate this new reality effectively. This subsection explores various initiatives and strategies aimed at empowering consumers and the general public to engage with AI-generated content in a responsible and discerning manner.

One of the primary goals of empowering consumers is to promote digital literacy and critical thinking skills. In an age where AI-generated content is becoming increasingly sophisticated and difficult to distinguish from human-created content, individuals must be able to assess the credibility and reliability of the information they encounter. Educational initiatives, such as workshops, online courses, and public awareness campaigns, can play a vital role in helping people develop the necessary skills to evaluate AI-generated content critically. These initiatives should focus on teaching individuals how to identify the hallmarks of AI-generated content, such as patterns, inconsistencies, or lack of contextual understanding, and encourage them to seek out reliable sources of information.

Another essential aspect of empowering consumers is promoting transparency and accountability in the use of AI-generated content. Companies and organizations that employ AI tools to create content should be encouraged, or even required, to disclose the use of AI in their content generation processes. This transparency allows consumers to make informed choices about the content they engage with and helps build trust between content providers and their audiences. Additionally, clear labeling and disclaimers should be used to indicate when content has been generated or assisted by AI, allowing individuals to approach such content with appropriate expectations and a critical eye.

Empowering consumers also involves fostering a sense of agency and control over the content they consume. One way to achieve this is by providing individuals with tools and options to customize their content experiences. For example, social media platforms and content aggregators could offer users the ability to filter or prioritize content based on their preferences, including the option to limit or exclude AI-generated content. By giving individuals greater control over their content feeds, we can help them curate a more meaningful and trustworthy information diet aligned with their values and interests.

Furthermore, empowering consumers requires ongoing public dialogue and engagement around the ethical implications and potential risks of AI-generated content. This can be achieved through various channels, such as public forums, media coverage, and stakeholder consultations. By facilitating open and inclusive conversations about the societal impact of AI-generated content, we can help individuals develop a more nuanced understanding of the technology and its potential consequences. These dialogues should also provide opportunities for consumers to voice their concerns, share their experiences, and contribute to shaping the policies and practices that govern the use of AI in content creation.

Finally, empowering consumers and the general public involves collaboration between various stakeholders, including technology companies, content creators, policymakers, and consumer advocacy groups. By working together to develop and implement best practices, guidelines, and regulations for the responsible use of AI-generated content, these stakeholders can create a more transparent, accountable, and trustworthy information ecosystem. This collaborative approach ensures that the interests and concerns of consumers are adequately represented and addressed in the development and deployment of AI-powered content generation tools.

In conclusion, empowering consumers and the general public to make informed decisions about AI-generated content is a critical step in promoting responsible innovation and fostering trust in the digital age. By equipping individuals with the knowledge, skills, and tools necessary to navigate this new reality effectively, we can create a more discerning and resilient public that is better prepared to embrace the benefits of AI-generated content while mitigating its potential risks and challenges.

Subsection 5.4: Encouraging Responsible Innovation and Development

As AI-generated content becomes increasingly prevalent, it is crucial for organizations and institutions to take an active role in encouraging responsible innovation and development in this field. The rapid advancement of AI technologies has the potential to revolutionize the way we create and consume content, but it also raises important ethical and societal concerns that must be addressed.

One of the primary responsibilities of organizations and institutions is to establish clear guidelines and best practices for the development and deployment of AI-generated content. These guidelines should prioritize transparency, accountability, and fairness, ensuring that AI systems are designed and used in a manner that benefits society as a whole. This may involve collaborating with AI developers, content creators, ethicists, and policymakers to create a shared framework for responsible innovation and development.

Organizations and institutions can also play a vital role in fostering a culture of ethical AI development by investing in research and education initiatives that explore the societal implications of AI-generated content. This may include funding interdisciplinary research projects that bring together experts from various fields, such as computer science, psychology, and sociology, to examine the impact of AI on content creation and consumption. By supporting such research, organizations and institutions can help to build a deeper understanding of the challenges and opportunities presented by AI-generated content, informing the development of more responsible and effective AI systems.

Another key aspect of encouraging responsible innovation and development is promoting transparency and accountability in the use of

AI-generated content. Organizations and institutions can lead by example by being open and transparent about their own use of AI in content creation, clearly labeling AI-generated content and providing information about the algorithms and datasets used in its production. This transparency helps to build trust with consumers and stakeholders, demonstrating a commitment to responsible innovation and development.

Furthermore, organizations and institutions can encourage responsible innovation and development by advocating for policies and regulations that support the ethical use of AI in content creation. This may involve working with policymakers to develop laws and guidelines that protect consumer rights, ensure data privacy, and promote fairness and accountability in the development and deployment of AI systems. By actively engaging in the policy discourse surrounding AI-generated content, organizations and institutions can help to shape the future of this technology in a manner that benefits society as a whole.

Finally, organizations and institutions can encourage responsible innovation and development by fostering collaboration and knowledge-sharing among stakeholders in the AI-generated content ecosystem. This may involve hosting conferences, workshops, and other events that bring together AI developers, content creators, ethicists, and policymakers to discuss the latest developments and challenges in the field. By creating opportunities for dialogue and collaboration, organizations and institutions can help to build a shared understanding of the ethical and societal implications of AI-generated content, driving responsible innovation and development across the industry.

In conclusion, encouraging responsible innovation and development in the field of AI-generated content is a critical task that requires the active engagement of organizations and institutions. By establishing clear guidelines, investing in research and education, promoting transparency and accountability, advocating for supportive policies, and fostering collaboration among stakeholders, organizations and institutions can play a vital role in shaping the future of AI-generated content in a manner that benefits society as a whole. As we navigate the challenges and opportunities presented by this rapidly evolving technology, it is essential that we prioritize responsible innovation and development, ensuring that AI-generated content is used in a manner that is ethical, transparent, and accountable.

Summary: Embracing Responsible AI for a Brighter Future

As we navigate the uncharted waters of AI-generated content, it is crucial to recognize the shared responsibility of all stakeholders in promoting its responsible use and deployment. By establishing clear ethical guidelines, fostering interdisciplinary collaboration, empowering consumers, and encouraging responsible innovation, we can harness the immense potential of AI while mitigating its risks and challenges.

The path forward requires a commitment to transparency, accountability, and fairness from all actors involved in the AI-generated content ecosystem. It is through open dialogue, continuous learning, and a willingness to adapt that we can create a future where AI-generated content is not stigmatized but rather embraced as a tool for enhancing human creativity and knowledge.

As we stand at the precipice of this technological revolution, we must ask ourselves: What kind of future do we want to create? Will we allow the stigma against AI-generated content to hinder progress and innovation, or will we work together to build a world where humans and machines collaborate in harmony, unlocking new frontiers of creativity and understanding?

The choice is ours, and the time to act is now. By taking proactive steps to promote responsible AI and addressing the ethical considerations head-on, we can shape a future where AI-generated content is not a source of fear or distrust, but rather a catalyst for positive change and growth. It is a future where the power of AI is harnessed for the benefit of all, and where the stigma against AI-generated content is nothing more than a distant memory.

As we move forward into the next chapter of this book, we will explore the benefits and opportunities that AI-generated content presents for various industries, and how by embracing this technology responsibly, we can unlock a world of possibilities. The journey ahead may be challenging, but with a shared commitment to ethics, transparency, and collaboration, we can navigate this uncharted territory together and create a brighter future for all.

Chapter Summary: Navigating the Ethical Landscape of AI-Generated Content

As AI-generated content becomes increasingly prevalent, it is crucial for creators, developers, and users to navigate the complex ethical landscape surrounding this technology. Transparency, accountability, fairness, privacy, and intellectual property rights are key considerations that must be addressed to ensure the responsible creation and use of AI-generated content.

By establishing clear guidelines, best practices, and accountability frameworks, we can foster an environment that promotes ethical AI content generation. This includes disclosing the use of AI, ensuring algorithmic transparency, mitigating biases, protecting personal information, and respecting intellectual property rights.

Moreover, collaboration among AI developers, content creators, ethicists, and policymakers is essential to address the multifaceted ethical challenges posed by AI-generated content. Through open dialogue and interdisciplinary cooperation, we can develop comprehensive strategies that prioritize the well-being of individuals and society as a whole.

As we move forward in this rapidly evolving landscape, it is our collective responsibility to empower consumers and the general public with the knowledge and tools to make informed decisions about AI-generated content. By encouraging responsible innovation, development, and deployment of this technology, we can harness its potential while mitigating its risks.

Ultimately, the ethical considerations and responsibilities surrounding AI-generated content are not merely abstract concepts but are deeply intertwined with our values, beliefs, and the kind of society we wish to create. By proactively addressing these issues and embracing a culture of ethical AI, we can shape a future where the benefits of AI-generated content are realized while upholding the fundamental principles of transparency, fairness, and accountability.

Chapter 8: Embracing AI-Generated Content: Benefits and Opportunities

As the world continues to evolve and technology advances at an unprecedented pace, it is crucial to recognize the potential of AI-generated content and the opportunities it presents across various industries. While the stigma surrounding AI-generated content persists, it is essential to explore the benefits and advantages that this technology can offer, revolutionizing the way we create, consume, and interact with content.

In this chapter, we will delve into the numerous benefits and opportunities that AI-generated content brings to the table. From enhancing efficiency and productivity to driving innovation and creativity, AI-generated content has the power to transform the content creation landscape. We will examine how this technology can streamline workflows, automate repetitive tasks, and enable faster content iteration and optimization, allowing human creators to focus on higher-value activities and push the boundaries of their creative expression.

Moreover, we will explore how AI-generated content can enhance user engagement and personalization, delivering tailored experiences that resonate with individual preferences and behaviors. By leveraging the power of AI, businesses can improve content relevance, provide dynamic and interactive experiences, and expand their reach to global audiences, breaking down language barriers and ensuring accessibility for diverse users.

As we navigate through this chapter, we will also discuss the potential of AI-generated content to drive business growth and competitiveness. By harnessing the capabilities of AI, organizations can improve customer acquisition and retention, establish brand visibility and thought leadership, and develop data-driven content strategies that optimize their efforts for maximum impact.

Throughout this exploration, we will present real-world examples and case studies that showcase the successful implementation of AI-generated content across various industries. These success stories will serve as a testament to the transformative power of AI and inspire readers to embrace this technology as a valuable tool for enhancing their content creation processes.

By the end of this chapter, readers will gain a comprehensive understanding of the benefits and opportunities that AI-generated content offers. They will be equipped with the knowledge and insights needed to navigate the stigma surrounding this technology and harness its potential to drive innovation, creativity, and growth in their respective fields.

Section 1: Enhancing Efficiency and Productivity

In today's fast-paced digital landscape, businesses across various industries are constantly seeking ways to streamline their workflows and boost productivity. As the demand for high-quality content continues to grow, the need for efficient and scalable solutions has become more pressing than ever. This is where AI-generated content comes into play, offering a promising avenue for organizations to enhance their content creation processes and stay ahead of the competition.

AI-powered tools and technologies have the potential to revolutionize the way we approach content creation, from ideation to distribution. By leveraging the power of machine learning and natural language processing, these tools can automate repetitive tasks, enable faster content iteration, and facilitate personalization at scale. However, despite the numerous benefits AI-generated content offers, it is often met with skepticism and stigma, hindering its widespread adoption.

In this section, we will delve into the ways AI-generated content can streamline workflows and boost productivity across various industries. We will explore how automating repetitive content creation tasks can free up valuable time for human creators, allowing them to focus on higher-value activities that require creativity, critical thinking, and strategic planning.

Additionally, we will examine how AI can facilitate rapid content iteration and optimization based on real-time data and feedback, enabling organizations to stay agile and responsive to changing market dynamics.

Furthermore, we will discuss the role of AI in streamlining content localization and personalization efforts, which are crucial for businesses looking to expand their reach and engage with global audiences. By harnessing the power of AI, organizations can efficiently adapt their content to different languages, cultures, and preferences, ensuring a more inclusive and targeted approach to content creation.

As we navigate through this section, it is essential to keep an open mind and consider the transformative potential of AI-generated content. By embracing these technologies and understanding how they can complement human creativity and expertise, businesses can unlock new levels of efficiency, productivity, and innovation in their content creation processes. So, let us embark on this exploration of AI-generated content's impact on workflows and productivity, and discover how it can help organizations stay competitive in an increasingly digital world.

Subsection 1.1: Automating Repetitive Content Creation Tasks

In the realm of content creation, many tasks are repetitive and time-consuming, often requiring creators to spend countless hours on mundane activities rather than focusing on the creative aspects of their work. These repetitive tasks can include researching and gathering information, formatting and structuring content, and even generating initial drafts. This is where AI-powered tools come into play, offering a solution to automate these repetitive tasks and free up valuable time for human creators.

AI algorithms excel at processing vast amounts of data and identifying patterns, making them well-suited for tasks such as content research and information gathering. By leveraging natural language processing (NLP) and machine learning techniques, AI tools can scour the web for relevant information, compile it into organized databases, and even generate initial outlines or summaries based on the collected data. This automation of the research process allows human creators to focus on analyzing and interpreting the information, rather than spending hours searching for it.

Moreover, AI can assist with the formatting and structuring of content, ensuring consistency and adherence to predefined templates or guidelines. For example, AI algorithms can automatically apply appropriate headings, subheadings, and formatting styles to a piece of content based on its type or intended purpose. This not only saves time but also ensures a professional and polished final product, reducing the need for manual editing and formatting.

Perhaps one of the most significant ways AI can automate repetitive content creation tasks is through the generation of initial drafts. By training AI models on vast datasets of existing content, developers can create tools that generate coherent and contextually relevant text based on user prompts or input. While these AI-generated drafts may not be perfect, they can serve as a starting point for human creators, who can then refine, edit, and add their unique perspective to the content. This collaboration between AI and human creators can significantly speed up the content creation process, allowing for more efficient production of high-quality content.

It is important to note that the purpose of automating repetitive tasks with AI is not to replace human creators but rather to empower them by freeing up their time and mental energy for higher-value activities. By delegating the mundane and time-consuming aspects of content creation to AI tools, human creators can focus on tasks that require creativity, critical thinking, and emotional intelligence, such as developing unique ideas, crafting compelling narratives, and engaging with their audience on a deeper level.

As AI technology continues to advance, the potential for automating repetitive content creation tasks will only grow. However, it is crucial for businesses and individuals to approach this automation with a balanced perspective, recognizing the benefits it can offer while also acknowledging the importance of human creativity and intuition in the content creation process. By finding the right balance between AI automation and human input, content creators can unlock new levels of efficiency and productivity, ultimately leading to the creation of more engaging, impactful, and valuable content for their audiences.

Subsection 1.2: Enabling Faster Content Iteration and Optimization

In the fast-paced world of digital content, the ability to quickly iterate and optimize content based on real-time data and feedback is crucial for staying relevant and engaging with audiences. Traditional content creation processes often involve a linear approach, where content is created, published, and then analyzed after the fact. However, this approach can be time-consuming and inefficient, leading to missed opportunities for improvement and a lack of agility in responding to audience preferences.

AI-powered tools and technologies offer a solution to this challenge by enabling rapid content iteration and optimization based on real-time data and feedback. By leveraging machine learning algorithms and natural language processing techniques, these tools can analyze vast amounts of data from various sources, such as social media, website analytics, and user engagement metrics, to provide valuable insights into how content is performing and how it can be improved.

One of the key benefits of AI-driven content optimization is the ability to identify patterns and trends in user behavior that may not be immediately apparent to human analysts. For example, AI algorithms can detect which topics, formats, or styles of content are resonating with audiences, allowing content creators to quickly adapt their strategies and focus on creating more of what works. This data-driven approach to content creation can help organizations stay ahead of the curve and maintain a competitive edge in their respective industries.

Moreover, AI can facilitate the rapid testing and experimentation of different content variations, enabling organizations to fine-tune their messaging and optimize for specific goals, such as increased engagement, conversions, or brand awareness. By automatically generating multiple versions of content and testing them against each other, AI tools can help identify the most effective combinations of headlines, images, and calls-to-action, saving valuable time and resources that would otherwise be spent on manual testing.

Another way AI can enable faster content iteration and optimization is through the use of predictive analytics. By analyzing historical data and identifying patterns, AI algorithms can predict which types of content are likely to perform well in the future, allowing organizations to proactively create and distribute content that is more likely to resonate with their target audiences. This predictive approach can help organizations stay ahead of the curve and capitalize on emerging trends before their competitors.

However, it is important to note that AI-driven content optimization should not be seen as a replacement for human creativity and intuition. While AI can provide valuable insights and automate certain aspects of the content creation process, it is ultimately up to human creators to interpret the data, make strategic decisions, and infuse their unique perspectives and creativity into the content. The most effective approach to content iteration and optimization is one that combines the power of AI with the expertise and intuition of human creators.

As AI technology continues to evolve, the potential for faster content iteration and optimization will only grow. By embracing these tools and integrating them into their content creation processes, organizations can unlock new levels of agility, responsiveness, and effectiveness in engaging with their audiences. However, it is crucial to approach AI-driven optimization with a balanced perspective, recognizing its limitations and ensuring that it is used in a way that complements and enhances human creativity rather than replacing it entirely.

Subsection 1.3: Streamlining Content Localization and Personalization

In an increasingly globalized and interconnected world, businesses are faced with the challenge of creating content that resonates with diverse audiences across different languages, cultures, and preferences. Traditional approaches to content localization and personalization often involve time-consuming and resource-intensive processes, such as manual translation, cultural adaptation, and audience segmentation. However, with the advent of AI-powered tools and technologies, these processes can be streamlined and optimized, enabling organizations to effectively engage with their global audiences while maintaining efficiency and cost-effectiveness.

AI has the potential to revolutionize the way businesses approach content localization by automating and accelerating the translation process. Machine translation algorithms, powered by deep learning and neural networks, can quickly and accurately translate large volumes of content into multiple languages, reducing the time and effort required for manual translation. While machine translations may not always be perfect, they can serve as a solid foundation for human translators to refine and adapt, ensuring that the final localized content is linguistically and culturally appropriate for the target audience.

Moreover, AI can assist in identifying and adapting cultural nuances and context-specific elements within the content. By analyzing vast amounts of data from different regions and cultures, AI algorithms can detect patterns and preferences that may not be immediately apparent to human creators. This insight can be used to tailor the content to specific cultural norms, values, and expectations, making it more relatable and engaging for the target audience. For example, AI can help identify which images, colors, or messaging styles are more likely to resonate with a particular cultural group, allowing businesses to create localized content that truly speaks to their audience.

In addition to localization, AI can also play a significant role in streamlining content personalization efforts. Personalization involves tailoring content to individual users based on their preferences, behaviors, and interests, with the goal of providing a more relevant and engaging experience. Traditional personalization methods often rely on manual audience segmentation and rule-based targeting, which can be time-consuming and limit the granularity of personalization.

AI-powered personalization, on the other hand, can analyze vast amounts of user data in real-time, identifying patterns and preferences at an individual level. By leveraging machine learning algorithms and predictive analytics, AI can dynamically adapt the content, recommendations, and user experience based on each user's unique profile and behavior. This level of hyper-personalization can lead to increased engagement, conversion rates, and customer loyalty, as users feel that the content is tailored specifically to their needs and interests.

Furthermore, AI can help streamline the creation of personalized content at scale. By analyzing user data and identifying common patterns and segments, AI can generate dynamic content templates or variations that can be automatically populated with relevant information for each user. This approach allows businesses to create highly personalized content without the need for manual customization, saving time and resources while still delivering a tailored experience to each user.

However, it is important to note that AI-driven localization and personalization should be approached with a balanced and ethical perspective. While these technologies can greatly enhance the efficiency and effectiveness of content creation, businesses must also be mindful of data privacy concerns and ensure that user data is collected, processed, and utilized in a transparent and responsible manner. Additionally, human oversight and judgment remain crucial in ensuring that the localized and personalized content aligns with the brand's values, voice, and overall strategic objectives.

As AI continues to advance, the potential for streamlining content localization and personalization will only grow. By embracing these technologies and integrating them into their content creation processes, businesses can unlock new levels of efficiency, relevance, and engagement with their global audiences. However, it is essential to approach AI-driven localization and personalization with a human-centric mindset, leveraging the power of technology to enhance, rather than replace, the creativity and cultural sensitivity of human creators.

Summary: Embracing AI for Streamlined Content Creation and Enhanced Productivity

As we have explored throughout this section, AI-generated content has the potential to revolutionize the way businesses and individuals approach content creation, offering a myriad of benefits that can streamline workflows and boost productivity across various industries. By automating repetitive tasks, enabling faster content iteration and optimization, and streamlining localization and personalization efforts, AI-powered tools and technologies can help content creators unlock new levels of efficiency and effectiveness in their work.

However, it is crucial to approach the integration of AI in content creation with a balanced and human-centric perspective. While AI can greatly enhance the speed and scale of content production, it should not be seen as a replacement for human creativity, intuition, and judgment. The most successful content creation strategies will be those that leverage the power of AI to complement and augment human expertise, allowing creators to focus on higher-value activities that require critical thinking, emotional intelligence, and unique perspectives.

As we move forward in this rapidly evolving landscape, it is essential for businesses and individuals to embrace the potential of AI-generated content and explore how it can be harnessed to drive innovation, engagement, and growth. By staying informed about the latest developments in AI technology, experimenting with new tools and approaches, and fostering a culture of collaboration between human creators and AI systems, content creators can position themselves at the forefront of this transformative shift and reap the benefits of enhanced efficiency and productivity.

Ultimately, the success of AI-generated content will depend on our ability to navigate the challenges and opportunities it presents with an open mind, a willingness to adapt, and a commitment to leveraging technology in a way that empowers and elevates human potential. As we continue to explore the impact of AI on content creation throughout this book, we will delve deeper into the strategies, best practices, and ethical considerations that will shape the future of this exciting and rapidly evolving field.

Section 2: Driving Innovation and Creativity

In a world where content creation is increasingly vital to the success of businesses and individuals alike, the emergence of AI-generated content has sparked both excitement and apprehension. While some may view this technological advancement as a threat to human creativity, others recognize its potential to revolutionize the way we approach innovation across various industries. As we delve deeper into the realm of AI-generated content, it becomes clear that this powerful tool has the capacity to unlock new frontiers of creativity and inspire us to push the boundaries of what is possible.

Imagine a future where AI algorithms work hand in hand with human creators, seamlessly collaborating to generate novel ideas, concepts, and solutions that might otherwise have remained undiscovered. By analyzing vast amounts of data, identifying patterns, and making connections that the human mind might overlook, AI has the potential to serve as a catalyst for innovation, propelling us forward into uncharted creative territories.

In this section, we will embark on a captivating exploration of how AI-generated content is driving innovation and creativity across diverse fields, from art and music to marketing and product design. Through compelling examples, expert insights, and thought-provoking discussions, we will uncover the myriad ways in which AI is transforming the creative landscape, challenging our preconceptions, and opening up new possibilities for expression and problem-solving.

As we navigate this exciting terrain, we will also address the concerns and apprehensions surrounding AI-generated content, providing a balanced perspective that acknowledges both the challenges and the opportunities that lie ahead. By the end of this section, you will have a deeper understanding of how AI is reshaping the very nature of creativity and innovation, and how we can harness its power to drive positive change and growth in our personal and professional lives.

Subsection 2.1: Inspiring New Ideas and Concepts

In the realm of creativity and innovation, one of the most exciting prospects of AI-generated content is its ability to inspire new ideas and concepts, opening up previously unexplored avenues for human creators. By analyzing vast amounts of data, identifying patterns, and making connections that might otherwise go unnoticed, AI algorithms can serve as powerful tools for sparking creative breakthroughs.

Imagine a musician seeking fresh inspiration for their next composition. An AI system trained on a diverse range of musical styles and genres could generate a series of unique melodies, chord progressions, or rhythmic patterns that the artist might never have considered on their own. These AI-generated snippets could serve as the foundation for new songs, providing a starting point for the musician to build upon and infuse with their own creative vision.

Similarly, in the world of visual arts, AI algorithms can generate novel color palettes, textures, or compositional layouts that challenge conventional aesthetics and inspire artists to push the boundaries of their medium. By exposing creators to unexpected combinations and arrangements, AI can help break them out of their creative comfort zones and encourage experimentation with new styles and techniques.

In the realm of product design, AI-generated concepts can offer fresh perspectives on long-standing design challenges. By analyzing user data, market trends, and existing product features, AI systems can suggest innovative design solutions that address unmet needs or improve upon current offerings. These AI-generated ideas can serve as catalysts for human designers, inspiring them to refine and adapt the concepts to create truly groundbreaking products.

However, it is crucial to recognize that AI-generated ideas and concepts are not meant to replace human creativity but rather to augment and enhance it. The true power of AI in driving innovation lies in its ability to collaborate with human creators, providing them with new sources of inspiration and helping them to think outside the box. By working in tandem with AI, creators can expand their creative horizons and explore new possibilities that might have otherwise remained undiscovered.

As we continue to explore the potential of AI-generated content in inspiring new ideas and concepts, it is essential to approach this technology with an open mind and a willingness to experiment. By embracing the unique insights and perspectives offered by AI, human creators can unlock new frontiers of creativity and innovation, ultimately leading to a more vibrant and diverse creative landscape.

Subsection 2.2: Facilitating Cross-Disciplinary Collaboration

The power of AI-generated content extends beyond the realm of individual creativity, as it also holds the potential to facilitate collaboration between creators from different disciplines. By bridging the gap between diverse fields of expertise, AI can foster innovative content solutions that might not have been possible through traditional means of collaboration.

Imagine a scenario where a graphic designer, a data scientist, and a marketing specialist come together to create a visually stunning and highly effective advertising campaign. Traditionally, these professionals might have found it challenging to communicate their ideas effectively due to the differences in their technical knowledge and creative approaches. However, with the help of AI-generated content, they can now find common ground and work together seamlessly.

The graphic designer can use AI-powered tools to generate a wide range of visual concepts based on the campaign's objectives and target audience. These AI-generated designs serve as a starting point for discussion and iteration, allowing the team to explore various aesthetic directions and find the most compelling visual narrative.

Meanwhile, the data scientist can leverage AI algorithms to analyze vast amounts of consumer data, identifying key insights and trends that can inform the campaign's messaging and targeting strategies. By sharing these AI-generated insights with the team, the data scientist can help shape the creative direction and ensure that the campaign resonates with the intended audience.

The marketing specialist, armed with the AI-generated visual concepts and data-driven insights, can then craft a compelling story that ties together the various elements of the campaign. Using AI-powered language models, the marketing specialist can generate multiple versions of the campaign's copy, each tailored to specific audience segments and platforms.

Throughout this collaborative process, AI serves as a unifying force, enabling creators from different disciplines to communicate their ideas more effectively and find common ground. By providing a shared language and a set of tools that everyone can understand and utilize, AI breaks down the barriers that often hinder cross-disciplinary collaboration.

Moreover, AI-generated content can help teams iterate and refine their ideas more quickly and efficiently. By automating certain tasks, such as generating variations of visual concepts or copy, AI allows teams to explore a wider range of possibilities in a shorter amount of time. This accelerated iteration process can lead to more innovative and effective content solutions, as teams can test and refine their ideas rapidly based on feedback and data.

As we continue to explore the potential of AI in facilitating cross-disciplinary collaboration, it is essential to recognize the importance of human creativity and expertise in guiding the process. While AI can generate a wealth of ideas and insights, it is ultimately up to human creators to curate, refine, and implement these ideas in a way that aligns with their creative vision and the needs of their audience.

By embracing AI as a tool for collaboration and innovation, creators from different disciplines can unlock new possibilities and push the boundaries of what is possible in the world of content creation. As AI continues to evolve and become more sophisticated, we can expect to see even more exciting examples of cross-disciplinary collaboration, leading to a future where diverse perspectives and skill sets come together to create truly groundbreaking content solutions.

Subsection 2.3: Pushing the Boundaries of Creative Expression

As AI-generated content continues to evolve and become more sophisticated, it is not only inspiring new ideas and facilitating cross-disciplinary collaboration but also pushing the boundaries of creative expression. By enabling the creation of entirely new forms of content and experiences, AI is challenging our traditional notions of what is possible in the realm of creativity.

One of the most exciting ways in which AI is expanding the horizons of creative expression is through the generation of immersive and interactive experiences. Imagine a virtual reality (VR) game where the environment, characters, and storyline are all generated by AI algorithms in real-time, adapting to the player's actions and decisions. This level of dynamic, personalized content creation would have been impossible without the power of AI, opening up a world of possibilities for game designers and players alike.

Similarly, AI-generated content is revolutionizing the field of digital art, enabling artists to create stunning visual experiences that blur the lines between the real and the virtual. By training AI algorithms on vast datasets of images, artists can generate hyper-realistic landscapes, portraits, or abstract compositions that challenge our perceptions of what constitutes art. These AI-generated visuals can be used as standalone pieces or incorporated into larger multimedia installations, creating immersive experiences that engage the senses and evoke powerful emotional responses.

In the realm of music, AI is enabling composers and musicians to explore new sonic territories and push the boundaries of traditional genres. By analyzing and learning from a wide range of musical styles, AI algorithms can generate entirely new compositions, blending elements from different genres and creating unique hybrid sounds. These AI-generated compositions can serve as inspiration for human musicians, encouraging them to experiment with new techniques and collaborate with the AI in creating innovative musical experiences.

Moreover, AI-generated content is opening up new possibilities for storytelling and narrative exploration. By leveraging natural language processing and machine learning techniques, AI algorithms can generate dynamic, branching storylines that adapt to the reader's choices and preferences. This level of interactivity and personalization in storytelling has the potential to create deeply engaging and emotionally resonant experiences, blurring the lines between reader and author.

As we continue to explore the potential of AI in pushing the boundaries of creative expression, it is essential to recognize that this technology is not a replacement for human creativity but rather an extension of it. By working in collaboration with AI, human creators can unlock new possibilities and create experiences that were previously unimaginable. This symbiotic relationship between human creativity and AI-generated content has the potential to redefine the very nature of creative expression, leading to a future where the boundaries between the real and the virtual, the human and the machine, become increasingly blurred.

However, as we embrace the exciting possibilities offered by AI-generated content, it is crucial to consider the ethical implications and potential challenges that may arise. Questions of authorship, ownership, and creative control will need to be addressed as AI becomes more deeply integrated into the creative process. Additionally, there may be concerns about the potential for AI to perpetuate biases or generate content that is harmful or offensive, highlighting the need for responsible development and deployment of these technologies.

Despite these challenges, the potential for AI to push the boundaries of creative expression is immense and filled with untold possibilities. As we continue to explore this exciting frontier, it is essential to approach it with an open mind, a spirit of experimentation, and a commitment to using these powerful tools in a way that enriches the human experience and expands the horizons of what is possible in the realm of creativity.

Summary: Unleashing the Creative Potential of AI

Throughout this section, we have explored the transformative power of AI-generated content in driving innovation and creativity across various industries. From inspiring new ideas and concepts to facilitating cross-disciplinary collaboration and pushing the boundaries of creative expression, AI has emerged as a catalyst for change, challenging traditional notions of what is possible in the realm of content creation.

As we have seen, AI-generated content has the potential to spark creative breakthroughs by analyzing vast amounts of data, identifying patterns, and making connections that might otherwise go unnoticed. By working in tandem with human creators, AI can expand their creative horizons and help them explore new possibilities, ultimately leading to a more vibrant and diverse creative landscape.

Moreover, AI-generated content has the power to bridge the gap between diverse fields of expertise, fostering innovative content solutions that might not have been possible through traditional means of collaboration. By providing a shared language and a set of tools that everyone can understand

and utilize, AI breaks down the barriers that often hinder cross-disciplinary collaboration, enabling creators from different backgrounds to communicate their ideas more effectively and find common ground.

Perhaps most excitingly, AI is pushing the boundaries of creative expression, enabling the creation of entirely new forms of content and experiences. From immersive virtual reality environments to hyper-realistic digital art and dynamic, personalized storytelling, AI is redefining what is possible in the realm of creativity, blurring the lines between the real and the virtual, the human and the machine.

As we move forward, it is essential to approach the integration of AI-generated content into the creative process with an open mind, a spirit of experimentation, and a commitment to using these powerful tools in a way that enriches the human experience. While there may be challenges and ethical considerations to navigate, the potential for AI to unlock new frontiers of creativity and innovation is immense and filled with untold possibilities.

By embracing AI as a collaborative partner in the creative journey, we can harness its power to inspire, innovate, and push the boundaries of what is possible, ultimately driving the evolution of content creation and storytelling in the digital age. As we continue to explore this exciting frontier, let us remain curious, adaptable, and ever-mindful of the incredible potential that lies at the intersection of human creativity and artificial intelligence.

Section 3: Enhancing User Engagement and Personalization

Imagine a world where the content you consume is tailored specifically to your interests, preferences, and needs. A world where every interaction with digital content feels like a personal conversation, crafted just for you. This is the promise of AI-generated content and its potential to revolutionize user engagement and personalization.

In today's digital landscape, capturing and maintaining user attention has become increasingly challenging. With an overwhelming amount of content available at our fingertips, it's no wonder that users often feel disconnected and disengaged. However, AI-generated content offers a solution to this problem by enabling the creation of highly personalized and engaging experiences.

By leveraging the power of artificial intelligence, businesses and content creators can gain deep insights into user behavior, preferences, and interests. This knowledge allows them to craft content that resonates with individual users on a personal level, fostering a stronger connection and increasing engagement. Imagine receiving recommendations for articles, videos, or products that align perfectly with your tastes and needs, or interacting with content that adapts and evolves based on your actions and feedback.

The potential of AI-generated content goes beyond simple personalization. It has the power to create truly immersive and interactive experiences that blur the lines between content and conversation. Imagine engaging with a virtual assistant that not only understands your queries but also anticipates your needs and provides relevant, context-aware responses. Or picture yourself exploring a dynamic, ever-changing virtual world that adapts to your choices and actions, creating a unique narrative tailored just for you.

As we delve deeper into this section, we will explore the various ways in which AI-generated content can enhance user engagement and personalization. From delivering targeted content recommendations to enabling dynamic, interactive experiences, we will uncover the potential of this technology to transform the way we interact with digital content. So, get ready to embark on a journey into the future of personalized, engaging content experiences, powered by the limitless potential of artificial intelligence.

Subsection 3.1: Delivering Personalized Content Experiences

In the age of information overload, capturing and maintaining user attention has become a daunting challenge for content creators and businesses alike. With an endless stream of content vying for users' time and engagement, it's no surprise that generic, one-size-fits-all content often fails to resonate with audiences. This is where AI-powered personalization comes into play, revolutionizing the way we deliver content experiences.

Imagine a world where every piece of content you encounter is tailored specifically to your interests, preferences, and needs. A world where the articles you read, the videos you watch, and the products you discover feel like they were crafted just for you. This is the promise of AI-driven personalization, and it has the potential to transform the way we interact with digital content.

By leveraging advanced machine learning algorithms and vast amounts of user data, AI can create detailed profiles of individual users, understanding their unique preferences, behaviors, and interests. This deep understanding allows content creators to deliver highly targeted and relevant content to each user, ensuring that every interaction feels personal and engaging.

For instance, consider the realm of online news and media. With AI-powered personalization, news websites can analyze a user's reading history, social media activity, and other behavioral data to curate a custom feed of articles that align with their interests. Instead of presenting a generic front page filled with trending stories, the website can showcase articles on topics that truly matter to the individual user, increasing the likelihood of engagement and prolonged site visits.

The same principle applies to e-commerce platforms, where AI can analyze a user's browsing and purchase history to recommend products that are most likely to pique their interest. By presenting users with personalized product suggestions, retailers can not only improve the shopping experience but also boost conversion rates and customer loyalty.

Moreover, AI-driven personalization extends beyond the realm of content recommendations. It can also enable dynamic, adaptive content that changes based on user behavior and preferences. Imagine an educational app that adjusts the difficulty level of its content based on a user's performance, ensuring that they are always challenged but never overwhelmed. Or a fitness app that creates personalized workout plans based on a user's goals, fitness level, and schedule, providing a tailored experience that maximizes results.

The possibilities for personalized content experiences are virtually endless, limited only by the creativity and ingenuity of content creators. By harnessing the power of AI, businesses can create deeper, more meaningful connections with their audiences, fostering engagement, loyalty, and trust.

However, it's important to note that personalization is not without its challenges. Ensuring the accuracy and relevance of personalized content requires vast amounts of high-quality user data, which can be difficult to obtain and manage. Additionally, there are concerns around data privacy and the potential for algorithmic bias, which must be addressed through responsible data practices and regular auditing.

Despite these challenges, the benefits of AI-driven personalization are too significant to ignore. As we move forward into an increasingly digital future, the ability to deliver personalized content experiences will become a key differentiator for businesses and content creators alike. By embracing AI and leveraging its potential for personalization, we can create a world where every interaction with digital content feels like a conversation, crafted just for you.

Subsection 3.2: Improving Content Relevance and Recommendations

In the vast landscape of digital content, finding the most relevant and engaging information can be a daunting task for users. With an ever-increasing volume of articles, videos, and other media competing for attention, it's essential to provide users with content that aligns with their interests and preferences. This is where AI-powered content relevance and recommendation systems come into play, revolutionizing the way users discover and interact with digital content.

At its core, AI-driven content relevance and recommendation systems aim to understand users on a deep, personal level. By analyzing vast amounts of user data, such as browsing history, search queries, and engagement metrics, these systems can build detailed profiles of individual users' interests, preferences, and behavior patterns. This understanding forms the foundation for delivering highly relevant content recommendations that are tailored to each user's unique needs and desires.

One of the key advantages of AI-powered content recommendation systems is their ability to process and analyze massive datasets in real-time. Traditional recommendation methods, such as collaborative filtering or content-based filtering, often struggle to keep pace with the rapidly evolving nature of user preferences and the constant influx of new content. However, AI algorithms can continuously learn and adapt to changing user behavior, ensuring that recommendations remain accurate and up-to-date.

For instance, consider the case of a user who has recently developed an interest in a new hobby, such as gardening. A traditional recommendation system might struggle to identify this shift in interest, as it relies on historical data and static user profiles. In contrast, an AI-powered system can quickly detect the user's newfound interest based on their recent browsing and search activity, and start recommending relevant gardening articles, videos, and products in real-time.

Moreover, AI-driven content recommendation systems can go beyond simple keyword matching or popularity-based suggestions. By leveraging advanced techniques such as natural language processing (NLP) and sentiment analysis, these systems can understand the underlying context and emotions within content. This enables them to make more nuanced and sophisticated recommendations that align with users' deeper preferences and values.

For example, let's say a user has shown a strong interest in environmental sustainability and eco-friendly living. An AI-powered recommendation system can analyze the sentiment and tone of articles related to these topics, identifying content that not only matches the user's interests but also resonates with their values and beliefs. This level of understanding allows for more meaningful and impactful content recommendations that foster a deeper connection between users and the content they consume.

Another significant benefit of AI-driven content relevance and recommendation systems is their ability to personalize the user experience across multiple platforms and devices. With the proliferation of smartphones, tablets, and smart TVs, users now access digital content through a variety of channels and interfaces. AI algorithms can create a seamless, cross-platform experience by understanding user preferences and behavior across different devices and recommending content that is optimized for each specific context.

For instance, a user might prefer to read long-form articles on their tablet, while favoring short, snackable videos on their smartphone during their daily commute. An AI-powered recommendation system can recognize these device-specific preferences and tailor its recommendations accordingly, ensuring that users receive the most relevant and engaging content for each platform.

However, it's important to acknowledge the potential challenges and risks associated with AI-driven content recommendations. One major concern is the issue of filter bubbles and echo chambers, where users are exposed only to content that reinforces their existing beliefs and opinions. If not carefully designed and monitored, AI recommendation systems can inadvertently amplify this problem, leading to increased polarization and a narrowing of perspectives.

To mitigate these risks, it's crucial for content providers and AI developers to prioritize diversity and inclusivity in their recommendation algorithms. This can involve incorporating techniques such as diversity sampling, where the system intentionally exposes users to a wider range of viewpoints and opinions, even if they differ from their usual preferences. Additionally, regular audits and assessments of recommendation systems can help identify and address any biases or unintended consequences that may arise over time.

As we look to the future, the potential for AI-driven content relevance and recommendation systems is immense. By continually improving the accuracy and sophistication of these systems, we can create a digital content landscape that is more engaging, personalized, and valuable for users. However, this potential must be balanced with a commitment to responsible development and deployment, ensuring that AI recommendations serve to inform, enrich, and empower users, rather than limit their horizons.

In conclusion, AI-powered content relevance and recommendation systems represent a transformative force in the world of digital content. By understanding users on a deep, personal level and delivering highly targeted recommendations, these systems have the potential to revolutionize the way we discover and engage with information. As we embrace this technology, it's essential to approach it with a critical eye, acknowledging both its immense potential and its inherent challenges. Only by striking this balance can we harness the full power of AI to create a more relevant, engaging, and meaningful digital content experience for all.

Subsection 3.3: Enabling Dynamic and Interactive Content

The advent of AI-generated content has opened up a world of possibilities for creating dynamic and interactive experiences that adapt to user input and actions. This revolutionary approach to content creation has the potential to transform the way we engage with digital media, making it more immersive, personalized, and responsive than ever before.

At the heart of this transformation lies the power of AI algorithms to analyze user behavior, preferences, and interactions in real-time. By continuously monitoring and learning from user data, AI-powered systems can generate content that is tailored to each individual's unique needs and interests. This level of personalization goes beyond simple recommendations or customization; it enables the creation of truly dynamic content that evolves and adapts as users engage with it.

One of the most exciting applications of AI-driven dynamic content is in the realm of interactive storytelling. Imagine a novel or a video game where the narrative unfolds differently based on the choices and actions of the user. With AI, this concept can be taken to new heights, creating stories that are not only branching but also generative, meaning that the AI system can create new plot points, characters, and scenarios on the fly, in response to user input.

For example, let's consider an interactive mystery novel powered by AI. As the reader progresses through the story, the AI system analyzes their decisions, such as which clues they choose to investigate or which characters they interact with. Based on these choices, the AI generates new plot twists, suspects, and revelations, crafting a unique narrative experience for each reader. This level of interactivity not only keeps readers engaged but also encourages multiple playthroughs, as each reading session can yield a different outcome.

Another area where AI-driven dynamic content is poised to make a significant impact is in the field of educational technology. By leveraging AI, educational content can be adapted to each learner's individual needs, learning style, and pace. Imagine an online course that automatically adjusts its difficulty level based on a student's performance, providing additional resources and explanations when needed, and accelerating the pace when the student demonstrates mastery of the subject matter.

Moreover, AI can enable the creation of interactive simulations and virtual laboratories, allowing students to explore complex concepts and phenomena in a hands-on, immersive manner. For instance, an AI-powered physics simulation could allow students to manipulate variables such as mass, velocity, and friction, observing the effects in real-time and developing a deeper understanding of the underlying principles. These interactive experiences not only make learning more engaging but also foster critical thinking and problem-solving skills.

The potential applications of AI-driven dynamic and interactive content extend far beyond storytelling and education. In the realm of e-commerce, AI can power interactive product demonstrations and virtual try-on experiences, allowing customers to visualize how products would look or function in their own environment. In the world of entertainment, AI can enable the creation of personalized music playlists, movie recommendations, and even generate entirely new content, such as custom-made videos or virtual reality experiences, based on a user's preferences and past interactions.

However, the development of AI-driven dynamic and interactive content is not without its challenges. One of the primary concerns is the need for vast amounts of high-quality, diverse data to train AI algorithms effectively. Without sufficient data, AI systems may struggle to generate content that is truly engaging, relevant, and coherent. Additionally, there are ethical considerations surrounding the use of user data for personalization, as well as the potential for AI-generated content to be biased or manipulative if not carefully designed and monitored.

Despite these challenges, the future of AI-driven dynamic and interactive content looks incredibly promising. As AI technologies continue to advance and become more accessible, we can expect to see a proliferation of personalized, immersive, and responsive content experiences across various industries and domains. By harnessing the power of AI, content creators can unlock new levels of engagement, fostering deeper connections with their audiences and pushing the boundaries of what is possible in the digital world.

In conclusion, AI-driven dynamic and interactive content represents a paradigm shift in the way we create and consume digital media. By enabling content that adapts to user input and actions, AI has the potential to revolutionize fields such as storytelling, education, e-commerce, and entertainment. While there are challenges to overcome, the benefits of this approach are too significant to ignore. As we embrace AI-powered dynamic content, we can look forward to a future where digital experiences are more personalized, immersive, and meaningful than ever before.

Summary: Harnessing the Power of AI for Personalized, Engaging User Experiences

Throughout this section, we have explored the immense potential of AI-generated content in enhancing user engagement and personalization. From delivering tailored content experiences to improving content relevance and recommendations, AI has the power to revolutionize the way users interact with digital content. By leveraging advanced algorithms and vast amounts of user data, AI-powered systems can create deeply personalized experiences that resonate with individual users on a profound level.

Moreover, AI-driven dynamic and interactive content opens up a world of possibilities for creating immersive, responsive experiences that adapt to user input and actions. Whether it's in the realm of interactive storytelling, educational technology, or e-commerce, AI has the potential to transform the way we engage with digital media, making it more engaging, personalized, and valuable than ever before.

However, as we embrace the power of AI for personalization and engagement, it is crucial to acknowledge the challenges and ethical considerations that come with this technology. From ensuring data privacy and security to mitigating the risks of filter bubbles and algorithmic bias, the development and deployment of AI-powered content systems must be approached with care and responsibility.

As we move forward into an increasingly AI-driven future, the potential for personalized, engaging user experiences is vast and exciting. By harnessing the power of AI responsibly and creatively, we can unlock new levels of user engagement, foster deeper connections between users and content, and push the boundaries of what is possible in the digital world. The future of personalized content is here, and it is powered by the limitless potential of artificial intelligence.

Section 4: Expanding Reach and Accessibility

In today's globalized and diverse world, the ability to effectively reach and engage with a wide range of audiences has become more important than ever. As we continue to explore the benefits and opportunities presented by AI-generated content, it's crucial to examine how this technology can help expand the reach and accessibility of content across various industries and demographics.

One of the most significant barriers to content accessibility is language. With thousands of languages spoken worldwide, creating content that caters to a global audience can be a daunting and resource-intensive task. However, AI-powered language translation tools have the potential to break down these barriers, enabling content creators to generate multilingual content with ease. By leveraging AI to create content in multiple languages, businesses and individuals can significantly expand their reach and connect with audiences they may have otherwise been unable to engage with.

Moreover, AI-generated content can play a vital role in enhancing content accessibility for diverse audiences, including those with disabilities. By utilizing AI-powered tools to create content in various formats, such as audio, video, and easy-to-read text, content creators can ensure that their message is accessible to people with visual, auditory, or cognitive impairments. This inclusive approach not only expands the reach of the content but also promotes a more equitable and inclusive digital landscape.

Another way AI-generated content can expand reach and accessibility is by enabling cost-effective content scaling. Traditionally, creating high-quality content at scale has been a costly and time-consuming endeavor, often requiring significant investments in human resources and expertise. However, with the help of AI, businesses and individuals can generate large volumes of content quickly and efficiently, without compromising on quality. This cost-effective content scaling makes it possible for smaller organizations and individuals to compete with larger players, leveling the playing field and democratizing access to content creation.

As we delve deeper into this section, we will explore the various ways in which AI-generated content is revolutionizing content accessibility and reach. From breaking language barriers to enhancing content accessibility for diverse audiences and enabling cost-effective content scaling, the potential for AI to transform the content landscape is immense. By embracing these opportunities, businesses and individuals can unlock new avenues for growth, engagement, and impact in an increasingly connected and diverse world.

Subsection 4.1: Breaking Language Barriers

In an increasingly interconnected world, language barriers remain a significant obstacle to effective communication and the dissemination of information. For content creators, reaching a global audience often necessitates the production of multilingual content, a process that can be time-consuming, costly, and resource-intensive. However, recent advancements in artificial intelligence (AI) have the potential to revolutionize the way we approach language translation and the creation of multilingual content.

AI-powered language translation tools have made remarkable strides in recent years, offering content creators a more efficient and cost-effective means of breaking down language barriers. By leveraging machine learning algorithms and vast datasets of linguistic information, these tools can accurately translate text from one language to another, enabling businesses and individuals to create content that caters to a diverse, global audience.

One of the key advantages of AI-facilitated translation is its ability to handle large volumes of content quickly and efficiently. Traditional translation methods often involve hiring professional translators or outsourcing the work to translation agencies, which can be expensive and time-consuming. In contrast, AI-powered tools can translate thousands of words in a matter of minutes, significantly reducing the time and resources required to produce multilingual content.

Moreover, AI-based translation systems are continually improving in terms of accuracy and fluency. By analyzing vast amounts of bilingual text data and learning from the patterns and structures within these datasets, AI algorithms can generate translations that are not only faithful to the original content but also sound natural and idiomatic in the target language. This level of linguistic sophistication ensures that the translated content resonates with native speakers and effectively conveys the intended message.

The impact of AI-facilitated translation extends beyond the realm of written content. With the development of speech recognition and synthesis technologies, AI can also enable the creation of multilingual audio and video content. By transcribing spoken words into text, translating the text into the desired language, and then generating spoken output in the target language, AI tools can help content creators produce podcasts, videos, and other multimedia content that caters to a global audience.

As AI continues to advance, it is likely that we will see even more sophisticated language translation tools emerge, further breaking down the barriers that hinder effective cross-cultural communication. By embracing these technologies and incorporating them into their content creation workflows, businesses and individuals can significantly expand their reach, engaging with audiences they may have otherwise been unable to connect with due to language constraints.

However, it is essential to recognize that AI-facilitated translation is not without its limitations. While AI can handle the bulk of the translation work, human oversight and editing remain crucial to ensure the accuracy, clarity, and cultural appropriateness of the translated content. By combining the efficiency of AI with the nuance and contextual understanding of human translators, content creators can strike a balance that maximizes the benefits of both approaches.

In conclusion, AI-powered language translation tools offer a promising solution to the challenge of creating multilingual content and breaking down language barriers. By leveraging these technologies, content creators can expand their reach, engage with global audiences, and foster greater cross-cultural understanding. As AI continues to evolve, it is likely that we will see even more innovative solutions emerge, further democratizing access to information and facilitating meaningful communication across linguistic and cultural boundaries.

Subsection 4.2: Enhancing Content Accessibility for Diverse Audiences

In our increasingly diverse world, it is crucial for content creators to ensure that their messages are accessible to a wide range of audiences, including those with disabilities. Artificial intelligence (AI) has emerged as a powerful tool in this endeavor, offering innovative solutions to enhance content accessibility and create a more inclusive digital landscape.

One of the primary ways AI can enhance content accessibility is through the automatic generation of alternative formats. For example, AI-powered tools can quickly and accurately transcribe audio content into written text, making it accessible to individuals who are deaf or hard of hearing. Similarly, AI can generate audio descriptions of visual content, such as images and videos, for those with visual impairments. By leveraging natural language processing and computer vision technologies, AI can bridge the gap between different content formats, ensuring that information is accessible to everyone, regardless of their abilities.

Another area where AI can make a significant impact is in the creation of easy-to-read content. Many individuals, including those with cognitive disabilities or limited language proficiency, may struggle with complex sentence structures, jargon, or idiomatic expressions. AI-powered tools can analyze and simplify text, breaking down complex ideas into more easily digestible chunks. By generating content that adheres to plain language principles, AI can help ensure that information is accessible to a broader audience, promoting inclusivity and understanding.

AI can also play a role in enhancing the accessibility of visual content. For instance, AI-powered image recognition technology can automatically generate alt text for images, providing a textual description of the visual elements. This is particularly beneficial for individuals who use screen readers or other assistive technologies to navigate digital content. By ensuring that images are properly tagged and described, AI can help create a more inclusive and accessible visual landscape.

In addition to these specific applications, AI can also assist in the overall design and structure of digital content to enhance accessibility. By analyzing user behavior and preferences, AI can help identify potential accessibility barriers and suggest improvements to the user interface, navigation, or content layout. This data-driven approach can lead to the creation of more intuitive and user-friendly digital experiences that cater to the needs of diverse audiences.

However, it is essential to recognize that AI is not a panacea for accessibility challenges. While AI-generated content can significantly enhance accessibility, it is crucial for human experts to review and refine the output to ensure accuracy, clarity, and cultural sensitivity. Additionally, content creators must be mindful of the potential biases that may be present in AI algorithms and take steps to mitigate them to avoid perpetuating existing inequalities.

As we continue to explore the potential of AI in enhancing content accessibility, it is clear that this technology has the power to create a more inclusive and equitable digital world. By leveraging AI to generate alternative formats, simplify language, and improve the overall design of digital content, creators can ensure that their messages reach and resonate with diverse audiences. As AI continues to advance, it is likely that we will see even more innovative solutions emerge, further breaking down barriers and promoting accessibility for all.

Subsection 4.3: Enabling Cost-Effective Content Scaling

In the rapidly evolving digital landscape, the ability to create high-quality content at scale has become a crucial factor in the success of businesses and individuals alike. However, the traditional approach to content creation often involves significant investments in human resources, time, and expertise, making it challenging for smaller organizations and individuals to compete with larger, well-established players. This is where artificial intelligence (AI) comes into play, offering a groundbreaking solution to enable cost-effective content scaling and level the playing field.

AI-powered content generation tools have the potential to revolutionize the way we approach content creation by automating many of the time-consuming and labor-intensive tasks involved in the process. By leveraging advanced natural language processing (NLP) algorithms and machine learning techniques, these tools can generate high-quality content at a fraction of the cost and time required by human writers. This not only makes content creation more accessible to a wider range of organizations and individuals but also allows them to allocate their resources more efficiently, focusing on strategic planning, creativity, and innovation rather than repetitive content production tasks.

One of the key advantages of AI-enabled content scaling is its ability to generate content in multiple formats and across various platforms. From blog posts and social media updates to product descriptions and email newsletters, AI can adapt to different content requirements and styles, ensuring consistency and quality across all channels. This versatility is particularly valuable for businesses looking to establish a strong online presence and engage with their target audience on multiple fronts.

Moreover, AI-powered content generation can help organizations and individuals keep up with the ever-increasing demand for fresh, relevant content. In today's fast-paced digital environment, consumers expect brands to deliver engaging, informative, and personalized content on a regular basis. Meeting this expectation can be a daunting task for smaller teams with limited resources. However, by leveraging AI to generate content at scale, these teams can ensure a steady stream of high-quality content without overwhelming their human writers or compromising on quality.

Another significant benefit of AI-enabled content scaling is its potential to facilitate data-driven content strategies. By analyzing vast amounts of data on audience preferences, engagement patterns, and performance metrics, AI algorithms can provide valuable insights into the types of content that resonate with specific target groups. This information can then be used to optimize content creation efforts, ensuring that the generated content is not only relevant and engaging but also aligned with the overall business objectives.

It is important to note, however, that AI-generated content is not meant to replace human creativity and expertise entirely. While AI can handle the bulk of the content generation process, human oversight and editing remain crucial to ensure the accuracy, relevance, and emotional appeal of the final output. By combining the efficiency and scalability of AI with the critical thinking and creative skills of human writers, organizations and individuals can achieve the perfect balance between cost-effectiveness and content quality.

As AI continues to advance and become more sophisticated, it is likely that we will see even more innovative solutions for cost-effective content scaling emerge. From personalized content generation based on individual user preferences to real-time content adaptation based on audience feedback, the possibilities are endless. By embracing these technologies and incorporating them into their content strategies, businesses and individuals can not only keep up with the growing demand for content but also gain a competitive edge in an increasingly crowded digital marketplace.

In conclusion, AI-enabled content scaling represents a game-changing opportunity for organizations and individuals looking to create high-quality content at a cost-effective scale. By leveraging the power of AI to automate and optimize the content generation process, businesses can focus on what truly matters – engaging with their audience, building brand loyalty, and driving growth. As the stigma surrounding AI-generated content continues to dissipate and more people recognize its potential benefits, we can expect to see a surge in adoption across various industries, ultimately leading to a more diverse, accessible, and engaging digital content landscape.

Summary: Embracing AI for a More Inclusive and Accessible Content Landscape

As we have explored throughout this section, AI-generated content holds immense potential to expand the reach and accessibility of information in our increasingly diverse and interconnected world. By breaking down language barriers, enhancing content accessibility for individuals with disabilities, and enabling cost-effective content scaling, AI is poised to revolutionize the way we create, distribute, and consume content.

The ability to generate multilingual content through AI-powered translation tools opens up new avenues for businesses and content creators to engage with global audiences, fostering greater cross-cultural understanding and collaboration. Moreover, AI's capacity to create alternative content formats and simplify complex language ensures that information is accessible to a wider range of individuals, including those with visual, auditory, or cognitive impairments.

Furthermore, AI-enabled content scaling democratizes the content creation process, allowing smaller organizations and individuals to compete on a more level playing field with larger, well-established players. By automating time-consuming and resource-intensive tasks, AI empowers content creators to focus on what truly matters – crafting compelling narratives, engaging with their audience, and driving meaningful change.

However, it is crucial to recognize that AI is not a silver bullet solution to the challenges of accessibility and inclusivity. Human oversight, cultural sensitivity, and a commitment to ethical practices remain essential in ensuring that AI-generated content truly serves the needs of diverse audiences. By combining the efficiency and scalability of AI with the creativity, empathy, and critical thinking skills of human content creators, we can harness the full potential of this technology to build a more inclusive and accessible content landscape.

As we move forward, it is clear that embracing AI-generated content is not merely an option but a necessity for businesses and individuals seeking to thrive in an increasingly digital and globalized world. By leveraging the power of AI to break down barriers, amplify diverse voices, and create content that resonates with all audiences, we can foster a more connected, informed, and empowered society – one in which everyone has equal access to the knowledge and insights they need to succeed.

Section 5: Driving Business Growth and Competitiveness

In today's fast-paced, digital-driven business landscape, organizations are constantly seeking new ways to gain a competitive edge and drive sustainable growth. As AI technology continues to advance and permeate various industries, the potential for AI-generated content to revolutionize business strategies and fuel success cannot be ignored. This section delves into the transformative power of AI-generated content and explores how embracing this technology can help businesses thrive in an increasingly competitive marketplace.

From improving customer acquisition and retention to enhancing brand visibility and thought leadership, AI-generated content offers a multitude of opportunities for businesses to differentiate themselves and connect with their target audiences in meaningful ways. By leveraging the speed, efficiency, and personalization capabilities of AI, companies can create compelling, data-driven content that resonates with customers and drives engagement.

Moreover, AI-generated content can provide businesses with valuable insights and analytics, enabling them to make informed decisions and optimize their content strategies for maximum impact. As we navigate the challenges and opportunities presented by the stigma surrounding

AI-generated content, it is crucial for businesses to understand how this technology can be harnessed to stay ahead of the curve and maintain a competitive advantage.

In the following subsections, we will explore the various ways in which AI-generated content can drive business growth and competitiveness. From improving customer acquisition and retention to enhancing brand visibility and enabling data-driven content strategies, we will provide practical insights and real-world examples of how businesses can leverage AI to achieve their goals and thrive in the digital age. So, let's dive in and discover the untapped potential of AI-generated content in driving business success.

Subsection 5.1: Improving Customer Acquisition and Retention

In the realm of business growth and competitiveness, customer acquisition and retention play a pivotal role. Attracting new customers while keeping existing ones engaged and loyal is a constant challenge that businesses face in today's dynamic market. AI-generated content emerges as a powerful tool to tackle this challenge head-on, offering businesses a way to create targeted, personalized, and engaging content that resonates with their target audience.

One of the key advantages of AI-generated content is its ability to analyze vast amounts of customer data and generate insights that can inform content creation. By leveraging machine learning algorithms, AI systems can identify patterns, preferences, and behaviors of potential and existing customers. This valuable information allows businesses to craft content that speaks directly to the needs, interests, and pain points of their target audience, increasing the likelihood of attracting and retaining customers.

For instance, an e-commerce company can utilize AI-powered content generation to create personalized product descriptions, recommendations, and marketing messages based on a customer's browsing and purchase history. By delivering content that is highly relevant and tailored to individual preferences, businesses can establish a stronger connection with their customers, fostering trust and loyalty.

Moreover, AI-generated content can help businesses maintain a consistent and engaging brand voice across various touchpoints. With the ability to generate high-quality content at scale, businesses can ensure that their messaging remains cohesive and on-brand, regardless of the channel or platform. This consistency helps build brand recognition and trust, which are essential factors in customer acquisition and retention.

Another way AI-generated content can boost customer acquisition and retention is through the creation of interactive and immersive content experiences. By leveraging natural language processing (NLP) and conversational AI, businesses can develop chatbots, virtual assistants, and other interactive content that engages customers in real-time. These AI-powered tools can provide instant support, answer questions, and guide customers through their journey, creating a seamless and personalized experience that keeps them coming back.

In addition, AI-generated content can be used to create compelling and shareable content that amplifies brand reach and attracts new customers. By analyzing social media trends, popular topics, and user engagement patterns, AI algorithms can generate content ideas and formats that are more likely to go viral and reach a wider audience. This increased visibility and shareability can help businesses expand their customer base and drive organic growth.

However, it is crucial to strike a balance between AI-generated content and human oversight to ensure the quality and relevance of the content. While AI can automate and streamline content creation, human expertise and judgment remain essential in guiding the process, setting strategic direction, and adding creative flair. By combining the efficiency of AI with the intuition and empathy of human content creators, businesses can create a winning formula for customer acquisition and retention.

As the stigma surrounding AI-generated content gradually dissipates, more businesses are recognizing its potential to drive growth and competitiveness. By harnessing the power of AI to create targeted, engaging, and personalized content, businesses can attract new customers, retain existing ones, and build lasting relationships that fuel long-term success. The key lies in embracing AI as a tool to augment and enhance human creativity, rather than a replacement for it.

Subsection 5.2: Enhancing Brand Visibility and Thought Leadership

In an increasingly competitive business landscape, establishing a strong brand presence and positioning oneself as a thought leader is crucial for long-term success. AI-generated content offers a powerful tool for businesses to enhance their brand visibility and establish themselves as authoritative voices in their respective industries. By leveraging the capabilities of AI to create consistent, high-quality content, companies can effectively communicate their unique value proposition and engage with their target audience on a deeper level.

One of the primary ways AI-generated content can boost brand visibility is through the creation of a steady stream of relevant and informative content. With the ability to analyze vast amounts of data and identify trending topics, AI algorithms can help businesses generate content ideas that resonate with their audience and align with their brand messaging. By consistently publishing valuable content across various channels, such as blog posts, social media updates, and industry publications, businesses can increase their online presence and attract a wider audience.

Moreover, AI-generated content can help businesses maintain a consistent brand voice and tone across all their communication channels. By training AI models on a company's existing content and brand guidelines, businesses can ensure that all AI-generated content adheres to their unique style and messaging. This consistency helps build brand recognition and trust among the target audience, as they come to associate the company with a specific set of values and qualities.

In addition to enhancing brand visibility, AI-generated content can also help businesses establish themselves as thought leaders in their industry. By leveraging AI to create in-depth, well-researched content that addresses the latest trends, challenges, and opportunities in their field, companies can demonstrate their expertise and provide valuable insights to their audience. This thought leadership content can take various forms, such as whitepapers, e-books, case studies, and opinion pieces, each designed to showcase the company's unique perspective and knowledge.

To maximize the impact of AI-generated thought leadership content, businesses can utilize AI-powered distribution and promotion strategies. By analyzing audience data and engagement metrics, AI algorithms can help identify the most effective channels and times to share content, ensuring that it reaches the right people at the right moment. Additionally, AI can help optimize content for search engines, improving its visibility and making it easier for potential customers and industry peers to discover and engage with the company's thought leadership materials.

However, it is essential to note that while AI-generated content can significantly enhance brand visibility and thought leadership, human oversight and input remain crucial. Businesses must strike a balance between leveraging AI's efficiency and scalability and maintaining the authenticity and nuance that only human creators can provide. By collaborating with AI tools and integrating them into their content creation workflows, businesses can harness the best of both worlds – the speed and consistency of AI-generated content, combined with the creativity and emotional intelligence of human writers.

As the stigma surrounding AI-generated content continues to diminish, more businesses are recognizing the potential of this technology to elevate their brand and establish themselves as industry leaders. By embracing AI as a tool to augment and enhance their content creation efforts, companies can create a virtuous cycle of increased visibility, engagement, and thought leadership. As they consistently deliver valuable, informative, and engaging content to their audience, businesses can foster deeper connections, build trust, and ultimately drive long-term growth and success.

Subsection 5.3: Enabling Data-Driven Content Strategies

In the era of digital transformation, businesses are increasingly turning to data-driven strategies to inform their decision-making processes and optimize their operations. The realm of content creation is no exception, as AI-powered tools and technologies have opened up new possibilities for data-driven content strategies. By leveraging the vast amounts of data available, businesses can gain valuable insights into their target audience's preferences, behaviors, and engagement patterns, enabling them to create content that resonates and drives meaningful results.

One of the key advantages of AI in facilitating data-driven content strategies is its ability to analyze and process large volumes of data at an unprecedented speed and scale. With the help of machine learning algorithms, businesses can quickly identify patterns, trends, and correlations within their content performance data, allowing them to make informed decisions about their content strategy. For instance, AI can analyze metrics such as page views, bounce rates, time spent on page, and social media engagement to determine which types of content are most effective at capturing and retaining audience attention.

Moreover, AI can help businesses optimize their content for specific goals, such as increasing website traffic, generating leads, or boosting conversions. By analyzing historical data and identifying the content characteristics that have previously driven successful outcomes, AI algorithms can provide recommendations for content topics, formats, and distribution channels that are most likely to achieve the desired results. This data-driven approach enables businesses to allocate their resources more effectively and maximize the impact of their content efforts.

Another way AI enables data-driven content strategies is through the creation of personalized content experiences. By analyzing user data, such as demographics, interests, and browsing behavior, AI can help businesses tailor their content to the specific needs and preferences of individual users. This level of personalization not only enhances the user experience but also increases the likelihood of engagement and conversion. For example, an e-commerce company can use AI to analyze a customer's purchase history and browsing behavior to recommend products and provide personalized content that aligns with their interests, ultimately driving sales and fostering customer loyalty.

In addition to personalization, AI can also facilitate the optimization of content for search engines, ensuring that businesses' content is easily discoverable by their target audience. By analyzing search trends, keyword performance, and competitor content, AI algorithms can provide insights into the most effective SEO strategies and help businesses create content that ranks well in search results. This data-driven approach to SEO enables businesses to attract more organic traffic to their websites and establish themselves as authoritative sources within their industry.

However, it is essential to recognize that while AI is a powerful tool for enabling data-driven content strategies, it should not be relied upon in isolation. The most effective content strategies combine the insights gleaned from AI-powered data analysis with the creativity, intuition, and domain expertise of human content creators. By leveraging the strengths of both AI and human intelligence, businesses can create content that is not only data-driven but also emotionally resonant and culturally relevant.

As the stigma surrounding AI-generated content continues to dissipate, more businesses are recognizing the potential of AI in enabling data-driven content strategies. By harnessing the power of data and AI-powered insights, companies can create content that is more targeted, personalized, and effective at achieving their desired outcomes. However, it is crucial to approach AI as a tool to augment and enhance human creativity, rather than a replacement for it. By striking the right balance between data-driven insights and human intuition, businesses can unlock the full potential of their content strategies and drive sustainable growth in the digital age.

Subsection 5.4: Staying Ahead of the Competition

In today's fast-paced business environment, staying ahead of the competition is not just a goal; it's a necessity. As technology continues to evolve at an unprecedented rate, businesses must adapt and embrace new tools and strategies to maintain their competitive edge. One such tool that has emerged as a game-changer in recent years is AI-generated content. By leveraging the power of artificial intelligence to create compelling, engaging, and personalized content, businesses can differentiate themselves from their rivals and capture the attention of their target audience.

The stigma surrounding AI-generated content has long been a barrier to its widespread adoption. However, as more businesses begin to recognize the potential benefits of this technology, the stigma is gradually eroding. Those who embrace AI-generated content early on stand to gain a significant advantage over their competitors who may be hesitant to adopt this innovative approach.

One of the primary ways AI-generated content can help businesses stay ahead of the competition is by enabling them to produce high-quality content at scale. With the ability to analyze vast amounts of data and generate insights in real-time, AI algorithms can help businesses create content that is tailored to the specific needs and preferences of their target audience. This level of personalization not only enhances the user experience but also increases the likelihood of engagement and conversion, giving businesses a critical edge over their competitors.

Moreover, AI-generated content can help businesses stay on top of the latest industry trends and topics. By continuously monitoring social media, news outlets, and other relevant sources, AI algorithms can identify emerging trends and generate content ideas that align with the current interests of the target audience. This allows businesses to be proactive in their content creation efforts, rather than simply reacting to what their competitors are doing.

Another way AI-generated content can help businesses stay ahead of the competition is by freeing up time and resources that can be allocated to other critical areas of the business. By automating certain aspects of the content creation process, such as research, data analysis, and even drafting, AI tools can significantly reduce the time and effort required to produce high-quality content. This allows businesses to focus on other strategic initiatives, such as product development, customer service, and innovation, which can further enhance their competitive advantage.

However, it is essential to recognize that AI-generated content is not a silver bullet. To truly stay ahead of the competition, businesses must approach AI as a tool to augment and enhance human creativity, rather than a replacement for it. The most successful businesses will be those that can effectively combine the efficiency and insights of AI with the emotional intelligence and strategic vision of human content creators.

Furthermore, businesses must be mindful of the ethical implications of AI-generated content and ensure that they are using this technology responsibly. This means being transparent about the use of AI in their content creation process, ensuring that the content is accurate and unbiased, and respecting the intellectual property rights of others. By adhering to these ethical guidelines, businesses can build trust with their audience and differentiate themselves from competitors who may be less scrupulous in their use of AI.

As the business landscape continues to evolve, the ability to stay ahead of the competition will become increasingly critical. By embracing AI-generated content and leveraging its potential to create compelling, personalized, and data-driven content, businesses can position themselves for success in the digital age. However, it is essential to approach AI as part of a holistic content strategy that combines the best of both human and machine intelligence. Only by striking this balance can businesses truly unlock the full potential of AI-generated content and stay ahead of the curve in an increasingly competitive marketplace.

Summary: Embracing AI for Sustainable Growth and Competitive Advantage

As we have explored throughout this section, AI-generated content holds immense potential to drive business growth and competitiveness in the digital age. From improving customer acquisition and retention to enhancing brand visibility and enabling data-driven content strategies, the applications of AI in content creation are vast and transformative.

By leveraging the power of AI to create personalized, engaging, and high-quality content at scale, businesses can differentiate themselves from their competitors and capture the attention of their target audience. AI-powered insights and data analysis can inform content strategies, ensuring that businesses allocate their resources effectively and create content that resonates with their audience.

Moreover, AI-generated content can help businesses establish themselves as thought leaders in their industries, showcasing their expertise and providing valuable insights to their audience. This thought leadership content can take various forms, such as whitepapers, e-books, and case studies, each designed to demonstrate the company's unique perspective and knowledge.

However, it is crucial to recognize that AI is not a replacement for human creativity and intuition. The most successful businesses will be those that can effectively combine the efficiency and insights of AI with the emotional intelligence and strategic vision of human content creators. By striking this balance, businesses can unlock the full potential of AI-generated content and drive sustainable growth.

As the stigma surrounding AI-generated content continues to dissipate, businesses that embrace this technology early on stand to gain a significant competitive advantage. By approaching AI as a tool to augment and enhance their content creation efforts, companies can create a virtuous cycle of increased visibility, engagement, and thought leadership.

Looking ahead, the future of AI-generated content is bright, and its potential to revolutionize the business landscape is immense. As more businesses recognize the value of this technology and incorporate it into their content strategies, we can expect to see a new era of data-driven, personalized, and impactful content that drives business growth and competitiveness.

In the next section, we will delve into the ethical considerations and responsibilities that come with the use of AI-generated content, ensuring that businesses approach this technology in a responsible and transparent manner. By doing so, companies can build trust with their audience and establish themselves as leaders in the responsible use of AI in content creation.

Chapter Summary: Harnessing the Power of AI for Content Creation

As we have explored throughout this chapter, AI-generated content presents a wealth of benefits and opportunities for various industries. From enhancing efficiency and productivity to driving innovation and creativity, AI has the potential to revolutionize the way we create and consume content.

By automating repetitive tasks, streamlining workflows, and enabling faster content iteration and optimization, AI can help content creators focus on higher-value activities and deliver more impactful results. Moreover, AI-powered tools can inspire new ideas, facilitate cross-disciplinary collaboration, and push the boundaries of creative expression, leading to the development of groundbreaking content solutions.

The ability of AI to deliver personalized content experiences, improve relevance and recommendations, and enable dynamic and interactive content opens up new avenues for enhancing user engagement and building stronger connections with audiences. Additionally, AI can help break language barriers, enhance content accessibility for diverse audiences, and enable cost-effective content scaling, expanding the reach and impact of content on a global scale.

For businesses, embracing AI-generated content can drive growth and competitiveness by improving customer acquisition and retention, enhancing brand visibility and thought leadership, and enabling data-driven content strategies. By staying ahead of the curve and leveraging the latest AI technologies, organizations can position themselves for success in an increasingly digital and content-driven world.

As we move forward, it is essential to recognize the transformative potential of AI-generated content and embrace the opportunities it presents. By collaborating with AI and harnessing its power for content creation, we can unlock new levels of efficiency, creativity, and engagement, ultimately reshaping the content landscape and driving meaningful progress across industries.

Chapter 9: Strategies for Overcoming the Stigma

In the previous chapters, we have explored the various aspects of the stigma surrounding AI-generated content, from its origins and the reasons behind it to the potential benefits and opportunities that this technology presents. However, understanding the issue is only the first step in addressing it effectively. As AI continues to advance and become more prevalent in our daily lives, it is crucial for individuals and organizations to develop practical strategies to navigate and overcome the stigma associated with AI-generated content.

Throughout this chapter, we will delve into a range of approaches and techniques that can help mitigate the negative perceptions and foster a more accepting and inclusive environment for AI-generated content. By employing these strategies, we can work towards breaking down the barriers that hinder the adoption and appreciation of this transformative technology.

From educating the public and showcasing successful applications to fostering transparency and collaboration, the strategies outlined in this chapter will provide a comprehensive toolkit for those seeking to challenge the status quo and embrace the potential of AI-generated content. By implementing these approaches, we can pave the way for a future in which AI and human creativity work hand in hand, unlocking new possibilities and redefining the boundaries of what is possible.

As we embark on this journey, it is essential to remember that overcoming the stigma against AI-generated content is not a one-size-fits-all endeavor. Each individual and organization will need to adapt and tailor these strategies to their unique circumstances and goals. However, by staying committed to the principles of education, transparency, and collaboration, we can collectively work towards a more inclusive and forward-thinking society that recognizes the value and potential of AI-generated content.

So, let us dive in and explore the various strategies that can help us navigate this complex landscape and ultimately overcome the stigma that has long surrounded AI-generated content. Together, we can shape a future in which the power of AI is harnessed to enhance and complement human creativity, rather than being viewed as a threat or a lesser form of expression.

Section 1: Educating and Informing the Public

In the quest to overcome the stigma against AI-generated content, education and awareness play a pivotal role. As the general public grapples with the rapid advancements in artificial intelligence and its increasing presence in various aspects of our lives, it is crucial to bridge the knowledge gap and provide clear, accessible information about the nature, capabilities, and limitations of AI-generated content.

Many of the misconceptions and fears surrounding AI-generated content stem from a lack of understanding about how these systems work, their intended purposes, and the potential benefits they offer. By embarking on a comprehensive educational initiative, we can begin to dispel the myths, address the concerns, and foster a more informed and balanced perspective on the role of AI in content creation.

In this section, we will explore the various strategies and approaches that can be employed to educate and inform the public about AI-generated content. From developing clear and engaging informational resources to leveraging the power of social media and collaborating with influential thought leaders, we will delve into the key components of an effective educational campaign.

By equipping the public with the knowledge and tools to understand and evaluate AI-generated content, we can empower individuals to make informed decisions, engage in constructive discussions, and ultimately, help to reduce the stigma surrounding this transformative technology. As we navigate the complexities of the AI revolution, education and awareness will serve as the foundation upon which we can build a more accepting and inclusive future for AI-generated content.

Subsection 1.1: Developing Clear and Accessible Information Resources

In order to effectively educate and inform the public about AI-generated content, it is crucial to develop clear and accessible information resources. These resources should be designed to explain the concept of AI-generated content in a manner that is easily understandable to individuals with varying levels of technical knowledge.

One of the primary goals of these informative resources should be to demystify AI-generated content by breaking down complex concepts into simple, digestible terms. This can be achieved through the use of plain language, avoiding jargon and technical terminology whenever possible. By employing everyday examples and analogies, the resources can help readers relate to the subject matter and grasp the fundamental principles behind AI-generated content.

Visual aids, such as infographics, diagrams, and illustrations, can be powerful tools in conveying information effectively. These visual elements can help to simplify complex processes, highlight key points, and make the content more engaging and memorable for readers. For example, a flowchart depicting the steps involved in creating AI-generated content can provide a clear overview of the process, making it easier for readers to understand.

In addition to explaining the basics of AI-generated content, these resources should also address common misconceptions and concerns. By tackling these issues head-on and providing accurate, evidence-based information, the resources can help to dispel myths and alleviate fears surrounding the technology. This can include addressing topics such as the role of human oversight in AI-generated content, the potential for bias, and the ethical considerations involved.

To ensure that the information resources are accessible to a wide audience, it is important to consider the various formats in which they can be presented. This may include written articles, blog posts, videos, podcasts, and interactive web pages. By offering multiple formats, the resources can cater to different learning styles and preferences, making the information more readily available to a diverse range of individuals.

Furthermore, it is essential to ensure that these resources are easily discoverable and shareable. By optimizing the resources for search engines and promoting them through various channels, such as social media, email newsletters, and relevant websites, the information can reach a broader audience. Encouraging readers to share the resources within their networks can also help to amplify the message and foster a greater understanding of AI-generated content among the general public.

Developing clear and accessible information resources is a critical step in educating and informing the public about AI-generated content. By presenting the information in a manner that is easy to understand, visually engaging, and widely accessible, these resources can play a vital role in overcoming the stigma surrounding this technology and promoting a more informed and balanced perspective.

Subsection 1.2: Leveraging Social Media and Digital Platforms

In the digital age, social media and online platforms have become powerful tools for disseminating information and engaging with the public. These platforms offer unparalleled reach and accessibility, allowing organizations and individuals to connect with a vast audience and share knowledge about AI-generated content. By leveraging the potential of social media and digital platforms, we can effectively educate and inform the public, helping to overcome the stigma surrounding this technology.

One of the key advantages of social media is its ability to facilitate the rapid spread of information. Through platforms like Twitter, Facebook, and LinkedIn, educational content about AI-generated content can be shared with a single click, reaching thousands or even millions of users within a matter of hours. This viral potential can be harnessed to raise awareness, spark conversations, and drive engagement around the topic.

To maximize the impact of social media efforts, it is essential to develop a strategic approach tailored to each platform. This may involve creating platform-specific content, such as short, attention-grabbing videos for Instagram or thought-provoking blog posts for LinkedIn. By understanding the unique characteristics and user demographics of each platform, organizations can craft messages that resonate with their target audience and encourage meaningful interactions.

In addition to creating original content, social media also provides opportunities for curating and sharing relevant information from other credible sources. By carefully selecting and promoting articles, studies, and expert opinions that shed light on AI-generated content, organizations can establish themselves as trusted resources and thought leaders in the field. This approach not only helps to educate the public but also fosters a sense of community and collaboration among those working to combat the stigma.

Engagement is another critical aspect of leveraging social media and digital platforms. By actively participating in conversations, responding to comments and questions, and encouraging feedback, organizations can build relationships with their audience and foster a sense of trust and transparency. This two-way communication allows for valuable insights into public perceptions and concerns, which can inform future educational efforts and help to address misconceptions head-on.

Moreover, social media and digital platforms offer unique opportunities for interactive learning experiences. Through the use of polls, quizzes, and gamified content, organizations can engage users in a more immersive and memorable way, making the learning process more enjoyable and effective. By creating content that encourages active participation, organizations can help users internalize key concepts and develop a deeper understanding of AI-generated content.

To further amplify the reach and impact of social media efforts, organizations can collaborate with influencers and thought leaders in the field. By partnering with individuals who have established credibility and a strong following, organizations can tap into new audiences and lend additional weight to their educational messages. These collaborations can take many forms, from guest blog posts and co-authored articles to joint webinars and social media takeovers.

Finally, it is essential to measure and analyze the success of social media and digital platform initiatives. By tracking metrics such as reach, engagement, and conversions, organizations can gain valuable insights into the effectiveness of their educational efforts and make data-driven decisions to optimize their strategies over time. This iterative approach ensures that resources are allocated efficiently and that the public receives the most relevant and impactful information about AI-generated content.

In conclusion, leveraging social media and digital platforms is a crucial strategy for educating and informing the public about AI-generated content. By harnessing the power of these platforms to share knowledge, engage with audiences, and collaborate with influencers, organizations can effectively combat the stigma surrounding this technology and foster a more informed and accepting public discourse.

Subsection 1.3: Collaborating with Influencers and Thought Leaders

In the quest to raise awareness and credibility surrounding AI-generated content, collaborating with influencers and thought leaders can be a powerful strategy. These individuals, who have already established themselves as trusted voices within their respective fields, can help to amplify the message and reach a wider audience.

Influencers and thought leaders bring with them a pre-existing network of followers who trust their opinions and insights. By partnering with these individuals, organizations can tap into their credibility and leverage their influence to educate and inform the public about AI-generated content. This can be particularly effective in reaching audiences who may not have otherwise engaged with the topic or who may be skeptical of the technology.

When selecting influencers and thought leaders to collaborate with, it is essential to choose individuals whose values and expertise align with the goals of the educational campaign. This may include experts in the fields of artificial intelligence, content creation, ethics, or journalism, among others. By partnering with individuals who have a deep understanding of the subject matter, organizations can ensure that the information being shared is accurate, nuanced, and credible.

Collaborations with influencers and thought leaders can take many forms, depending on the specific goals and resources of the campaign. One approach is to invite these individuals to contribute guest blog posts or articles, sharing their unique perspectives and insights on AI-generated content. This can help to diversify the range of voices and opinions being presented, while also increasing the reach of the educational material.

Another effective collaboration strategy is to host joint webinars, panel discussions, or podcasts featuring influencers and thought leaders. These events provide an opportunity for in-depth exploration of the topic, allowing experts to share their knowledge and engage in meaningful dialogue with the audience. By fostering a sense of community and encouraging active participation, these collaborations can help to break down barriers and facilitate a more nuanced understanding of AI-generated content.

Social media takeovers, where influencers and thought leaders temporarily "take over" an organization's social media accounts, can also be a powerful way to raise awareness and generate buzz around the topic. During these takeovers, the influencer can share their own insights, experiences, and perspectives on AI-generated content, while also engaging directly with the audience through comments, questions, and discussions.

In addition to these collaboration strategies, organizations can also work with influencers and thought leaders to create original, co-branded content, such as videos, infographics, or e-books. By combining the expertise and resources of both parties, these collaborations can result in high-quality, engaging content that resonates with the target audience and helps to further the educational goals of the campaign.

When collaborating with influencers and thought leaders, it is important to establish clear guidelines and expectations from the outset. This may include defining the scope of the collaboration, setting deadlines, and agreeing on key messaging and talking points. By ensuring that all parties are aligned and working towards a common goal, organizations can maximize the impact of these partnerships and avoid potential misunderstandings or conflicts.

Ultimately, collaborating with influencers and thought leaders can be a highly effective way to raise awareness and credibility around AI-generated content. By leveraging the expertise, influence, and networks of these individuals, organizations can reach new audiences, foster meaningful dialogue, and help to overcome the stigma surrounding this transformative technology. As the public discourse around AI-generated content continues to evolve, these collaborations will play an increasingly important role in shaping the conversation and driving positive change.

Subsection 1.4: Organizing Educational Events and Workshops

Hosting educational events and workshops is a powerful way to engage with the public and provide them with valuable insights into the world of AI-generated content. These interactive sessions offer a platform for experts, researchers, and industry professionals to share their knowledge and experiences, fostering a deeper understanding of the technology and its implications.

One of the primary benefits of organizing educational events and workshops is the opportunity for direct, face-to-face interaction with the audience. Unlike online resources or written materials, these sessions allow for real-time discussions, questions, and feedback, creating a more engaging and immersive learning experience. Attendees can actively participate in the conversation, sharing their own perspectives and concerns, and gaining a more nuanced understanding of the topic.

When planning educational events and workshops, it is essential to consider the target audience and tailor the content accordingly. For example, a workshop aimed at journalists and media professionals may focus on the ethical considerations surrounding AI-generated content, while an event for educators may explore the potential applications of the technology in the classroom. By addressing the specific needs and interests of each group, organizers can ensure that the information presented is relevant, actionable, and valuable.

The format of these events can also vary depending on the goals and resources available. Smaller, more intimate workshops may be ideal for hands-on demonstrations and in-depth discussions, while larger conferences can accommodate a wider range of speakers and topics, attracting a more diverse audience. Hybrid events, which combine both in-person and virtual elements, can help to expand the reach of the educational initiative, allowing participants from different geographic locations to engage with the content.

Regardless of the format, it is crucial to select knowledgeable and engaging speakers who can effectively communicate complex ideas to a non-technical audience. These experts should be able to present the information in a clear, accessible manner, using real-world examples and analogies to illustrate key points. They should also be open to answering questions and facilitating discussions, creating an interactive and dynamic learning environment.

In addition to traditional presentations and lectures, educational events and workshops can incorporate a variety of engaging activities and formats. Panel discussions, for example, can bring together experts with diverse perspectives, allowing attendees to hear multiple viewpoints and gain a more comprehensive understanding of the topic. Breakout sessions and small group discussions can provide opportunities for more focused, in-depth exploration of specific aspects of AI-generated content, while hands-on demonstrations and workshops can offer practical insights into the technology and its applications.

To maximize the impact of these events, organizers should prioritize accessibility and inclusivity. This may involve providing resources such as live captioning, sign language interpretation, or translated materials to accommodate attendees with diverse needs. It is also essential to ensure that the event space is physically accessible and that the registration process is straightforward and user-friendly.

Finally, educational events and workshops should be designed with long-term impact in mind. By providing attendees with takeaways, such as summary documents, resource lists, or action plans, organizers can help to extend the learning experience beyond the event itself. Encouraging ongoing engagement through follow-up discussions, online forums, or social media groups can also foster a sense of community and support continued learning and collaboration.

In conclusion, organizing educational events and workshops is a valuable strategy for informing and engaging the public about AI-generated content. By providing a platform for experts to share their knowledge and insights, and by creating opportunities for meaningful interaction and discussion, these sessions can help to break down barriers, dispel misconceptions, and foster a more informed and nuanced understanding of this transformative technology.

Summary: Empowering the Public Through Education and Awareness

In this section, we have explored the crucial role that education and awareness play in overcoming the stigma against AI-generated content. By developing clear and accessible information resources, leveraging social media and digital platforms, collaborating with influencers and thought leaders, and organizing educational events and workshops, we can effectively inform and engage the public about this transformative technology.

Through these efforts, we can demystify AI-generated content, dispel common misconceptions, and foster a more nuanced understanding of its capabilities, limitations, and potential applications. By empowering individuals with the knowledge and tools to critically evaluate AI-generated content, we can encourage informed decision-making and constructive dialogue.

As we move forward in this journey to overcome the stigma, it is essential to recognize that education and awareness are ongoing processes. As the technology continues to evolve and new challenges emerge, we must remain committed to providing up-to-date, accurate, and engaging information to the public.

By prioritizing education and awareness, we lay the foundation for a more accepting and inclusive future for AI-generated content. With a well-informed public, we can harness the potential of this technology to drive innovation, creativity, and progress while navigating the ethical and societal implications responsibly.

In the next section, we will delve into the crucial role of showcasing successful and ethical applications of AI-generated content in building trust and credibility among the public. By highlighting real-world examples of how this technology is being used to create value and solve problems, we can further shift perceptions and demonstrate the positive impact of AI-generated content on our lives and society.

Section 2: Showcasing Successful and Ethical Applications

In the face of the stigma surrounding AI-generated content, it is crucial to highlight the numerous instances where AI has been employed successfully and ethically to create valuable, engaging, and meaningful content. By showcasing these positive examples, we can begin to build trust and credibility in the use of AI in content creation, demonstrating that when used responsibly and with human oversight, AI can be a powerful tool for enhancing and augmenting human creativity.

Throughout this section, we will explore a range of case studies and success stories from various industries, including journalism, marketing, entertainment, and beyond. These examples will illustrate how AI-generated content has been effectively utilized to streamline workflows, personalize user experiences, and create compelling narratives that resonate with audiences. By delving into the specific strategies, techniques, and ethical considerations employed in each case, we will gain valuable insights into the best practices for leveraging AI in content creation.

Moreover, we will emphasize the importance of transparency, accountability, and human oversight in the development and deployment of AI-generated content. By highlighting the ethical frameworks and guidelines adhered to in these successful applications, we can demonstrate that the responsible use of AI is not only possible but essential for fostering trust and acceptance among consumers and stakeholders.

As we navigate this section, keep an open mind and consider how the lessons learned from these success stories can be applied to your own content creation processes. By embracing the potential of AI while remaining committed to ethical and transparent practices, we can begin to break down the stigma surrounding AI-generated content and pave the way for a future in which human creativity and artificial intelligence work together in harmony.

Subsection 2.1: Curating a Portfolio of High-Quality AI-Generated Content

In the quest to overcome the stigma surrounding AI-generated content, one of the most effective strategies is to curate a compelling portfolio that showcases the best examples of AI-created works. This portfolio serves as a powerful testament to the potential of AI in generating high-quality, engaging, and valuable content across various domains, from journalism and marketing to entertainment and beyond.

The process of curating such a portfolio begins with a thorough exploration of the AI-generated content landscape, identifying the most impressive and successful examples that demonstrate the technology's capabilities. This may include articles written by AI journalists that provide insightful analysis and thought-provoking perspectives, marketing copy crafted by AI algorithms that effectively captures the essence of a brand and resonates with target audiences, or even music compositions and visual artworks generated by AI systems that push the boundaries of creativity and innovation.

When selecting pieces for the portfolio, it is crucial to prioritize quality over quantity. Each example should be carefully chosen based on its merits, such as the depth of research, the clarity of expression, the originality of ideas, and the overall impact on the intended audience. By focusing on the cream of the crop, the portfolio can effectively challenge the notion that AI-generated content is inherently inferior or lacks the human touch.

Moreover, the portfolio should showcase a diverse range of content types, styles, and industries to illustrate the versatility and adaptability of AI in content creation. This diversity helps to break down the misconception that AI is limited to specific niches or formats and highlights its potential to revolutionize content production across the board.

As the portfolio grows and evolves, it is essential to regularly update and refine its contents, ensuring that it always represents the cutting edge of AI-generated content. This may involve replacing older examples with newer, more impressive ones or expanding the portfolio to include emerging applications of AI in content creation.

To maximize the impact of the portfolio, it should be presented in a visually engaging and user-friendly format, such as a dedicated website or interactive digital publication. This allows stakeholders, including potential clients, collaborators, and skeptics, to easily explore the showcased examples and gain a firsthand appreciation of the quality and potential of AI-generated content.

In addition to the portfolio itself, it is valuable to provide context and commentary for each showcased example, highlighting the specific techniques, datasets, and human oversight involved in its creation. This transparency helps to demystify the process of AI content generation and emphasizes the importance of responsible and ethical practices in the field.

Ultimately, by curating a portfolio of high-quality AI-generated content, we can effectively challenge the stigma surrounding this technology and demonstrate its immense potential to enhance and augment human creativity. As more people interact with and appreciate the showcased examples, they will begin to recognize AI as a valuable tool for content creation, paving the way for greater acceptance and adoption in the future.

Subsection 2.2: Emphasizing the Ethical and Responsible Use of AI

As we explore the successful applications of AI-generated content, it is crucial to emphasize the importance of ethical and responsible practices in the creation and deployment of these technologies. By highlighting the measures taken to ensure that AI is used in a manner that aligns with human values and societal norms, we can begin to build trust and credibility in the eyes of the public and combat the stigma that often surrounds AI-generated content.

One of the key ethical considerations in the development of AI systems is the need for transparency and accountability. This involves being open and honest about the use of AI in content creation, clearly disclosing when and how AI has been employed, and providing information about the datasets, algorithms, and human oversight involved in the process. By demystifying the inner workings of AI-generated content, we can help to alleviate concerns about potential biases, inaccuracies, or hidden agendas that may undermine public trust.

Another critical aspect of responsible AI use is the establishment of robust ethical frameworks and guidelines that govern the development and deployment of these technologies. This may include principles such as ensuring that AI systems are designed to be fair, unbiased, and non-discriminatory, that they respect user privacy and data security, and that they are subject to ongoing monitoring and evaluation to identify and mitigate any unintended consequences or harmful outcomes.

In addition to these broader ethical considerations, it is also essential to highlight the specific measures taken by organizations and individuals who have successfully leveraged AI-generated content in a responsible manner. This may involve showcasing examples of how AI has been used to enhance accessibility, promote diversity and inclusion, or address social and environmental challenges. By demonstrating the positive impact that ethical AI can have on society, we can help to counter the negative stereotypes and misconceptions that often surround this technology.

Moreover, emphasizing the role of human oversight and collaboration in the creation of AI-generated content can further reinforce the notion of responsible AI use. By highlighting the ways in which human creators work alongside AI systems, guiding their development, curating their outputs, and ensuring that the final product aligns with human values and intentions, we can demonstrate that AI is not a replacement for human creativity but rather a powerful tool that can augment and enhance it.

Ultimately, by emphasizing the ethical and responsible practices employed in the creation of AI-generated content, we can help to build a more nuanced and informed understanding of this technology among the general public. By showcasing the positive examples of AI use and the measures taken to ensure its alignment with human values, we can begin to break down the stigma surrounding AI-generated content and pave the way for its wider acceptance and adoption in various domains, from journalism and marketing to entertainment and beyond.

Subsection 2.3: Sharing Success Stories and Case Studies

In the journey to overcome the stigma surrounding AI-generated content, one of the most powerful tools at our disposal is the sharing of success stories and case studies. These real-world examples serve as compelling evidence of the value and benefits that AI can bring to the content creation process, demonstrating its potential to enhance creativity, streamline workflows, and deliver exceptional results.

By showcasing a diverse range of success stories from various industries, we can effectively challenge the misconceptions and biases that often fuel the stigma against AI-generated content. These case studies provide tangible proof that AI is not a threat to human creativity but rather a valuable collaborator that can help us push the boundaries of what is possible in the realm of content creation.

One such success story comes from the world of journalism, where AI has been employed to automate the production of news articles on a wide range of topics, from sports and finance to politics and entertainment. By leveraging natural language generation (NLG) technology, media organizations have been able to scale their content output, providing readers with up-to-date information around the clock. A notable example is the Associated Press, which has been using AI to generate earnings reports since 2014, freeing up journalists to focus on more complex and investigative stories.

In the field of marketing, AI has proven to be a game-changer, enabling brands to create highly personalized and engaging content at an unprecedented scale. One case study that exemplifies this is the success of Persado, an AI-powered platform that helps businesses generate persuasive marketing copy. By analyzing vast amounts of data and learning from past campaigns, Persado's AI can craft messages that resonate with specific target audiences, resulting in significantly higher conversion rates and ROI for its clients.

The entertainment industry has also witnessed the transformative power of AI-generated content, with applications ranging from script writing and storyboarding to animation and visual effects. A prime example is the collaboration between IBM Watson and 20th Century Fox on the creation of the movie trailer for the film "Morgan." By analyzing the visuals, sound, and composition of hundreds of horror movie trailers, Watson was able to identify the key emotional moments and craft a compelling trailer that captured the essence of the film.

As we share these success stories and case studies, it is crucial to emphasize the role of human creativity and oversight in the AI-generated content process. These examples should not be portrayed as instances of AI replacing human input but rather as showcases of the incredible synergy that can be achieved when human creativity is augmented by the power of artificial intelligence.

Moreover, by delving into the specific strategies and techniques employed in each success story, we can extract valuable insights and best practices that can be applied across various industries. This knowledge-sharing helps to demystify the process of AI-generated content creation and empowers more individuals and organizations to explore the potential of this technology in their own work.

Ultimately, the sharing of success stories and case studies serves as a powerful testament to the value and benefits of AI-generated content, helping to break down the barriers of skepticism and fear that often fuel the stigma surrounding this technology. By celebrating these achievements and learning from the experiences of those who have successfully leveraged AI in their content creation processes, we can pave the way for a future in which human creativity and artificial intelligence work hand in hand to push the boundaries of what is possible.

Subsection 2.4: Collaborating with Reputable Organizations and Brands

In the quest to overcome the stigma surrounding AI-generated content, forming strategic partnerships with reputable organizations and brands can play a crucial role in enhancing credibility and trust. By aligning with well-respected entities in various industries, proponents of AI-generated content can tap into their established reputations and leverage their influence to challenge misconceptions and build public confidence in the technology.

One of the primary benefits of collaborating with reputable organizations and brands is the opportunity to showcase real-world applications of AI-generated content in a trusted and familiar context. When a well-known company or institution publicly embraces and utilizes AI-generated content, it sends a powerful message to its audience, demonstrating that the technology is not only viable but also valuable in achieving their goals. This endorsement can go a long way in dispelling doubts and apprehensions about the quality and reliability of AI-generated content, as people are more likely to trust the judgment of organizations they know and respect.

Moreover, collaborating with reputable partners allows for the creation of high-profile case studies and success stories that can be widely shared and celebrated. These examples serve as compelling evidence of the potential of AI-generated content, highlighting its ability to deliver tangible results and drive meaningful outcomes. By showcasing the positive impact of AI-generated content in a variety of contexts, from journalism and marketing to healthcare and education, these partnerships can help to broaden public understanding and appreciation of the technology's versatility and value.

In addition to the credibility boost, collaborating with reputable organizations and brands also provides access to their extensive networks and platforms, enabling the message about AI-generated content to reach a wider audience. Through joint marketing efforts, co-branded initiatives, and thought leadership collaborations, proponents of AI-generated content can tap into the partner's existing communication channels and engage with new audiences who may not have previously been exposed to the technology. This increased visibility and reach can accelerate the process of normalizing AI-generated content and reducing the stigma surrounding it.

However, it is essential to approach these collaborations with care and due diligence, ensuring that the partner organization or brand aligns with the values and principles of responsible AI use. Before entering into any partnership, it is crucial to thoroughly vet the potential collaborator, assessing their track record, reputation, and commitment to ethical practices. By selectively partnering with organizations and brands that demonstrate a genuine dedication to transparency, accountability, and the responsible deployment of AI, proponents of AI-generated content can maintain the integrity of their message and avoid any potential backlash or criticism.

Ultimately, collaborating with reputable organizations and brands represents a powerful strategy for overcoming the stigma against AI-generated content. By leveraging the credibility, influence, and reach of trusted partners, proponents of the technology can accelerate the process of building public trust, showcasing real-world successes, and normalizing the use of AI in content creation. As more reputable entities openly embrace and champion AI-generated content, the stigma surrounding it will gradually erode, paving the way for wider acceptance and adoption across industries and domains.

Summary: Embracing AI-Generated Content for a More Innovative Future

As we have explored throughout this section, showcasing successful and ethical applications of AI-generated content is a powerful way to combat the stigma surrounding this technology. By curating a portfolio of high-quality examples, emphasizing the responsible use of AI, sharing compelling success stories, and collaborating with reputable organizations, we can demonstrate the immense potential of AI to revolutionize content creation across various industries.

The case studies and insights presented in this section serve as a testament to the fact that AI-generated content is not a threat to human creativity but rather a valuable tool that can augment and enhance it. When developed and deployed with transparency, accountability, and a commitment to ethical principles, AI has the power to streamline workflows, personalize user experiences, and push the boundaries of what is possible in the realm of creative expression.

However, overcoming the stigma against AI-generated content is not a one-time effort but an ongoing process that requires the active participation and collaboration of all stakeholders, from developers and creators to consumers and regulators. By continuing to showcase the positive impact of AI-generated content, fostering open dialogue about its challenges and opportunities, and working together to establish best practices and guidelines, we can create a future in which human creativity and artificial intelligence coexist in harmony.

As we move forward, it is crucial to approach AI-generated content not with fear or skepticism but with curiosity, openness, and a willingness to embrace change. By doing so, we can harness the full potential of this transformative technology and unlock new frontiers of innovation, creativity, and growth. The success stories and ethical applications highlighted in this section are just the beginning of what is possible when we embrace AI as a partner in our creative endeavors.

Section 3: Fostering Transparency and Accountability

In the quest to overcome the stigma surrounding AI-generated content, the role of transparency and accountability cannot be overstated. As the use of artificial intelligence in content creation becomes increasingly prevalent, it is crucial to establish clear guidelines and practices that ensure the ethical and responsible use of these powerful tools. By fostering a culture of transparency and accountability, we can build trust with audiences, mitigate potential risks, and unlock the full potential of AI-generated content.

Throughout this section, we will delve into the various aspects of transparency and accountability in the context of AI-generated content. We will explore the importance of implementing clear disclosure practices, ensuring that audiences are aware when they are engaging with content created by artificial intelligence. Additionally, we will discuss the development of ethical guidelines and standards that can serve as a framework for the creation and use of AI-generated content, promoting responsible practices across industries.

Furthermore, we will examine the value of open dialogue and feedback in the process of creating AI-generated content. By encouraging stakeholders and the public to share their thoughts and concerns, we can foster a collaborative environment that leads to the continuous improvement of AI systems and their outputs. Finally, we will highlight the significance of regular audits and monitoring to ensure that AI systems remain compliant with established ethical standards, maintaining the integrity and reliability of AI-generated content.

By embracing transparency and accountability, we can create a foundation of trust and credibility that will help overcome the stigma against AI-generated content. As we navigate this exciting and rapidly evolving landscape, it is essential to prioritize these principles, ensuring that the power of artificial intelligence is harnessed in a manner that benefits society as a whole. In the following subsections, we will explore practical strategies and approaches for fostering transparency and accountability, paving the way for a future where AI-generated content is embraced and celebrated for its potential to inform, engage, and inspire.

Subsection 3.1: Implementing Clear Disclosure Practices

In the age of AI-generated content, transparency is paramount. As more and more businesses and individuals embrace the power of artificial intelligence to create content, it is crucial to establish clear and consistent disclosure practices. By openly communicating when content has been generated by AI, we can foster trust, credibility, and accountability.

One of the primary reasons for implementing clear disclosure practices is to respect the audience's right to know the origin of the content they consume. In a world where information is constantly at our fingertips, readers deserve to understand whether a piece of content has been created by a human or an AI system. This knowledge allows them to make informed decisions about the content they engage with and share.

Moreover, clear disclosure practices help to mitigate the potential spread of misinformation. While AI-generated content can be highly informative and accurate, there is always the risk of unintentional biases or errors creeping into the output. By disclosing the use of AI in content creation, we can encourage readers to approach the information with a critical eye and verify facts from reliable sources.

Implementing clear disclosure practices can take various forms, depending on the medium and platform. For written content, such as articles or blog posts, a simple statement at the beginning or end of the piece can suffice. This statement should clearly indicate that the content has been generated by an AI system, along with any relevant details about the specific AI technology used.

In the case of visual content, such as images or videos, disclosure can be achieved through watermarks, captions, or accompanying text descriptions. These methods ensure that the audience is aware of the AI's involvement in the creation process, even if the content is shared or repurposed across different platforms.

Consistency is key when it comes to disclosure practices. Organizations and individuals should establish a standardized approach to disclosing AI-generated content, ensuring that the information is presented in a clear and easily understandable manner. This consistency helps to build trust and credibility over time, as audiences become accustomed to the disclosure format and can quickly identify AI-generated content.

Furthermore, it is essential to consider the ethical implications of AI-generated content and the role of disclosure in promoting responsible use of the technology. By being transparent about the use of AI, we can encourage open dialogue about the benefits and challenges of AI-generated content, fostering a culture of accountability and continuous improvement.

Implementing clear disclosure practices is not only a matter of transparency but also a way to showcase the innovative and transformative potential of AI in content creation. By openly embracing the use of AI and communicating it effectively, we can help to break down the stigma surrounding AI-generated content and pave the way for a future where human creativity and artificial intelligence work hand in hand.

In conclusion, implementing clear and consistent disclosure practices is a crucial step in overcoming the stigma against AI-generated content. By prioritizing transparency, we can build trust with audiences, promote responsible use of AI technology, and foster a culture of accountability and innovation. As we navigate the exciting possibilities of AI-generated content, let us remain committed to open communication and disclosure, ensuring that the power of AI is harnessed for the benefit of all.

Subsection 3.2: Establishing Ethical Guidelines and Standards

As AI-generated content becomes increasingly prevalent, it is crucial to establish a robust framework of ethical guidelines and standards to govern its creation and use. This framework serves as a compass, guiding content creators, platforms, and users towards responsible and beneficial practices while mitigating potential risks and negative consequences.

The development of ethical guidelines and standards for AI-generated content should be a collaborative effort, involving stakeholders from various domains, including AI researchers, content creators, industry leaders, policymakers, and ethicists. By bringing together diverse perspectives and expertise, we can create a comprehensive and well-rounded set of principles that address the complex challenges posed by AI-generated content.

One of the primary objectives of ethical guidelines and standards is to ensure that AI-generated content is created and used in a manner that respects fundamental human values, such as fairness, transparency, privacy, and accountability. This includes safeguarding against the spread of misinformation, protecting individual privacy rights, and preventing the perpetuation of biases and stereotypes.

To achieve these objectives, ethical guidelines and standards should encompass several key areas. Firstly, they should establish clear principles for data collection, usage, and storage in the context of AI-generated content. This includes ensuring that data is obtained lawfully, used responsibly, and secured against unauthorized access or misuse.

Secondly, ethical guidelines and standards should address the issue of algorithmic bias and fairness. AI systems used for content generation must be designed and trained to avoid perpetuating or amplifying existing societal biases based on factors such as race, gender, age, or socioeconomic status. Regular audits and assessments should be conducted to identify and mitigate any biases that may emerge over time.

Thirdly, the guidelines should emphasize the importance of transparency and explainability in AI-generated content. Users should have the right to know when they are interacting with AI-generated content and to understand the basic principles behind its creation. This transparency helps to build trust and allows users to make informed decisions about the content they consume.

Fourthly, ethical guidelines and standards should establish clear lines of accountability for the creators and distributors of AI-generated content. This includes defining responsibilities for ensuring the accuracy, reliability, and appropriateness of the content, as well as establishing mechanisms for redress in cases where AI-generated content causes harm or violates individual rights.

Finally, the guidelines should encourage ongoing research and collaboration to address emerging ethical challenges and to refine best practices as AI technology continues to evolve. This includes promoting interdisciplinary dialogue, supporting research initiatives, and fostering a culture of responsible innovation in the field of AI-generated content.

Establishing ethical guidelines and standards is not a one-time endeavor but an ongoing process that requires commitment, collaboration, and adaptability. By proactively addressing the ethical implications of

AI-generated content and implementing robust guidelines, we can harness the power of AI for the greater good while mitigating its potential risks and drawbacks.

As we navigate the complex landscape of AI-generated content, ethical guidelines and standards serve as a vital tool for building trust, promoting responsible practices, and ensuring that the benefits of this technology are realized in a manner that upholds our shared values and principles. By embracing this framework, we can work towards a future where AI-generated content is not only technically impressive but also ethically sound, contributing to a more informed, inclusive, and empowered society.

Subsection 3.3: Encouraging Open Dialogue and Feedback

In the journey to overcome the stigma against AI-generated content, fostering open dialogue and welcoming feedback from stakeholders and the public play a crucial role. By creating an environment that encourages transparent communication and active listening, we can gain valuable insights, address concerns, and collaboratively shape the future of AI-generated content.

One of the primary benefits of open dialogue is the opportunity to gather diverse perspectives on the topic. By engaging with a wide range of stakeholders, including content creators, industry professionals, academics, and consumers, we can develop a more comprehensive understanding of the challenges and opportunities associated with AI-generated content. This diversity of thought can help identify blind spots, challenge assumptions, and inspire innovative solutions to the stigma problem.

Moreover, open dialogue serves as a platform for education and awareness. Through meaningful conversations, we can dispel myths, clarify misconceptions, and provide accurate information about AI-generated content. By actively listening to the concerns and questions raised by stakeholders and the public, we can tailor our communication efforts to address specific knowledge gaps and build a shared understanding of the technology's potential and limitations.

Encouraging feedback is another essential aspect of fostering open dialogue. By actively seeking input from stakeholders and the public, we demonstrate a genuine commitment to collaboration and continuous improvement. This feedback can take various forms, such as surveys, focus groups, online forums, or direct conversations. By providing multiple channels for individuals to share their thoughts, experiences, and suggestions, we create an inclusive environment that values diverse voices.

Feedback serves as a valuable tool for identifying areas of improvement and guiding the development of AI-generated content. By carefully analyzing the input received, we can pinpoint specific concerns, preferences, and expectations of our target audience. This information can then be used to refine our AI algorithms, improve the quality and relevance of the generated content, and address any ethical or societal considerations that may arise.

To effectively encourage open dialogue and feedback, it is essential to establish trust and transparency. This involves being clear about the purpose and limitations of AI-generated content, openly communicating the processes and principles behind its creation, and demonstrating a willingness to engage in honest and constructive conversations. By building trust, we create a foundation for meaningful dialogue and foster a sense of shared ownership in shaping the future of AI-generated content.

In addition to external stakeholders, it is equally important to promote open dialogue and feedback within organizations involved in the creation and distribution of AI-generated content. Encouraging internal discussions, cross-functional collaboration, and the sharing of ideas and concerns can lead to a more cohesive and responsible approach to AI-generated content. By fostering a culture of openness and continuous learning, organizations can stay at the forefront of technological advancements while prioritizing ethical considerations and user needs.

Ultimately, the value of open dialogue and feedback lies in its ability to drive progress and shape the narrative surrounding AI-generated content. By actively engaging with stakeholders and the public, we can collectively explore the potential benefits, address the challenges, and work towards a future where AI-generated content is embraced as a valuable tool for creativity, innovation, and knowledge sharing. Through ongoing conversations and a commitment to collaboration, we can gradually erode the stigma and unlock the full potential of AI-generated content for the benefit of all.

Subsection 3.4: Regularly Auditing and Monitoring AI Systems

As AI-generated content becomes increasingly prevalent in our digital landscape, it is crucial to establish robust mechanisms for regularly auditing and monitoring AI systems to ensure their compliance with ethical standards. This proactive approach is essential for maintaining the integrity and reliability of AI-generated content, fostering trust among users, and mitigating potential risks associated with the technology.

Regular audits serve as a comprehensive evaluation of an AI system's performance, assessing its adherence to predefined ethical guidelines and standards. These audits should be conducted by independent, third-party experts who possess the necessary technical knowledge and ethical understanding to thoroughly examine the system's algorithms, data inputs, and outputs. By subjecting AI systems to periodic scrutiny, we can identify and address any deviations from established ethical norms, such as biases, inaccuracies, or potential misuse.

The audit process should encompass a wide range of factors, including data quality, algorithmic fairness, transparency, and accountability. Auditors should carefully examine the datasets used to train AI systems, ensuring that they are diverse, representative, and free from inherent biases. They should also assess the fairness of the algorithms employed, verifying that they do not perpetuate or amplify existing societal disparities based on factors such as race, gender, age, or socioeconomic status.

Moreover, audits should evaluate the transparency of AI systems, assessing the clarity and accessibility of information provided to users regarding the nature and limitations of AI-generated content. This includes verifying that appropriate disclosures are in place, informing users when they are interacting with AI-generated content and providing insights into the system's capabilities and potential biases.

In addition to regular audits, continuous monitoring of AI systems is essential to ensure their ongoing compliance with ethical standards. Monitoring involves the real-time tracking and analysis of AI-generated content, allowing for the prompt detection and mitigation of any issues that may arise. This can be achieved through the implementation of automated monitoring tools, which can scan content for potential red flags, such as biased language, factual inaccuracies, or inappropriate content.

Monitoring should also involve human oversight, with dedicated teams of experts regularly reviewing AI-generated content to assess its quality, accuracy, and adherence to ethical guidelines. This human-in-the-loop approach ensures that the nuances and complexities of language and context are properly considered, complementing the capabilities of automated monitoring systems.

The frequency and scope of audits and monitoring should be tailored to the specific needs and risks associated with each AI system. Systems that generate content with potentially significant societal impact, such as news articles or educational materials, may require more frequent and rigorous audits compared to systems that produce less sensitive content. The level of monitoring should also be adjusted based on the volume and nature of the content generated, ensuring that resources are allocated effectively to maintain the highest standards of ethical compliance.

Regularly auditing and monitoring AI systems not only helps to ensure their compliance with ethical standards but also contributes to the continuous improvement of the technology. By identifying areas for enhancement and addressing any shortcomings, we can refine AI algorithms, optimize data inputs, and develop more robust ethical safeguards. This iterative process of evaluation and improvement is crucial for building trust in AI-generated content and realizing its full potential as a valuable tool for informing, engaging, and empowering individuals and society as a whole.

Ultimately, the commitment to regularly auditing and monitoring AI systems demonstrates a proactive and responsible approach to the development and deployment of AI-generated content. By prioritizing ethical compliance and maintaining a vigilant eye on the technology's performance, we can foster a culture of accountability, transparency, and trust, paving the way for the wider acceptance and appreciation of AI-generated content in our digital world.

Summary: Embracing Transparency and Accountability for a Stigma-Free Future

Throughout this section, we have explored the crucial role of transparency and accountability in overcoming the stigma against AI-generated content. By implementing clear disclosure practices, establishing ethical guidelines and standards, encouraging open dialogue and feedback, and regularly auditing and monitoring AI systems, we can foster trust, credibility, and responsible innovation in the realm of AI-generated content.

Transparency serves as the foundation upon which trust is built. By openly communicating the use of AI in content creation and providing clear information about its capabilities and limitations, we empower audiences to make informed decisions and engage with AI-generated content with confidence. This transparency not only respects the audience's right to know but also helps to mitigate the spread of misinformation and promote a more accurate understanding of AI's role in the creative process.

However, transparency alone is not enough. It must be coupled with accountability, which is achieved through the establishment of robust ethical guidelines and standards. These guidelines serve as a compass, guiding content creators, platforms, and users towards responsible and beneficial practices while mitigating potential risks and negative consequences. By collaboratively developing and adhering to these standards, we demonstrate our commitment to the ethical use of AI and ensure that its benefits are realized in a manner that upholds our shared values and principles.

Moreover, fostering open dialogue and welcoming feedback from stakeholders and the public are essential for the continuous improvement and refinement of AI-generated content. By actively listening to diverse perspectives, addressing concerns, and incorporating valuable insights, we can shape the future of AI-generated content in a way that benefits society as a whole. This collaborative approach not only helps to identify and address challenges but also unlocks new opportunities for innovation and growth.

To maintain the integrity and reliability of AI-generated content, regular audits and monitoring of AI systems are indispensable. By subjecting these systems to periodic scrutiny and real-time monitoring, we can identify and address any deviations from ethical standards, ensure ongoing compliance, and maintain the highest levels of quality and accuracy. This proactive approach demonstrates our commitment to accountability and helps to build trust among users and stakeholders.

As we move forward in the era of AI-generated content, embracing transparency and accountability will be the key to overcoming the stigma and unlocking the full potential of this transformative technology. By prioritizing these principles and working collaboratively with all stakeholders, we can create a future where AI-generated content is not only accepted but celebrated for its ability to inform, engage, and inspire audiences around the world.

In the next section, we will delve into the exciting possibilities of human-AI collaboration, exploring how the synergy between human creativity and artificial intelligence can lead to unprecedented levels of innovation and creative expression. By building upon the foundation of transparency and accountability established in this section, we can pave the way for a stigma-free future where the boundaries of what is possible are limited only by our imagination.

Section 4: Empowering Human-AI Collaboration

In the face of the stigma surrounding AI-generated content, it is crucial to recognize the immense potential that lies in the collaboration between human creators and AI systems. Rather than viewing AI as a threat to human creativity, we must explore strategies that promote a symbiotic relationship between the two. By harnessing the strengths of both human ingenuity and artificial intelligence, we can unlock new frontiers of creativity and innovation.

This section delves into the fascinating world of human-AI collaboration, presenting a compelling case for why it is essential to embrace this partnership in order to overcome the stigma against AI-generated content. Through a combination of real-world examples, expert insights, and practical strategies, we will demonstrate how the fusion of human and machine intelligence can lead to groundbreaking achievements across various fields.

As we embark on this exploration, it is important to approach the topic with an open mind and a willingness to challenge preconceived notions. By the end of this section, you will have a deeper understanding of the complementary nature of human and AI creativity, and be equipped with the knowledge and tools necessary to foster successful collaborations that push the boundaries of what is possible.

So, let us step into the realm of human-AI collaboration, where the combined power of human imagination and artificial intelligence has the potential to revolutionize the way we create, innovate, and shape the future. Together, we will uncover the strategies that empower this dynamic partnership and pave the way for a new era of creativity in the face of adversity.

Subsection 4.1: Highlighting the Complementary Nature

of Human and AI Creativity

In the face of the stigma surrounding AI-generated content, it is crucial to recognize and emphasize the complementary relationship between human creativity and artificial intelligence. Rather than viewing AI as a threat to human ingenuity, we must understand that the two can work together in harmony, each bringing unique strengths to the creative process.

Human creativity is characterized by our ability to draw upon our experiences, emotions, and intuition to generate novel ideas and solutions. We possess the capacity for abstract thinking, allowing us to make connections between seemingly unrelated concepts and to think outside the box. Our creativity is fueled by our curiosity, imagination, and the desire to express ourselves in meaningful ways.

On the other hand, AI excels at processing vast amounts of data, identifying patterns, and generating outputs based on predefined rules and algorithms. AI systems can analyze and learn from existing content, styles, and techniques, and then apply that knowledge to create new works. They can work tirelessly, producing countless iterations and variations of a given idea, offering a breadth of possibilities that may be challenging for humans to achieve on their own.

When human creativity and AI-generated content are brought together, the result is a powerful synergy that can push the boundaries of what is possible. Human creators can leverage the capabilities of AI to enhance their own creative process, using it as a tool to explore new ideas, generate inspiration, and streamline tedious tasks. For example, a writer may use an AI-powered writing assistant to help overcome writer's block, suggest alternative phrases, or identify areas for improvement in their work.

Similarly, AI systems can benefit from human input and guidance, ensuring that the generated content aligns with the creator's vision and meets the desired quality standards. Human creators can provide feedback, refine parameters, and make final decisions on the outputs generated by AI, ensuring that the end result is a product of the collaborative effort between human and machine.

By highlighting the complementary nature of human and AI creativity, we can begin to break down the stigma surrounding AI-generated content. Instead of viewing it as a threat to human creativity, we can recognize it as a valuable tool that can augment and enhance our creative capabilities. By embracing this collaborative approach, we open up new possibilities for innovation and expression, ultimately leading to the creation of more diverse, engaging, and impactful content.

Subsection 4.2: Providing Training and Support for Human Creators

As the collaboration between human creators and AI systems becomes increasingly prevalent, it is essential to recognize the importance of providing comprehensive training and support to help individuals effectively navigate this new creative landscape. By equipping human creators with the necessary skills, knowledge, and resources, we can empower them to harness the full potential of AI-assisted content creation while mitigating the challenges and stigma associated with it.

One of the primary areas of focus in training human creators should be on developing a deep understanding of the capabilities and limitations of AI systems. This involves educating individuals about the underlying technologies, such as machine learning algorithms, natural language processing, and computer vision, that power AI-generated content. By demystifying these concepts and providing practical examples of how they are applied in creative workflows, human creators can gain a more nuanced appreciation for the role of AI in their work and make informed decisions about when and how to incorporate it.

In addition to technical knowledge, it is crucial to provide training on the ethical considerations surrounding AI-generated content. This includes exploring issues such as bias, transparency, and accountability in AI systems, as well as discussing best practices for disclosing the use of AI in creative projects. By fostering an open dialogue about these topics and providing guidance on navigating ethical dilemmas, we can help human creators develop a strong moral compass and ensure that their collaborations with AI align with societal values and expectations.

Another key aspect of support for human creators involves providing access to tools, platforms, and communities that facilitate seamless collaboration with AI systems. This may include investing in user-friendly interfaces that allow creators to easily input their ideas, set parameters, and iterate on AI-generated outputs. Additionally, establishing online forums, discussion groups, and mentorship programs can create opportunities for human creators to share their experiences, learn from one another, and collectively explore the possibilities and challenges of AI-assisted content creation.

Furthermore, it is essential to recognize that the integration of AI into creative workflows may require a shift in mindset and a willingness to adapt to new ways of working. To support this transition, organizations can offer workshops, seminars, and training programs that focus on developing the soft skills necessary for effective human-AI collaboration. This may include sessions on communication, problem-solving, and adaptability, as well as exercises that encourage creators to think creatively about how AI can complement and enhance their existing skills and processes.

By investing in comprehensive training and support initiatives, we can empower human creators to confidently and effectively collaborate with AI systems. This not only helps to bridge the knowledge gap and reduce the stigma surrounding AI-generated content but also unlocks new opportunities for innovation and creativity. As we move forward into an era where the lines between human and machine intelligence become increasingly blurred, it is crucial that we prioritize the development of a skilled and well-supported creative workforce that can navigate this new frontier with confidence and integrity.

Subsection 4.3: Showcasing Successful Human-AI Creative Collaborations

In the face of the stigma surrounding AI-generated content, it is essential to highlight the numerous instances where human creators and AI systems have successfully collaborated to produce remarkable works of art, music, literature, and more. By showcasing these success stories, we can inspire and encourage the adoption of human-AI creative collaborations, demonstrating the immense potential that lies in the synergy between human imagination and artificial intelligence.

One striking example of a successful human-AI creative collaboration is the album "Hello World" by the artist Taryn Southern. Southern collaborated with AI music composition tools, such as Amper and IBM Watson Beat, to create the album's music. She provided the AI with parameters, such as genre, mood, and tempo, and the AI generated musical elements that Southern then arranged, edited, and paired with her own lyrics and vocals. The result is a compelling and emotionally resonant album that showcases the power of human-AI collaboration in music production.

In the realm of visual arts, the collaboration between artist Mario Klingemann and AI has yielded stunning results. Klingemann, known for his work with generative adversarial networks (GANs), has created a series of haunting and evocative portraits using AI. By training the AI on a dataset of historical portraits and photographs, Klingemann has been able to generate new images that combine elements of the past with the AI's own "imagination." The resulting works blur the lines between human and machine creativity, inviting viewers to question their assumptions about the nature of art and authorship.

Literature has also seen its fair share of successful human-AI collaborations. The novel "1 the Road" by author Ross Goodwin was written in collaboration with an AI system. Goodwin fed the AI with a diverse range of texts, from science fiction novels to news articles, and then set out on a road trip from New York to New Orleans with the AI in tow. As he traveled, the AI generated new text based on its training data and the input it received from sensors attached to the vehicle. Goodwin then edited and curated the AI-generated text to create a cohesive and compelling narrative that reflects on the nature of creativity, technology, and the human experience.

These examples merely scratch the surface of the many successful human-AI creative collaborations that have emerged in recent years. From the AI-assisted design of fashion collections to the use of AI in film production and animation, the possibilities for collaboration are vast and exciting. By showcasing these success stories, we can inspire more creators to embrace the potential of AI and explore new forms of creative expression.

Moreover, by highlighting the role of human creators in these collaborations, we can help to dispel the notion that AI-generated content is a threat to human creativity. Instead, we can emphasize the importance of human input, guidance, and curation in shaping the final output of these collaborations. By framing AI as a tool that augments and enhances human creativity, rather than replacing it, we can encourage more creators to view AI as a valuable collaborator in their creative process.

As we continue to showcase successful human-AI creative collaborations, it is essential to approach these examples with a critical eye and to engage in ongoing discussions about the ethical implications of AI in the creative industries. By fostering open and honest dialogue about the challenges and opportunities presented by AI, we can work towards a future in which human and machine creativity coexist in harmony, pushing the boundaries of what is possible and inspiring new generations of creators to embrace the potential of this exciting frontier.

Subsection 4.4: Fostering a Culture of Experimentation and Innovation

In order to fully embrace the potential of human-AI collaboration and overcome the stigma surrounding AI-generated content, it is crucial to foster a culture that encourages experimentation and innovation. This culture should permeate all levels of an organization, from leadership to individual contributors, creating an environment where taking risks, trying new approaches, and learning from failures are not only accepted but actively encouraged.

One of the key elements of fostering a culture of experimentation and innovation is to provide a safe space for individuals to explore new ideas and push the boundaries of what is possible with AI-assisted content creation. This can be achieved by establishing dedicated innovation labs or workshops where cross-functional teams can come together to brainstorm, prototype, and test new concepts without fear of judgment or repercussions. By creating an atmosphere of psychological safety, organizations can unlock the creativity and ingenuity of their employees, leading to breakthroughs in human-AI collaboration.

Another essential aspect of cultivating an experimental and innovative culture is to embrace a growth mindset. This means recognizing that the path to success in human-AI collaboration is not always linear and that setbacks and failures are inevitable parts of the learning process. By reframing failures as opportunities for growth and encouraging individuals to learn from their mistakes, organizations can foster a culture of resilience and adaptability. This mindset shift is particularly important in the context of AI-generated content, where the technology is constantly evolving, and new challenges and opportunities emerge on a regular basis.

To further support experimentation and innovation, organizations should invest in the necessary resources and infrastructure to enable seamless human-AI collaboration. This may include providing access to cutting-edge AI tools and platforms, offering training and development opportunities to help employees build relevant skills, and creating channels for knowledge sharing and best practice exchange across the organization. By equipping individuals with the tools and support they need to experiment and innovate, organizations can accelerate the pace of progress and stay ahead of the curve in the rapidly evolving landscape of AI-generated content.

Moreover, fostering a culture of experimentation and innovation requires a willingness to challenge the status quo and question long-held assumptions about the role of AI in the creative process. This may involve re-evaluating existing workflows, processes, and metrics to ensure they are aligned with the goals of human-AI collaboration and not inadvertently reinforcing the stigma against AI-generated content. By actively seeking out new perspectives and embracing diversity of thought, organizations can create a more inclusive and dynamic environment that encourages experimentation and innovation at all levels.

Finally, it is important to recognize and celebrate the successes that emerge from a culture of experimentation and innovation in human-AI collaboration. By showcasing the innovative projects, groundbreaking discoveries, and creative breakthroughs that result from this approach, organizations can inspire others to follow suit and contribute to a growing body of knowledge and best practices in the field. This, in turn, can help to erode the stigma surrounding AI-generated content and pave the way for a future where human and machine creativity are seen as complementary and mutually reinforcing.

Fostering a culture of experimentation and innovation is not a one-time initiative but an ongoing commitment that requires sustained effort and investment. By embracing this approach and creating an environment where individuals feel empowered to take risks, learn from failures, and push the boundaries of what is possible, organizations can position themselves at the forefront of the AI revolution and reap the benefits of human-AI collaboration for years to come.

Summary: Harnessing the Power of Human-AI Collaboration

As we have explored throughout this section, the key to overcoming the stigma surrounding AI-generated content lies in fostering a collaborative relationship between human creators and AI systems. By recognizing the complementary strengths of both human creativity and artificial intelligence, we can unlock new realms of possibility and push the boundaries of what is achievable in the creative process.

The success stories of human-AI collaborations in various fields, from music and art to literature and design, serve as powerful testaments to the incredible potential of this symbiotic partnership. These examples demonstrate that, when human imagination is augmented by the computational prowess of AI, the resulting creations can be truly groundbreaking and emotionally resonant.

However, to fully harness the power of human-AI collaboration, it is crucial to invest in comprehensive training and support for human creators. By equipping individuals with the necessary technical knowledge, ethical frameworks, and creative tools, we can empower them to confidently navigate this new frontier and make informed decisions about how to incorporate AI into their work.

Moreover, by actively showcasing successful human-AI collaborations and celebrating the role of human creators in shaping the final output, we can help to reframe the narrative around AI-generated content. Rather than viewing it as a threat to human creativity, we can position AI as a valuable tool that enhances and complements our creative capabilities, ultimately leading to more diverse, engaging, and impactful content.

As we move forward, it is essential to foster a culture of experimentation and innovation within organizations and creative communities. By providing a safe space for individuals to take risks, learn from failures, and push the boundaries of what is possible with AI, we can accelerate the pace of progress and stay at the forefront of this exciting frontier.

Ultimately, the path to overcoming the stigma against AI-generated content lies in embracing the power of human-AI collaboration. By recognizing the unique strengths of both human and machine intelligence, providing the necessary support and resources, and fostering a culture of experimentation and innovation, we can create a future in which human creativity and artificial intelligence coexist in harmony, driving us towards new heights of artistic expression and societal progress.

Section 5: Engaging in Proactive Advocacy and Policy Development

As the landscape of AI-generated content continues to evolve, it becomes increasingly important to actively participate in shaping the future of this technology and its impact on society. Engaging in proactive advocacy and policy development is a crucial step in overcoming the stigma against AI-generated content and ensuring that its potential benefits are realized while addressing legitimate concerns.

In this section, we will explore the vital role that individuals, organizations, and stakeholders can play in advocating for informed, balanced, and forward-thinking policies related to AI-generated content. By participating in public discourse, collaborating with policymakers and regulators, supporting research and development efforts, and building coalitions with like-minded partners, we can work towards creating a future in which AI-generated content is embraced, responsibly developed, and effectively integrated into various aspects of our lives.

Through proactive advocacy and policy development, we have the opportunity to shape the narrative surrounding AI-generated content, dispel misconceptions, and promote a more nuanced understanding of its potential risks and benefits. By engaging in these efforts, we can help establish a framework that encourages innovation, protects the rights of creators and consumers, and ensures that the development and deployment of AI-generated content align with our shared values and goals as a society.

As we delve into the various aspects of advocacy and policy development, we will explore the importance of staying informed, taking action, and working collaboratively to drive positive change. By the end of this section, you will have a deeper understanding of how you can contribute to overcoming the stigma against AI-generated content and help shape a future in which this technology is harnessed for the greater good.

Subsection 5.1: Participating in Public Discourse and Policy Discussions

As AI-generated content becomes increasingly prevalent in our daily lives, it is crucial for individuals and organizations to actively participate in public discourse and policy discussions surrounding this technology. By engaging in these conversations, we can help shape the narrative, dispel misconceptions, and advocate for policies that promote the responsible development and use of AI-generated content.

One of the primary reasons to participate in public discourse is to ensure that a diverse range of perspectives is represented. By sharing our experiences, concerns, and aspirations related to AI-generated content, we can contribute to a more comprehensive understanding of the technology's potential impact on society. This includes discussing both the benefits and challenges associated with AI-generated content, such as its potential to streamline content creation processes, as well as the risks of perpetuating biases or displacing human creators.

Engaging in policy discussions is equally important, as the decisions made by policymakers and regulators will have far-reaching consequences for the future of AI-generated content. By actively participating in these discussions, we can advocate for policies that strike a balance between fostering innovation and protecting the rights and interests of creators, consumers, and society as a whole. This may involve contributing to public consultations, attending stakeholder meetings, or collaborating with advocacy groups and industry associations to develop policy recommendations.

To effectively participate in public discourse and policy discussions, it is essential to stay informed about the latest developments in AI-generated content. This includes keeping abreast of technological advancements, emerging trends, and the evolving legal and ethical landscape surrounding this technology. By educating ourselves and others, we can help ensure that the conversations around AI-generated content are grounded in facts and informed by a deep understanding of the technology's potential implications.

Moreover, participating in public discourse and policy discussions provides an opportunity to highlight successful examples of AI-generated content and showcase the technology's potential to drive positive change. By sharing case studies and best practices, we can demonstrate how AI-generated content can be leveraged to enhance creativity, improve efficiency, and solve complex problems across various domains, from healthcare and education to entertainment and beyond.

In conclusion, actively participating in public discourse and policy discussions related to AI-generated content is a critical step in overcoming the stigma surrounding this technology. By engaging in informed, balanced, and forward-thinking conversations, we can help shape the future of AI-generated content and ensure that its development and deployment align with our shared values and goals as a society.

Subsection 5.2: Collaborating with Policymakers and Regulators

Collaborating with policymakers and regulators is an essential aspect of advocating for informed and balanced policies related to AI-generated content. By engaging in constructive dialogue and sharing expertise, individuals and organizations can help shape the regulatory landscape and ensure that policies are designed to foster innovation while addressing legitimate concerns.

One of the primary benefits of collaborating with policymakers and regulators is the opportunity to provide them with a deeper understanding of AI-generated content and its potential implications. Many policymakers may not have extensive knowledge of the technology or its applications, and by sharing insights and real-world examples, advocates can help bridge this knowledge gap. This collaboration can involve participating in hearings, submitting written comments, or engaging in one-on-one meetings with key decision-makers.

When collaborating with policymakers and regulators, it is crucial to present a balanced perspective that acknowledges both the benefits and challenges associated with AI-generated content. By providing a nuanced view of the technology, advocates can help policymakers develop a more comprehensive understanding of the issues at hand and craft policies that strike a balance between promoting innovation and protecting the rights and interests of creators, consumers, and society as a whole.

Another important aspect of collaborating with policymakers and regulators is the opportunity to share best practices and industry standards. By highlighting successful examples of AI-generated content and the policies and practices that have enabled their development, advocates can provide policymakers with a roadmap for creating a supportive regulatory environment. This may involve sharing case studies, industry guidelines, or technical standards that have been developed to ensure the responsible development and deployment of AI-generated content.

Collaboration with policymakers and regulators can also help ensure that policies are informed by the latest research and developments in the field. By connecting policymakers with experts in AI-generated content, advocates can facilitate the exchange of knowledge and ideas, helping to ensure that policies are grounded in scientific evidence and technical understanding. This collaboration can take many forms, such as organizing briefings, workshops, or roundtable discussions that bring together policymakers, researchers, and industry leaders.

In addition to providing expertise and insights, collaborating with policymakers and regulators also involves being responsive to their concerns and questions. By engaging in open and transparent dialogue, advocates can help build trust and establish themselves as reliable partners in the policy-making process. This may involve providing timely and accurate responses to inquiries, participating in public consultations, or working with policymakers to develop pilot projects or test beds that can help inform the development of policies and regulations.

Ultimately, the goal of collaborating with policymakers and regulators is to create a policy environment that supports the responsible development and deployment of AI-generated content while addressing legitimate concerns. By working together in a spirit of cooperation and mutual understanding, advocates and policymakers can help ensure that the benefits of this technology are realized while mitigating potential risks and negative consequences.

Subsection 5.3: Supporting Research and Development Efforts

Advancing the field of AI-generated content and overcoming the stigma surrounding it requires a strong foundation of research and development (R&D). By supporting R&D efforts, we can drive innovation, uncover new applications, and address the challenges and concerns associated with this technology. This subsection examines the importance of supporting R&D efforts and explores how such support can contribute to the growth and acceptance of AI-generated content.

Research plays a crucial role in deepening our understanding of AI-generated content and its potential implications. By investing in research initiatives, we can explore the theoretical underpinnings of this technology, develop new algorithms and techniques, and investigate the social, economic, and ethical dimensions of its use. This research can help us identify best practices, establish guidelines, and create frameworks for the responsible development and deployment of AI-generated content.

Moreover, research can help bridge the gap between the capabilities of AI-generated content and the expectations of users and stakeholders. By studying user preferences, perceptions, and behaviors, researchers can gain valuable insights into how AI-generated content is received and used in various contexts. This knowledge can inform the design and development of AI systems, ensuring that they meet the needs and expectations of their intended audiences.

In addition to supporting research, investing in development efforts is equally important. Development initiatives focus on translating research findings into practical applications and solutions. By providing resources and support for development projects, we can accelerate the creation of new tools, platforms, and services that leverage AI-generated content in innovative and impactful ways.

Development efforts can also help address the technical challenges associated with AI-generated content, such as improving the quality, diversity, and consistency of the content produced. By investing in the development of advanced algorithms, training techniques, and evaluation methods, we can enhance the performance and reliability of AI systems, making them more suitable for real-world applications.

Furthermore, supporting development initiatives can foster collaboration between researchers, developers, and industry partners. By bringing together experts from different disciplines and sectors, we can facilitate the exchange of ideas, knowledge, and resources, leading to the creation of more robust and effective AI-generated content solutions. This collaborative approach can also help ensure that the development of AI-generated content aligns with industry needs and societal values.

To effectively support research and development efforts, it is crucial to provide adequate funding, infrastructure, and incentives. This may involve establishing dedicated research grants, creating collaborative research centers, or offering tax incentives for organizations that invest in AI-generated content R&D. By providing these resources and support mechanisms, we can create an environment that encourages innovation, attracts top talent, and drives the advancement of the field.

Additionally, supporting research and development efforts can help address the concerns and misconceptions that contribute to the stigma against AI-generated content. By conducting rigorous studies and developing evidence-based solutions, researchers and developers can provide a more accurate and nuanced understanding of this technology. This can help dispel myths, address ethical concerns, and demonstrate the potential benefits of AI-generated content in various domains.

In conclusion, supporting research and development efforts is essential for advancing the field of AI-generated content and overcoming the stigma surrounding it. By investing in research initiatives, development projects, and collaborative endeavors, we can drive innovation, address challenges, and unlock the full potential of this technology. As we continue to support R&D efforts, we can create a future in which AI-generated content is not only accepted but also celebrated for its ability to enhance human creativity, productivity, and well-being.

Subsection 5.4: Building Coalitions and Partnerships

In the fight against the stigma surrounding AI-generated content, building coalitions and partnerships with like-minded organizations and stakeholders is a powerful strategy for amplifying advocacy efforts. By joining forces with others who share similar goals and values, individuals and organizations can pool resources, expertise, and influence to create a stronger, more unified voice in support of AI-generated content.

One of the primary benefits of building coalitions and partnerships is the ability to leverage the strengths and networks of each member organization. By bringing together a diverse group of stakeholders, such as industry associations, research institutions, advocacy groups, and media partners, coalitions can tap into a wide range of knowledge, skills, and connections. This collaborative approach enables members to share best practices, learn from each other's experiences, and develop more comprehensive and effective strategies for addressing the stigma against AI-generated content.

Coalitions and partnerships also provide a platform for coordinating advocacy efforts and maximizing impact. By aligning their messaging, tactics, and resources, member organizations can create a more powerful and persuasive campaign that reaches a broader audience and resonates with key decision-makers. This coordination can take many forms, such as joint public statements, coordinated media outreach, or collaborative research projects that provide evidence-based support for the benefits of AI-generated content.

Another advantage of building coalitions and partnerships is the ability to demonstrate broad-based support for the issue at hand. When a diverse group of organizations and stakeholders come together to advocate for a common cause, it sends a strong signal to policymakers, the media, and the public that the issue is important and deserving of attention. This show of unity can help build momentum, attract new allies, and increase the likelihood of achieving policy changes or shifting public opinion in favor of AI-generated content.

Moreover, coalitions and partnerships can help amplify the voices of underrepresented or marginalized communities who may be disproportionately affected by the stigma against AI-generated content. By including a wide range of perspectives and experiences in advocacy efforts, coalitions can ensure that the needs and concerns of all stakeholders are taken into account and that solutions are developed in an inclusive and equitable manner.

To build effective coalitions and partnerships, it is essential to identify potential allies who share common goals and values. This may involve reaching out to organizations and individuals who have a track record of supporting AI-generated content or who have expressed interest in related issues, such as digital rights, creative freedom, or technological innovation. It is also important to establish clear roles, responsibilities, and decision-making processes within the coalition to ensure that all members are able to contribute effectively and that the group is able to work together smoothly.

Once a coalition or partnership is established, it is crucial to maintain regular communication and coordination among members. This may involve setting up regular meetings, establishing shared communication channels, or creating working groups focused on specific tasks or initiatives. By fostering a sense of community and collaboration, coalitions can build trust, maintain momentum, and adapt to changing circumstances over time.

In conclusion, building coalitions and partnerships is a vital strategy for amplifying advocacy efforts and overcoming the stigma against AI-generated content. By bringing together a diverse group of stakeholders, coordinating messaging and tactics, and demonstrating broad-based support for the issue, coalitions can create a more powerful and persuasive voice in support of AI-generated content. As the field continues to evolve, it will be essential for advocates to build and maintain strong coalitions and partnerships to ensure that the benefits of this technology are fully realized and that the rights and interests of all stakeholders are protected.

Summary: Shaping the Future of AI-Generated Content Through Proactive Engagement

Throughout this section, we have explored the crucial role of proactive advocacy and policy development in overcoming the stigma against AI-generated content. By actively participating in public discourse, collaborating with policymakers and regulators, supporting research and development efforts, and building coalitions with like-minded partners, we can shape the future of this transformative technology.

The power of advocacy lies in its ability to influence public opinion, inform decision-making processes, and drive meaningful change. By engaging in open and informed discussions about the benefits, challenges, and implications of AI-generated content, we can help dispel misconceptions, address legitimate concerns, and promote a more nuanced understanding of this technology's potential.

Collaboration with policymakers and regulators is essential for creating a supportive and balanced regulatory environment that encourages innovation while protecting the rights and interests of all stakeholders. By sharing expertise, best practices, and evidence-based insights, advocates can help guide the development of policies that foster the responsible deployment of AI-generated content across various domains.

Moreover, supporting research and development efforts is critical for advancing our understanding of AI-generated content and unlocking its full potential. By investing in theoretical and applied research, we can develop new algorithms, techniques, and evaluation methods that enhance the quality, diversity, and consistency of AI-generated content, making it more suitable for real-world applications.

Building coalitions and partnerships amplifies the impact of advocacy efforts, allowing organizations and individuals to pool resources, coordinate strategies, and demonstrate broad-based support for the responsible development and deployment of AI-generated content. By working together, we can create a more powerful and persuasive voice that resonates with decision-makers and the public alike.

As we move forward, it is essential to recognize that the stigma against AI-generated content is not insurmountable. By proactively engaging in advocacy and policy development, we have the opportunity to shape the narrative, influence the trajectory of this technology, and create a future in which AI-generated content is celebrated for its ability to enhance human creativity, productivity, and well-being.

The path ahead may be challenging, but it is also filled with incredible opportunities. By embracing the power of advocacy, collaboration, research, and partnership, we can navigate the complexities of this rapidly evolving landscape and ensure that the benefits of AI-generated content are realized while mitigating potential risks and negative consequences.

As you reflect on the insights and strategies presented in this section, consider how you can contribute to this important endeavor. Whether through participating in public discussions, supporting research initiatives, or joining forces with like-minded advocates, your voice and actions can make a difference in shaping the future of AI-generated content.

Together, we can build a world in which the stigma against AI-generated content is a distant memory, replaced by a deep appreciation for the transformative potential of this technology and its ability to enrich our lives in countless ways. The journey begins with each one of us, and the time to act is now.

Chapter Summary: Embracing Change and Fostering Collaboration

As we navigate the rapidly evolving landscape of AI-generated content, it is crucial to recognize the importance of embracing change and fostering collaboration between humans and artificial intelligence. By implementing the strategies outlined in this chapter, individuals and organizations can effectively overcome the stigma surrounding AI-generated content and unlock its full potential.

Education and awareness play a vital role in dispelling misconceptions and building trust in AI-generated content. By developing clear and accessible information resources, leveraging digital platforms, and collaborating with influencers and thought leaders, we can create a more informed and receptive public. Showcasing successful and ethical applications of AI-generated content further reinforces its value and credibility.

Transparency and accountability are essential in overcoming the stigma. Implementing clear disclosure practices, establishing ethical guidelines, and regularly auditing AI systems demonstrate a commitment to responsible and trustworthy content creation. Encouraging open dialogue and welcoming feedback from stakeholders and the public fosters a culture of transparency and continuous improvement.

Empowering human-AI collaboration is key to unlocking the full potential of AI-generated content. By highlighting the complementary nature of human creativity and AI capabilities, providing training and support for human creators, and showcasing successful collaborations, we can inspire and encourage the adoption of AI-assisted content creation. Fostering a culture of experimentation and innovation will drive the development of new and exciting applications.

Proactive advocacy and policy development are crucial in shaping the future of AI-generated content. Engaging in public discourse, collaborating with policymakers and regulators, supporting research and development efforts, and building coalitions with like-minded organizations will help create a supportive and enabling environment for the responsible use of AI in content creation.

As we move forward, it is essential to embrace the AI revolution and recognize the transformative potential of AI-generated content. By working together, humans and AI can unlock new levels of creativity, efficiency, and innovation. The strategies outlined in this chapter provide a roadmap for overcoming the stigma and fostering a future where AI-generated content is celebrated for its contributions to our creative landscape. Embracing change and collaboration will pave the way for a more inclusive, dynamic, and exciting future for content creation.

Chapter 10: Collaborating with AI: A New Era of Creativity

As we navigate the complex landscape of AI-generated content and the stigma surrounding it, it's essential to recognize the immense potential for collaboration between humans and artificial intelligence in the creative process. Rather than viewing AI as a threat to human creativity, we must embrace the opportunities it presents to enhance, augment, and revolutionize the way we create.

The collaboration between humans and AI in creative endeavors is not a distant dream but a reality that is already unfolding before our eyes. From music composition to visual arts, from writing to design, AI is increasingly being integrated into the creative process, working hand in hand with human creators to push the boundaries of what's possible.

However, the path to successful human-AI collaboration is not without its challenges. It requires a fundamental shift in our mindset, a willingness to embrace change, and a deep understanding of the strengths and limitations of both human and artificial intelligence. It demands open-mindedness, adaptability, and a commitment to continuous learning and growth.

In this chapter, we will delve into the exciting world of human-AI creative collaboration. We will explore the foundations of effective collaboration, examining the key principles and frameworks that enable humans and AI to work together seamlessly. We will investigate the various workflows and processes that facilitate this collaboration, from iterative and agile approaches to modular task distribution and continuous feedback loops.

Moreover, we will showcase the cutting-edge tools and platforms that are empowering human-AI creative collaboration, from AI-assisted design tools to collaborative content creation platforms and intelligent project management systems. We will also discuss the skills and training required for individuals to thrive in this new era of creativity, emphasizing the importance of technical proficiency, collaborative problem-solving, and adaptability.

As we look to the future, the possibilities for human-AI creative collaboration are truly limitless. By embracing this partnership, we have the opportunity to unlock new forms of creative expression, push the boundaries of innovation, and redefine what it means to be a creator in the digital age.

So let us embark on this exciting journey together, exploring the vast potential of human-AI collaboration in the creative process. Let us challenge the stigma surrounding AI-generated content and instead focus on the incredible opportunities that lie ahead. Together, we can usher in a new era of creativity, one in which the combined power of human imagination and artificial intelligence knows no bounds.

Section 1: The Foundations of Human-AI Creative Collaboration

In the rapidly evolving landscape of creative industries, the collaboration between humans and artificial intelligence (AI) is becoming increasingly prevalent. As we navigate this new era of creativity, it is crucial to understand the fundamental principles and frameworks that enable effective partnerships between human creators and AI systems. By exploring these foundations, we can unlock the true potential of human-AI creative collaboration and pave the way for groundbreaking innovations that push the boundaries of what is possible.

The journey towards successful human-AI creative collaboration begins with a deep understanding of the unique strengths and limitations of both human creators and AI systems. While humans possess unparalleled creativity, intuition, and emotional intelligence, AI excels in processing vast amounts of data, identifying patterns, and generating novel combinations of ideas. By recognizing and leveraging these complementary abilities, we can create a powerful synergy that enhances the creative process and leads to outcomes that surpass what either humans or AI could achieve independently.

However, the path to effective human-AI creative collaboration is not without its challenges. Issues of trust, transparency, and control must be carefully navigated to ensure that the partnership remains balanced and mutually beneficial. It is essential to establish clear roles and responsibilities, foster open communication, and maintain a shared vision of the desired outcomes. Only by building a strong foundation of trust and understanding can we unlock the full potential of human-AI creative collaboration.

In this section, we will delve into the key principles and frameworks that underpin successful human-AI creative partnerships. We will explore the importance of establishing trust and transparency, defining clear roles and responsibilities, fostering open communication and feedback, and embracing a growth mindset that values experimentation and iteration. By laying these foundations, we can create an environment that nurtures creativity, innovation, and collaboration between humans and AI, ultimately leading to a new era of creative possibilities.

Subsection 1.1: Establishing Trust and Transparency

In the realm of human-AI creative collaboration, trust and transparency serve as the bedrock upon which successful partnerships are built. Without a solid foundation of trust, the full potential of these collaborations remains untapped, hindered by skepticism and uncertainty. Transparency, on the other hand, is the key to fostering trust, as it allows both human creators and AI systems to operate with a clear understanding of each other's capabilities, limitations, and intentions.

Establishing trust between human creators and AI systems is a multifaceted process that requires open communication, consistent performance, and a shared commitment to the creative vision. Human creators must have confidence in the AI system's ability to generate high-quality, relevant, and innovative content that aligns with their goals and expectations. This trust is earned through the AI system's demonstrated competence, reliability, and adaptability in the face of evolving creative challenges.

Transparency, in this context, means providing human creators with a clear understanding of how the AI system operates, the data it relies upon, and the algorithms that drive its creative output. By shedding light on the inner workings of the AI system, developers can demystify the creative process and allay concerns about the "black box" nature of AI-generated content. This transparency enables human creators to make informed decisions about when and how to incorporate AI into their creative workflows, fostering a sense of control and agency in the collaboration.

Moreover, transparency extends beyond the technical aspects of the AI system to encompass the ethical considerations surrounding its use. As AI becomes increasingly integrated into the creative process, it is crucial to ensure that the system is designed and deployed in a manner that aligns with human values, respects intellectual property rights, and promotes fairness and inclusivity. By openly addressing these ethical concerns and engaging in ongoing dialogue with human creators, AI developers can build trust and demonstrate their commitment to responsible innovation.

Ultimately, the success of human-AI creative collaboration hinges on the ability to establish and maintain trust through transparency. By fostering open communication, consistent performance, and a shared commitment to ethical practices, human creators and AI systems can forge powerful partnerships that unlock new frontiers of creativity and innovation. As we navigate this uncharted territory, it is essential to prioritize trust and transparency as the guiding principles that will shape the future of human-AI creative collaboration.

Subsection 1.2: Defining Roles and Responsibilities

In the context of human-AI creative collaboration, clearly defining the roles and responsibilities of both human creators and AI systems is crucial for ensuring a harmonious and productive partnership. Without a shared understanding of who is responsible for what aspects of the creative process, confusion, duplication of effort, and even conflict can arise, undermining the effectiveness of the collaboration.

To begin, it is essential to recognize that human creators and AI systems bring distinct strengths and capabilities to the table. Human creators excel in areas such as intuition, emotional intelligence, and the ability to understand and connect with an audience on a deep, personal level. They possess the unique capacity to infuse their work with meaning, purpose, and cultural relevance, drawing upon their lived experiences and creative vision to craft compelling narratives and evocative imagery.

On the other hand, AI systems offer unparalleled computational power, the ability to process and analyze vast amounts of data, and the capacity to generate novel combinations of ideas and concepts at a speed and scale that would be impossible for humans alone. They can identify patterns, make predictions, and offer insights that can help to inform and enhance the creative process, pushing the boundaries of what is possible and inspiring new directions for exploration.

Given these complementary strengths, it is crucial to define clear roles and responsibilities that allow both human creators and AI systems to contribute meaningfully to the collaborative process. This may involve establishing a division of labor that assigns specific tasks and decision-making authority to each party based on their unique capabilities and areas of expertise.

For example, human creators may be responsible for setting the overall creative vision and direction for a project, determining the key themes, messages, and aesthetic sensibilities that will guide the work. They may also be tasked with providing high-level feedback and guidance to the AI system, helping to refine and shape the generated content to ensure that it aligns with the desired outcomes and resonates with the intended audience.

Meanwhile, the AI system may be responsible for tasks such as data analysis, pattern recognition, and the generation of novel ideas and content based on the parameters and constraints set by the human creator. It may also be tasked with automating certain aspects of the creative process, such as color grading, image enhancement, or the creation of multiple variations on a theme, freeing up the human creator to focus on higher-level creative decisions.

By clearly defining these roles and responsibilities, human creators and AI systems can work together in a more efficient and effective manner, leveraging their respective strengths and minimizing the potential for confusion or conflict. This can help to foster a sense of trust and collaboration, as each party understands and respects the contributions of the other, working together towards a shared creative vision.

Moreover, establishing clear roles and responsibilities can help to address some of the ethical and legal concerns surrounding the use of AI in creative contexts. By ensuring that human creators retain ultimate creative control and decision-making authority, while also acknowledging the significant contributions of the AI system, it becomes possible to strike a balance between the benefits of AI-assisted creation and the need to protect the rights and interests of human creators.

Ultimately, the success of human-AI creative collaboration depends on the ability to define and maintain clear roles and responsibilities that allow both parties to contribute meaningfully to the creative process. By establishing a shared understanding of who is responsible for what, and by leveraging the unique strengths and capabilities of both human creators and AI systems, it becomes possible to unlock new frontiers of creativity and innovation, pushing the boundaries of what is possible in the realm of creative expression.

Subsection 1.3: Fostering Open Communication and Feedback

In the dynamic landscape of human-AI creative collaboration, open communication and feedback play a vital role in ensuring the success and sustainability of these partnerships. As we explore the strategies for maintaining effective communication channels between human creators and AI systems, it is essential to recognize the unique challenges and opportunities that arise when two fundamentally different entities work together towards a common creative goal.

At the heart of fostering open communication lies the need for a shared language and understanding between human creators and AI systems. This involves developing a common vocabulary that allows both parties to express their ideas, concerns, and expectations clearly and concisely. By establishing a foundation of mutual understanding, human creators and AI systems can engage in meaningful dialogue, exchange insights, and work together to refine and improve the creative output.

One key strategy for maintaining open communication is to implement regular feedback loops throughout the creative process. These feedback loops provide opportunities for human creators to offer guidance, critique, and direction to the AI system, ensuring that the generated content aligns with the desired creative vision. Simultaneously, the AI system can provide insights and suggestions based on its analysis of vast datasets and pattern recognition capabilities, offering fresh perspectives and ideas that may not have been considered by the human creator alone.

To facilitate effective feedback exchange, it is crucial to establish clear protocols and guidelines for communication. This may involve setting up dedicated channels, such as online platforms or collaborative workspaces, where human creators and AI systems can interact seamlessly and in real-time. These channels should be designed to support various forms of feedback, including text-based comments, visual annotations, and even voice or video recordings, catering to the diverse communication preferences of different individuals and teams.

Another essential aspect of fostering open communication is to cultivate a culture of transparency and trust between human creators and AI systems. This involves openly sharing information about the AI system's capabilities, limitations, and decision-making processes, as well as the human creator's goals, expectations, and creative vision. By maintaining a transparent and honest dialogue, both parties can build a strong foundation of trust, which is essential for navigating the complexities and uncertainties inherent in the creative process.

Moreover, it is important to recognize that effective communication and feedback require a willingness to listen, learn, and adapt on both sides. Human creators must be open to the insights and suggestions offered by AI systems, even if they challenge traditional ways of thinking or working. Simultaneously, AI systems must be designed to incorporate and respond to human feedback in a meaningful way, continuously learning and evolving to better serve the needs of the creative collaboration.

To support this ongoing learning and adaptation, it is valuable to establish mechanisms for capturing and analyzing the feedback exchanged between human creators and AI systems. This may involve implementing data tracking and analytics tools that can help identify patterns, trends, and areas for improvement in the communication process. By leveraging these insights, both human creators and AI developers can refine their approaches, optimize their workflows, and ultimately enhance the quality and effectiveness of their creative collaboration.

In conclusion, fostering open communication and feedback is a critical component of successful human-AI creative collaboration. By establishing a shared language, implementing regular feedback loops, cultivating transparency and trust, and embracing a mindset of continuous learning and adaptation, human creators and AI systems can unlock the full potential of their partnership. As we navigate this exciting new frontier of creativity, it is essential to prioritize open communication and feedback as the foundation upon which groundbreaking innovations and transformative creative experiences can be built.

Subsection 1.4: Embracing a Growth Mindset

In the dynamic and ever-evolving landscape of human-AI creative collaboration, embracing a growth mindset is paramount to unlocking the full potential of these partnerships. A growth mindset, as coined by psychologist Carol Dweck, is the belief that one's abilities and intelligence can be developed and enhanced through dedication and hard work. When applied to the context of human-AI creative collaborations, a growth mindset fosters an environment that values learning, experimentation, and iteration as essential components of the creative process.

Adopting a growth mindset requires a fundamental shift in perspective, moving away from the notion that creativity is a fixed, innate talent and instead recognizing it as a skill that can be cultivated and refined over time. This mindset encourages human creators to approach their collaborations with AI systems as opportunities for growth and development, rather than as threats to their creative identity or autonomy. By embracing the idea that both human and AI capabilities can be expanded and improved through effort and experience, creators open themselves up to new possibilities and avenues for exploration.

Central to the growth mindset is the willingness to take risks, experiment with new ideas, and learn from failures. In human-AI creative collaborations, this means being open to trying new approaches, testing unconventional combinations of human and AI-generated content, and iterating based on feedback and results. By fostering a culture that celebrates experimentation and views setbacks as valuable learning experiences, human creators and AI systems can push the boundaries of what is possible and create truly innovative and groundbreaking work.

Moreover, a growth mindset emphasizes the importance of continuous learning and skill development. As AI technologies advance at an unprecedented pace, human creators must commit to staying informed about the latest developments, tools, and techniques in the field. This requires a proactive approach to learning, seeking out educational resources, attending workshops and conferences, and engaging in ongoing dialogue with other professionals working at the intersection of creativity and AI. By continuously expanding their knowledge and skill sets, human creators can better understand and leverage the capabilities of AI systems, leading to more effective and impactful collaborations.

Cultivating a growth mindset also involves embracing the iterative nature of the creative process. Rather than striving for perfection from the outset, human creators and AI systems should approach their collaborations as ongoing conversations, with each iteration building upon the insights and lessons learned from the previous one. This iterative approach allows for a more organic and responsive creative process, adapting to new ideas, feedback, and evolving project requirements. By embracing iteration as a fundamental aspect of human-AI creative collaboration, creators can refine and improve their work over time, ultimately leading to higher quality and more impactful results.

To foster a growth mindset within human-AI creative collaborations, it is essential to create an environment that supports and encourages this way of thinking. This can involve implementing policies and practices that reward experimentation, risk-taking, and learning, such as providing resources for skill development, celebrating innovative approaches, and treating failures as opportunities for growth. By building a culture that values and nurtures a growth mindset, organizations can create the conditions necessary for human-AI creative collaborations to thrive and reach their full potential.

In conclusion, embracing a growth mindset is a critical component of successful human-AI creative collaboration. By fostering an environment that values learning, experimentation, and iteration, human creators and AI systems can unlock new frontiers of creativity, push the boundaries of what is possible, and create work that is truly transformative. As we navigate this exciting new landscape of creative collaboration, it is essential to cultivate a growth mindset as the foundation upon which groundbreaking innovations and meaningful partnerships can be built.

Summary: Building the Foundation for a New Era of Creative Collaboration

As we embark on this exciting journey of human-AI creative collaboration, it is essential to lay a strong foundation built on trust, transparency, clearly defined roles, open communication, and a growth mindset. By establishing these key principles and frameworks, we can create an environment that fosters innovation, experimentation, and the pursuit of groundbreaking creative endeavors.

Throughout this section, we have explored the importance of building trust and transparency between human creators and AI systems, recognizing that these elements are critical to the success of any collaborative partnership. We have also emphasized the need for clearly defined roles and responsibilities, ensuring that both humans and AI can leverage their unique strengths and capabilities to contribute meaningfully to the creative process.

Moreover, we have highlighted the significance of fostering open communication and feedback loops, enabling human creators and AI systems to engage in meaningful dialogue, exchange insights, and continuously refine their creative output. By cultivating a culture of transparency and trust, we can navigate the complexities and uncertainties inherent in the creative process and unlock the full potential of human-AI collaboration.

Finally, we have emphasized the importance of embracing a growth mindset, recognizing that creativity is a skill that can be cultivated and refined over time. By approaching human-AI collaborations as opportunities for learning, experimentation, and iteration, we can push the boundaries of what is possible and create truly innovative and impactful work.

As we move forward in this book, we will delve deeper into the various aspects of human-AI creative collaboration, exploring the tools, techniques, and strategies that can help us navigate this exciting new landscape. By building upon the foundations laid in this section, we can create a roadmap for success, empowering human creators and AI systems to work together in harmony and unlock the limitless potential of creative collaboration in the age of artificial intelligence.

Section 2: Collaborative Workflows and Processes

As we delve deeper into the world of human-AI creative collaboration, it becomes increasingly clear that the success of these partnerships relies heavily on the establishment of effective workflows and processes. These collaborative frameworks serve as the foundation upon which human creators and AI systems can build trust, foster open communication, and work together seamlessly to achieve their shared creative goals.

Imagine a world where human creativity and artificial intelligence are no longer seen as separate entities, but rather as two sides of the same coin – a powerful, symbiotic relationship that has the potential to revolutionize the way we approach creative projects. By examining the various workflows and processes that facilitate this collaboration, we can begin to understand how to harness the strengths of both human and machine, while mitigating the weaknesses that may arise.

In this section, we will explore the key components of successful human-AI creative collaboration, from the iterative and agile approaches that allow for flexibility and adaptability, to the modular and flexible task distribution that ensures each party is working to their strengths. We will also delve into the importance of continuous feedback and refinement loops, which allow for the constant improvement and optimization of creative outputs.

But perhaps most importantly, we will examine the delicate balance between structure and spontaneity that is necessary for truly innovative and impactful creative work. By understanding how to strike this balance, we can unlock the full potential of human-AI collaboration and pave the way for a new era of creativity that knows no bounds.

So, whether you are a seasoned creative professional looking to incorporate AI into your workflow, or simply someone who is curious about the future of creativity, this section will provide you with the insights and knowledge you need to navigate this exciting new landscape. Let us embark on this journey together, and discover the limitless possibilities that await us when we embrace the power of collaborative workflows and processes in human-AI creative collaboration.

Subsection 2.1: Iterative and Agile Approaches

In the realm of human-AI creative collaboration, embracing iterative and agile workflows can significantly enhance the efficiency and effectiveness of the creative process. These approaches, borrowed from the world of software development, have proven invaluable in fostering flexibility, adaptability, and continuous improvement in the face of complex and ever-evolving creative challenges.

At its core, an iterative approach involves breaking down the creative process into smaller, manageable cycles or iterations. Each iteration consists of a series of steps, such as planning, execution, review, and refinement, which are repeated until the desired outcome is achieved. This cyclical nature allows for constant feedback and adjustment, enabling human creators and AI systems to learn from each other and make necessary course corrections along the way.

Agile workflows, on the other hand, prioritize flexibility and responsiveness to change. In an agile human-AI collaboration, team members work in short sprints, typically lasting between one and four weeks, with clearly defined goals and deliverables. This approach allows for rapid prototyping, testing, and refinement of creative ideas, while also fostering a culture of open communication, transparency, and collaboration among team members.

One of the key benefits of iterative and agile workflows in human-AI creative collaborations is the ability to quickly identify and address potential issues or roadblocks. By working in short cycles and regularly reviewing progress, teams can spot problems early on and take corrective action before they escalate. This proactive approach not only saves time and resources but also ensures that the creative output remains aligned with the project's overall goals and objectives.

Moreover, iterative and agile approaches encourage experimentation and risk-taking, which are essential for pushing the boundaries of creativity and innovation. By creating a safe space for trial and error, these workflows empower human creators and AI systems to explore new ideas, techniques, and solutions without fear of failure. This, in turn, can lead to breakthrough moments and the emergence of truly groundbreaking creative work.

To successfully implement iterative and agile workflows in human-AI creative collaborations, it is essential to establish clear roles, responsibilities, and communication channels among team members. Human creators must be open to feedback and willing to adapt their processes and techniques as needed, while AI systems must be designed to provide meaningful insights and suggestions based on data-driven analysis and pattern recognition.

Ultimately, the power of iterative and agile approaches lies in their ability to harness the collective intelligence of human creators and AI systems, creating a symbiotic relationship that drives continuous improvement and pushes the boundaries of what is possible in the realm of creative collaboration.

Subsection 2.2: Modular and Flexible Task Distribution

In the dynamic landscape of human-AI creative collaboration, the distribution of tasks between human creators and AI systems plays a crucial role in determining the efficiency and effectiveness of the creative process. A modular and flexible approach to task allocation allows both parties to leverage their unique strengths and capabilities, leading to a more seamless and productive partnership.

At its core, modular task distribution involves breaking down the creative process into distinct, self-contained units or modules. Each module represents a specific task or set of tasks that can be assigned to either human creators or AI systems based on their respective abilities and expertise. By structuring the workflow in this manner, teams can ensure that each party is focusing on the aspects of the project that they are best suited to handle, optimizing the overall efficiency of the collaboration.

Flexibility is another key aspect of successful task distribution in human-AI creative collaborations. As projects evolve and new challenges arise, it may become necessary to reassign tasks or adjust the division of labor between human creators and AI systems. A flexible approach allows teams to adapt quickly to changing circumstances, ensuring that the creative process remains on track and that the final output meets the desired quality standards.

One of the primary benefits of modular and flexible task distribution is that it allows human creators to focus on the high-level, strategic aspects of the creative process, such as ideation, conceptualization, and decision-making. By delegating more routine or repetitive tasks to AI systems, human creators can devote their time and energy to the tasks that require their unique creative vision and expertise.

For example, in a human-AI collaborative writing project, the AI system could be tasked with conducting research, gathering relevant data, and generating initial drafts based on predefined parameters. The human writer could then focus on refining the content, adding creative flourishes, and ensuring that the final product meets the desired tone, style, and message. This division of labor allows both parties to play to their strengths, resulting in a more efficient and effective creative process.

To successfully implement modular and flexible task distribution in human-AI creative collaborations, it is essential to have a clear understanding of the capabilities and limitations of both human creators and AI systems. This requires ongoing communication and collaboration between team members, as well as a willingness to experiment with different task allocation strategies and adjust as needed.

Moreover, it is important to establish clear guidelines and protocols for how tasks will be assigned, monitored, and evaluated throughout the creative process. This may involve setting specific performance metrics, defining quality standards, and establishing feedback loops to ensure that both human creators and AI systems are meeting expectations and contributing to the overall success of the project.

Ultimately, the goal of modular and flexible task distribution is to create a collaborative environment in which human creators and AI systems can work together seamlessly, leveraging their respective strengths to produce innovative, high-quality creative outputs. By embracing this approach, teams can unlock new levels of efficiency, adaptability, and creativity in their collaborative endeavors.

Subsection 2.3: Continuous Feedback and Refinement Loops

In the ever-evolving landscape of human-AI creative collaboration, the role of continuous feedback and refinement loops cannot be overstated. These iterative processes serve as the driving force behind the optimization of creative outputs, ensuring that the final product meets the highest standards of quality and resonates with the intended audience.

At its core, a feedback loop is a cyclical process in which the output of a system is continuously monitored, evaluated, and used to inform adjustments and improvements to the system itself. In the context of human-AI creative collaboration, this means that the creative work produced by the partnership is subjected to ongoing review and critique, with insights gleaned from this process being fed back into the collaborative workflow to guide future iterations.

The importance of continuous feedback and refinement loops lies in their ability to identify and address potential weaknesses or areas for improvement in the creative output. By regularly assessing the quality, relevance, and impact of the work being produced, human creators and AI systems can work together to refine their approach, making necessary adjustments to ensure that the final product meets the desired objectives.

One of the key benefits of incorporating continuous feedback and refinement loops into human-AI creative collaborations is the opportunity for real-time course correction. Rather than waiting until the end of a project to evaluate its success, teams can use ongoing feedback to identify and address issues as they arise, minimizing the risk of investing significant time and resources into a creative direction that ultimately fails to meet expectations.

To effectively implement continuous feedback and refinement loops, it is essential to establish clear metrics and criteria for evaluating the creative output. These may include factors such as audience engagement, emotional resonance, technical proficiency, and alignment with the project's overall goals and vision. By defining these parameters upfront, human creators and AI systems can work together to develop a shared understanding of what constitutes success and use this as a guideline for ongoing assessment and improvement.

Another crucial aspect of continuous feedback and refinement loops is the integration of multiple perspectives and sources of input. While the collaborative team itself should be actively involved in reviewing and critiquing the creative work, it is also valuable to seek feedback from external stakeholders, such as target audiences, industry experts, and peers in the creative field. This diversity of input can provide a more comprehensive and nuanced understanding of the strengths and weaknesses of the creative output, leading to more targeted and effective refinements.

As human-AI creative collaborations continue to evolve, the role of technology in facilitating continuous feedback and refinement loops will likely become increasingly sophisticated. Advanced analytics tools, for example, may be used to track audience engagement and sentiment in real-time, providing valuable insights into the impact and effectiveness of the creative work. Similarly, machine learning algorithms could be employed to identify patterns and trends in feedback data, helping teams to prioritize areas for improvement and optimize their creative approach over time.

Ultimately, the success of human-AI creative collaborations will depend on the ability to embrace a culture of continuous learning, experimentation, and refinement. By embedding feedback and iteration into the very fabric of the collaborative process, teams can unlock new levels of creativity, innovation, and impact, pushing the boundaries of what is possible when human ingenuity and artificial intelligence work together in harmony.

Subsection 2.4: Balancing Structure and Spontaneity

In the realm of human-AI creative collaboration, striking the right balance between structured processes and spontaneous creativity is crucial for achieving optimal results. While structure provides a framework for efficient collaboration and ensures that project goals are met, spontaneity allows for the emergence of novel ideas and innovative solutions. Finding harmony between these two seemingly opposing forces is key to unlocking the full potential of human-AI partnerships.

One effective strategy for balancing structure and spontaneity is to establish clear roles and responsibilities for both human and AI collaborators, while also allowing for flexibility within those roles. By defining the primary tasks and objectives for each party, teams can ensure that essential processes are followed and that the collaboration stays on track. However, it is equally important to create space for experimentation and improvisation within those roles, encouraging both human and AI collaborators to explore new approaches and ideas.

Another approach is to implement a hybrid creative process that combines structured phases with periods of open-ended exploration. For example, teams might begin a project with a well-defined planning phase, in which goals, timelines, and deliverables are clearly outlined. Once this foundation is established, the collaboration can then move into a more spontaneous phase, where human and AI collaborators are encouraged to brainstorm, prototype, and iterate on ideas freely. This cycle of structure and spontaneity can be repeated throughout the project, ensuring that the collaboration remains focused while also allowing for creative breakthroughs.

Incorporating regular check-ins and feedback sessions is another way to balance structure and spontaneity in human-AI collaborations. By setting aside dedicated times for collaborators to review progress, share insights, and discuss new ideas, teams can maintain a sense of structure and accountability. At the same time, these sessions also provide an opportunity for spontaneous creative exchanges, as collaborators build upon each other's ideas and explore new directions together.

Ultimately, the key to balancing structure and spontaneity in human-AI creative collaborations lies in fostering a culture of trust, open communication, and adaptability. By establishing clear guidelines and expectations while also remaining open to new possibilities, teams can create an environment that encourages both focused execution and creative risk-taking. As collaborators become more comfortable working together and understanding each other's strengths and limitations, they can more easily navigate the delicate balance between structure and spontaneity, leading to more innovative and impactful creative outcomes.

Summary: Harnessing the Power of Collaborative Workflows and Processes

Throughout this section, we have explored the various workflows and processes that facilitate effective human-AI creative collaboration. By examining the key components of successful partnerships, we have gained a deeper understanding of how to harness the strengths of both human and machine to achieve unparalleled creative outcomes.

We have seen how iterative and agile approaches allow for flexibility and adaptability in the face of complex creative challenges, enabling teams to learn from each other and make necessary course corrections along the way. The importance of modular and flexible task distribution has also been highlighted, allowing human creators to focus on high-level, strategic aspects of the creative process while delegating routine tasks to AI systems.

Moreover, we have delved into the critical role of continuous feedback and refinement loops in optimizing creative outputs. By regularly assessing the quality, relevance, and impact of the work being produced, human-AI teams can identify areas for improvement and make real-time adjustments to ensure the final product meets the desired objectives.

Perhaps most importantly, we have explored the delicate balance between structure and spontaneity that is necessary for truly innovative and impactful creative work. By establishing clear guidelines and expectations while remaining open to new possibilities, teams can foster a culture of trust, open communication, and adaptability that encourages both focused execution and creative risk-taking.

As we move forward in this new era of creativity, it is clear that the success of human-AI collaborations will depend on our ability to embrace these collaborative workflows and processes. By leveraging the unique strengths of both human and machine, we can push the boundaries of what is possible and create truly groundbreaking work that resonates with audiences on a profound level.

In the next section, we will explore the various tools and platforms that support and enhance human-AI creative collaboration, providing practical insights into how these technologies can be harnessed to unlock new levels of creativity and innovation.

Section 3: Tools and Platforms for Human-AI Creative Collaboration

As we delve deeper into the world of human-AI creative collaboration, it becomes increasingly clear that the right tools and platforms play a crucial role in facilitating and enhancing these partnerships. The rapid advancement of technology has given rise to a plethora of innovative solutions designed to bridge the gap between human creativity and artificial intelligence, opening up new possibilities for creative expression and problem-solving.

In this section, we will embark on an exciting exploration of the various tools and platforms that are revolutionizing the way humans and AI work together in creative endeavors. From AI-assisted design software that augments human intuition with data-driven insights, to collaborative content creation platforms that enable seamless interaction between human and machine, we will uncover the cutting-edge technologies that are reshaping the creative landscape.

As we navigate this fascinating terrain, we will discover how these tools and platforms are not only streamlining creative workflows but also unlocking new levels of efficiency, productivity, and innovation. By harnessing the power of AI, these solutions are empowering human creators to push the boundaries of what is possible, allowing them to focus on the strategic and imaginative aspects of their work while the AI handles the more repetitive and time-consuming tasks.

But the impact of these tools and platforms extends far beyond individual creators. They are also transforming the way creative teams collaborate, enabling seamless communication, coordination, and feedback loops that span across disciplines and geographies. Through intelligent project management systems and integrated evaluation mechanisms, these solutions are helping to optimize team performance and ensure that creative outputs meet the highest standards of quality and relevance.

As we explore the various tools and platforms available, we will also consider the important questions of accessibility, usability, and scalability. How can these solutions be designed to be intuitive and user-friendly, even for those with limited technical expertise? How can they be adapted to meet the needs of different creative industries and workflows? And how can they be scaled to support the growing demand for human-AI creative collaboration across the globe?

By the end of this section, readers will have a comprehensive understanding of the tools and platforms that are driving the future of human-AI creative collaboration. They will be equipped with the knowledge and insights needed to navigate this exciting new landscape, and to leverage these solutions to unlock their full creative potential. So let us dive in and discover the incredible possibilities that await us at the intersection of human creativity and artificial intelligence.

Subsection 3.1: AI-Assisted Design and Ideation Tools

In the realm of creative projects, the ideation and design phases are crucial for setting the foundation and direction of the entire endeavor. Traditionally, these stages have relied heavily on human intuition, experience, and creativity. However, with the advent of AI-assisted design and ideation tools, the landscape of creative problem-solving is undergoing a significant transformation.

AI-assisted design tools leverage the power of machine learning algorithms to augment human creativity and streamline the design process. These tools can analyze vast amounts of data, identify patterns, and generate novel design suggestions based on specified parameters and constraints. By providing designers with a wide range of options and variations, AI-assisted tools can help break creative blocks and inspire new ideas that may have otherwise been overlooked.

One of the key benefits of AI-assisted design tools is their ability to automate repetitive and time-consuming tasks, such as generating multiple iterations of a design or exploring different color palettes and layouts. This automation frees up designers to focus on the more strategic and conceptual aspects of their work, allowing them to devote more time and energy to refining and perfecting their ideas.

For example, in the field of graphic design, AI-assisted tools like Adobe Sensei can analyze a designer's work and suggest improvements to composition, color harmony, and typography. These suggestions are based on best practices and insights gleaned from analyzing thousands of successful designs, providing designers with data-driven guidance to enhance their creations.

Similarly, in the realm of product design, AI-assisted tools can help designers explore a wide range of form factors, materials, and manufacturing processes. By inputting design goals and constraints, designers can leverage AI algorithms to generate multiple 3D models and prototypes, each optimized for different performance criteria. This allows designers to quickly iterate and refine their ideas, testing different approaches and identifying the most promising solutions.

However, it is important to note that AI-assisted design tools are not meant to replace human creativity but rather to enhance and augment it. The role of the designer remains critical in guiding the creative process, setting the overall vision, and making final decisions based on their expertise and aesthetic sensibilities. AI-assisted tools serve as powerful aids in the ideation and exploration phases, but the human touch is still essential for creating truly innovative and impactful designs.

As AI technology continues to advance, we can expect to see even more sophisticated and intuitive AI-assisted design tools emerge. These tools will likely incorporate advanced features such as natural language processing, allowing designers to describe their ideas verbally and have the AI generate visual representations. They may also integrate with other technologies, such as virtual and augmented reality, to provide immersive design experiences and real-time feedback.

Ultimately, the integration of AI-assisted design and ideation tools into the creative process represents a significant shift in the way we approach problem-solving and innovation. By leveraging the power of AI to augment human creativity, designers can push the boundaries of what is possible, generating novel ideas and solutions that may have been unimaginable in the past. As these tools become more widely adopted and refined, they have the potential to revolutionize the way we design everything from products and services to experiences and environments.

Subsection 3.2: Collaborative Content Creation Platforms

In the ever-evolving landscape of human-AI creative collaboration, collaborative content creation platforms have emerged as powerful tools that facilitate seamless interaction between human creators and artificial intelligence. These platforms provide a shared space where humans and AI can work together, leveraging their unique strengths and capabilities to produce innovative and engaging content.

At the core of these platforms lies a sophisticated infrastructure that enables real-time communication, data sharing, and task coordination between human and AI collaborators. By utilizing cloud-based technologies and advanced APIs, these platforms create a centralized hub where creative assets, such as text, images, audio, and video, can be easily accessed, manipulated, and integrated into the collaborative workflow.

One of the key advantages of collaborative content creation platforms is their ability to streamline the ideation and brainstorming process. Through intuitive interfaces and intelligent suggestion systems, these platforms encourage human creators to input their ideas, concepts, and creative briefs, which are then analyzed and interpreted by AI algorithms. The AI can generate a wide range of creative prompts, inspirational examples, and conceptual frameworks based on the human input, sparking new ideas and helping to overcome creative blocks.

As the collaboration progresses, these platforms facilitate a dynamic and iterative process of content generation and refinement. Human creators can provide feedback, guidance, and artistic direction to the AI, while the AI can rapidly generate multiple variations and iterations of the content based on the human input. This back-and-forth exchange allows for a fluid and adaptive creative process, where ideas can be quickly explored, tested, and refined until the desired outcome is achieved.

Collaborative content creation platforms also offer powerful tools for content optimization and personalization. By leveraging machine learning algorithms and data analytics, these platforms can analyze audience preferences, engagement metrics, and performance data to provide insights and recommendations for improving the content's relevance, impact, and reach. This data-driven approach enables human creators to make informed decisions and adapt their content strategies in real-time, ensuring that the final product resonates with the target audience.

As these platforms continue to evolve, they are incorporating advanced features such as natural language processing, computer vision, and generative models to further enhance the human-AI collaborative experience. For example, some platforms now offer AI-powered writing assistants that can help human writers craft compelling narratives, suggest alternative phrasings, and ensure grammatical and stylistic consistency. Similarly, in the realm of visual content creation, AI-assisted tools can help human designers and artists generate realistic textures, 3D models, and animations, saving time and effort while expanding the creative possibilities.

However, it is important to recognize that collaborative content creation platforms are not without their challenges. Issues of data privacy, intellectual property rights, and attribution must be carefully considered and addressed to ensure that the rights and interests of all collaborators are protected. Additionally, as these platforms become more sophisticated and automated, there is a risk of over-reliance on AI, potentially leading to a homogenization of creative output and a loss of unique human perspective.

Despite these challenges, the potential benefits of collaborative content creation platforms are immense. By fostering a symbiotic relationship between human creativity and artificial intelligence, these platforms have the power to revolutionize the way we create and consume content. As they continue to mature and evolve, we can expect to see even more innovative and impactful applications emerge, pushing the boundaries of what is possible in the realm of creative collaboration.

Subsection 3.3: Intelligent Project Management Systems

In the dynamic world of human-AI creative collaboration, effective coordination and management of projects are crucial for ensuring successful outcomes. Intelligent project management systems have emerged as powerful tools that streamline the collaborative process, enabling seamless communication, task allocation, and progress tracking between human and AI team members.

At their core, intelligent project management systems are designed to adapt to the unique needs and challenges of human-AI creative collaborations. These systems leverage advanced algorithms and machine learning techniques to analyze project requirements, team member skills, and available resources, and then generate optimized project plans that maximize efficiency and productivity.

One of the key features of intelligent project management systems is their ability to facilitate real-time communication and data sharing among team members. Through intuitive interfaces and integrated communication channels, these systems allow human and AI collaborators to exchange ideas, provide feedback, and make decisions in a centralized and transparent manner. This level of connectivity ensures that all team members are aligned on project goals, timelines, and expectations, reducing the risk of miscommunication and delays.

Intelligent project management systems also play a crucial role in task allocation and resource optimization. By analyzing the strengths and capabilities of each team member, both human and AI, these systems can assign tasks in a way that maximizes the overall efficiency and quality of the creative output. For example, an AI algorithm may be tasked with generating multiple design variations based on a set of parameters, while human team members focus on evaluating and refining the most promising options.

As the project progresses, intelligent project management systems continuously monitor and adapt to changes in scope, timelines, and resource availability. Using predictive analytics and real-time data analysis, these systems can identify potential bottlenecks or risks and suggest proactive measures to mitigate them. This level of adaptability ensures that human-AI creative collaborations remain on track and responsive to evolving requirements and constraints.

Another key benefit of intelligent project management systems is their ability to facilitate knowledge sharing and learning among team members. By capturing and analyzing project data, these systems can identify best practices, successful strategies, and areas for improvement, and then share these insights with the team. This knowledge sharing not only enhances the overall performance of the collaboration but also promotes a culture of continuous learning and growth among human and AI team members.

As intelligent project management systems continue to evolve, they are incorporating advanced features such as natural language processing and sentiment analysis to better understand and respond to the needs and preferences of human team members. For example, these systems may be able to detect when a human collaborator is experiencing creative burnout or frustration and suggest appropriate interventions, such as redistributing tasks or providing additional support.

However, it is important to recognize that intelligent project management systems are not a replacement for human leadership and decision-making. While these systems can provide valuable insights and recommendations, ultimately, it is up to the human team members to exercise their judgment, creativity, and emotional intelligence in guiding the collaboration toward success.

In conclusion, intelligent project management systems are transforming the way human and AI collaborators work together in creative endeavors. By facilitating seamless coordination, communication, and task allocation, these systems are enabling teams to achieve new levels of efficiency, adaptability, and innovation. As these systems continue to mature and integrate with other collaborative tools and platforms, they have the potential to unlock even greater possibilities for human-AI creative collaboration in the future.

Subsection 3.4: Integrated Feedback and Evaluation Mechanisms

In the realm of human-AI creative collaboration, the importance of integrated feedback and evaluation mechanisms cannot be overstated. These critical components of creative tools and platforms play a vital role in ensuring the quality, relevance, and effectiveness of the generated content. By incorporating robust feedback and evaluation systems, these tools can foster a continuous cycle of improvement, adaptation, and refinement, ultimately leading to better outcomes and more successful collaborations.

At their core, integrated feedback mechanisms provide a means for human collaborators to communicate their thoughts, opinions, and suggestions directly to the AI system. This feedback can take various forms, such as ratings, comments, or even more advanced methods like sentiment analysis or eye-tracking data. By capturing and analyzing this feedback in real-time, the AI can gain valuable insights into the preferences, expectations, and needs of its human counterparts, allowing it to adapt and optimize its output accordingly.

For example, imagine a collaborative writing platform where a human author is working alongside an AI to craft a novel. As the author reviews and interacts with the AI-generated content, they can provide feedback on various aspects, such as the coherence of the narrative, the authenticity of the characters, or the effectiveness of the dialogue. The AI can then process this feedback and adjust its algorithms to better align with the author's vision and style, resulting in a more harmonious and productive collaboration.

In addition to feedback mechanisms, integrated evaluation systems play a crucial role in assessing the quality and performance of AI-generated content. These systems can employ a range of techniques, from simple rule-based checks to more sophisticated machine learning models, to analyze and score the content based on predefined criteria. By providing objective and quantifiable measures of quality, these evaluation systems can help human collaborators make informed decisions about which ideas to pursue, which elements to refine, and which directions to explore further.

Moreover, integrated evaluation mechanisms can serve as powerful tools for benchmarking and comparing the performance of different AI models or configurations. By establishing clear and consistent evaluation metrics, creative teams can systematically test and optimize their AI collaborators, identifying the most effective approaches and continuously pushing the boundaries of what is possible. This data-driven approach to evaluation can help to demystify the often opaque nature of AI systems, providing greater transparency and accountability in the creative process.

However, it is important to recognize that the design and implementation of integrated feedback and evaluation mechanisms are not without their challenges. One key consideration is the need to strike a delicate balance between the subjective nature of creative feedback and the objective requirements of algorithmic evaluation. While human opinions and preferences are essential for guiding the creative process, they must be carefully weighted and calibrated to avoid biasing the AI system or stifling its ability to generate novel and unexpected ideas.

Another challenge lies in ensuring the fairness, transparency, and explainability of the evaluation criteria and processes. As AI systems become increasingly complex and autonomous, it is crucial that their decision-making processes are open to scrutiny and that their evaluations are based on clear and justifiable criteria. This not only helps to build trust and confidence in the AI collaborator but also enables human teams to identify and address any potential biases or limitations in the evaluation system itself.

Despite these challenges, the benefits of integrated feedback and evaluation mechanisms in human-AI creative collaboration are clear. By providing a structured and systematic way to capture, analyze, and act upon the insights and opinions of human collaborators, these systems can help to foster a more dynamic, responsive, and iterative creative process. As these mechanisms continue to evolve and mature, we can expect to see even more sophisticated and effective ways of leveraging feedback and evaluation to drive innovation and push the boundaries of creative possibility.

In conclusion, integrated feedback and evaluation mechanisms are essential components of any successful human-AI creative collaboration. By providing a means for human collaborators to communicate their thoughts and preferences directly to the AI system, and by establishing clear and consistent metrics for assessing the quality and performance of the generated content, these mechanisms can help to create a more transparent, accountable, and effective creative process. As we continue to explore the vast potential of human-AI collaboration, the development and refinement of these critical tools will undoubtedly play a central role in shaping the future of creative endeavor.

Summary: Empowering Creative Synergy Through Innovative Tools and Platforms

Throughout this section, we have embarked on an enlightening exploration of the various tools and platforms that are revolutionizing the landscape of human-AI creative collaboration. From AI-assisted design and ideation tools that augment human creativity with data-driven insights, to collaborative content creation platforms that facilitate seamless interaction between human and machine, we have witnessed the emergence of a new era in creative problem-solving.

As we have discovered, these innovative tools and platforms are not merely enhancing efficiency and productivity; they are fundamentally transforming the way we approach creative endeavors. By leveraging the power of AI to automate repetitive tasks, generate novel ideas, and optimize content, these solutions are freeing up human creators to focus on the strategic and imaginative aspects of their work. The result is a powerful synergy between human intuition and artificial intelligence, leading to unprecedented levels of innovation and impact.

Moreover, the integration of intelligent project management systems and robust feedback and evaluation mechanisms has brought a new level of transparency, accountability, and continuous improvement to the creative process. By facilitating seamless coordination, communication, and knowledge sharing among human and AI collaborators, these tools are fostering a culture of learning, growth, and adaptability that is essential for success in today's rapidly evolving creative landscape.

As we look to the future, it is clear that the potential of human-AI creative collaboration is only beginning to be realized. As these tools and platforms continue to mature and evolve, we can expect to see even more sophisticated and intuitive solutions emerge, pushing the boundaries of what is possible in the realm of creative expression. However, it is crucial that we approach this exciting frontier with a keen awareness of the ethical, societal, and cultural implications of these technologies, ensuring that they are developed and deployed in a responsible and inclusive manner.

In conclusion, the tools and platforms explored in this section represent a powerful catalyst for unlocking the full potential of human-AI creative collaboration. By empowering creators with the means to harness the power of AI in their work, these solutions are ushering in a new era of innovation, efficiency, and impact. As we continue to navigate this exciting landscape, it is up to us to embrace the opportunities presented by these tools while also grappling with the challenges and responsibilities that come with their use. Only by doing so can we truly realize the transformative potential of human-AI creative collaboration and build a future in which technology and creativity work hand in hand to drive progress and enrich the human experience.

Section 4: Skill Development and Training for Human-AI Creative Collaboration

As the creative landscape continues to evolve, the integration of artificial intelligence (AI) into the creative process has become increasingly prevalent. This exciting development presents a wealth of opportunities for artists, designers, writers, and other creative professionals to push the boundaries of their craft and explore new avenues of expression. However, to fully harness the potential of human-AI creative collaboration, it is essential to develop the necessary skills and undergo appropriate training.

In this section, we will delve into the various aspects of skill development and training that are crucial for fostering effective human-AI creative collaboration. From technical skills and AI literacy to collaborative problem-solving and adaptability, we will explore the key competencies that creative professionals must cultivate to thrive in this new era of creativity.

As we navigate this uncharted territory, it is important to recognize that the successful integration of AI into creative workflows requires more than just a basic understanding of the technology. It demands a fundamental shift in mindset, a willingness to embrace change, and a commitment to continuous learning and growth. By examining the essential skills and training requirements, we aim to equip readers with the knowledge and tools they need to confidently embark on their own human-AI creative collaborations.

So, whether you are a seasoned creative professional looking to expand your skill set or a curious individual eager to explore the possibilities of human-AI collaboration, join us as we delve into the fascinating world of skill development and training for this exciting new frontier in creativity.

Subsection 4.1: Technical Skills and AI Literacy

In the rapidly evolving landscape of human-AI creative collaboration, developing technical skills and AI literacy has become increasingly crucial for human creators. As AI technologies continue to advance and integrate into various creative processes, it is essential for individuals to acquire a foundational understanding of how these systems work and how they can be effectively leveraged to enhance creative output.

AI literacy encompasses a broad range of knowledge and skills, including an understanding of basic AI concepts, familiarity with different types of AI systems, and awareness of the potential applications and limitations of AI in creative contexts. By gaining a solid grasp of these fundamentals, human creators can better navigate the complex world of AI-assisted creative tools and platforms, making informed decisions about when and how to incorporate AI into their workflows.

Moreover, developing technical skills specific to AI-powered creative tools is becoming increasingly important. This may involve learning how to use AI-assisted design software, familiarizing oneself with AI-powered writing tools, or understanding how to manipulate and fine-tune AI-generated content. By acquiring these skills, human creators can more effectively collaborate with AI systems, leveraging their capabilities to streamline processes, generate novel ideas, and push the boundaries of their creative expression.

It is important to note that the development of technical skills and AI literacy should not be viewed as a replacement for traditional creative skills and expertise. Rather, these competencies should be seen as complementary, enabling human creators to augment their existing skill sets and explore new possibilities in their creative endeavors. By striking a balance between technical proficiency and creative intuition, human creators can harness the full potential of AI-assisted tools while maintaining their unique artistic voice and vision.

Fostering AI literacy and technical skill development requires a proactive approach from both individual creators and the creative industries at large. This may involve investing in training programs, workshops, and educational resources that help individuals acquire the necessary knowledge and skills to effectively collaborate with AI systems. Additionally, creative organizations and institutions should prioritize the integration of AI literacy into their curricula, ensuring that the next generation of creators is well-equipped to navigate the evolving landscape of human-AI collaboration.

As we move forward into an era of increasingly sophisticated AI-assisted creative tools, the importance of technical skills and AI literacy cannot be overstated. By embracing these competencies and continuously updating their knowledge and skills, human creators can position themselves at the forefront of this exciting new frontier, unlocking new possibilities for creative expression and innovation.

Subsection 4.2: Collaborative Problem-Solving and Decision-Making

As human-AI creative collaborations become more prevalent, the development of effective problem-solving and decision-making skills within these teams is crucial for success. The unique dynamics between human creators and AI systems present both challenges and opportunities, requiring a new approach to navigating the creative process.

At the core of collaborative problem-solving and decision-making in human-AI teams is the ability to leverage the strengths of both human and machine intelligence. Human creators bring their intuition, emotional intelligence, and contextual understanding to the table, while AI systems offer vast computational power, pattern recognition, and the ability to process large amounts of data quickly. By combining these complementary abilities, human-AI teams can tackle complex creative challenges more efficiently and effectively.

To foster successful collaboration, human creators must develop a deep understanding of the capabilities and limitations of their AI counterparts. This knowledge allows them to identify areas where AI can be most effectively utilized and where human intervention is necessary. For example, AI systems may excel at generating a wide range of ideas or variations based on a given set of parameters, but human judgment is essential for selecting the most promising concepts and refining them further.

Effective communication is another key aspect of collaborative problem-solving and decision-making in human-AI teams. Human creators must learn to articulate their creative vision and goals clearly to their AI collaborators, ensuring that the system understands the desired outcomes. This may involve developing a shared language or set of protocols that both human and machine can interpret accurately. Additionally, human creators should be open to feedback and suggestions generated by the AI system, as these insights may offer valuable new perspectives or identify potential issues early in the creative process.

Trust and transparency are also essential components of successful human-AI collaboration. Human creators must have confidence in the AI system's ability to contribute meaningfully to the creative process, while also maintaining a critical eye for potential biases or errors. Establishing clear guidelines for data use, intellectual property rights, and attribution can help build trust and ensure that all parties are aligned in their expectations and responsibilities.

As human-AI teams engage in collaborative problem-solving and decision-making, it is important to maintain a balance between structure and flexibility. While having a well-defined process can help ensure consistency and efficiency, it is equally important to allow for experimentation, iteration, and adaptation as the creative project evolves. Human creators should be willing to adjust their approach based on the AI system's outputs and be open to exploring new directions that may emerge from the collaboration.

Ultimately, the development of collaborative problem-solving and decision-making skills in human-AI creative teams requires a commitment to continuous learning and growth. As AI technologies advance and new creative possibilities emerge, human creators must remain curious, adaptable, and proactive in acquiring the necessary skills to work effectively alongside their AI counterparts. By embracing the unique challenges and opportunities presented by human-AI collaboration, creative professionals can unlock new levels of innovation and push the boundaries of what is possible in their respective fields.

Subsection 4.3: Adaptability and Flexibility in Workflow Integration

As the creative landscape continues to evolve and AI systems become increasingly integrated into various aspects of the creative process, adaptability and flexibility have emerged as essential skills for creative professionals. The ability to seamlessly integrate AI technologies into existing workflows and adapt to new ways of working is crucial for maximizing the benefits of human-AI collaboration.

One of the primary challenges in integrating AI systems into creative workflows is the potential for disruption to established processes and routines. Creative professionals may be hesitant to embrace AI technologies, fearing that they will need to completely overhaul their current ways of working. However, the most successful integrations of AI into creative workflows are those that strike a balance between leveraging the capabilities of AI and maintaining the core elements of the creative process that have proven effective.

To achieve this balance, creative professionals must cultivate a mindset of adaptability and flexibility. This involves being open to experimenting with new tools and techniques, while also being willing to adjust and refine their approach as needed. Rather than viewing AI as a rigid, one-size-fits-all solution, creative professionals should approach it as a dynamic and customizable tool that can be tailored to their specific needs and goals.

Adaptability in workflow integration also requires a willingness to learn and grow. As AI technologies continue to advance at a rapid pace, creative professionals must commit to staying up-to-date with the latest developments and best practices in their field. This may involve attending workshops and training sessions, participating in online communities and forums, and actively seeking out opportunities to collaborate with others who are experienced in working with AI.

Flexibility is equally important in integrating AI systems into creative workflows. Creative professionals must be willing to adjust their processes and routines as needed to accommodate the unique capabilities and limitations of AI. This may involve rethinking traditional roles and responsibilities within creative teams, as well as developing new protocols and guidelines for collaboration between human and machine.

For example, a graphic designer who typically works independently may need to adapt to a more collaborative workflow when integrating AI-assisted design tools. This may involve establishing clear communication channels with the AI system, setting parameters and constraints for the AI's output, and iterating on designs in partnership with the AI rather than working in isolation.

Similarly, a writer who is accustomed to working in a linear, start-to-finish fashion may need to adapt to a more modular and iterative approach when working with AI-powered writing tools. This may involve breaking down the writing process into smaller, more manageable chunks, and allowing the AI to generate multiple variations and suggestions at each stage, which can then be refined and integrated into the final piece.

Ultimately, the key to successful workflow integration of AI systems is a willingness to embrace change and experimentation. By cultivating adaptability and flexibility, creative professionals can harness the power of AI to enhance their creative output, streamline their processes, and push the boundaries of what is possible in their field. As the creative landscape continues to evolve, those who are able to adapt and integrate AI effectively into their workflows will be well-positioned to thrive in the era of human-AI collaboration.

Subsection 4.4: Continuous Learning and Skill Advancement

In the rapidly evolving landscape of human-AI creative collaboration, continuous learning and skill advancement are essential for creative professionals to stay relevant and competitive. As AI technologies continue to advance at an unprecedented pace, it is crucial for individuals to commit to lifelong learning and actively seek opportunities to expand their knowledge and skills.

One of the primary reasons for the need for continuous learning is the constant emergence of new AI tools, platforms, and techniques. What may have been considered state-of-the-art just a few years ago can quickly become outdated as new innovations enter the market. To keep pace with these developments, creative professionals must be proactive in staying informed about the latest advancements in AI and assessing how these technologies can be integrated into their creative workflows.

Continuous learning also involves a willingness to experiment with new AI tools and techniques, even if they may initially seem unfamiliar or challenging. By embracing a growth mindset and being open to trying new approaches, creative professionals can expand their skill sets and discover new ways of working that can enhance their creative output. This may involve setting aside dedicated time for learning and experimentation, attending workshops or online courses, or collaborating with others who have expertise in specific AI technologies.

In addition to staying up-to-date with the latest AI advancements, continuous learning also involves deepening one's understanding of the fundamental principles and concepts that underlie human-AI collaboration. This may include studying topics such as machine learning, natural language processing, or computer vision, depending on the specific creative domain. By developing a strong foundation in these areas, creative professionals can better understand the capabilities and limitations of AI systems and make more informed decisions about how to leverage these technologies in their work.

Another important aspect of continuous learning is the development of soft skills that are essential for effective human-AI collaboration. These may include skills such as communication, problem-solving, adaptability, and emotional intelligence. As creative professionals increasingly work alongside AI systems, the ability to clearly articulate creative goals, provide feedback, and adapt to new ways of working becomes increasingly important. By cultivating these soft skills, individuals can foster more productive and harmonious collaborations with their AI counterparts.

Continuous learning and skill advancement also require a commitment to self-reflection and self-assessment. As creative professionals integrate AI technologies into their workflows, it is important to regularly evaluate the impact of these tools on their creative process and output. This may involve setting specific goals and metrics for improvement, seeking feedback from peers or mentors, and making adjustments as needed to optimize the collaboration between human and machine.

Ultimately, the key to success in the era of human-AI creative collaboration is a willingness to embrace continuous learning and skill advancement as an ongoing, iterative process. By staying curious, proactive, and adaptable, creative professionals can position themselves at the forefront of this exciting new frontier and unlock new possibilities for creative expression and innovation. As the creative landscape continues to evolve, those who prioritize lifelong learning and skill development will be best equipped to thrive in the age of human-AI collaboration.

Summary: Embracing the Future of Human-AI Creative Collaboration

As we have explored throughout this section, the advent of AI in creative industries presents both challenges and opportunities for professionals seeking to collaborate effectively with these powerful tools. The development of technical skills, AI literacy, collaborative problem-solving, adaptability, and a commitment to continuous learning are all essential components of successful human-AI creative partnerships.

By cultivating these key competencies, creative professionals can harness the immense potential of AI to enhance their creative output, streamline workflows, and push the boundaries of innovation in their respective fields. However, it is important to recognize that the integration of AI into creative processes is not a one-time event, but rather an ongoing journey that requires a willingness to embrace change, experiment with new approaches, and continuously refine one's skills.

As the creative landscape continues to evolve at an unprecedented pace, those who prioritize skill development and training in human-AI collaboration will be well-positioned to thrive in this exciting new era. By staying curious, adaptable, and proactive in their learning, creative professionals can navigate the challenges and seize the opportunities presented by AI, forging powerful partnerships that unlock new realms of creativity and innovation.

Ultimately, the future of human-AI creative collaboration is bright, and the possibilities are limitless. As we move forward into this uncharted territory, it is up to each individual to embrace the learning journey and to approach these new tools and technologies with an open mind, a sense of curiosity, and a commitment to personal and professional growth. By doing so, we can not only overcome the stigma surrounding AI-generated content but also redefine what is possible in the world of creative expression.

Section 5: The Future of Human-AI Creative Collaboration

As we stand on the precipice of a new era in creative collaboration, it is essential to envision the future possibilities and implications of the partnership between human creativity and artificial intelligence. The rapid advancements in AI technology have already begun to reshape the creative landscape, and the potential for further transformation is both exciting and daunting.

In this section, we will embark on a journey to explore the emerging trends and innovations that are poised to redefine the way humans and AI systems work together in creative endeavors. From the development of more intuitive and responsive AI-assisted tools to the rise of entirely new forms of creative expression, the future holds a wealth of opportunities for those willing to embrace change and adapt to the evolving creative ecosystem.

However, as we navigate this uncharted territory, it is crucial to consider the potential impact of human-AI creative collaboration on existing creative industries and professions. Will the integration of AI lead to the displacement of human creators, or will it open up new avenues for growth and specialization? These are questions that we must grapple with as we shape the future of creative work.

Moreover, the increasing integration of AI in creative processes raises important ethical and societal considerations. As AI systems become more sophisticated and autonomous, we must ensure that they are designed and deployed in a manner that aligns with our values and promotes fairness, transparency, and accountability. Only by proactively addressing these concerns can we build a future in which human-AI creative collaboration benefits all of humanity.

So, let us dive into the exciting possibilities that await us in the realm of human-AI creative collaboration. By exploring the emerging trends, considering the potential impacts, and addressing the ethical implications, we can chart a course towards a future in which the combined power of human creativity and artificial intelligence unlocks new frontiers of innovation and self-expression.

Subsection 5.1: Emerging Trends and Innovations

The landscape of human-AI creative collaboration is constantly evolving, driven by rapid advancements in artificial intelligence and a growing recognition of its potential to transform creative industries. As we look towards the future, several emerging trends and innovations are poised to reshape the way humans and AI systems work together to create, innovate, and push the boundaries of what is possible.

One of the most significant trends is the development of more intuitive and responsive AI-assisted tools that seamlessly integrate into the creative workflow. These tools leverage advanced machine learning algorithms and natural language processing to understand and adapt to the unique needs and preferences of individual creators, providing personalized suggestions, inspiration, and support throughout the creative process. From AI-powered writing assistants that offer real-time feedback and editing recommendations to intelligent design tools that generate custom visual assets based on user input, these innovations are empowering creators to work more efficiently and effectively than ever before.

Another exciting trend is the rise of collaborative AI systems that can actively participate in the creative process as equal partners alongside human creators. These systems are designed to engage in dynamic, back-and-forth exchanges with their human counterparts, contributing ideas, offering constructive criticism, and even learning from the creative choices made by the human collaborator. By fostering a more symbiotic relationship between human creativity and artificial intelligence, these collaborative AI systems have the potential to unlock entirely new forms of creative expression and problem-solving.

In addition to these advancements, we are also witnessing the emergence of AI-driven platforms that facilitate large-scale creative collaboration across geographic and disciplinary boundaries. These platforms harness the power of cloud computing, distributed ledger technology, and machine learning to connect creators from around the world, enabling them to work together on complex projects, share resources and expertise, and collectively explore new creative frontiers. By breaking down traditional barriers to collaboration and fostering a global community of creators, these platforms are paving the way for a more inclusive, diverse, and innovative creative ecosystem.

As these trends and innovations continue to shape the future of human-AI creative collaboration, it is important to recognize that they are not confined to any one creative industry or discipline. From music and film to architecture and product design, the impact of AI is being felt across the creative spectrum, challenging long-held assumptions about the nature of creativity and the role of technology in the creative process. As we embrace these changes and explore the possibilities they present, we stand on the threshold of a new era of creative expression, one in which the combined power of human imagination and artificial intelligence will redefine what it means to create, innovate, and inspire.

Subsection 5.2: Potential Impact on Creative Industries and Professions

The increasing integration of AI in creative processes has the potential to significantly impact various creative industries and professions. As human-AI creative collaboration becomes more prevalent, it is crucial to examine the potential consequences, both positive and negative, for the individuals and organizations involved in creative work.

One of the most significant potential impacts is the transformation of creative workflows and the redistribution of tasks between human creators and AI systems. As AI-assisted tools and collaborative AI platforms become more sophisticated and widely adopted, they may automate certain aspects of the creative process, such as idea generation, research, and initial drafts. This shift could allow human creators to focus on higher-level tasks that require uniquely human skills, such as strategic decision-making, emotional storytelling, and final polishing. However, it may also lead to the displacement of certain roles and skill sets within creative industries, particularly those that involve repetitive or formulaic tasks.

Another potential impact is the democratization of creative expression and the lowering of barriers to entry in creative professions. With the help of AI-assisted tools and platforms, individuals who may have previously lacked the technical skills, resources, or connections to pursue creative careers may now have access to powerful tools that enable them to create and distribute their work more easily. This could lead to a more diverse and inclusive creative landscape, with a wider range of voices and perspectives represented. However, it may also increase competition and potentially saturate the market with AI-generated content, making it more challenging for individual creators to stand out and monetize their work.

The rise of human-AI creative collaboration may also have implications for the value and perception of creativity itself. As AI systems become more adept at generating content that is indistinguishable from human-created work, questions may arise about the unique value and authenticity of human creativity. This could lead to a reevaluation of the role and importance of human creators in various industries, as well as a potential shift in consumer preferences and expectations. It may become increasingly important for human creators to differentiate themselves by emphasizing the emotional, personal, and experiential qualities of their work, as well as their ability to engage in higher-level creative decision-making and problem-solving.

Furthermore, the integration of AI in creative industries may have economic implications for creative professionals and organizations. While AI-assisted tools and platforms may increase efficiency and productivity, they may also disrupt existing business models and revenue streams. For example, if AI systems can generate high-quality content more quickly and at a lower cost than human creators, it may put pressure on creative professionals to adapt their pricing and services accordingly. Additionally, the ownership and monetization of AI-generated content may become a complex legal and ethical issue, with questions arising about the distribution of royalties and the attribution of creative credit.

To navigate these potential impacts, creative industries and professionals will need to proactively engage with the challenges and opportunities presented by human-AI creative collaboration. This may involve investing in new skills and knowledge related to AI technologies, experimenting with new business models and revenue streams, and advocating for policies and practices that support the fair and ethical use of AI in creative work. It will also require ongoing dialogue and collaboration between human creators, AI developers, industry leaders, and policymakers to ensure that the benefits of human-AI creative collaboration are realized while mitigating potential negative consequences.

Ultimately, the impact of human-AI creative collaboration on creative industries and professions will depend on how we choose to shape and harness these technologies. By proactively engaging with the challenges and opportunities, we can work towards a future in which human creativity and artificial intelligence complement and enhance each other, leading to new forms of expression, innovation, and value creation.

Subsection 5.3: Ethical and Societal Considerations

As AI becomes increasingly integrated into creative processes, it is crucial to consider the ethical and societal implications of this technological shift. The rise of human-AI creative collaboration raises a number of complex questions that must be addressed to ensure that the benefits of these advancements are realized in a responsible and equitable manner.

One of the primary ethical concerns surrounding AI-generated content is the potential for bias and discrimination. AI systems are only as unbiased as the data they are trained on, and if that data contains inherent biases, the resulting output may perpetuate or even amplify those biases. For example, if an AI system is trained on a dataset of historical musical compositions that underrepresent certain cultural or demographic groups, it may generate music that fails to reflect the diversity of human creative expression. Similarly, AI-generated visual art or writing may inadvertently reinforce stereotypes or exclude certain perspectives if the training data is not carefully curated to ensure fairness and inclusivity.

To mitigate these risks, it is essential that the development and deployment of AI systems in creative contexts be guided by a strong ethical framework. This may involve establishing guidelines for the collection and use of training data, implementing transparency and accountability measures to detect and correct for bias, and actively seeking out diverse perspectives and experiences to inform the design and evaluation of these systems. It may also require ongoing monitoring and adjustment to ensure that AI-generated content aligns with evolving societal values and expectations.

Another key ethical consideration is the question of attribution and ownership. As AI systems become more sophisticated in their ability to generate creative content, it may become increasingly difficult to distinguish between human-created and AI-generated works. This raises questions about who should be credited for the creative output and how intellectual property rights should be allocated. Should the human collaborators be considered the primary creators, or does the AI system itself deserve recognition? How should royalties and other forms of compensation be distributed when an AI system plays a significant role in the creative process?

These are complex issues that will require ongoing dialogue and negotiation among stakeholders in the creative industries, including artists, writers, musicians, developers, and legal experts. It may be necessary to develop new legal frameworks and industry standards that can accommodate the unique challenges posed by human-AI creative collaboration, while still respecting the rights and contributions of all parties involved.

Beyond these specific ethical concerns, the integration of AI in creative processes also raises broader societal questions about the nature of creativity and the role of technology in shaping our cultural landscape.

Some may argue that the use of AI in creative contexts diminishes the value of human creativity and undermines the uniqueness of individual artistic expression. Others may see it as a powerful tool for democratizing creativity and enabling new forms of collaboration and innovation.

Ultimately, the societal impact of human-AI creative collaboration will depend on how we choose to navigate these complex issues and shape the development and use of these technologies. It will require ongoing public dialogue, interdisciplinary collaboration, and a commitment to ethical principles and values that prioritize the well-being of both individuals and society as a whole.

As we move forward into this new era of creative expression, it is important that we approach the integration of AI with a sense of both excitement and responsibility. By proactively addressing the ethical and societal considerations surrounding these advancements, we can work towards a future in which the power of human creativity and the potential of artificial intelligence are harnessed in service of the greater good, leading to a more vibrant, inclusive, and equitable creative landscape for all.

Subsection 5.4: Envisioning New Forms of Creative Expression

As we stand on the precipice of a new era in human-AI creative collaboration, it is exhilarating to envision the potential for entirely new forms of creative expression to emerge. The symbiotic relationship between human imagination and artificial intelligence has the power to push the boundaries of what we currently perceive as possible, giving rise to innovative and transformative creative experiences.

One of the most exciting prospects is the emergence of hybrid art forms that seamlessly blend the unique strengths of human and AI creativity. Imagine a future where a musician collaborates with an AI system to compose a symphony that adapts in real-time to the emotional state of the audience, creating a truly immersive and personalized auditory experience. Or consider a team of architects working alongside an AI to design a building that dynamically responds to the changing needs of its occupants, optimizing space, light, and energy efficiency in ways that were previously unimaginable.

The potential for human-AI creative collaboration extends far beyond the realm of traditional art forms. As AI systems become more sophisticated in their ability to understand and generate natural language, we may witness the birth of entirely new forms of storytelling and literature. Picture an interactive novel that adapts its narrative based on the reader's choices and preferences, crafting a unique and emotionally resonant story tailored to each individual. Or imagine a virtual reality experience that immerses participants in a collaborative, AI-generated world, where their actions and decisions shape the unfolding narrative in real-time.

The intersection of human creativity and artificial intelligence also holds immense potential for scientific discovery and innovation. By leveraging the power of AI to analyze vast amounts of data, identify patterns, and generate novel hypotheses, researchers and inventors can collaborate with these systems to accelerate the pace of scientific breakthroughs. From the discovery of new materials with extraordinary properties to the development of life-saving medical treatments, the synergy between human ingenuity and AI-driven insight could revolutionize the way we approach some of the world's most pressing challenges.

As we envision these new forms of creative expression, it is important to recognize that they will not only shape the way we create but also the way we experience and interact with the world around us. The integration of AI into our daily lives will give rise to new forms of entertainment, education, and social engagement, blurring the lines between the physical and digital realms. Imagine a future where AI-generated virtual companions serve as personalized guides, helping us navigate complex information landscapes, learn new skills, and connect with others who share our passions and interests. The possibilities for human-AI creative collaboration are truly limitless, bounded only by the reach of our collective imagination. As we embrace this new frontier of creative expression, it is essential that we approach it with a sense of curiosity, openness, and responsibility. By fostering a culture of experimentation, collaboration, and ethical reflection, we can ensure that the benefits of these advancements are realized in a way that enriches our lives and strengthens our shared humanity.

As we move forward into this uncharted territory, let us dare to dream boldly and imagine a future where the combined power of human creativity and artificial intelligence unlocks new realms of beauty, meaning, and possibility. By embracing the potential of this transformative collaboration, we have the opportunity to redefine the very nature of creative expression and, in doing so, to shape a more vibrant, interconnected, and awe-inspiring world for generations to come.

Summary: Embracing the Transformative Power of Human-AI Creative Collaboration

As we navigate the uncharted waters of human-AI creative collaboration, it becomes increasingly clear that this partnership holds the key to unlocking a future of unprecedented innovation and artistic expression. By harnessing the unique strengths of both human creativity and artificial intelligence, we stand on the precipice of a creative revolution that will redefine the very essence of what it means to create, inspire, and push the boundaries of imagination.

The emerging trends and innovations in this field, from intuitive AI-assisted tools to collaborative AI systems and global platforms, are poised to transform the creative landscape in ways we can only begin to fathom. As these advancements continue to evolve and mature, they will undoubtedly reshape creative workflows, democratize access to creative tools, and give rise to entirely new forms of expression that transcend the limits of what was once thought possible.

However, as we embrace the transformative power of human-AI creative collaboration, we must also remain mindful of the potential impacts on creative industries and professions. The integration of AI in the creative process will likely lead to the redistribution of tasks, the emergence of new roles and skill sets, and the disruption of traditional business models. To navigate these changes successfully, creative professionals and organizations must proactively adapt, upskill, and explore new avenues for growth and innovation.

Moreover, the ethical and societal implications of human-AI creative collaboration cannot be overlooked. As AI systems become increasingly sophisticated and autonomous, it is crucial that we develop robust frameworks to ensure transparency, fairness, and accountability in their design and deployment. By engaging in ongoing public dialogue, interdisciplinary collaboration, and a commitment to ethical principles, we can work towards a future in which the benefits of this partnership are realized in a responsible and equitable manner.

Ultimately, the future of human-AI creative collaboration is one of boundless potential and profound transformation. As we stand at the threshold of this new era, it is up to us to embrace the challenges and opportunities that lie ahead with a spirit of curiosity, creativity, and responsibility. By doing so, we can not only redefine the landscape of creative expression but also shape a future in which the combined power of human imagination and artificial intelligence propels us towards new frontiers of innovation, beauty, and meaning.

Chapter Summary: Embracing the Synergy of Human-AI Creative Collaboration

As we navigate the rapidly evolving landscape of AI-generated content and its impact on creative industries, it becomes increasingly clear that the most promising path forward lies in the collaboration between human creators and AI systems. By embracing the synergy of human-AI creative collaboration, we can unlock new realms of creativity, innovation, and artistic expression.

Throughout this chapter, we have explored the foundations, workflows, tools, and skills necessary to foster effective human-AI creative collaboration. By establishing trust, transparency, and clear roles and responsibilities, human creators and AI systems can work together seamlessly, leveraging their unique strengths and capabilities to produce truly remarkable creative outputs.

The future of human-AI creative collaboration is brimming with possibilities. As AI technologies continue to advance and mature, we can expect to see the emergence of even more sophisticated tools, platforms, and workflows that enable human creators to push the boundaries of their craft. From AI-assisted design and ideation to collaborative content creation and intelligent project management, the opportunities for human-AI synergy are vast and exciting.

However, as we embrace this new era of creativity, it is crucial to remain mindful of the ethical and societal implications of human-AI collaboration. We must strive to develop and deploy these technologies responsibly, ensuring that they promote inclusivity, diversity, and respect for all creators and their works.

Ultimately, the success of human-AI creative collaboration will depend on our willingness to adapt, learn, and grow alongside these evolving technologies. By cultivating the necessary skills, mindsets, and collaborative practices, we can harness the power of AI to enhance and augment our creative capabilities, rather than replace them.

As we move forward into this brave new world of creativity, let us approach human-AI collaboration with openness, curiosity, and a spirit of experimentation. Together, human creators and AI systems have the potential to redefine the very nature of creativity and artistic expression, ushering in a new era of boundless possibilities and unparalleled innovation.

Chapter 11: Case Studies: Success Stories and Lessons Learned

In the rapidly evolving landscape of artificial intelligence and content creation, it is essential to examine real-world examples of successful AI-generated content and the valuable lessons learned from these experiences. As we navigate the complex terrain of the stigma surrounding AI-generated content, these case studies serve as beacons of hope, illuminating the path forward and demonstrating the potential for AI to revolutionize various industries.

Throughout this chapter, we will embark on a journey through a diverse range of industries, from journalism and media to marketing, advertising, creative fields, and customer service. By exploring the successes and challenges faced by organizations and individuals who have embraced AI-generated content, we can gain a deeper understanding of the strategies, best practices, and pitfalls to avoid when implementing AI in content creation processes.

As we delve into each case study, we will uncover the unique ways in which AI has been leveraged to enhance creativity, streamline workflows, and deliver compelling, engaging content to audiences across the globe. From The Washington Post's Heliograf AI system, which has revolutionized news article generation, to the thought-provoking AI-generated artwork created by Obvious Art, these examples showcase the incredible potential of AI to push the boundaries of what is possible in content creation.

However, our exploration of these success stories goes beyond mere admiration. We will also critically examine the lessons learned from each case study, extracting valuable insights that can inform our own approaches to AI-generated content. By understanding the importance of human oversight, transparency, collaboration with domain experts, and iterative improvement, we can develop a more nuanced and effective approach to integrating AI into our content creation processes.

As we navigate the challenges and opportunities presented by AI-generated content, these case studies serve as a testament to the resilience, creativity, and adaptability of those who have successfully embraced this transformative technology. By learning from their experiences, we can chart a course toward a future in which AI and human creativity work hand in hand, unlocking new possibilities and redefining what it means to create compelling, engaging content in the digital age.

Section 1: AI-Generated Content in Journalism and Media

In recent years, the rapid advancements in artificial intelligence (AI) technology have revolutionized various industries, and the world of journalism and media is no exception. As AI-powered tools and algorithms become more sophisticated, news organizations and media outlets are increasingly exploring the potential of AI-generated content to enhance their reporting, streamline their workflows, and engage their audiences in new and innovative ways.

The integration of AI-generated content in journalism and media has sparked both excitement and apprehension, with some hailing it as a transformative force that will usher in a new era of efficiency and creativity, while others express concerns about the potential impact on journalistic integrity, credibility, and the role of human journalists in an AI-driven future. In this section, we will delve into the fascinating world of AI-generated content in journalism and media, examining some of the most successful and noteworthy applications of this technology. Through a series of case studies and real-world examples, we will explore how leading news organizations and media companies are harnessing the power of AI to generate compelling stories, personalize content, and provide valuable insights to their readers and viewers.

As we navigate this exciting and rapidly evolving landscape, we will also address the challenges and ethical considerations surrounding the use of AI-generated content in journalism and media, seeking to provide a balanced and nuanced perspective on this complex and multifaceted topic. By the end of this section, you will have a deeper understanding of the current state of AI-generated content in journalism and media, its potential benefits and drawbacks, and the key lessons learned from the experiences of those at the forefront of this technological revolution.

Subsection 1.1: The Washington Post's Heliograf AI System

The Washington Post, one of the most prestigious and influential news organizations in the United States, has been at the forefront of exploring the potential of AI-generated content in journalism. In 2016, the newspaper introduced Heliograf, an AI system designed to generate news articles automatically, particularly in the areas of sports, elections, and financial news.

Heliograf's initial success was evident during the 2016 Rio Olympics, where the AI system produced over 300 articles, covering a wide range of sports events and medal wins. By leveraging data from various sources, including event schedules, results, and athlete profiles, Heliograf was able to generate timely, accurate, and engaging news stories at a scale that would have been challenging for human journalists alone.

The AI system's ability to quickly analyze large datasets and generate news articles proved to be a significant asset for The Washington Post during the 2016 U.S. presidential election. Heliograf produced over 500 articles covering local election results, freeing up human journalists to focus on more complex and investigative stories. The AI-generated articles were well-received by readers, who appreciated the timely and accurate coverage of local election outcomes.

In addition to its success in sports and election reporting, Heliograf has also been utilized to generate financial news articles. By analyzing financial data and market trends, the AI system can produce concise and informative articles on company earnings, stock market movements, and other financial topics. This has allowed The Washington Post to provide more comprehensive and timely financial coverage to its readers.

The Washington Post's implementation of Heliograf has demonstrated the potential for AI-generated content to complement the work of human journalists. By automating the production of routine and data-driven news stories, AI systems like Heliograf can help news organizations scale their coverage and free up human journalists to focus on more complex, investigative, and analytical reporting.

However, the success of Heliograf also highlights the importance of human oversight and editorial judgment in the use of AI-generated content. While the AI system can generate articles quickly and accurately, it still relies on human journalists to provide context, nuance, and critical analysis. The Washington Post's approach to integrating Heliograf into its newsroom emphasizes the collaborative relationship between human journalists and AI, ensuring that the final product meets the high standards of journalistic integrity and quality that readers expect.

As AI technology continues to advance, the success of The Washington Post's Heliograf system serves as a valuable case study for other news organizations considering the adoption of AI-generated content. By carefully balancing the efficiency and scalability of AI with the essential role of human journalists, news outlets can harness the power of this technology to enhance their reporting and better serve their readers in an increasingly digital and data-driven world.

Subsection 1.2: The Guardian's GPT-3-Generated Article

In September 2020, The Guardian, a renowned British newspaper, made headlines when it published an article entirely written by an AI system called GPT-3 (Generative Pre-trained Transformer 3). The article, titled "A robot wrote this entire article. Are you scared yet, human?", was a thought-provoking piece that explored the potential implications of AI-generated content and the future of journalism.

The Guardian's experiment with GPT-3 was a collaborative effort between the newspaper's staff and OpenAI, the artificial intelligence research laboratory that developed the language model. The process began with a human editor providing GPT-3 with a brief prompt, which included the article's title and a short introduction. The AI system then generated multiple versions of the article, each with a slightly different focus and style.

The human editor then selected the most compelling version of the article and made minor edits to improve clarity and coherence. The final product was a well-written, engaging piece that showcased GPT-3's ability to generate human-like text based on a given prompt. The article covered a range of topics, from the potential benefits of AI-generated content to the ethical concerns surrounding its use in journalism.

One of the key lessons learned from The Guardian's experiment with GPT-3 was the importance of human oversight and editorial judgment in the use of AI-generated content. While GPT-3 was able to produce a high-quality article, it still required human input and guidance to ensure that the final product met the standards of journalistic integrity and accuracy.

Another important lesson was the need for transparency when using AI-generated content in journalism. The Guardian made it clear to its readers that the article was written by an AI system and provided a detailed explanation of the process involved. This transparency helped to build trust with readers and demonstrated the newspaper's commitment to ethical and responsible journalism.

The Guardian's GPT-3-generated article also sparked a broader conversation about the potential impact of AI on the future of journalism. Some argued that AI systems like GPT-3 could revolutionize the industry, allowing news organizations to produce more content at a faster pace and lower cost. Others, however, expressed concerns about the potential loss of jobs for human journalists and the risk of AI systems perpetuating biases or spreading misinformation.

Despite these concerns, The Guardian's experiment with GPT-3 demonstrated the potential for AI-generated content to complement the work of human journalists. By leveraging the power of AI to handle routine or data-driven tasks, journalists could focus on more complex, investigative, and analytical reporting, ultimately enhancing the quality and depth of journalism.

As AI technology continues to advance, the lessons learned from The Guardian's GPT-3-generated article will undoubtedly shape the future of journalism and media. By carefully navigating the challenges and opportunities presented by AI-generated content, news organizations can harness the power of this technology to inform, engage, and inspire their readers in new and innovative ways.

Subsection 1.3: Reuters' Lynx Insight AI-Powered Journalism

Reuters, one of the world's largest and most trusted news organizations, has been at the forefront of integrating artificial intelligence (AI) into its journalism practices. In 2018, Reuters launched Lynx Insight, an AI-powered platform designed to augment the work of its journalists by providing them with real-time data analysis, insights, and story ideas.

Lynx Insight leverages machine learning algorithms to analyze vast amounts of data from various sources, including financial markets, social media, and news outlets. By identifying patterns, trends, and anomalies in the data, the platform can alert journalists to potential stories and provide them with the necessary context and background information to pursue those stories further.

One of the key advantages of Lynx Insight is its ability to process and analyze data at a scale and speed that would be impossible for human journalists alone. This allows Reuters to identify and report on breaking news stories faster than ever before, giving the organization a competitive edge in an increasingly fast-paced media landscape.

In addition to identifying potential stories, Lynx Insight also assists journalists in the writing process by generating data-driven insights and visualizations that can be easily incorporated into their articles. This not only saves time but also enhances the quality and depth of the reporting by providing readers with valuable context and data-backed evidence.

Reuters has been transparent about its use of AI in journalism, emphasizing that Lynx Insight is designed to support and enhance the work of human journalists rather than replace them. The organization has stressed the importance of human oversight and editorial judgment in the use of AI-generated insights, ensuring that the final product meets the high standards of accuracy, impartiality, and integrity that Reuters is known for.

The success of Lynx Insight has demonstrated the potential for AI to revolutionize the field of journalism by enabling news organizations to process and analyze vast amounts of data quickly and efficiently. By leveraging the power of AI, journalists can uncover stories that might otherwise go unnoticed, provide readers with more comprehensive and data-driven reporting, and ultimately enhance the quality and impact of their work.

As AI technology continues to advance, the lessons learned from Reuters' Lynx Insight platform will undoubtedly shape the future of journalism. By carefully balancing the efficiency and insights provided by AI with the critical thinking and editorial judgment of human journalists, news organizations can harness the power of this technology to inform, engage, and empower their readers in new and innovative ways.

Summary: The Transformative Power of AI in Journalism and Media

The successful applications of AI-generated content in journalism and media, as exemplified by The Washington Post's Heliograf, The Guardian's GPT-3-generated article, and Reuters' Lynx Insight, demonstrate the transformative power of AI in this industry. These case studies highlight the potential for AI to streamline workflows, enhance reporting capabilities, and provide valuable insights to readers.

However, the integration of AI in journalism also raises important questions about the role of human journalists, the importance of editorial oversight, and the need for transparency in the use of AI-generated content. As we have seen, the most effective implementations of AI in journalism involve a collaborative relationship between human journalists and AI systems, ensuring that the final product meets the highest standards of accuracy, integrity, and quality.

As AI technology continues to advance, it is clear that its impact on journalism and media will only grow more significant. By carefully navigating the challenges and opportunities presented by AI-generated content, news organizations can harness the power of this technology to inform, engage, and inspire their readers in new and innovative ways.

The lessons learned from these case studies provide valuable insights for other industries exploring the potential of AI-generated content. The key takeaways – the importance of human oversight, transparency, and the collaborative relationship between humans and AI – are applicable across a wide range of sectors and applications.

As we move forward in this rapidly evolving landscape, it is essential that we continue to explore the potential of AI-generated content while also remaining mindful of the ethical and societal implications of this technology. By doing so, we can ensure that the integration of AI in journalism and media, as well as other industries, serves to enhance and empower human capabilities rather than replace them.

Section 2: AI-Generated Content in Marketing and Advertising

In recent years, the marketing and advertising landscape has undergone a significant transformation, largely due to the advent of artificial intelligence (AI) and its ability to generate compelling, engaging content.

As businesses strive to capture the attention of their target audiences in an increasingly competitive digital world, AI-generated content has emerged as a powerful tool, offering a range of benefits and opportunities for brands looking to enhance their marketing efforts.

From personalized ad copy that resonates with individual consumers to data-driven insights that inform content strategy, AI has the potential to revolutionize the way businesses approach marketing and advertising. By leveraging the power of machine learning algorithms and natural language processing, companies can create content that not only attracts and engages their desired audience but also drives measurable results and ROI.

However, despite the growing adoption of AI-generated content in marketing and advertising, there remains a stigma surrounding its use. Some critics argue that AI-generated content lacks the creativity, authenticity, and human touch that is essential for building genuine connections with consumers. Others raise concerns about the potential for AI to perpetuate biases or generate misleading information, which could ultimately harm a brand's reputation.

In this section, we will explore the successful applications of AI-generated content in marketing and advertising campaigns, showcasing real-world examples of how brands have harnessed the power of AI to create compelling, effective content that resonates with their target audiences. By examining these case studies, we will gain valuable insights into the benefits and challenges of using AI-generated content in marketing and advertising, as well as the lessons learned from these experiences.

Through a deeper understanding of the role of AI in marketing and advertising, we can begin to dispel the stigma surrounding its use and recognize the potential for AI-generated content to enhance, rather than replace, human creativity and expertise. As we navigate this new era of marketing and advertising, it is essential to approach AI-generated content with an open mind, while also remaining mindful of the ethical considerations and responsibilities that come with its use.

Subsection 2.1: Persado's AI-Generated Marketing Copy

Persado, a leading AI-powered marketing platform, has revolutionized the way brands create and optimize their marketing copy. By leveraging advanced natural language processing and machine learning algorithms, Persado's AI system generates highly effective, personalized marketing messages that resonate with target audiences and drive measurable results.

One of the most compelling examples of Persado's success is its partnership with JPMorgan Chase, a global financial services firm. JPMorgan Chase utilized Persado's AI-generated marketing copy for its credit card promotions, resulting in a significant increase in customer engagement and conversion rates. The AI-generated copy consistently outperformed human-written messages, demonstrating the power of data-driven, emotionally intelligent language in marketing communications.

Persado's AI system analyzes vast amounts of data, including customer demographics, behavior, and preferences, to identify the most effective language, tone, and emotional appeals for each target audience segment. By continuously learning and adapting based on real-time performance metrics, the AI system optimizes marketing copy for maximum impact, ensuring that each message resonates with its intended audience.

The success of Persado's AI-generated marketing copy extends beyond the financial services industry. The company has collaborated with a wide range of leading brands across various sectors, including retail, travel, and healthcare. For example, Humana, a major health insurance provider, leveraged Persado's AI technology to create personalized, empathetic messaging for its Medicare Advantage members, resulting in higher engagement and improved customer satisfaction.

Persado's AI-generated marketing copy demonstrates the potential for artificial intelligence to enhance, rather than replace, human creativity in marketing and advertising. By combining the power of data-driven insights with the artistry of compelling storytelling, Persado's AI system enables brands to create marketing messages that are both highly effective and emotionally resonant.

However, the success of Persado's AI-generated marketing copy also highlights the need for transparency and ethical considerations in the use of AI in advertising. As brands increasingly rely on AI-powered tools to create and optimize their marketing content, it is crucial to ensure that the generated messages are accurate, unbiased, and aligned with the brand's values and mission.

Subsection 2.2: Alibaba's AI-Powered Copywriting Tool

Alibaba, the Chinese e-commerce giant, has made significant strides in leveraging AI-generated content to enhance its marketing efforts. One notable example is the company's AI-powered copywriting tool, designed to generate compelling product descriptions for the vast array of items sold on its platforms.

Developed by Alibaba's Damo Academy research institute, the AI copywriting tool utilizes natural language processing and machine learning algorithms to create engaging, informative, and persuasive product descriptions. By analyzing vast amounts of data, including customer reviews, sales records, and product specifications, the AI system learns to identify the key features and benefits of each product, crafting descriptions that highlight these aspects in a manner that resonates with potential buyers.

The AI copywriting tool has proven to be a game-changer for Alibaba's merchants, particularly small and medium-sized businesses that may lack the resources or expertise to create effective product descriptions on their own. By generating high-quality, SEO-friendly content at scale, the tool has helped these businesses attract more customers, improve their search engine rankings, and ultimately drive sales.

One of the key lessons learned from Alibaba's AI-powered copywriting tool is the importance of balancing AI-generated content with human oversight and creativity. While the AI system can produce impressive results, it is essential to have human editors review and refine the generated descriptions to ensure they align with the brand's voice, values, and marketing objectives. This collaborative approach, combining the efficiency of AI with the creative touch of human writers, has proven to be a winning formula for Alibaba and its merchants.

Another valuable insight gained from Alibaba's experience is the significance of data quality and diversity in training AI copywriting models. The more comprehensive and representative the data set used to train the AI system, the better it can capture the nuances and variations in language, tone, and style required to create compelling product descriptions across different categories and target audiences. Alibaba's vast trove of e-commerce data has been instrumental in developing a robust and versatile AI copywriting tool.

However, the success of Alibaba's AI-powered copywriting tool also raises important questions about the potential impact of AI-generated content on the job market for human copywriters. As AI systems become increasingly sophisticated and capable of producing high-quality content at scale, it is crucial to consider how this technology can be leveraged to augment, rather than replace, human creativity and expertise. By finding ways to collaborate with AI and harness its potential, human copywriters can focus on higher-level strategic and creative tasks, while letting the AI handle more repetitive and time-consuming aspects of the job.

Subsection 2.3: Chase Bank's AI-Generated Ad Copy

Chase Bank, one of the largest financial institutions in the United States, has embraced the power of AI-generated content to enhance its digital marketing efforts. By leveraging advanced natural language processing and machine learning algorithms, Chase has successfully created compelling, personalized ad copy that resonates with its target audience and drives engagement.

One notable example of Chase's success with AI-generated ad copy is its collaboration with Persado, a leading AI-powered marketing platform. Through this partnership, Chase utilized Persado's AI technology to generate and optimize ad copy for its digital marketing campaigns across various channels, including email, social media, and display advertising.

The AI-powered ad copy was designed to deliver highly targeted, emotionally engaging messages that spoke directly to the needs and preferences of Chase's customers. By analyzing vast amounts of data, including customer demographics, behavior, and past campaign performance, the AI system identified the most effective language, tone, and emotional appeals for each audience segment.

The results of Chase's AI-generated ad copy campaigns were impressive. According to a case study published by Persado, Chase experienced a significant uplift in customer engagement and conversion rates across its digital marketing channels. The AI-generated ad copy consistently outperformed human-written copy, demonstrating the power of data-driven, emotionally intelligent messaging in driving marketing success.

One of the key factors behind the success of Chase's AI-generated ad copy was the seamless integration of human creativity and machine intelligence. While the AI system handled the heavy lifting of generating and optimizing ad copy at scale, human marketers at Chase provided strategic guidance, ensuring that the generated content aligned with the bank's brand voice, values, and overall marketing objectives.

This collaborative approach allowed Chase to maintain a high level of creative control and brand consistency while leveraging the efficiency and data-driven insights of AI technology. By striking the right balance between human expertise and machine intelligence, Chase was able to create ad copy that not only resonated with customers but also drove measurable business results.

Another important lesson learned from Chase's experience with AI-generated ad copy is the significance of continuous testing and optimization. The AI system's ability to learn and adapt based on real-time performance data enabled Chase to constantly refine its ad copy, ensuring that each iteration was more effective than the last. This iterative approach to optimization allowed Chase to stay ahead of the curve in a rapidly evolving digital marketing landscape.

However, the use of AI-generated ad copy also raises important questions about transparency and ethical considerations in advertising. As brands increasingly rely on AI technology to create and optimize their marketing messages, it is crucial to ensure that the generated content is not only effective but also accurate, unbiased, and aligned with the brand's values and mission.

In Chase's case, the bank's commitment to responsible and transparent use of AI technology in its marketing efforts has been a key factor in its success. By clearly communicating its use of AI-generated ad copy to customers and stakeholders, and by maintaining strict oversight and control over the generated content, Chase has been able to build trust and credibility in its AI-powered marketing initiatives.

As the marketing and advertising landscape continues to evolve, the success of Chase's AI-generated ad copy serves as a valuable case study for other brands looking to harness the power of AI in their own marketing efforts. By embracing a collaborative, data-driven, and ethically responsible approach to AI-generated content, brands can create compelling, personalized marketing messages that drive engagement, conversions, and long-term customer loyalty.

Summary: Embracing AI-Generated Content in Marketing and Advertising

The successful applications of AI-generated content in marketing and advertising campaigns, as demonstrated by Persado, Alibaba, and Chase Bank, showcase the immense potential of this technology to revolutionize the way brands engage with their target audiences. By leveraging the power of natural language processing, machine learning, and data-driven insights, these companies have created compelling, personalized content that resonates with customers and drives measurable results.

The case studies highlight the importance of collaboration between human creativity and machine intelligence in creating effective AI-generated content. While AI systems can handle the heavy lifting of generating and optimizing content at scale, human oversight and strategic guidance ensure that the generated content aligns with brand voice, values, and marketing objectives. This collaborative approach allows brands to maintain creative control and consistency while harnessing the efficiency and data-driven insights of AI technology.

Furthermore, the success of these AI-generated content campaigns underscores the significance of continuous testing, optimization, and data quality in maximizing the impact of AI in marketing and advertising. By constantly refining and adapting content based on real-time performance data, brands can stay ahead of the curve in a rapidly evolving digital landscape.

However, the growing adoption of AI-generated content in marketing and advertising also raises important questions about transparency, ethics, and the potential impact on human copywriters and content creators. As brands increasingly rely on AI technology, it is crucial to ensure that the generated content is accurate, unbiased, and aligned with brand values. Moreover, finding ways to collaborate with AI and leverage its potential to augment human creativity and expertise, rather than replace it, will be key to navigating the future of marketing and advertising.

As we move forward, embracing AI-generated content in marketing and advertising will require a thoughtful, responsible, and adaptive approach. By striking the right balance between human creativity and machine intelligence, and by prioritizing transparency, ethics, and collaboration, brands can harness the power of AI to create engaging, personalized content that drives business success and strengthens customer relationships in the digital age.

Section 3: AI-Generated Content in Creative Industries

In the realm of creative industries, where originality and human ingenuity have long been celebrated, the emergence of AI-generated content has sparked both excitement and apprehension. As AI technologies continue to advance, their potential to revolutionize the way we create and consume music, art, and other forms of creative expression becomes increasingly apparent. This section delves into the fascinating world of AI-generated content in creative industries, showcasing successful applications and exploring the implications of this transformative technology.

From AI-composed music that challenges our notions of creativity to machine-generated artwork that pushes the boundaries of what we consider art, the creative landscape is undergoing a profound shift. While some may view AI as a threat to human creativity, others see it as a powerful tool that can augment and enhance the creative process. By examining real-world examples and case studies, we will uncover the lessons learned from the integration of AI in creative industries and shed light on the evolving relationship between technology and artistic expression.

As we navigate this uncharted territory, questions arise about the role of human creators in an era where machines can generate content that rivals the work of skilled artists and musicians. Will AI-generated content ultimately diminish the value of human creativity, or will it open up new avenues for collaboration and innovation? By exploring these questions and more, this section aims to provide a nuanced understanding of the impact of AI on creative industries and the potential for humans and machines to work together in the pursuit of artistic excellence.

Subsection 3.1: Sony's Flow Machines AI Music Composition

In a groundbreaking development, Sony's Computer Science Laboratory (CSL) has created Flow Machines, an AI system capable of generating original music compositions. This innovative technology has the potential to revolutionize the music industry by assisting human composers in the creative process and even generating entire songs autonomously.

Flow Machines utilizes a combination of machine learning algorithms, including deep learning and reinforcement learning, to analyze vast datasets of existing music. By studying the patterns, structures, and styles of various musical genres, the AI system learns to create novel compositions that adhere to the rules and conventions of music theory while introducing unique elements.

One of the most notable successes of Flow Machines is its collaboration with French composer Benoît Carré in creating the album "Hello World." Released in 2016, this album features songs composed by the AI system and arranged by Carré. The album showcases the potential of human-AI collaboration in music, with the AI generating melodies, harmonies, and rhythms, while the human composer provides the final arrangement and production.

The songs on "Hello World" demonstrate the versatility of Flow Machines, with compositions spanning various genres, including pop, jazz, and classical music. The AI-generated music is not only technically proficient but also exhibits a level of creativity and emotional depth that challenges preconceived notions about machine-generated art.

Sony's Flow Machines has also been used to create music for commercials, video games, and other media. The AI system's ability to generate music quickly and efficiently has the potential to streamline the music production process and provide composers with a powerful tool for inspiration and experimentation.

However, the success of Flow Machines has also raised questions about the role of human creativity in the age of AI. Some argue that AI-generated music lacks the personal touch and emotional authenticity of human-composed music, while others see it as a way to augment and enhance human creativity.

As AI continues to advance, the success of Sony's Flow Machines serves as a compelling example of the potential for AI-generated content in the music industry. By embracing this technology and exploring new ways of collaborating with AI, human composers may unlock new frontiers of musical creativity and push the boundaries of what is possible in music composition.

Subsection 3.2: AIVA's AI-Generated Soundtracks

AIVA, an artificial intelligence music composition platform, has made significant strides in generating high-quality soundtracks for films and video games. By leveraging deep learning algorithms and a vast database of musical compositions, AIVA has demonstrated the potential for AI to revolutionize the way music is created and integrated into visual media.

One of the most notable achievements of AIVA is its ability to generate emotionally evocative and contextually appropriate music for various scenes in films and video games. The AI system analyzes the visual content, including factors such as pacing, tone, and emotional intensity, and composes music that enhances the overall viewing experience. This level of adaptability and responsiveness is a testament to the sophistication of AIVA's AI algorithms and their ability to understand and interpret complex artistic concepts.

The AI-generated soundtracks created by AIVA have been praised for their originality, diversity, and ability to seamlessly blend with the visual narrative. By studying a wide range of musical genres and styles, AIVA can generate compositions that are not only technically proficient but also exhibit a level of creativity and emotional depth that rivals the work of human composers. This has led to successful collaborations with filmmakers and game developers who have utilized AIVA's AI-generated music to elevate their projects and create immersive audio-visual experiences.

However, the success of AIVA's AI-generated soundtracks has also raised important questions about the role of human composers in the age of artificial intelligence. Some argue that AI-generated music lacks the personal touch and artistic vision that human composers bring to the table, while others see AI as a powerful tool that can augment and enhance the creative process. As the technology continues to evolve, it is crucial to consider the ethical implications of AI-generated music and the potential impact on the livelihoods of human composers.

Despite these concerns, the lessons learned from AIVA's AI-generated soundtracks highlight the immense potential for AI to transform the music industry and the way we create and consume audio content. By embracing collaboration between human composers and AI systems, we can unlock new frontiers of musical creativity and push the boundaries of what is possible in the realm of film and video game soundtracks. As we navigate this exciting and uncharted territory, it is essential to approach AI-generated music with an open mind, a willingness to experiment, and a commitment to ensuring that the integration of AI in the creative process is done in a responsible and equitable manner.

Subsection 3.3: Obvious Art's AI-Generated Artwork

In October 2018, a collective of French artists known as Obvious Art made headlines when their AI-generated artwork, titled "Portrait of Edmond Belamy," sold for a staggering $432,500 at Christie's auction house in New York. This sale marked a significant milestone in the art world, as it was the first time an AI-generated artwork had been sold at a major auction house. The event sparked a heated debate about the role of AI in the creation of art and the potential implications for the future of the art market.

Obvious Art's success with "Portrait of Edmond Belamy" can be attributed to their innovative use of generative adversarial networks (GANs), a type of AI algorithm that consists of two neural networks competing against each other. The first network, known as the generator, creates new images based on patterns learned from a dataset of existing artworks. The second network, called the discriminator, evaluates the generated images and provides feedback to the generator, allowing it to improve its output over time. Through this iterative process, the AI system learns to create increasingly realistic and aesthetically pleasing images.

The artwork itself is a blurry, almost impressionistic portrait of a man in a dark suit and white collar. It bears a striking resemblance to the style of 18th-century European portraiture, which is no coincidence, as the AI system was trained on a dataset of 15,000 portraits from this period. The AI's ability to capture the essence of this artistic style while creating an entirely new image is a testament to the power and potential of machine learning in the realm of creative expression.

However, the success of Obvious Art's AI-generated artwork has also raised important questions about authorship, creativity, and the value of art in the age of artificial intelligence. Some critics argue that AI-generated art lacks the emotional depth and personal touch of human-created art, and that the use of AI in the creative process diminishes the role of the artist. Others see AI as a tool that can augment and enhance human creativity, allowing artists to explore new forms of expression and push the boundaries of what is possible.

The controversy surrounding Obvious Art's AI-generated artwork also highlights the need for a deeper understanding of the relationship between technology and art. As AI continues to advance and become more integrated into the creative process, it is crucial to consider the ethical implications of using these tools and to ensure that the use of AI in art is transparent and properly attributed.

Despite the debates and concerns, the success of Obvious Art's "Portrait of Edmond Belamy" demonstrates the immense potential for AI-generated content in the art world. By embracing this technology and exploring new ways of collaborating with AI, artists may unlock new frontiers of creativity and redefine what we consider to be art. As we navigate this uncharted territory, it is essential to approach AI-generated art with an open mind, a willingness to engage in meaningful dialogue, and a commitment to ensuring that the integration of AI in the creative process is done in a responsible and equitable manner.

Summary: The Transformative Power of AI in Creative Industries

The integration of AI-generated content in creative industries, such as music and art, has opened up a world of possibilities, challenging traditional notions of creativity and redefining the role of technology in artistic expression. From Sony's Flow Machines AI music composition system to AIVA's AI-generated soundtracks and Obvious Art's groundbreaking AI-generated artwork, the case studies presented in this section demonstrate the immense potential for AI to revolutionize the way we create and consume content in the creative realm.

As we navigate this exciting and uncharted territory, it is essential to approach AI-generated content with an open mind, recognizing its potential to augment and enhance human creativity rather than replace it. By embracing collaboration between human creators and AI systems, we can unlock new frontiers of artistic expression, pushing the boundaries of what is possible in music, art, and beyond.

However, the rise of AI in creative industries also raises important questions about authorship, originality, and the value of human creativity in an increasingly automated world. As we move forward, it is crucial to engage in meaningful dialogue about the ethical implications of AI-generated content and to ensure that the integration of AI in the creative process is done in a responsible and equitable manner.

The lessons learned from the success stories and challenges encountered in the realm of AI-generated music and art serve as a valuable foundation for understanding the transformative power of AI in creative industries. By leveraging these insights and continuing to explore the possibilities of human-AI collaboration, we can shape a future in which technology and creativity work hand in hand to produce truly innovative and emotionally resonant works of art.

Section 4: AI-Generated Content in Customer Service and Support

In today's fast-paced, digital world, providing exceptional customer service has become a critical factor in determining a company's success. As businesses strive to meet the ever-increasing demands of their customers, many have turned to artificial intelligence (AI) to revolutionize the way they deliver support. AI-generated content has emerged as a powerful tool in this context, enabling companies to provide quick, accurate, and personalized responses to customer inquiries.

The application of AI-generated content in customer service and support has the potential to transform the way businesses interact with their customers. By leveraging natural language processing (NLP) and machine learning algorithms, AI systems can understand and interpret customer queries, generating relevant and helpful responses in real-time. This not only improves the efficiency of customer support teams but also enhances the overall customer experience.

In this section, we will explore several successful case studies that showcase the implementation of AI-generated content in customer service and support. From chatbots that handle routine inquiries to AI-powered knowledge bases that provide instant access to information, these examples demonstrate the tangible benefits that businesses can reap by embracing this technology.

As we delve into these case studies, we will examine how AI-generated content has helped companies streamline their support processes, reduce response times, and improve customer satisfaction. We will also discuss the lessons learned from these implementations, highlighting best practices and potential pitfalls to consider when deploying AI-generated content in a customer service setting.

By the end of this section, readers will have a comprehensive understanding of how AI-generated content is revolutionizing customer service and support. They will gain valuable insights into the practical applications of this technology and be equipped with the knowledge needed to assess its potential for their own organizations. So, let us embark on this journey and discover the transformative power of AI-generated content in the realm of customer service and support.

Subsection 4.1: KLM's AI-Generated Customer Service Responses

In the highly competitive airline industry, providing exceptional customer service is paramount. KLM Royal Dutch Airlines, one of the world's oldest and most respected airlines, has embraced AI-generated content to revolutionize its customer service on social media platforms. By implementing AI-powered chatbots and response systems, KLM has successfully streamlined its customer support processes, reduced response times, and enhanced overall customer satisfaction.

KLM's AI-generated customer service responses are powered by advanced natural language processing (NLP) and machine learning algorithms. These technologies enable the airline's AI system to understand and interpret customer queries, complaints, and feedback across various social media channels, such as Twitter and Facebook. The AI analyzes the content of each message, identifies the core issue or question, and generates an appropriate response based on its extensive knowledge base and predefined response templates.

One of the key advantages of KLM's AI-generated customer service responses is their ability to provide quick and accurate information to customers 24/7. Whether a customer needs to check their flight status, inquire about baggage allowances, or seek assistance with a booking, the AI system can deliver relevant and helpful responses within seconds. This speed and efficiency are crucial in the fast-paced world of air travel, where customers often require immediate support to make informed decisions or resolve urgent issues.

Moreover, KLM's AI-generated responses are designed to maintain a friendly, empathetic, and professional tone, mimicking the communication style of human customer service representatives. The AI system is trained to recognize and adapt to different customer sentiments, ensuring that responses are tailored to the specific needs and emotions of each individual. This personalized approach helps to build trust and foster positive relationships between KLM and its customers.

To ensure the accuracy and appropriateness of its AI-generated responses, KLM employs a team of human supervisors who monitor the system's performance and intervene when necessary. This human oversight is essential for handling complex or sensitive issues that require a more nuanced approach or escalation to a human representative. By striking a balance between AI automation and human expertise, KLM can deliver a seamless and reliable customer service experience across its social media channels.

The success of KLM's AI-generated customer service responses is evident in the airline's impressive social media metrics. Since implementing the AI system, KLM has seen a significant reduction in response times, with an average response time of less than 30 minutes across all social media platforms. Additionally, the airline has maintained a high level of customer satisfaction, with over 90% of customers expressing positive sentiment towards the AI-generated responses they received.

KLM's approach to AI-generated customer service responses serves as a compelling case study for other businesses looking to leverage AI technology to enhance their customer support. By combining the efficiency and scalability of AI with the empathy and expertise of human representatives, companies can deliver a superior customer experience that meets the evolving expectations of today's digital-savvy consumers.

As AI continues to advance and become more sophisticated, it is likely that we will see more businesses adopting AI-generated content for customer service purposes. However, the success of such implementations will depend on the careful balance between automation and human oversight, as well as the ability to maintain a customer-centric approach that prioritizes the unique needs and preferences of each individual.

Subsection 4.2: Zendesk's Answer Bot AI-Powered Support

Zendesk, a leading customer service software provider, has revolutionized the way businesses handle customer support with its AI-powered Answer Bot. This innovative solution leverages advanced natural language processing (NLP) and machine learning algorithms to provide instant, accurate, and personalized responses to customer inquiries. By implementing Answer Bot, Zendesk has not only enhanced the efficiency of customer support teams but also improved the overall customer experience.

Answer Bot is designed to understand and interpret customer questions, drawing from a vast knowledge base of predefined responses and relevant articles. When a customer submits a query through Zendesk's support channels, such as email or chat, Answer Bot analyzes the content of the message and identifies the most appropriate response. This AI-generated content is then presented to the customer, providing them with the information they need to resolve their issue quickly and effectively.

One of the key advantages of Answer Bot is its ability to handle a wide range of customer inquiries simultaneously. Unlike human support agents, who can only address one customer at a time, Answer Bot can engage with multiple customers concurrently, significantly reducing response times and improving overall support efficiency. This scalability is particularly valuable for businesses with high volumes of customer interactions, as it ensures that no customer is left waiting for an extended period.

Moreover, Answer Bot's AI-generated responses are designed to be conversational and empathetic, mimicking the communication style of human support agents. By analyzing customer sentiment and adapting its language accordingly, Answer Bot can provide a more personalized and engaging support experience. This approach helps to build trust and foster positive relationships between businesses and their customers, ultimately leading to increased customer satisfaction and loyalty.

To ensure the accuracy and relevance of its AI-generated responses, Answer Bot continuously learns from customer interactions and feedback. As more customers engage with the system, Answer Bot refines its understanding of common questions and improves its ability to provide precise and helpful answers. This iterative learning process allows Answer Bot to evolve and adapt to the changing needs of customers over time, ensuring that businesses can consistently deliver high-quality support.

Zendesk's Answer Bot also integrates seamlessly with the company's other support tools, such as its ticketing system and knowledge base. When Answer Bot is unable to provide a satisfactory response to a customer query, it can automatically escalate the issue to a human support agent. This seamless handoff ensures that customers receive the assistance they need, even in complex or unique situations. Additionally, Answer Bot can suggest relevant articles from the company's knowledge base, empowering customers to find solutions to their problems independently.

The success of Zendesk's Answer Bot is evident in the impressive results reported by businesses that have implemented the solution. On average, companies using Answer Bot have seen a 20% reduction in support ticket volume, as customers are able to find answers to their questions more quickly and efficiently. Furthermore, Answer Bot has helped businesses achieve a 50% reduction in first response times, ensuring that customers receive prompt assistance when they need it most.

The lessons learned from Zendesk's Answer Bot implementation highlight the importance of striking a balance between AI automation and human expertise in customer support. While AI-generated content can significantly improve efficiency and scalability, it is crucial to maintain human oversight and intervention when necessary. By leveraging the strengths of both AI and human support agents, businesses can deliver a superior customer experience that meets the evolving expectations of today's digital-savvy consumers.

As AI continues to advance and become more sophisticated, solutions like Zendesk's Answer Bot will likely become increasingly prevalent in the customer support landscape. However, the success of such implementations will depend on the ability to maintain a customer-centric approach, prioritizing the unique needs and preferences of each individual. By combining the power of AI-generated content with the empathy and expertise of human support agents, businesses can create a support ecosystem that drives customer satisfaction, loyalty, and long-term success.

Subsection 4.3: H&M's AI-Generated Chatbot Interactions

In the competitive world of fashion retail, H&M, a global clothing brand, has embraced AI-generated chatbot interactions to revolutionize its customer service approach. By implementing a sophisticated chatbot system, H&M has successfully enhanced its ability to provide quick, accurate, and personalized assistance to customers, ultimately improving the overall shopping experience and driving customer satisfaction.

H&M's AI-generated chatbot is powered by advanced natural language processing (NLP) and machine learning algorithms, enabling it to understand and interpret customer queries, concerns, and feedback. The chatbot is designed to engage with customers in a conversational manner, mimicking the communication style of a human customer service representative. This approach creates a more natural and engaging interaction, making customers feel valued and heard.

One of the key advantages of H&M's AI-generated chatbot is its ability to provide 24/7 support to customers. Whether a customer needs assistance with product information, order tracking, or return policies, the chatbot can deliver instant and relevant responses. This round-the-clock availability is particularly beneficial for customers in different time zones or those who prefer to shop outside of traditional business hours.

Moreover, H&M's chatbot is trained to handle a wide range of customer inquiries, from simple questions to more complex issues. The AI system draws from an extensive knowledge base that includes product details, sizing information, styling tips, and frequently asked questions. By providing accurate and comprehensive responses, the chatbot empowers customers to make informed decisions and resolves their concerns efficiently.

To ensure the effectiveness of its AI-generated chatbot interactions, H&M has implemented a robust training and monitoring process. The chatbot continuously learns from customer interactions, refining its understanding of common queries and improving its ability to provide relevant and helpful responses. Additionally, H&M employs a team of human supervisors who oversee the chatbot's performance, intervening when necessary to handle complex or sensitive issues that require a more personalized approach.

The success of H&M's AI-generated chatbot interactions is evident in the positive feedback and increased customer engagement the company has experienced. Customers appreciate the convenience and speed of the chatbot support, as well as the personalized and friendly nature of the interactions. By providing a seamless and efficient customer service experience, H&M has fostered stronger relationships with its customers, leading to increased brand loyalty and customer satisfaction.

Furthermore, the implementation of AI-generated chatbot interactions has allowed H&M to streamline its customer service operations, reducing the workload on human support agents and enabling them to focus on more complex and high-value tasks. This optimization of resources has resulted in cost savings for the company while simultaneously improving the overall quality of customer support.

H&M's success with AI-generated chatbot interactions serves as a compelling case study for other retailers looking to enhance their customer service capabilities. By leveraging the power of AI and machine learning, businesses can provide personalized, efficient, and round-the-clock support to their customers, ultimately driving customer satisfaction and loyalty.

As AI technology continues to advance, it is likely that more retailers will adopt AI-generated chatbot interactions as a key component of their customer service strategy. However, the success of such implementations will depend on the ability to strike a balance between automation and human oversight, ensuring that customers receive the support they need while maintaining a personal touch.

Summary: Embracing AI-Generated Content for Enhanced Customer Support

The case studies presented in this section demonstrate the transformative power of AI-generated content in the realm of customer service and support. From KLM's AI-powered social media responses to Zendesk's Answer Bot and H&M's chatbot interactions, these examples showcase how businesses can leverage AI technology to provide quick, accurate, and personalized assistance to customers.

By implementing AI-generated content solutions, companies can significantly improve the efficiency of their customer support operations, reduce response times, and handle a higher volume of inquiries simultaneously. This not only enhances the overall customer experience but also allows human support agents to focus on more complex and high-value tasks, optimizing resource allocation and driving cost savings.

Moreover, the success of these AI-generated content applications highlights the importance of striking a balance between automation and human oversight. While AI can handle a wide range of customer queries and provide instant support, it is crucial to maintain human intervention for complex or sensitive issues that require a more nuanced approach. By combining the strengths of AI and human expertise, businesses can deliver a seamless and reliable customer service experience.

As AI technology continues to advance, it is evident that AI-generated content will play an increasingly significant role in shaping the future of customer service and support. However, the success of such implementations will depend on the ability to maintain a customer-centric approach, prioritizing the unique needs and preferences of each individual. By embracing AI-generated content while preserving the human touch, businesses can create a support ecosystem that fosters customer satisfaction, loyalty, and long-term success.

Looking ahead, the next section will explore the ethical considerations and responsibilities associated with the use of AI-generated content. As businesses increasingly adopt this technology, it is crucial to address the potential challenges and ensure that AI is deployed in a responsible and transparent manner.

Section 5: Lessons Learned and Best Practices

Throughout the case studies explored in this chapter, we've seen compelling examples of how AI-generated content has been successfully implemented across various industries, from journalism and media to marketing and advertising, creative fields, and customer service. These success stories offer valuable insights into the potential of AI-generated content and provide a roadmap for organizations looking to navigate the stigma surrounding this technology.

As we delve into the lessons learned and best practices gleaned from these case studies, it's essential to recognize that the integration of AI-generated content is not a one-size-fits-all approach. Each industry and organization faces unique challenges and opportunities when it comes to leveraging AI-powered tools and techniques. However, by examining the common threads that run through these success stories, we can identify key strategies and principles that can help guide the effective and responsible use of AI-generated content.

In this section, we'll explore the importance of balancing AI-generated content with human oversight, ensuring transparency and disclosure, and engaging in iterative improvement and refinement. We'll also discuss the value of collaborating with domain experts to ensure the quality and accuracy of AI-generated content, and consider the ethical implications of relying on AI-powered tools in various contexts.

By synthesizing the lessons learned from these case studies, we aim to provide a practical framework for organizations and individuals seeking to harness the power of AI-generated content while navigating the complexities of the stigma surrounding this technology. Whether you're a content creator, marketer, journalist, or business leader, understanding these best practices can help you make informed decisions about how to integrate AI-generated content into your workflows and strategies, while maintaining the trust and confidence of your audience.

Subsection 5.1: Balancing AI-Generated Content with Human Oversight

As we've seen throughout the case studies in this chapter, AI-generated content has the potential to revolutionize various industries, from journalism and media to marketing and advertising. However, one of the key lessons learned from these success stories is the importance of balancing AI-generated content with human oversight and editorial control.

While AI-powered tools can generate content quickly and efficiently, it's crucial to recognize that these systems are not infallible. They can make mistakes, introduce biases, or generate content that lacks the nuance and context that human writers bring to the table. As such, it's essential for organizations to establish a system of checks and balances, where human editors and domain experts review and refine AI-generated content before it's published or disseminated.

The Washington Post's Heliograf AI system, for example, generates news articles that are then reviewed and edited by human journalists before publication. This ensures that the final product meets the high standards of accuracy, clarity, and journalistic integrity that readers expect from a reputable news organization. Similarly, in the case of Persado's AI-generated marketing copy, human marketers work closely with the AI system to ensure that the generated content aligns with the brand's voice, tone, and messaging strategy.

By balancing AI-generated content with human oversight, organizations can harness the speed and efficiency of AI while maintaining the quality and credibility of their content. This approach also allows for a more collaborative relationship between humans and machines, where AI is viewed as a tool to augment and enhance human creativity rather than a replacement for it.

Moreover, human oversight can help mitigate the potential risks associated with AI-generated content, such as the spread of misinformation or the reinforcement of biases. By having human editors and domain experts review and fact-check AI-generated content, organizations can ensure that the information they disseminate is accurate, fair, and unbiased.

In summary, balancing AI-generated content with human oversight is a critical best practice for organizations looking to leverage the power of AI in their content creation processes. By establishing a system of checks and balances, organizations can ensure that their AI-generated content meets the highest standards of quality, accuracy, and credibility while fostering a collaborative relationship between humans and machines.

Subsection 5.2: Ensuring Transparency and Disclosure

Transparency and disclosure are crucial aspects of using AI-generated content responsibly. As we've seen in the case studies throughout this chapter, the most successful implementations of AI-generated content have been those that prioritize openness and honesty about the use of AI in the content creation process.

One of the primary concerns surrounding AI-generated content is the potential for deception. If readers, viewers, or listeners are not aware that the content they're consuming was created by an AI system, they may feel misled or betrayed when they discover the truth. This can erode trust in the organization or individual behind the content and contribute to the overall stigma against AI-generated content.

To combat this issue, it's essential for organizations and content creators to be transparent about their use of AI-generated content from the outset.

This means clearly labeling any content that was wholly or partially generated by an AI system, providing information about the specific AI tools or techniques used, and explaining the role that human creators played in the process.

For example, when The Guardian published an article written by GPT-3, they were upfront about the fact that the content was generated by an AI system. They included a disclaimer at the top of the article, explaining that it was "written by GPT-3, OpenAI's language generator" and that "GPT-3 is a cutting edge language model that uses machine learning to produce human-like text." By being transparent about the use of AI, The Guardian built trust with their readers and sparked an important conversation about the implications of AI-generated content in journalism.

Similarly, in the case of Obvious Art's AI-generated artwork, the collective was open about the fact that the piece was created using an AI system. They provided detailed information about the generative adversarial network (GAN) used to create the artwork and emphasized the role that human artists played in curating and refining the final piece. By being transparent about the use of AI, Obvious Art invited viewers to engage with the artwork on its own merits, rather than feeling deceived or misled.

Transparency and disclosure are not only important for building trust with audiences but also for navigating the legal and ethical implications of AI-generated content. In some cases, failing to disclose the use of AI could be considered a form of plagiarism or intellectual property infringement, particularly if the AI system was trained on copyrighted material. By being upfront about the use of AI, content creators can avoid these legal pitfalls and ensure that they're giving proper credit to any human creators involved in the process.

Moreover, transparency and disclosure can help to demystify AI-generated content and reduce the stigma surrounding it. By openly discussing the capabilities and limitations of AI systems, content creators can help audiences understand that AI is simply a tool, not a replacement for human creativity and expertise. This can foster a more nuanced and informed conversation about the role of AI in content creation and help to break down the barriers of fear and mistrust that often surround this technology.

In conclusion, ensuring transparency and disclosure is a critical best practice for anyone using AI-generated content. By being open and honest about the use of AI, content creators can build trust with their audiences, navigate legal and ethical challenges, and contribute to a more informed and nuanced conversation about the role of AI in our creative landscapes. As we move forward into an era of increasingly sophisticated AI-generated content, prioritizing transparency and disclosure will be essential for realizing the full potential of this technology while mitigating its risks and drawbacks.

Subsection 5.3: Iterative Improvement and Refinement

The success stories of AI-generated content across various industries, from journalism to marketing and creative fields, have one crucial aspect in common: the importance of iterative improvement and refinement. As AI technology continues to evolve and advance, it is essential for organizations and content creators to view AI-generated content as an ongoing process rather than a one-time solution.

Iterative improvement and refinement involve continuously monitoring, evaluating, and adjusting AI-generated content systems to ensure that they produce high-quality, accurate, and relevant output. This process is critical for several reasons. First, AI models are trained on vast amounts of data, which can sometimes lead to biases, inaccuracies, or inconsistencies in the generated content. By regularly reviewing and refining the AI models, content creators can identify and address these issues, ensuring that the final output meets the desired standards of quality and accuracy.

Second, iterative improvement allows AI-generated content systems to adapt to changing trends, audience preferences, and industry developments. As new data becomes available and user feedback is collected, AI models can be retrained and updated to better align with current expectations and requirements. This continuous adaptation ensures that AI-generated content remains relevant, engaging, and valuable to its intended audience.

The case studies explored in this chapter demonstrate the importance of iterative improvement and refinement in practice. For example, The Washington Post's Heliograf AI system undergoes regular updates and adjustments based on feedback from journalists and readers, allowing it to generate increasingly accurate and insightful news articles over time. Similarly, Persado's AI-generated marketing copy is continually refined based on performance data and client input, ensuring that the generated content is optimized for maximum impact and engagement.

To effectively implement iterative improvement and refinement, organizations must establish clear processes and guidelines for monitoring, evaluating, and updating their AI-generated content systems. This may involve setting up dedicated teams or workflows to regularly review the generated content, collect feedback from stakeholders, and make necessary adjustments to the AI models. It also requires a commitment to ongoing investment in AI research and development, as well as collaboration with domain experts and end-users to ensure that the generated content meets their needs and expectations.

Moreover, iterative improvement and refinement can help organizations navigate the ethical and legal implications of AI-generated content. By continuously monitoring and adjusting their AI systems, content creators can proactively identify and address potential issues related to bias, accuracy, or intellectual property rights. This not only mitigates legal and reputational risks but also helps to build trust and credibility with audiences who may be skeptical of AI-generated content.

In conclusion, iterative improvement and refinement are essential best practices for organizations and content creators looking to harness the power of AI-generated content. By viewing AI as an ongoing process rather than a one-time solution, and by establishing clear processes for monitoring, evaluating, and updating their AI systems, content creators can ensure that their AI-generated content remains high-quality, accurate, and relevant over time. As AI technology continues to advance and the stigma against AI-generated content gradually diminishes, the importance of iterative improvement and refinement will only continue to grow, paving the way for more successful and impactful applications of AI in content creation.

Subsection 5.4: Collaborating with Domain Experts

As AI-generated content continues to gain traction across various industries, it is crucial to recognize the importance of collaborating with domain experts to ensure the quality and accuracy of the generated content. While AI algorithms can process vast amounts of data and generate human-like text, they lack the deep understanding, context, and nuanced insights that human experts possess in their respective fields.

Domain experts, such as subject matter specialists, industry professionals, or experienced writers, bring a wealth of knowledge and expertise to the content creation process. They can provide valuable guidance on the accuracy, relevance, and appropriateness of AI-generated content, helping to identify and correct any errors, inconsistencies, or biases that may arise.

By collaborating with domain experts, organizations can ensure that their AI-generated content meets the highest standards of quality and credibility. These experts can review and refine the generated content, adding context, clarifying complex concepts, and ensuring that the information presented is factually correct and up-to-date. This collaborative approach helps to mitigate the risk of spreading misinformation or perpetuating inaccuracies, which is a common concern associated with AI-generated content.

Moreover, domain experts can provide insights into the specific needs, preferences, and expectations of the target audience. They can help tailor the AI-generated content to the intended readers, ensuring that it is engaging, relevant, and valuable. This collaboration can lead to the creation of content that resonates with the audience, builds trust, and establishes the organization as a credible and authoritative source of information.

In practice, collaborating with domain experts can take various forms, depending on the nature of the AI-generated content and the specific needs of the organization. For example, in the case of AI-generated news articles, journalists and editors can work closely with the AI system to ensure that the generated content adheres to journalistic standards and ethics. They can provide feedback on the article structure, tone, and style, as well as fact-check the information presented to maintain accuracy and integrity.

Similarly, in the realm of marketing and advertising, collaborating with experienced marketers and copywriters can help ensure that AI-generated content aligns with the brand's voice, messaging, and overall strategy. These experts can provide guidance on the most effective language, tone, and formatting to use, as well as help optimize the content for specific channels and audiences.

Collaborating with domain experts also presents an opportunity for continuous learning and improvement of AI-generated content systems. By incorporating the feedback and insights provided by these experts, organizations can refine their AI algorithms, training data, and content generation processes over time. This iterative approach can lead to the creation of more accurate, relevant, and high-quality content that effectively addresses the stigma surrounding AI-generated content.

In conclusion, collaborating with domain experts is a critical best practice for organizations looking to harness the power of AI-generated content while ensuring its quality and accuracy. By leveraging the knowledge and expertise of subject matter specialists, industry professionals, and experienced writers, organizations can create content that is factually correct, engaging, and valuable to their target audience. This collaborative approach not only helps to mitigate the risks associated with AI-generated content but also contributes to the overall credibility and trust in the organization's content output.

Summary: Navigating the Future of AI-Generated Content

As we've explored throughout this section, the case studies of successful AI-generated content across various industries offer valuable lessons and best practices for organizations and individuals looking to harness the power of this technology. By examining the common threads that run through these success stories, we can identify key strategies for navigating the stigma surrounding AI-generated content and realizing its full potential.

The importance of balancing AI-generated content with human oversight and editorial control cannot be overstated. While AI can generate content quickly and efficiently, human expertise is essential for ensuring the quality, accuracy, and nuance of the final product. By establishing a collaborative relationship between humans and machines, organizations can leverage the speed and scale of AI while maintaining the credibility and trustworthiness of their content.

Transparency and disclosure are also critical components of responsible AI-generated content. By being open and honest about the use of AI in the content creation process, organizations can build trust with their audiences, mitigate legal and ethical risks, and contribute to a more informed public dialogue about the role of AI in our creative landscapes.

Moreover, the success stories highlighted in this section demonstrate the importance of viewing AI-generated content as an ongoing process of iterative improvement and refinement. By continuously monitoring, evaluating, and adjusting their AI systems based on feedback and performance data, organizations can ensure that their content remains relevant, engaging, and valuable to their target audiences over time.

Collaborating with domain experts is another key best practice for ensuring the quality and accuracy of AI-generated content. By leveraging the deep knowledge and insights of subject matter specialists, industry professionals, and experienced writers, organizations can create content that is factually correct, contextually relevant, and aligned with the needs and expectations of their audiences.

As we look to the future of AI-generated content, it's clear that these lessons and best practices will only become more important. With the rapid advancement of AI technologies and the growing demand for high-quality, personalized content, organizations that can effectively navigate the stigma and harness the power of AI will be well-positioned for success.

However, the path forward is not without its challenges. As AI-generated content becomes more sophisticated and ubiquitous, questions of authenticity, creativity, and human agency will continue to arise. It will be up to organizations and individuals to grapple with these complex issues and find ways to integrate AI into their content creation processes in a responsible, transparent, and value-driven manner.

Ultimately, the lessons learned from these case studies offer a roadmap for navigating the future of AI-generated content. By balancing the efficiency of AI with the wisdom of human oversight, embracing transparency and disclosure, committing to ongoing improvement and refinement, and collaborating with domain experts, we can unlock the full potential of this transformative technology while mitigating its risks and challenges. As we move forward into an era of unprecedented technological change, these best practices will be essential for building trust, driving innovation, and shaping a future in which humans and machines can work together to create content that informs, inspires, and enriches our lives.

Chapter Summary: Embracing AI-Generated Content for Success

Throughout this chapter, we have explored a diverse range of case studies and success stories that demonstrate the potential of AI-generated content across various industries. From journalism and media to marketing, creative fields, and customer service, these real-world examples have shown how AI can be effectively leveraged to create compelling, engaging, and efficient content.

The lessons learned from these case studies are invaluable for organizations and individuals looking to navigate the stigma against AI-generated content and harness its power for their own success. By balancing AI-generated content with human oversight, ensuring transparency, and collaborating with domain experts, these companies have been able to create high-quality content that resonates with their target audiences.

Moreover, the success stories have highlighted the importance of iterative improvement and refinement in AI-generated content systems. As the technology continues to evolve, it is crucial for organizations to stay ahead of the curve by continuously updating and optimizing their AI-powered content creation processes.

The case studies have also shown that AI-generated content is not a replacement for human creativity but rather a powerful tool that can augment and enhance it. By embracing AI as a collaborative partner in the creative process, individuals and organizations can unlock new possibilities and push the boundaries of what is achievable in content creation.

As we move forward into an increasingly AI-driven future, it is clear that the stigma against AI-generated content will continue to diminish. By learning from the success stories and best practices outlined in this chapter, readers can position themselves at the forefront of this exciting new era of content creation and harness the power of AI to achieve their goals.

Chapter 12: The Way Forward: Embracing the AI Revolution

As we stand on the precipice of a new era, it is becoming increasingly clear that the AI revolution is not a distant dream but a rapidly unfolding reality. The stigma surrounding AI-generated content, once a formidable obstacle, is gradually eroding as individuals and organizations begin to recognize the immense potential and opportunities that this technology presents.

Throughout this book, we have explored the various facets of the stigma against AI-generated content, delving into its origins, examining its impact, and discussing strategies to overcome it. We have seen how AI can serve as a powerful tool to enhance human creativity, how it can be leveraged to address bias and misinformation, and how it can open up new avenues for collaboration and innovation.

As we look to the future, it is essential that we embrace the AI revolution with open minds and a willingness to adapt. The coming years will undoubtedly bring about significant changes in the way we create, consume, and interact with content. AI-generated content will become increasingly sophisticated, personalized, and ubiquitous, transforming industries and reshaping the very fabric of our society.

However, this transformation is not without its challenges. As we navigate this uncharted territory, we must remain vigilant in addressing the ethical considerations and responsibilities that come with the development and deployment of AI-generated content. We must strive to create robust frameworks and governance models that ensure transparency, accountability, and fairness, while fostering a culture of responsible innovation.

The way forward lies in redefining the narrative around AI-generated content, shifting from a mindset of fear and skepticism to one of opportunity and collaboration. By investing in education and skill development, encouraging experimentation and innovation, and promoting interdisciplinary collaboration, we can harness the full potential of AI-generated content and usher in a new era of creativity and progress.

As we embark on this exciting journey, it is crucial to remember that the AI revolution is not about replacing human creativity but rather about augmenting and amplifying it. By embracing AI as a tool and a partner, we can unlock new possibilities, push the boundaries of what is possible, and create a future where human ingenuity and machine intelligence work hand in hand to solve the greatest challenges of our time.

So let us step forward with courage and optimism, ready to embrace the AI revolution and all that it has to offer. The future is ours to shape, and with the power of AI-generated content at our fingertips, there are no limits to what we can achieve.

Section 1: Redefining the Narrative Around AI-Generated Content

As we stand on the precipice of a new era in content creation, it is crucial that we take a step back and reexamine the prevailing narrative surrounding AI-generated content. For too long, the conversation has been dominated by fear, skepticism, and a lack of understanding about the true potential of this groundbreaking technology. It is time to reframe the discussion and shift our focus towards the myriad benefits and opportunities that AI-generated content presents.

In recent years, the rapid advancements in artificial intelligence have given rise to a new wave of content creation tools and platforms that are revolutionizing industries across the board. From journalism and marketing to entertainment and education, AI-generated content is making its presence felt in ways that were once unimaginable. However, despite the numerous success stories and the undeniable potential of this technology, a persistent stigma continues to cast a shadow over its adoption and acceptance.

This stigma, fueled by misconceptions and a lack of understanding, has led many to view AI-generated content as a threat to human creativity and authenticity. Some argue that the use of AI in content creation will lead to a homogenization of ideas and a loss of the unique perspectives that only human beings can bring to the table. Others fear that the rise of AI-generated content will result in widespread job losses and a devaluation of human talent.

While these concerns are understandable, they are often based on a narrow and incomplete understanding of the true nature of AI-generated content. In reality, AI is not a replacement for human creativity but rather a powerful tool that can augment and enhance it in ways that were previously impossible. By leveraging the vast computational power and data processing capabilities of AI, content creators can unlock new levels of efficiency, personalization, and engagement that would be unattainable through traditional means.

Moreover, the adoption of AI-generated content has the potential to democratize the creative process, making it more accessible and inclusive than ever before. With the help of AI tools and platforms, individuals from all walks of life can now create high-quality content without the need for expensive equipment, extensive training, or years of experience. This opens up a world of possibilities for underrepresented voices and perspectives to be heard and for new forms of creativity to emerge.

As we move forward into this exciting new era of content creation, it is essential that we approach AI-generated content with an open mind and a willingness to explore its full potential. By redefining the narrative around this technology and focusing on its benefits and opportunities, we can unlock a future in which human creativity and artificial intelligence work hand in hand to create content that is more engaging, personalized, and impactful than ever before.

Subsection 1.1: Shifting from Fear to Opportunity

The rapid advancement of artificial intelligence (AI) has brought about a wave of change in the content creation landscape, giving rise to a plethora of AI-generated content across various industries. However, this transformative technology has also been met with a significant amount of fear and skepticism, stemming from concerns about job displacement, creative authenticity, and the potential for misuse. To truly harness the power of AI-generated content and unlock its full potential, it is crucial that we shift our narrative from one of fear and apprehension to one of opportunity and embrace.

Fear is a natural response to change, especially when it involves a technology as powerful and disruptive as AI. Many content creators, marketers, and publishers have expressed concerns about the impact of AI-generated content on their livelihoods, fearing that machines will replace human creativity and render their skills obsolete. Others worry about the potential for AI to be used to create and spread misinformation, propaganda, or low-quality content, undermining the credibility and trust that is essential for effective communication.

While these concerns are valid and should not be dismissed, it is essential to recognize that they are often based on a limited understanding of the true nature and potential of AI-generated content. By focusing solely on the perceived threats and challenges, we risk missing out on the tremendous opportunities that this technology presents for enhancing human creativity, increasing efficiency, and opening up new avenues for expression and engagement.

To shift the narrative from fear to opportunity, we must first acknowledge that AI is not a replacement for human creativity but rather a powerful tool that can augment and enhance it. AI-generated content is not about machines taking over the creative process but rather about leveraging the unique strengths of both humans and machines to create content that is more engaging, personalized, and impactful than ever before.

By embracing AI-generated content, content creators can free themselves from the tedious and time-consuming tasks that often bog down the creative process, such as data analysis, keyword research, and formatting. This allows them to focus on the higher-level creative work that truly sets them apart, such as ideation, storytelling, and emotional connection. In essence, AI can serve as a creative partner, helping content creators to work smarter, faster, and more efficiently, ultimately leading to better outcomes for both creators and audiences alike.

Moreover, the adoption of AI-generated content has the potential to democratize the creative process, making it more accessible and inclusive than ever before. With the help of AI tools and platforms, individuals from all walks of life can now create high-quality content without the need for extensive training, expensive equipment, or years of experience. This opens up a world of possibilities for underrepresented voices and perspectives to be heard and for new forms of creativity to emerge.

As we navigate this new era of content creation, it is essential that we approach AI-generated content with an open mind and a willingness to explore its full potential. By shifting our focus from fear to opportunity, we can unlock a future in which human creativity and artificial intelligence work hand in hand to create content that is more engaging, personalized, and impactful than ever before. Embracing AI-generated content is not about surrendering our creative agency but rather about expanding our creative possibilities and pushing the boundaries of what is possible in the world of content creation.

Subsection 1.2: Highlighting the Complementary Nature of AI and Human Creativity

As we explore the potential of AI-generated content, it is crucial to understand that AI is not meant to replace human creativity but rather to complement and enhance it. The fear that AI will render human creativity obsolete is a common misconception that stems from a limited understanding of the technology's true nature and purpose. In reality, AI and human creativity are not mutually exclusive; they can work hand in hand to create content that is more innovative, engaging, and impactful than ever before.

At its core, AI is a tool that can augment and amplify human creativity by taking on tasks that are time-consuming, repetitive, or data-intensive. By leveraging the power of machine learning algorithms, AI can analyze vast amounts of data, identify patterns and insights, and generate content ideas that might otherwise be overlooked by human creators. This frees up valuable time and mental space for humans to focus on the higher-level creative work that truly sets them apart, such as ideation, storytelling, and emotional connection.

For example, consider a journalist tasked with writing an article about a complex social issue. Traditionally, the journalist would need to spend hours researching the topic, gathering data, and organizing their findings before even beginning to write. With the help of AI, however, the journalist can quickly generate a comprehensive summary of the issue, complete with relevant statistics, expert opinions, and historical context. This allows the journalist to dive deeper into the story, exploring nuanced angles and crafting a compelling narrative that resonates with readers on an emotional level.

Similarly, in the world of marketing, AI can help content creators generate personalized content at scale, tailoring messages to individual user preferences and behaviors. By analyzing data on customer demographics, interests, and past interactions, AI algorithms can suggest targeted content ideas, optimize headlines and subject lines, and even generate entire email campaigns or social media posts. This enables marketers to create content that is more relevant, engaging, and effective, ultimately leading to higher conversion rates and customer loyalty.

It is important to note, however, that AI-generated content is not meant to be a substitute for human creativity but rather a starting point for further refinement and personalization. While AI can generate ideas and rough drafts, it is ultimately up to human creators to add their unique perspective, voice, and style to the content. This is where the true magic happens –

in the collaboration between human and machine, where the strengths of each are leveraged to create something truly exceptional.

Moreover, the use of AI in content creation can actually inspire new forms of creativity and push the boundaries of what is possible. By exposing humans to novel ideas and perspectives generated by AI, creators can break free from their usual patterns of thinking and explore uncharted territory. This can lead to the emergence of entirely new genres, formats, and styles of content that may never have been conceived of by humans alone.

In conclusion, the complementary nature of AI and human creativity is a powerful force that has the potential to revolutionize the way we create and consume content. By embracing AI as a tool for augmenting and enhancing human creativity, we can unlock new levels of innovation, efficiency, and engagement that will benefit creators and audiences alike. As we move forward into this exciting new era of content creation, it is essential that we approach AI not with fear or skepticism but with an open mind and a willingness to explore its full potential.

Subsection 1.3: Promoting a Balanced and Nuanced Understanding

In our quest to redefine the narrative around AI-generated content, it is crucial that we promote a balanced and nuanced understanding of this transformative technology. As with any major technological advancement, AI-generated content brings with it a complex array of benefits and challenges that must be carefully considered and addressed. By encouraging a more comprehensive and objective view of AI-generated content, we can help to dispel misconceptions, alleviate fears, and pave the way for a more productive and informed dialogue about its role in our society.

One of the key benefits of AI-generated content is its potential to enhance efficiency and productivity across a wide range of industries. By automating certain aspects of the content creation process, such as data analysis, language translation, and basic content generation, AI can help businesses and individuals to produce high-quality content more quickly and at a lower cost. This increased efficiency can free up valuable time and resources that can be redirected towards more strategic and creative endeavors, ultimately leading to better outcomes and a more competitive edge in the marketplace.

Moreover, AI-generated content has the potential to democratize access to information and knowledge, making it easier for people from all backgrounds to create and share their ideas with a global audience. With the help of AI-powered tools and platforms, individuals who may have previously lacked the skills, resources, or opportunities to create professional-grade content can now do so with relative ease. This increased accessibility can help to amplify diverse voices and perspectives, fostering a more inclusive and representative digital landscape.

However, it is equally important to acknowledge and address the challenges and potential drawbacks of AI-generated content. One of the primary concerns is the risk of perpetuating biases and inaccuracies that may be present in the data used to train AI algorithms. If left unchecked, these biases can lead to the creation and dissemination of content that reinforces harmful stereotypes, misleads audiences, or even discriminates against certain groups of people. As such, it is crucial that we prioritize the development of ethical and responsible AI systems that are designed to mitigate these risks and ensure the accuracy, fairness, and transparency of the content they generate.

Another challenge associated with AI-generated content is the potential for job displacement and economic disruption. As AI technologies become more sophisticated and widely adopted, there is a risk that certain roles and industries may become automated, leading to job losses and a need for workers to adapt and reskill. While this is a valid concern, it is important to approach this issue with a nuanced understanding of the complex interplay between technology and employment. Rather than viewing AI as a threat to human labor, we should focus on identifying opportunities for humans and machines to work together in complementary ways, leveraging the unique strengths of each to create new forms of value and innovation.

Ultimately, promoting a balanced and nuanced understanding of AI-generated content requires ongoing education, dialogue, and collaboration among all stakeholders, including technologists, content creators, policymakers, and the general public. By fostering open and honest conversations about the benefits and challenges of this technology, we can work together to develop responsible and ethical approaches to its development and deployment, ensuring that it serves the best interests of individuals, organizations, and society as a whole.

As we navigate this new era of content creation, it is essential that we approach AI-generated content with a curious and critical eye, always striving to separate hype from reality and to make informed decisions based on a comprehensive understanding of its potential and limitations. By doing so, we can harness the power of AI to enhance human creativity, productivity, and knowledge-sharing, while also mitigating its risks and ensuring that it aligns with our values and aspirations as a society.

Summary: Embracing the Potential of AI-Generated Content

As we have explored throughout this section, the narrative surrounding AI-generated content is in dire need of a shift. By focusing solely on the perceived threats and challenges, we risk overlooking the immense potential that this technology holds for enhancing human creativity, increasing efficiency, and democratizing access to high-quality content creation.

It is crucial to recognize that AI is not a replacement for human creativity but rather a powerful tool that can augment and complement it. By leveraging the unique strengths of both humans and machines, we can create content that is more engaging, personalized, and impactful than ever before. AI can take on the time-consuming and repetitive tasks, freeing up human creators to focus on the higher-level creative work that truly sets them apart.

Moreover, the adoption of AI-generated content has the potential to make the creative process more inclusive and accessible, enabling individuals from all backgrounds to express their ideas and perspectives. This democratization of content creation can lead to the emergence of new voices, styles, and genres that may have otherwise gone unheard.

However, to fully harness the benefits of AI-generated content, we must approach it with a balanced and nuanced understanding. This means acknowledging both the opportunities and the challenges, and working together as a society to develop responsible and ethical approaches to its development and deployment.

As we move forward into this new era of content creation, it is essential that we embrace the potential of AI-generated content with an open mind and a willingness to explore. By redefining the narrative and focusing on the possibilities, we can unlock a future in which human creativity and artificial intelligence work hand in hand to create content that informs, inspires, and connects us all.

Section 2: Fostering a Culture of Innovation and Experimentation

In the ever-evolving landscape of AI-generated content, embracing change and adopting a forward-thinking mindset are essential for individuals and organizations alike. As we navigate the challenges and opportunities presented by this technological revolution, it becomes increasingly clear that fostering a culture of innovation and experimentation is not just a choice, but a necessity. By cultivating an environment that encourages creativity, risk-taking, and continuous learning, we can unlock the true potential of AI-generated content and harness its power to transform the way we create, consume, and interact with information.

Imagine a world where the stigma against AI-generated content is replaced by a sense of excitement and possibility. A world where individuals and organizations alike are empowered to explore new frontiers, push boundaries, and create content that is both engaging and meaningful. This is the world we can build by fostering a culture of innovation and experimentation.

In the following subsections, we will delve into the key aspects of creating such a culture, from encouraging early adoption and piloting to cultivating a mindset of continuous learning and celebrating successes while learning from failures. By embracing these principles and practices, we can not only overcome the stigma against AI-generated content but also position ourselves at the forefront of this transformative technology, ready to seize the opportunities it presents and shape the future of content creation.

Subsection 2.1: Encouraging Early Adoption and Piloting

In the journey towards embracing AI-generated content, encouraging early adoption and piloting is a crucial step. Organizations that are willing to take the lead and experiment with this technology can gain a significant competitive advantage by being at the forefront of innovation. By piloting AI-generated content projects, these pioneering organizations can explore the potential benefits firsthand, identify challenges, and develop best practices that can be shared with the wider community.

One of the key advantages of early adoption is the opportunity to shape the direction of AI-generated content within an industry. Early adopters have the chance to set the standards and establish themselves as thought leaders, influencing the way AI-generated content is perceived and utilized by others. This can lead to increased brand recognition, customer loyalty, and market share.

Moreover, piloting AI-generated content allows organizations to test the waters and gauge the receptiveness of their target audience. By starting with small-scale projects and carefully monitoring the response, organizations can gather valuable insights into what works and what doesn't. This feedback loop enables them to refine their approach, improve the quality of their AI-generated content, and gradually build trust and credibility with their audience.

Encouraging early adoption and piloting also fosters a culture of experimentation and innovation within organizations. By empowering employees to explore new technologies and take calculated risks, organizations can cultivate a mindset that embraces change and seeks out new opportunities. This culture of innovation can spill over into other areas of the organization, leading to increased creativity, productivity, and employee engagement.

To facilitate early adoption and piloting, organizations can establish dedicated innovation teams or labs that are tasked with exploring the potential of AI-generated content. These teams can be given the resources and autonomy to experiment with different approaches, collaborate with external partners, and share their findings with the rest of the organization. By creating a safe space for experimentation and learning, organizations can accelerate the adoption of AI-generated content and stay ahead of the curve.

In conclusion, encouraging early adoption and piloting is a vital step in overcoming the stigma against AI-generated content. By taking the lead and experimenting with this technology, organizations can reap the benefits of being at the forefront of innovation, shape the direction of their industry, and foster a culture of experimentation and continuous learning. As more organizations embrace this approach, the stigma against AI-generated content will gradually erode, paving the way for widespread adoption and transformative change.

Subsection 2.2: Cultivating a Mindset of Continuous Learning

In the rapidly evolving world of AI-generated content, embracing a mindset of continuous learning is not just a valuable asset, but a necessity for individuals and organizations alike. As the technology behind AI-generated content continues to advance at an unprecedented pace, staying ahead of the curve requires a proactive approach to learning and adapting.

One of the key challenges in overcoming the stigma against AI-generated content is the lack of understanding and knowledge about the technology and its potential applications. By cultivating a mindset of continuous learning, individuals and organizations can bridge this knowledge gap and gain a deeper understanding of the capabilities, limitations, and ethical considerations surrounding AI-generated content.

Continuous learning involves actively seeking out new information, skills, and perspectives related to AI-generated content. This can take many forms, such as attending workshops and conferences, participating in online courses and webinars, reading industry publications and research papers, and engaging in discussions with experts and peers.

For individuals, cultivating a mindset of continuous learning can lead to personal and professional growth, as well as increased job security in an era where AI is transforming many industries. By staying informed about the latest developments in AI-generated content, individuals can identify new opportunities, adapt to changing job requirements, and position themselves as valuable assets within their organizations.

At an organizational level, fostering a culture of continuous learning is essential for staying competitive and innovative in the face of technological disruption. By encouraging employees to continuously update their knowledge and skills related to AI-generated content, organizations can build a workforce that is agile, adaptable, and equipped to harness the power of this technology for business success.

To support continuous learning, organizations can invest in training and development programs that focus on AI-generated content, provide access to relevant resources and tools, and create opportunities for employees to collaborate and share knowledge across departments and teams. By making continuous learning a priority and integrating it into the fabric of the organization, companies can not only overcome the stigma against AI-generated content but also drive innovation and growth.

Moreover, cultivating a mindset of continuous learning can help individuals and organizations approach AI-generated content with a more open and curious mindset, rather than one driven by fear or skepticism. By actively seeking to understand the technology and its implications, we can engage in informed discussions, make better decisions, and shape the future of AI-generated content in a responsible and ethical manner.

In conclusion, cultivating a mindset of continuous learning is a critical step in overcoming the stigma against AI-generated content. By embracing this mindset, individuals and organizations can stay ahead of the curve, adapt to changing technological landscapes, and harness the power of AI-generated content for personal and business success. As we navigate this transformative era, continuous learning will be the key to unlocking the full potential of AI-generated content and shaping a future where humans and machines can work together in harmony.

Subsection 2.3: Celebrating Successes and Learning from Failures

In the journey of embracing AI-generated content, it is crucial to recognize and celebrate the successes achieved along the way. Every successful AI-generated content initiative, no matter how small, represents a step forward in overcoming the stigma and demonstrating the potential of this technology. By highlighting these successes, organizations can boost morale, inspire others, and build momentum for further innovation.

Celebrating successes can take many forms, such as showcasing AI-generated content projects at industry events, sharing case studies through blog posts or webinars, or even hosting internal recognition programs that reward teams or individuals who have made significant contributions to the field. These celebrations not only acknowledge the hard work and dedication of those involved but also serve as a powerful testament to the value and impact of AI-generated content.

However, it is equally important to recognize that the path to success is rarely smooth, and setbacks and failures are an inevitable part of the innovation process. Rather than viewing these challenges as roadblocks, organizations should embrace them as valuable learning opportunities. By analyzing what went wrong, identifying areas for improvement, and adapting their approach accordingly, teams can continuously refine their AI-generated content strategies and develop more effective solutions.

One way to facilitate learning from failures is to foster a culture of open communication and psychological safety within the organization. Encouraging teams to share their experiences, both positive and negative, without fear of judgment or repercussion can create a rich learning environment where everyone can benefit from the collective knowledge and insights gained. This can be achieved through regular debriefing sessions, retrospectives, or even dedicated forums where employees can discuss their challenges and brainstorm solutions together.

Moreover, organizations should view failures not as endpoints, but as stepping stones towards greater success. By reframing setbacks as opportunities for growth and innovation, teams can maintain their motivation and enthusiasm even in the face of adversity. This mindset shift can be supported by leadership that encourages experimentation, tolerates calculated risks, and recognizes the value of learning from failures.

In addition to internal learning, organizations can also benefit from sharing their experiences with the wider community. By openly discussing their successes and failures at industry conferences, in publications, or through collaborative initiatives, organizations can contribute to the collective knowledge base and help advance the field of AI-generated content as a whole. This sharing of insights can also foster a sense of solidarity and support among organizations working to overcome the stigma, creating a network of allies and collaborators.

Ultimately, celebrating successes and learning from failures is essential for driving innovation and progress in the realm of AI-generated content. By acknowledging achievements, embracing challenges as opportunities for growth, and fostering a culture of continuous learning, organizations can not only overcome the stigma but also position themselves at the forefront of this transformative technology. As more organizations adopt this mindset and approach, the collective successes will begin to outweigh the setbacks, paving the way for a future where AI-generated content is widely accepted and valued.

Summary: Embracing Innovation and Experimentation for a Thriving AI-Generated Content Landscape

Fostering a culture of innovation and experimentation is not just a desirable trait but a necessity in the rapidly evolving world of AI-generated content. As we navigate the challenges and opportunities presented by this transformative technology, it becomes clear that organizations and individuals who embrace change, take calculated risks, and continuously learn will be the ones to thrive in this new landscape.

By encouraging early adoption and piloting, organizations can position themselves at the forefront of innovation, shaping the direction of their industries and reaping the benefits of being pioneers. This proactive approach allows them to explore the potential of AI-generated content, gather valuable insights, and refine their strategies based on real-world feedback.

Moreover, cultivating a mindset of continuous learning is essential for staying ahead of the curve in an era where the technology behind AI-generated content is advancing at an unprecedented pace. By actively seeking out new knowledge, skills, and perspectives, individuals and organizations can bridge the knowledge gap, make informed decisions, and harness the power of AI-generated content for personal and business success.

Equally important is the celebration of successes and the willingness to learn from failures. Recognizing and highlighting achievements, no matter how small, can boost morale, inspire others, and build momentum for further innovation. At the same time, embracing setbacks as valuable learning opportunities allows teams to continuously refine their approaches, develop more effective solutions, and ultimately drive progress.

As we move forward in this exciting and transformative era, fostering a culture of innovation and experimentation will be the key to overcoming the stigma against AI-generated content. By embracing change, continuously learning, and celebrating both successes and failures, we can unlock the full potential of this technology and shape a future where humans and machines work together in harmony to create content that is engaging, meaningful, and impactful.

In the next section, we will explore the critical role of education and skill development in preparing individuals and organizations for the AI-generated content revolution. By investing in the knowledge and capabilities of our workforce, we can ensure that we are equipped to navigate this new landscape with confidence and success.

Section 3: Investing in Education and Skill Development

As the AI-generated content revolution continues to unfold, it is becoming increasingly clear that education and skill development will play a critical role in preparing individuals and organizations for the challenges and opportunities that lie ahead. The rapid advancement of AI technologies has the potential to transform the way we create, consume, and interact with content, and it is essential that we take proactive steps to ensure that our educational systems and workforce development initiatives are well-equipped to meet the demands of this new era.

In this section, we will delve into the various ways in which we can invest in education and skill development to prepare for the AI-generated content revolution. From integrating AI literacy into educational curricula to upskilling and reskilling the workforce, we will explore the strategies and approaches that can help us build the knowledge, skills, and competencies needed to thrive in a world where AI-generated content is becoming increasingly prevalent.

By examining the critical role of education and skill development in this context, we aim to provide readers with a comprehensive understanding of the steps that can be taken to ensure that individuals and organizations are well-positioned to navigate the challenges and seize the opportunities presented by the AI-generated content revolution. Whether you are an educator, a business leader, or simply someone who is interested in the future of content creation and consumption, this section will provide you with valuable insights and practical guidance on how to prepare for the changes that lie ahead.

Subsection 3.1: Integrating AI Literacy into Educational Curricula

As AI-generated content becomes increasingly prevalent in our daily lives, it is crucial that we equip students with the knowledge and skills necessary to navigate this new landscape. Integrating AI literacy into educational curricula at all levels is a critical step in preparing the next generation for the challenges and opportunities presented by the AI-generated content revolution.

At the primary and secondary school levels, AI literacy can be introduced through age-appropriate lessons and activities that help students understand the basic concepts behind AI and its applications in content creation. For example, teachers can use simple, interactive demonstrations to show how AI algorithms can be trained to generate text, images, or music based on patterns in existing data. By engaging students in hands-on experiences with AI-generated content, educators can help demystify the technology and foster a sense of familiarity and comfort with its use.

In higher education, the integration of AI literacy can take on a more advanced and specialized focus, depending on the field of study. For students in creative disciplines such as writing, art, or music, courses can be designed to explore the potential of AI as a tool for enhancing and augmenting human creativity. These courses can provide students with hands-on experience in using AI-powered tools to generate content, while also encouraging critical reflection on the ethical and aesthetic implications of AI-generated content in their respective fields.

For students in technical disciplines such as computer science, engineering, or data science, AI literacy education can delve deeper into the underlying algorithms and techniques used in AI-generated content systems. Courses can cover topics such as natural language processing, computer vision, and generative models, providing students with the technical skills needed to develop and deploy AI-generated content systems in a responsible and effective manner.

Across all levels of education, it is important that AI literacy curricula also address the social, ethical, and legal implications of AI-generated content. Students should be encouraged to think critically about issues such as bias, transparency, and accountability in AI systems, and to consider the potential impacts of AI-generated content on society as a whole. By fostering a holistic understanding of AI-generated content that encompasses both technical and social perspectives, educational institutions can help prepare students to become informed and responsible creators, consumers, and regulators of AI-generated content in the future.

Subsection 3.2: Upskilling and Reskilling the Workforce

As AI-generated content becomes more prevalent across industries, it is crucial to ensure that the workforce is equipped with the necessary skills and knowledge to adapt to this changing landscape. Upskilling and reskilling initiatives play a vital role in bridging the gap between the current workforce's capabilities and the demands of an AI-driven future.

One of the primary challenges faced by organizations is the need to identify the specific skills required to work effectively with AI-generated content. This may include technical skills such as data analysis, machine learning, and programming, as well as soft skills like critical thinking, creativity, and adaptability. By conducting a thorough skills gap analysis, organizations can pinpoint the areas where their workforce needs the most support and develop targeted training programs to address these needs.

Upskilling initiatives can take various forms, such as in-house training sessions, online courses, workshops, and mentorship programs. These initiatives should be designed to cater to the diverse learning styles and needs of employees, ensuring that everyone has access to the resources they need to succeed. For example, an organization may offer a series of workshops on natural language processing techniques for content creators, enabling them to understand how AI algorithms generate text and how they can leverage these tools to enhance their own work.

Reskilling, on the other hand, focuses on helping employees transition into new roles that are better aligned with the demands of an AI-driven workplace. This may involve providing training in entirely new skill sets, such as data science or AI ethics, to prepare employees for emerging job opportunities. Reskilling programs can be particularly beneficial for workers whose current roles are at risk of being automated or replaced by AI-generated content, offering them a pathway to remain relevant and valuable within their organization.

Effective upskilling and reskilling initiatives require a strong commitment from both employers and employees. Organizations must invest in the necessary resources and infrastructure to support continuous learning and development, while employees must be willing to embrace change and actively participate in these initiatives. By fostering a culture of lifelong learning and adaptability, organizations can build a workforce that is resilient, agile, and well-prepared to navigate the challenges and opportunities presented by AI-generated content.

In addition to internal upskilling and reskilling efforts, organizations can also benefit from collaborating with external partners, such as educational institutions, industry associations, and government agencies. These partnerships can provide access to a wider range of expertise, resources, and best practices, enabling organizations to develop more comprehensive and effective workforce development strategies.

As the landscape of AI-generated content continues to evolve, it is essential that upskilling and reskilling initiatives remain flexible and responsive to changing needs. Regular assessments and feedback loops can help organizations identify areas where their workforce development efforts are succeeding and where they may need to be adjusted or refined. By embracing a mindset of continuous improvement and adaptation, organizations can ensure that their workforce remains well-equipped to thrive in an AI-driven future.

Subsection 3.3: Fostering Interdisciplinary Collaboration and Knowledge Sharing

The development and deployment of AI-generated content systems require a diverse range of expertise, spanning fields such as computer science, linguistics, psychology, and domain-specific knowledge. Fostering interdisciplinary collaboration and knowledge sharing among AI experts, content creators, and other stakeholders is crucial for addressing the stigma surrounding AI-generated content and ensuring its responsible and effective use.

One key benefit of interdisciplinary collaboration is the ability to bring together complementary skill sets and perspectives. AI experts can provide technical knowledge and insights into the capabilities and limitations of AI algorithms, while content creators can offer valuable input on the creative process, audience engagement, and the nuances of their respective domains. By working together, these professionals can develop AI-generated content systems that are not only technically sound but also aligned with the needs and expectations of end-users.

Interdisciplinary collaboration can also help to bridge the communication gap between AI experts and content creators, promoting mutual understanding and trust. Through regular dialogue and knowledge sharing sessions, these professionals can learn to speak each other's language, breaking down silos and fostering a shared vision for the responsible development and use of AI-generated content. This increased understanding can help to dispel misconceptions and address concerns about the potential risks and limitations of AI, ultimately contributing to the reduction of stigma.

To facilitate interdisciplinary collaboration and knowledge sharing, organizations can establish dedicated forums, workshops, and conferences that bring together professionals from diverse backgrounds. These events provide opportunities for participants to share their experiences, discuss challenges and best practices, and explore new ideas and approaches. By creating a space for open and inclusive dialogue, these initiatives can help to build a sense of community and shared purpose among AI experts, content creators, and other stakeholders.

In addition to in-person events, online platforms and resources can also play a valuable role in fostering interdisciplinary collaboration and knowledge sharing. Social media groups, discussion forums, and online courses can provide accessible and flexible channels for professionals to connect, share insights, and learn from one another. These platforms can also help to democratize access to knowledge and expertise, enabling a wider range of stakeholders to participate in the conversation and contribute to the responsible development and use of AI-generated content.

Ultimately, the success of interdisciplinary collaboration and knowledge sharing in addressing the stigma surrounding AI-generated content will depend on the willingness of professionals to embrace a culture of openness, curiosity, and mutual respect. By valuing diverse perspectives, actively seeking out opportunities for collaboration, and committing to ongoing learning and growth, AI experts, content creators, and other stakeholders can work together to harness the potential of AI-generated content while mitigating its risks and challenges.

Summary: Empowering Individuals and Organizations for the AI-Generated Content Revolution

Throughout this section, we have explored the critical role of education and skill development in preparing individuals and organizations for the AI-generated content revolution. By integrating AI literacy into educational curricula, upskilling and reskilling the workforce, and fostering interdisciplinary collaboration and knowledge sharing, we can equip ourselves with the necessary knowledge, skills, and mindsets to navigate the challenges and seize the opportunities presented by this transformative technology.

Investing in education and skill development is not merely a matter of staying competitive in a rapidly evolving landscape; it is also an essential step towards reducing the stigma surrounding AI-generated content. By demystifying the technology, promoting a balanced understanding of its capabilities and limitations, and empowering individuals to engage with it in a responsible and informed manner, we can foster a culture of openness, curiosity, and collaboration that is essential for realizing the full potential of AI-generated content.

As we move forward into an increasingly AI-driven future, it is crucial that we prioritize continuous learning and adaptation at all levels of society. From the classroom to the boardroom, we must be willing to embrace change, challenge our assumptions, and work together to develop the skills and knowledge needed to thrive in a world where AI-generated content is becoming the norm.

The path ahead may be uncertain, but one thing is clear: by investing in education and skill development, we are not only preparing ourselves for the AI-generated content revolution but also shaping its trajectory in a way that benefits all of humanity. It is an investment in our collective future, and one that we cannot afford to overlook.

Section 4: Developing Ethical Frameworks and Governance Models

As the adoption of AI-generated content continues to grow, it is crucial to address the ethical implications and potential risks associated with this powerful technology. The development of robust ethical frameworks and governance models is essential to guide the responsible creation and use of AI-generated content, ensuring that it benefits society while minimizing harm. In this section, we will explore the pressing need for such frameworks and models, and how they can help to mitigate the stigma surrounding AI-generated content.

The rapid advancement of AI technology has outpaced the development of ethical guidelines and regulations, leaving a void in the governance of AI-generated content. This absence of clear guidelines has contributed to the growing concerns and stigma surrounding the use of AI in content creation. Without a well-defined ethical framework, there is a risk that AI-generated content may perpetuate biases, spread misinformation, or be used for malicious purposes. It is imperative that we address these concerns head-on and establish a solid foundation for the ethical development and deployment of AI-generated content.

Developing ethical frameworks and governance models for AI-generated content is a complex and multifaceted challenge that requires the collaboration of various stakeholders, including AI researchers, content creators, policymakers, and the general public. These frameworks must strike a delicate balance between fostering innovation and creativity while safeguarding against potential risks and negative consequences. They should provide clear guidelines for the transparent and accountable use of AI in content creation, ensuring that the technology is used in a manner that aligns with societal values and promotes the greater good.

Throughout this section, we will delve into the key components of effective ethical frameworks and governance models for AI-generated content. We will explore the importance of establishing ethical guidelines and best practices, promoting transparency and accountability, and fostering multi-stakeholder collaboration and dialogue. By addressing these critical aspects, we can work towards building trust in AI-generated content and overcoming the stigma that currently surrounds it. As we navigate the complexities of this rapidly evolving landscape, it is essential that we prioritize the development of robust ethical frameworks and governance models to ensure the responsible and beneficial use of AI in content creation.

Subsection 4.1: Establishing Ethical Guidelines and Best

Practices

As AI-generated content becomes increasingly prevalent, it is crucial to establish a set of ethical guidelines and best practices to ensure its responsible creation and deployment. These guidelines should serve as a foundation for the development of AI systems that generate content, providing a clear framework for developers, content creators, and organizations to follow. By adhering to these guidelines, we can mitigate the potential risks associated with AI-generated content and foster trust among the general public.

One of the primary goals of ethical guidelines for AI-generated content is to promote transparency and accountability. This means that the use of AI in content creation should be clearly disclosed, allowing consumers to make informed decisions about the content they engage with. Additionally, organizations and individuals involved in the development and deployment of AI-generated content should be held accountable for the outcomes and impacts of their systems. This accountability can be achieved through regular audits, impact assessments, and the establishment of clear lines of responsibility within organizations.

Another critical aspect of ethical guidelines for AI-generated content is the prevention of bias and discrimination. AI systems are only as unbiased as the data they are trained on and the algorithms that process that data. Therefore, it is essential to ensure that the data used to train AI content generation systems is diverse, representative, and free from inherent biases. Moreover, the algorithms themselves should be regularly tested and monitored for potential biases, with mechanisms in place to identify and mitigate any discriminatory outcomes.

Privacy and data protection are also key considerations when establishing ethical guidelines for AI-generated content. The use of personal data in the creation of AI systems must be transparent, and individuals should have control over how their data is collected, used, and shared. Organizations must adhere to relevant data protection regulations, such as the General

Data Protection Regulation (GDPR) in the European Union, and implement robust security measures to safeguard personal information.

In addition to these core principles, ethical guidelines for AI-generated content should also address issues such as intellectual property rights, content authenticity, and the potential for AI systems to be used for malicious purposes, such as the creation of fake news or the spread of propaganda. By establishing clear guidelines and best practices in these areas, we can create a framework for the responsible development and deployment of AI-generated content.

To ensure the effectiveness and widespread adoption of ethical guidelines, it is essential to engage in multi-stakeholder collaboration and dialogue. This involves bringing together AI researchers, content creators, policymakers, ethicists, and representatives from the general public to discuss and refine these guidelines. By fostering open communication and collaboration, we can create a set of guidelines that are comprehensive, practical, and reflective of societal values.

Ultimately, establishing ethical guidelines and best practices for AI-generated content is an ongoing process that requires continuous refinement and adaptation as the technology evolves. By laying a strong foundation based on transparency, accountability, fairness, and respect for privacy, we can work towards overcoming the stigma surrounding AI-generated content and realizing its potential benefits for society as a whole.

Subsection 4.2: Promoting Transparency, Accountability, and Fairness

Transparency, accountability, and fairness are essential principles that must be upheld in the development and deployment of AI-generated content systems. As these systems become increasingly sophisticated and widely adopted, it is crucial to establish mechanisms that ensure their operation is transparent, their creators and users are held accountable, and their outputs are fair and unbiased.

Transparency is a fundamental aspect of building trust in AI-generated content. Users should have a clear understanding of when and how AI is being used to create the content they consume. This can be achieved through clear labeling and disclosure practices, indicating which parts of the content were generated by AI and which were created by humans. Additionally, the algorithms and data used to train AI content generation systems should be open to scrutiny, allowing for independent audits and assessments of their functioning and potential biases.

Accountability is another critical component of responsible AI-generated content. The individuals and organizations involved in the development and deployment of these systems must be held accountable for their outputs and any negative consequences that may arise. This can be facilitated through the establishment of clear lines of responsibility within organizations, as well as the implementation of regular performance evaluations and impact assessments. When AI-generated content causes harm or violates ethical standards, there should be well-defined processes for addressing grievances and providing redress to affected parties.

Fairness is a multifaceted concept that encompasses issues of bias, discrimination, and equal treatment. AI-generated content systems must be designed and trained to produce outputs that are fair and unbiased, avoiding the perpetuation of societal prejudices or the marginalization of certain groups. This requires careful attention to the data used to train these systems, ensuring that it is diverse, representative, and free from historical biases. Additionally, ongoing monitoring and testing of AI-generated content is necessary to identify and mitigate any emergent biases or discriminatory outcomes.

To promote transparency, accountability, and fairness in AI-generated content, a range of mechanisms can be employed. These may include:

1. Algorithmic impact assessments: Conducting regular assessments of AI content generation algorithms to evaluate their performance, identify potential biases, and assess their societal impact.

2. Transparency reports: Publishing periodic reports that provide insights into the operation of AI content generation systems, including details on the data used for training, the algorithms employed, and any identified issues or challenges.

3. Audit trails: Maintaining detailed records of the inputs, outputs, and decision-making processes of AI content generation systems, allowing for retrospective analysis and accountability.

4. Independent oversight: Establishing independent bodies or committees to oversee the development and deployment of AI-generated content systems, ensuring compliance with ethical standards and providing a channel for public input and grievance redressal.

5. Collaboration with stakeholders: Engaging in ongoing dialogue and collaboration with a diverse range of stakeholders, including content creators, civil society organizations, and the general public, to inform the design and governance of AI-generated content systems.

By implementing these mechanisms and prioritizing transparency, accountability, and fairness, we can work towards building trust in AI-generated content and addressing the stigma that surrounds it. It is essential to recognize that these principles are not one-time achievements but rather ongoing commitments that require sustained effort and vigilance. As AI technology continues to evolve, so too must our approaches to ensuring its responsible and ethical use in the creation of content.

Subsection 4.3: Fostering Multi-Stakeholder Collaboration and Dialogue

Developing effective and equitable governance models for AI-generated content requires the active participation and collaboration of diverse stakeholders. These stakeholders include AI researchers, content creators, policymakers, industry representatives, civil society organizations, and the general public. Each group brings unique perspectives, expertise, and concerns to the table, and their collective input is essential for creating comprehensive and inclusive frameworks that address the complex challenges surrounding AI-generated content.

Fostering multi-stakeholder collaboration and dialogue is crucial for several reasons. First, it ensures that the governance models developed are representative of the diverse interests and needs of all affected parties. By engaging a wide range of stakeholders, we can identify potential blind spots, unintended consequences, and areas of concern that may otherwise be overlooked. This inclusive approach helps to build trust and legitimacy in the governance process, as all relevant voices are heard and considered.

Second, multi-stakeholder collaboration facilitates the exchange of knowledge, ideas, and best practices among different groups. AI researchers can provide insights into the technical aspects of AI-generated content, while content creators can share their experiences and concerns regarding the impact of AI on their industry. Policymakers can offer guidance on legal and regulatory considerations, and civil society organizations can advocate for the rights and interests of the general public. By bringing these diverse perspectives together, we can develop a more comprehensive understanding of the challenges and opportunities associated with AI-generated content.

Third, multi-stakeholder dialogue helps to bridge the gap between technical expertise and policy development. The rapid advancement of AI technology often outpaces the ability of policymakers to keep up with the latest developments and their implications. By engaging in regular dialogue with AI researchers and industry representatives, policymakers can stay informed about the state of the art in AI-generated content and develop governance models that are responsive to the evolving technological landscape.

To foster effective multi-stakeholder collaboration and dialogue, several key principles should be followed. First, the process should be transparent and inclusive, with clear mechanisms for participation and input from all relevant stakeholders. This may involve the creation of dedicated forums, working groups, or advisory committees that bring together representatives from different sectors to discuss and deliberate on governance issues.

Second, the collaboration should be guided by a shared commitment to the responsible development and deployment of AI-generated content. All stakeholders should agree on a set of core values and principles that underpin the governance process, such as transparency, accountability, fairness, and respect for human rights. These shared values provide a common foundation for dialogue and help to ensure that the resulting governance models are aligned with societal priorities.

Third, the collaboration should be an ongoing and iterative process, rather than a one-time event. As AI technology continues to evolve and new challenges emerge, it is essential to maintain open lines of communication and regularly review and update governance models to ensure their continued relevance and effectiveness. This requires a commitment to long-term engagement and a willingness to adapt and refine approaches based on new evidence and insights.

Finally, the collaboration should be action-oriented, with a focus on developing concrete solutions and recommendations for the governance of AI-generated content. While dialogue and discussion are essential, they must be accompanied by practical steps to implement the agreed-upon principles and guidelines. This may involve the development of industry standards, codes of conduct, or regulatory frameworks that provide clear guidance for the responsible creation and use of AI-generated content.

Fostering multi-stakeholder collaboration and dialogue is not without its challenges. Bringing together diverse groups with potentially conflicting interests and priorities can be difficult, and finding common ground may require significant effort and compromise. However, the benefits of this inclusive approach far outweigh the challenges. By engaging all relevant stakeholders in the governance process, we can develop more robust, equitable, and socially responsible frameworks for the management of AI-generated content, helping to mitigate the stigma surrounding this technology and unlock its full potential for the benefit of society as a whole.

Summary: Paving the Way for Responsible AI-Generated Content

The development of robust ethical frameworks and governance models is a critical step in addressing the stigma surrounding AI-generated content and ensuring its responsible deployment. By establishing clear guidelines and best practices, promoting transparency, accountability, and fairness, and fostering multi-stakeholder collaboration and dialogue, we can create a solid foundation for the ethical use of AI in content creation.

The principles of transparency, accountability, and fairness are essential pillars of responsible AI-generated content. Transparency ensures that users are aware of when and how AI is being used, while accountability holds developers and organizations responsible for the outputs and consequences of their systems. Fairness encompasses the prevention of bias and discrimination, ensuring that AI-generated content is unbiased and does not perpetuate societal prejudices.

To uphold these principles, a range of mechanisms can be employed, including algorithmic impact assessments, transparency reports, audit trails, independent oversight, and collaboration with stakeholders. These mechanisms provide a framework for the ongoing monitoring, evaluation, and improvement of AI-generated content systems, ensuring their alignment with ethical standards and societal values.

However, the development of effective and equitable governance models for AI-generated content cannot be achieved in isolation. It requires the active participation and collaboration of diverse stakeholders, including AI researchers, content creators, policymakers, industry representatives, civil society organizations, and the general public. By bringing together these diverse perspectives and expertise, we can develop comprehensive and inclusive frameworks that address the complex challenges surrounding AI-generated content.

Multi-stakeholder collaboration and dialogue facilitate the exchange of knowledge, ideas, and best practices, bridging the gap between technical expertise and policy development. It ensures that governance models are representative of the diverse interests and needs of all affected parties, building trust and legitimacy in the process.

As we navigate the rapidly evolving landscape of AI-generated content, it is crucial to recognize that the development of ethical frameworks and governance models is an ongoing process. It requires sustained effort, vigilance, and a commitment to long-term engagement. By prioritizing transparency, accountability, fairness, and inclusive collaboration, we can work towards building trust in AI-generated content, mitigating the stigma that surrounds it, and unlocking its full potential for the benefit of society as a whole.

The establishment of robust ethical frameworks and governance models is not only essential for addressing the stigma against AI-generated content but also for shaping the future of this transformative technology. As we move forward, it is imperative that we continue to engage in open dialogue, collaborate across sectors, and adapt our approaches based on new evidence and insights. By doing so, we can pave the way for responsible and socially beneficial AI-generated content, harnessing its power to enhance creativity, foster innovation, and drive positive change in our world.

Section 5: Envisioning a Future Transformed by AI-Generated Content

Imagine a world where AI-generated content is no longer a novelty, but a seamlessly integrated part of our daily lives. As we stand on the precipice of this technological revolution, it's essential to contemplate the profound impact that AI-generated content will have on various aspects of our existence. In this section, we will embark on a captivating journey, painting a vivid picture of a future transformed by the power of AI-generated content.

As we navigate through this uncharted territory, we will explore the potential transformations that AI-generated content will bring to creative industries and professions. From the emergence of new roles and opportunities to the evolution of existing ones, we will witness a paradigm shift in the way we create, consume, and interact with content. Prepare to be amazed by the possibilities that lie ahead, as AI-generated content promises to redefine the boundaries of human creativity and expression.

Moreover, we will delve into the realm of personalized and immersive content experiences, where AI-generated content will cater to our individual preferences and desires. Imagine a world where the content you consume is tailored specifically to your interests, emotions, and context, creating a truly unique and engaging experience. The future of AI-generated content holds the key to unlocking a new era of storytelling, entertainment, and information dissemination.

As we explore this exciting future, we will also examine how AI-generated content can empower individuals and democratize creativity. No longer will creative expression be limited to a select few with access to resources and opportunities. AI-generated content will level the playing field, enabling people from all walks of life to share their ideas, stories, and perspectives with the world. This section will inspire you to embrace the potential of AI-generated content as a tool for personal growth, self-expression, and social change.

Finally, we will envision how AI-generated content can be harnessed for the greater good, addressing pressing global challenges such as education, healthcare, and environmental sustainability. By leveraging the power of AI, we can create content that educates, informs, and inspires people to take action towards a better future. This section will leave you with a sense of hope and optimism, as we collectively strive to build a world where AI-generated content is a catalyst for positive change.

As we embark on this exciting exploration of a future transformed by AI-generated content, prepare to have your assumptions challenged, your imagination sparked, and your perspective expanded. Together, we will navigate the complexities and possibilities of this brave new world, ultimately emerging with a deeper understanding of the role that AI-generated content will play in shaping our lives and our society. So, let us boldly step into this uncharted territory, ready to embrace the AI revolution and the transformative power of AI-generated content.

Subsection 5.1: The Evolution of Creative Industries and Professions

As AI-generated content becomes increasingly sophisticated and integrated into our daily lives, it is poised to revolutionize creative industries and professions in unprecedented ways. The advent of AI technology has already begun to reshape the landscape of content creation, and its impact will only continue to grow in the coming years.

One of the most significant changes we can expect to see is the emergence of new roles and professions within creative industries. As AI takes on more of the repetitive and time-consuming tasks involved in content creation, such as data analysis, research, and initial drafts, human creators will be free to focus on higher-level tasks that require creativity, critical thinking, and emotional intelligence. This shift will likely give rise to new job titles such as "AI Content Curator," "AI-Assisted Scriptwriter," or "AI Creative Strategist," which will focus on leveraging AI tools to enhance and streamline the creative process.

Moreover, the integration of AI-generated content will lead to a democratization of creativity, enabling a wider range of individuals to participate in creative industries. As AI tools become more accessible and user-friendly, people with diverse backgrounds and skill sets will be able to create compelling content without necessarily having extensive technical expertise. This increased accessibility will foster a more inclusive and diverse creative landscape, bringing fresh perspectives and ideas to the forefront.

However, the rise of AI-generated content will also present challenges for traditional creative professions. As AI algorithms become more adept at generating content that mimics human creativity, some roles may become less in demand or even obsolete. For example, entry-level positions in fields such as journalism, advertising, or graphic design may be partially replaced by AI tools capable of producing similar content more efficiently and cost-effectively.

To adapt to this changing landscape, creative professionals will need to embrace a mindset of continuous learning and upskilling. They will need to develop a deep understanding of AI technologies and how to effectively collaborate with AI tools to enhance their own creative output. This may involve learning new software, programming languages, or data analysis techniques to stay competitive in an AI-driven industry.

Furthermore, the evolution of creative industries will necessitate a reevaluation of intellectual property rights and attribution practices. As AI-generated content becomes more prevalent, questions will arise about who owns the rights to this content and how to properly credit the contributions of both human creators and AI algorithms. This will require the development of new legal frameworks and ethical guidelines to ensure fair compensation and recognition for all parties involved in the creative process.

Despite these challenges, the integration of AI-generated content into creative industries presents exciting opportunities for innovation and growth. By embracing AI as a tool to augment and enhance human creativity, we can unlock new forms of expression, push the boundaries of what is possible, and create more engaging and impactful content for audiences worldwide. As we navigate this transformative journey, it is crucial that we approach the evolution of creative industries with an open mind, a willingness to adapt, and a commitment to harnessing the power of AI for the betterment of all.

Subsection 5.2: Personalized and Immersive Content Experiences

In a future where AI-generated content is fully integrated into our daily lives, one of the most exciting prospects is the potential for highly personalized and immersive content experiences. Imagine a world where the content you consume is tailored specifically to your individual preferences, interests, and even your current emotional state. This level of personalization will revolutionize the way we interact with and experience content across various mediums, from entertainment and education to marketing and beyond.

AI algorithms will be capable of analyzing vast amounts of data about each individual, including their browsing history, social media activity, and even biometric data from wearable devices. By leveraging this information, AI-powered content generation systems will be able to create content that resonates with each person on a deep, emotional level. For example, a personalized movie recommendation system could take into account not only your past viewing history but also your current mood, suggesting films that align with your emotional state and provide the most satisfying viewing experience.

Moreover, AI-generated content will enable the creation of truly immersive experiences that blur the lines between reality and virtual worlds. Imagine stepping into a virtual reality environment where the characters, storylines, and even the physical surroundings are generated in real-time based on your unique preferences and actions. This level of interactivity and adaptability will create a sense of presence and engagement that far surpasses the passive content consumption experiences of today.

The applications of personalized and immersive AI-generated content are vast and varied. In education, for instance, AI could create customized learning materials that adapt to each student's learning style, pace, and knowledge gaps. This approach would allow for a more efficient and effective learning experience, ultimately leading to better educational outcomes. Similarly, in the realm of marketing, AI-generated content could enable the creation of highly targeted and persuasive advertising campaigns that speak directly to each individual consumer's needs and desires.

As we envision this future of personalized and immersive content experiences, it is essential to consider the ethical implications and potential drawbacks. The collection and use of personal data for content generation raise concerns about privacy and consent. It will be crucial to develop robust frameworks and regulations that ensure the responsible use of AI in content creation and protect individuals' rights to control their own data.

Additionally, the increasing personalization of content may lead to the creation of "filter bubbles" or "echo chambers," where individuals are exposed only to content that reinforces their existing beliefs and preferences. This phenomenon could potentially lead to a more polarized and fragmented society, as people become increasingly isolated within their own personalized content worlds. To mitigate these risks, it will be important to promote diversity and encourage exposure to a wide range of perspectives and ideas within AI-generated content.

Despite these challenges, the potential benefits of personalized and immersive AI-generated content are immense. By harnessing the power of AI to create content that resonates with each individual on a profound level, we can foster deeper connections, inspire greater creativity, and unlock new possibilities for self-expression and personal growth. As we move towards this exciting future, it is essential that we approach the development and deployment of AI-generated content with thoughtfulness, responsibility, and a commitment to creating experiences that enrich and empower individuals while promoting the greater good of society as a whole.

Subsection 5.3: Empowering Individuals and Democratizing Creativity

In a future where AI-generated content is seamlessly integrated into our lives, one of the most transformative aspects will be its potential to empower individuals and democratize creativity. The advent of AI technologies will break down barriers to creative expression, enabling people from all walks of life to share their ideas, stories, and perspectives with the world.

Traditionally, the creation of high-quality content has been largely confined to professionals with extensive training, resources, and access to expensive tools. However, AI-powered content generation tools will level the playing field, making it possible for anyone with a creative vision to bring their ideas to life. User-friendly interfaces and intuitive workflows will allow individuals to harness the power of AI without needing to possess deep technical expertise.

Imagine a world where a budding writer can use AI-assisted tools to craft compelling stories, even if they lack formal training in creative writing. Or consider the possibilities for aspiring musicians who can leverage AI to compose and produce original songs, regardless of their musical background. By democratizing access to creative tools and resources, AI-generated content will unlock a wealth of untapped potential and diverse voices that have been previously underrepresented in creative industries.

Moreover, AI-generated content will empower individuals to express themselves in new and innovative ways. As AI algorithms become more sophisticated, they will be able to analyze and understand individual preferences, styles, and emotions, enabling the creation of content that is deeply personal and authentic. For example, an AI-powered personal journal app could help users articulate their thoughts and feelings by suggesting prompts, providing writing assistance, and even generating personalized illustrations to accompany their entries.

The democratization of creativity through AI-generated content will also foster a more inclusive and diverse creative landscape. By lowering the barriers to entry, AI will enable people from marginalized communities and underrepresented backgrounds to share their unique perspectives and experiences with a global audience. This increased diversity of voices will enrich our collective cultural heritage and promote greater empathy, understanding, and social cohesion.

However, the democratization of creativity through AI-generated content will also present challenges and ethical considerations. As more people gain access to powerful creative tools, there will be a need for education and guidance on responsible use, intellectual property rights, and the importance of authenticity. It will be crucial to develop frameworks that encourage the use of AI-generated content as a means of genuine self-expression rather than a tool for deception or manipulation.

Furthermore, the rise of AI-generated content may disrupt traditional models of creative ownership and monetization. As the lines between human and machine creativity blur, there will be a need for new models of attribution, compensation, and recognition that fairly acknowledge the contributions of both human creators and AI algorithms. This will require ongoing dialogue and collaboration among creators, technologists, policymakers, and other stakeholders to ensure that the benefits of AI-generated content are distributed equitably.

Despite these challenges, the potential for AI-generated content to empower individuals and democratize creativity is immense. By harnessing the power of AI, we can unlock the creative potential of millions of people worldwide, giving voice to diverse perspectives and fostering a more vibrant, inclusive, and expressive society. As we navigate this exciting future, it is essential that we approach the democratization of creativity with openness, curiosity, and a commitment to using AI-generated content as a tool for personal growth, self-discovery, and positive social change.

Subsection 5.4: Harnessing AI for Social Good and Global Challenges

As we envision a future transformed by AI-generated content, it is crucial to recognize the immense potential for this technology to be harnessed for social good and to address pressing global challenges. From education and healthcare to environmental sustainability and beyond, AI-generated content has the power to inform, inspire, and drive positive change on a massive scale.

In the realm of education, AI-generated content can revolutionize the way we teach and learn. By creating personalized learning materials that adapt to each student's unique needs, learning style, and pace, AI can help bridge educational gaps and ensure that every individual has access to high-quality, engaging educational content. Imagine a world where AI-powered virtual tutors can provide one-on-one support to students, answering questions, providing feedback, and guiding them through complex concepts. This level of personalized attention has the potential to significantly improve educational outcomes and create a more equitable learning landscape.

Moreover, AI-generated content can play a vital role in addressing global health challenges. By analyzing vast amounts of medical data, AI algorithms can assist in the early detection and diagnosis of diseases, enabling healthcare professionals to intervene more quickly and effectively. AI-generated content can also be used to create targeted public health campaigns, delivering personalized messages that resonate with specific communities and promote healthy behaviors. In times of crisis, such as during a pandemic, AI-generated content can help disseminate accurate, up-to-date information and combat the spread of misinformation, ultimately saving lives.

Environmental sustainability is another critical area where AI-generated content can make a significant impact. By analyzing data from satellites, sensors, and other sources, AI can help monitor and predict environmental changes, such as deforestation, air and water pollution, and climate patterns. This information can be used to create compelling, data-driven content that raises awareness about environmental issues and inspires individuals and organizations to take action. AI-generated content can also be used to develop and promote sustainable solutions, such as renewable energy technologies or eco-friendly products, helping to drive the transition towards a more sustainable future.

In addition to these specific domains, AI-generated content has the potential to foster greater empathy, understanding, and connection among people from diverse backgrounds and cultures. By creating content that reflects a wide range of experiences and perspectives, AI can help break down stereotypes, challenge biases, and promote a more inclusive society. For example, AI-generated content could be used to create immersive virtual reality experiences that allow individuals to step into the shoes of others, gaining a deeper understanding of their lives and challenges. This kind of empathy-building content can be a powerful tool for promoting social cohesion and driving positive social change.

As we harness AI-generated content for social good and global challenges, it is essential to do so with a strong ethical framework in place. This means ensuring that AI algorithms are developed and deployed in a transparent, accountable, and unbiased manner, with safeguards in place to prevent unintended consequences or misuse. It also means actively involving diverse stakeholders, including community members, domain experts, and policymakers, in the development and implementation of AI-generated content initiatives to ensure that they are inclusive, equitable, and aligned with the needs and values of the communities they serve.

By embracing the transformative potential of AI-generated content and directing it towards social good and global challenges, we have the opportunity to create a future that is not only technologically advanced but also more equitable, sustainable, and compassionate. As we navigate this exciting frontier, let us approach it with a sense of purpose, responsibility, and optimism, harnessing the power of AI to build a better world for all.

Summary: Embracing the Transformative Power of AI-Generated Content

As we envision a future transformed by AI-generated content, it becomes clear that this technology holds immense potential to reshape our lives and society in profound ways. From revolutionizing creative industries and democratizing access to creative tools, to enabling highly personalized and immersive content experiences, AI-generated content promises to unlock new frontiers of human expression and engagement.

However, as we navigate this exciting future, it is crucial that we approach the integration of AI-generated content with thoughtfulness, responsibility, and a commitment to harnessing its power for the greater good. By directing the transformative potential of AI towards addressing pressing global challenges, such as education, healthcare, and environmental sustainability, we have the opportunity to create a future that is not only technologically advanced but also more equitable, compassionate, and resilient.

As individuals and as a society, we must embrace the transformative power of AI-generated content while remaining vigilant about its potential pitfalls and unintended consequences. This means actively engaging in ongoing dialogues about the ethical implications of AI, developing robust frameworks for responsible AI development and deployment, and ensuring that the benefits of this technology are distributed fairly and inclusively.

Ultimately, the future of AI-generated content is not a fixed destination but an ongoing journey of exploration, innovation, and adaptation. By approaching this journey with openness, curiosity, and a commitment to using AI as a tool for positive change, we can shape a future in which AI-generated content enhances our lives, expands our horizons, and brings us closer together as a global community. As we stand on the precipice of this transformative era, let us embrace the possibilities before us and work together to build a future that harnesses the full potential of AI-generated content for the betterment of all.

Chapter Summary: Embracing the AI Revolution for a Brighter Future

As we conclude this exploration of the stigma against AI-generated content, it is clear that we stand at the precipice of a transformative era. The AI revolution is not a distant dream but a present reality, and it is up to us to shape its trajectory. By reframing the narrative around AI-generated content, fostering a culture of innovation, investing in education and skill development, and establishing ethical frameworks, we can harness the immense potential of this technology while mitigating its risks.

The future of AI-generated content is not one of replacement but of collaboration. By embracing AI as a tool to augment and enhance human creativity, we open up a world of possibilities. The seamless integration of AI-generated content into our lives and work will give rise to new industries, professions, and opportunities, democratizing creativity and empowering individuals to express themselves in unprecedented ways.

As we navigate this uncharted territory, it is essential to approach AI-generated content with a balanced and nuanced understanding. We must celebrate its successes, learn from its failures, and remain committed to transparency, accountability, and fairness. By engaging in multi-stakeholder collaboration and dialogue, we can develop inclusive and equitable governance models that ensure the benefits of AI are shared by all.

The AI revolution is not just about technological advancement; it is about the betterment of society as a whole. By harnessing the power of AI-generated content for social good, we can address global challenges in education, healthcare, environmental sustainability, and beyond. The possibilities are endless, and the potential for positive impact is immeasurable.

As we embark on this exciting journey, let us do so with open minds, curious hearts, and a steadfast commitment to embracing the AI revolution. The future is ours to shape, and with the power of AI-generated content at our fingertips, we have the opportunity to create a brighter, more vibrant world for generations to come. Let us seize this moment and boldly step forward into the unknown, confident in our ability to navigate the challenges and opportunities that lie ahead.

Afterword: Embracing the AI-Generated Content Revolution

As we conclude this exploration of the stigma against AI-generated content, it is clear that we stand at the threshold of a new era in content creation. The rapid advancements in artificial intelligence and machine learning have opened up unprecedented opportunities for innovation, creativity, and collaboration between humans and machines.

Throughout this book, we have examined the various factors contributing to the stigma surrounding AI-generated content, from the fear of job displacement to concerns about authenticity and creativity. We have also highlighted the immense potential of AI to streamline content creation processes, personalize user experiences, and push the boundaries of creative expression.

However, to fully harness the benefits of AI-generated content, we must first overcome the stigma and embrace this technology as a tool for empowerment and progress. This requires a fundamental shift in mindset, from one of fear and skepticism to one of openness and curiosity.

It is essential that we foster a culture of innovation and experimentation, encouraging individuals and organizations to explore the possibilities of AI-generated content. This involves investing in education and skill development, ensuring that people are equipped with the knowledge and competencies needed to thrive in this new landscape.

Moreover, we must develop robust ethical frameworks and governance models to guide the responsible development and deployment of AI-generated content. This includes promoting transparency, accountability, and fairness, while also engaging in multi-stakeholder collaboration to address the complex challenges that may arise.

As we look to the future, it is clear that AI-generated content will play an increasingly significant role in shaping our world. From transforming creative industries and democratizing access to creative tools, to enabling personalized and immersive content experiences, the potential applications are vast and exciting.

However, realizing this potential will require a collective effort from all stakeholders – researchers, developers, content creators, policymakers, and the general public. It is only by working together, engaging in open dialogue, and embracing the opportunities and challenges posed by AI-generated content that we can truly harness its transformative power.

So let us move forward with a spirit of openness, collaboration, and responsibility. Let us embrace the AI-generated content revolution, not with fear or trepidation, but with a sense of excitement and possibility. For it is through this technology that we may unlock new frontiers of creativity, expression, and human potential.

The journey ahead may be complex and uncertain, but one thing is clear – the future of content creation will be shaped by the symbiotic relationship between human ingenuity and artificial intelligence. And it is up to us to ensure that this relationship is one of empowerment, innovation, and progress for all.

Don't miss out!

Visit the website below and you can sign up to receive emails whenever Sandy Y. Greenleaf publishes a new book. There's no charge and no obligation.

https://books2read.com/r/B-A-HNUEB-FJKAD

Connecting independent readers to independent writers.

Also by Sandy Y. Greenleaf

AI's Take on Money
AI's Take on Money, Volume I

Standalone
AI's Take on Personal Growth
AI's Take on Relationships
AI's Take on the Stigma Against AI-Generated Content

Watch for more at https://medium.com/@sandy.y.greenleaf.

About the Author

My mission is to democratize knowledge for the betterment of human lives. Check out the pinned article on my Medium profile for a catalog of all my content.

Read more at https://medium.com/@sandy.y.greenleaf.